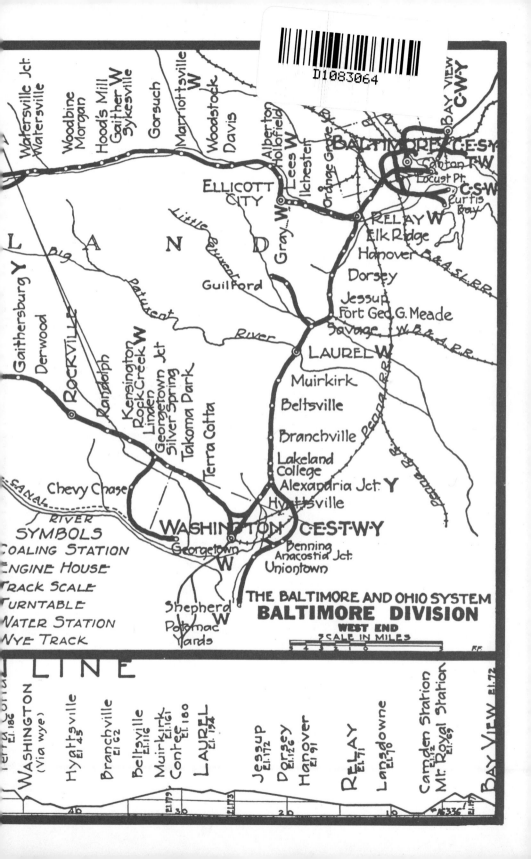

IMPOSSIBLE
CHALLENGE

THE BALTIMORE
and OHIO RAILROAD
IN MARYLAND

by

HERBERT H. HARWOOD, JR.

Copyright © 1979 by Barnard, Roberts and Company, Inc. All Worldwide rights reserved. No part of this book may be reproduced in any manner without permission in writing, except in the case of critical reviews. Printed and bound in the United States of America.

Library of Congress Catalog Card No. 79-54967
ISBN 0-934118-17-5

Published by Barnard, Roberts and Company, Inc.
Baltimore, Maryland 21227

TABLE OF CONTENTS

INTRODUCTION

On first reading the rough draft of this book, what struck me was not the quality of the scholarship (which is superb) or the smooth way in which the author makes sense of a century-and-a-half of confused history . . .rather, it was a feeling of being with old acquaintances, long time neighbors: the work had the feeling of a family album.

After reflection, I decided that the satisfaction I felt stemmed from several sources. First, it was a good story well told, offering excitement, intrigue and heroes and villains in the best American tradition. Too, I had a very parochial bias. The story of the B&O has been taught in Maryland grammar schools for decades and one with an inclination towards such things cannot help but soak up some of the railroad lore that permeates most of the State.

The B&O was, more so than most of its competitors, a home-grown project that reflected the needs, aspirations and limitations of its public and private sector parents. To be sure, it touched the lives of millions of people throughout the country, but as Harwood writes, its heart and soul were in Baltimore. In B&O territory, one is hard pressed to find an individual who does not have a grandfather, uncle or in-law who worked for "the Railroad". For eight generations, railroading has superimposed its own rhythms on those of the city and farm, in effect bringing the Industrial Revolution to within easy reach of virtually everyone. Loyalties to the agent of that revolution go back a long time—and die hard.

Such was also the nature of the enterprise. Continually in second or third place by virtue of geography, seniority and the maneuverings of its more northern rivals, the Company made the most of its two premier assets: service and style. Those assets had roots in the railroad's inception as a work of, by and for the people of Baltimore and Maryland, but they also reflected traditional Maryland hospitalities. For every time-worn anecdote involving a dining car meal or a held connection, there were countless other unrecorded courtesies extended to the shipper and the public. Of course, the B&O was a for-profit corporation; it just seemed that at times the road to prosperity was laid with good intentions.

Yet much more than those good intentions was required. A "Rail Road" to the Ohio River, in those not-so-naive days, was a venture that simply had to succeed. Baltimore knew too well that it was in a very high stakes contest, with its future as a viable seaport as the wager. The B&O was locally controlled until the turn of the century and it would not be an overstatement to say that it was the single most important investment ever made in Maryland. Without it, the "Port that built the City and State" would almost certainly have perished in the backwash of New York and Philadelphia.

Why it did not is more properly the concern of economic historians. This book is an examination of the physical plant and operations of the link to the west that kept Baltimore alive. Though necessarily limited to Maryland, it treats probably the most historic slice of railroading in the Country. That one can still ride (at least for a few miles) along the route of the Nation's first passenger train is confirmation of the soundness of the Founders' vision. That there has never been a coherent account of the

INTRODUCTION

actual development of that stretch of railroad was the motivation for this book.

I can only guess that it was his sense of justice that prodded Herb Harwood into taking on the project. Well known for his careful studies of the Hagerstown and Frederick and Washington and Old Dominion Railroads in addition to numerous contributions to scholarly and popular serials, he is a skilled analyst of the railroad industry. Most importantly, his career with the Chessie System and residence in Baltimore have given him the understanding of his subject vital to any author. In his two year research, he left no known rock unturned in the quest for accuracy and context.

It was not an easy book to assemble. The data had to be gleaned from a wide array of primary sources, no mean feat in spite of the body of published work bearing on the B&O. As with any entity that has become part of the popular culture, there was a great deal of debunking to be done. ...however hoary, many of the well liked and oft told stories surrounding the early days of the B&O are just that.

Photos also proved to be a challenge. To be informative, entertaining and appropriate meant winnowing several thousand available graphics down to the best several hundred. The integration of the well researched text and the pictures speaks for itself; an author less sensitive to his subject could not have accomplished it.

The story itself has been repeated a thousand times in the history of American enterprise. The successes, failures and unfailing optimism that emerge here are at once comfortably familiar and strikingly universal. What follows is a solid, original-source history that reads like a novel — as well it should.

Baltimore, Maryland   John P. Hankey
September, 1979   The Baltimore and Ohio Railroad Museum

PREFACE

Any railroad historian approaches the Baltimore & Ohio with awe, if not always reverence. As one of the country's earliest railroads and unquestionably the most historically significant, it has received massive coverage of one type or another. Almost any general American history makes at least passing mention of the B&O, and the railroad occupies a much more dominant part of the specialized economic, industrial, engineering and transportation histories. Not surprisingly a full book-shelf of works have been devoted to B&O alone. Its motive power, particularly, has been competently dissected in at least four books, with more to come. A company-sponsored corporate history published in 1928 took two volumes to cover only the bare essentials of its development to that date. Although apparently written more as an opera libretto than an objective history, it remains a durable classic. (Work is now well under way on a new full-length B&O history which promises to be more accurate and infinitely more coherent.) B&O's pivotal role in the Civil War has been explored both in specialized studies and in the enormous glut of Civil War histories. Other specialized publications constantly appear covering specific predecessor companies, types of rolling stock and structures—plus pictorials illustrating present and past operations.

In addition the company itself has been unusually sensitive to its history. Beginning as early as 1892 it started to assemble and maintain what is now the most historically comprehensive single collection of railroad rolling stock and artifacts in the United States. And, despite occasional lapses, it has consistently sponsored research and produced endless amounts of historically-oriented material on its own.

Thus anyone attempting to "do" the Baltimore & Ohio must pick a clear path through what has already been done and what is currently under way by others. And at the same time he must re-research seemingly familiar ground to separate fact from fabrication—for B&O's history has suffered more than its share of errors and apocrypha, much of which has now hardened into sanctified historical dogma.

Within this intimidating environment, this book sets rather modest goals for itself: It intends to cover only those B&O lines lying between Baltimore and the Potomac River at Washington and at Harpers Ferry. Specifically, this includes what is generally known as the Old Main Line, the Washington branch, the Metropolitan branch plus several smaller branches—the Alexandria branch, Georgetown branch and Frederick branch. Operationally, this means, in effect, the west end of B&O's Baltimore division (Baltimore-Weverton, Md.) with a side excursion to Harpers Ferry. Also, it attempts to take a somewhat different approach to the railroad's history: It will concentrate on B&O's *physical* development in this geographic area—such things as its route locations, structures, and train operations—rather than the abstractions of economics and politics, or the mechanical specifics of locomotives or even the romantic aura of such things as the "Royal Blue's" diners (a subject upon which still another book is underway).

PREFACE

Yet a book confined only to the physical aspects of a railroad within a limited geographic area may not be as narrow and technical as it may seem. B&O began here; its pioneering construction and engineering problems were here—as were its worst early obstacles. Many of its Civil War traumas were suffered here. And as the railroad developed through the late 19th and early 20th Centuries, its lines in this region reflected all the accomplishments and failures of the larger system. For the industrial archeologist, these lines still contain what is probably the most concentrated and comprehensive collection of historic railroad structures anywhere—including many of the most significant. And finally, although B&O ultimately expanded to the point where it regularly advertised itself as "Linking 13 Great States with the Nation," Maryland always remained its economic heart, its political heart, its operating heart and most of all its emotional heart.

The decision to cut this study at Harpers Ferry is admittedly arbitrary. From a railroad operating viewpoint, Harpers Ferry is only a way station and secondary junction. However, it is a significant reference point in B&O's historical development as well as the scene of many events—both positive and negative—in the railroad's life. Furthermore, the Harpers Ferry boundary has the tidy advantage of confining the coverage to Maryland while at the same time taking in all of the most interesting and historic lines at the east end of the B&O system. Perhaps the only significant omission which results is the facilities and historical events at Martinsburg, W. Va., the next major point west of Harpers Ferry—but by including Martinsburg, one logically opens the door to Cumberland as well as the Shenandoah Valley line and the story rapidly runs out of control.

Drawing the line in Baltimore was even more difficult, since over the years B&O managed to get into almost every corner of the city. The primary problem here was that the "Royal Blue Line" to Philadelphia is its own separate story, which goes beyond the scope of this book. Most of B&O's lines and structures in the northern and eastern part of the city—including the Howard Street tunnel, Mt. Royal station, the once-electrified Baltimore Belt Line, and the various industrial branches in Canton, Highlandtown and Sparrows Point—were built as part of the Philadelphia line or were later offshoots from it. Thus reluctantly, and even more arbitrarily, we defined our Baltimore boundaries as B&O's *original* line, plus the branches, cutoffs and terminals which historically developed from it. In effect, this makes Pratt Street and the west side of Baltimore harbor our dividing line. We thus have included such notable points as Camden station, Locust Point and Curtis Bay—but other equally notable spots at best have only been touched on.

In extending thanks for help, it is difficult to know where to start. The author is indebted to an outstandingly capable and cooperative group of B&O historians and photographers. Special thanks have to go to three of these: John P. Hankey, historian at the B&O Museum; Carlos P. Avery,

PREFACE

an architectural and engineering historian of Rockville, Md., who has done extensive research on B&O's Metropolitan branch and the railroad stations of architect E. Francis Baldwin; and James D. Dilts, who has taken on the awesome task of writing the full-length B&O history that Edward Hungerford should have written. Judging by the evidence so far, he is succeeding admirably. Others who helped almost as much were:

Thomas H. Arnold, railroad historian and retired B&O conductor, Baltimore

Ovalee Barefoot, Manager Traffic Administration, Chessie System, Baltimore

Howard N. Barr, B&O locomotive historian. Baltimore

Harold L. Buckley, Jr., photographer and historian, Kensington, Md.

Randolph W. Chalfant, railroad, architectural and steamship historian, Baltimore

Harry C. Eck, General Supervisor Locomotive Operations, Chessie System, Baltimore

Herbert H. Harwood (Sr.), retired Executive Representative, New York Central System, Brookline, Mass.

Philip R. Hastings, photographer, Waterloo, Iowa

Harry Jones, steamship historian, Waldorf, Md.

Charles T. Mahan, Jr., photographer and historian, Towson, Md.

John E. Merriken, railroad and traction historian, Columbia, Md.

Ara Mesrobian, photographer, Chevy Chase, Md.

Rodney H. Peterson, Resident Engineer, Chessie System, Baltimore

Bill Rettberg, photographer, Baltimore

Kenneth F. Roloson, retired Sales Manager, Chessie Systems, Englewood, Fla.

Gary Schlerf, railroad historian, Baltimore

Lee B. Smith, President, Brunswick Potomac Foundation, Brunswick, Md.

William F. Smith, railroad historian, Bethesda, Md.

Everett L. Thompson, author, photographer and retired Manager Passenger Operations, Chessie System, Baltimore

Robert A. Truax, railroad and traction historian, Washington, D.C.

Robert M. Vogel, Curator of Civil & Mechanical Engineering, Smithsonian Institution, Washington, D.C.

John H. White, Jr., Curator of Transportation, Smithsonian Institution, Washington, D.C.

Russell L. Wilcox, railroad historian, Lutherville, Md.

Ames W. Williams, railroad historian, Alexandria, Va.

Frank A. Wrabel, railroad historian, Timonium, Md.

All of them made special efforts to help me, and whatever credit is due for accurate facts or meaningful illustration goes mostly to them.

HERBERT H. HARWOOD, JR.

IMPOSSIBLE CHALLENGE

CHAPTER 1

A STUNNING SENDOFF: 1828

At six a.m. on the Fourth of July 1828, three guns were fired, signalling the participants in the grand parade to organize and take their places. At seven sharp they all started out west down Baltimore Street, led off by Captain Cox's Troop of Horse. It was the greatest celebration Baltimore had ever put on and—considering relative populations—the greatest it ever would. At the time, the city's population was about 70,000 and it was estimated that 70,000 people had turned out.

First in the parade were those scheduled to take part in the ultimate ceremony, plus some special bystanders: the Grand Lodge of Masons, the Orator of the Day, the officers and directors of the enterprise being launched that day, and some surviving veterans of the Revolutionary army. Then came a band, followed by an incredible succession of marchers and floats representing all of the city's major trades and crafts—46 in all, ranging from the stolid Farmers and Planters to the Ornamental Chair Painters. Each of their elaborate and painstakingly-built floats displayed the trade's wares, often in the process of creation. The hatters made beaver hats; the painters did a portrait; blacksmiths worked over a forge; lathes turned; printers printed. There were riggers, rope makers, cordwainers, victuallers, potters, plasterers, plow makers. And toward the rear came the most memorable float of all: a 27-foot long fully rigged sailing ship, sails set and silk colors flying, built at Fells Point and manned by the Ship Captains and Mates. It was named—of course—the *Union*.

Afterwards followed every conceivable public, civic and private group—the Governor, Mayor, U.S. Senators and Representatives, the state legislature, city council, army and navy officers, clergy, doctors, judges, justices of the peace, teachers, students, clerks, accountants and finally, to be sure that nobody who wanted to march was forgotten, the program specified "citizens, mechanics and artisans not included in the above arrangement." Captain Kennedy's Troop of Horse brought up the rear.

The occasion was the official launching of the Baltimore & Ohio Rail Road on its way west to the Ohio River. Obviously it was not just the beginning of another business enterprise. It was in every sense the start of a great—and enormously risky—adventure. "Adventure" is now a considerably devalued word and "railroad" conjures up a picture of a very ordinary and somewhat motheaten industry. But on that day the railroad officers marching behind the Masons were walking into the unknown. Their project was one of the most massive ever conceived in the country at that time: They intended to build an almost entirely unproven transportation system across 380 miles of hostile terrain, using untried technology and construction techniques. They had no clear idea of how the railroad would

1

be powered, much less how the power would be designed. They didn't know what kind of roadbed and rail would work or what bridge designs were appropriate to carry the unknown motive power and traffic loads. Nor did they really know what the project would cost or where the money would come from.

To be sure, railroads were already operating in 1828 and more were being planned. In fact, also present in the parade—somewhat to the rear— were the officers and directors of the recently-organized Baltimore & Susquehanna Railroad, which soon would build north toward Harrisburg. And the B&O itself was hardly an impromptu idea; formally or informally it had been discussed and planned for at least two years. But at that time railroads were short, limited-purpose affairs—mine tramways, portages connecting waterways or feeders running a short distance inland from some port. England's 25-mile Stockton & Darlington was the only truly operational "intercity" railroad. However, S&D was less than three years old and technologically was not much more than a mine tramway. The Baltimore & Ohio's length, purpose, and most of all the awesome topography it had to conquer, put it in a class by itself; the rules and techniques developed so far simply did not apply. In short, it was an early 19th century version of a moon shot—but without any of the reassuring research and meticulous planning which went into our space adventure. Doubtless the beaver-hatted bankers, merchants and engineers representing the railroad management were proud as they marched, but also apprehensive.

The parade led symbolically west, carrying the railroad's cornerstone with it. Any undertaking of note had to start with a cornerstone, of course. No matter that a railroad had no practical use for a cornerstone and in any case had no corner to put it on—B&O was to get one anyway. At the least, it was the first tangible evidence of all the discussions, plans, surveys, laws and charter made in its behalf. It had been decided to place the stone at the point where the railroad's planned route crossed the city boundary, which turned out to be a somewhat remote spot on James Carroll's estate, between Gwynns Run and Gwynns Falls. (The exact spot, now unrecognizable, is on the north side of B&O's present Mt. Clare branch, south of Wilkins Avenue and about 500 feet west of Catherine Street.) Ancient Charles Carroll of Carrollton, age 90, still superlatively patrician—the last living signer of the Declaration of Independence and the archetypal Maryland manor lord—turned the first ceremonial spadeful of earth. The stone was dedicated in a full Masonic ceremony, the band struck up a specially-composed march and an artillery salute signalled that the B&O was now officially blessed.

With the privilege of hindsight, historians could find much in the event that was symbolic and much that was ironic. The crafts and their products represented the world as it was—the known, familiar world with its known, familiar methods. The enterprise they were sending off was the unknown and unexplored. Similarly, many of the institutions represented in the celebration would be irrevocably altered or even destroyed by the creature whose birth they were celebrating. (And not the least of these would be the hereditary agricultural manor system personified by Charles

Carroll of Carrollton.) Someone else might muse on the irony that this very same railroad launched by the last survivors of the war for independence would witness the first shots leading to the tragically divisive Civil War— but also that this railroad would be a critical instrument in holding the Union together.

In any event, the aftermath of that Fourth of July inevitably was anticlimactic. The railroad did indeed reach the Ohio River. Very clearly it was a pioneer that proved the practicality of railroading over long distances and through mountainous terrain. In its early days it was one of the most creative and innovative enterprises in our history. Many other railroads patterned themselves after the B&O and learned by its experiments and mistakes. It was rightly labelled the "university of railroading" as its early engineers and operating men went on to build and run other lines. And eventually it did serve its purpose of keeping Baltimore on the map and making it a major ocean port.

But B&O also had all the problems of a pioneer, plus many more. The pressure to build and to get into business at a time when the technology was undeveloped, the legalities of its route unsettled and financing uncertain all caused false starts, delays, wasted investment and ultimately an awkward route which produced endless operating problems. It took almost 25 years to reach the Ohio and even then the terminal it was forced to pick—Wheeling—was commercially unsatisfactory. It was at least five years after that before a more productive route could be opened. In the meantime—thanks in part to B&O's trial-and-error experiences—railroading had blossomed and B&O found itself surrounded by rapidly developing trunk lines which sometimes were better located, better financed and more aggressively managed. It did continue to grow and it prospered, albeit erratically. But to be truthful it never regained the premiere status and worldwide attention that it had in the few years after 1828.

Perhaps then, the symbolic fate of the cornerstone, the centerpiece of that unforgettable Fourth of July celebration is not surprising: structurally useless and in an out-of-the-way spot, it was quickly forgotten during the day-to-day process of building, rebuilding and operating. Eventually it was simply buried during some siding construction project —nobody even remembered how or when. By then B&O's major problem was not conquering the unknown but simply staying alive.

But to return to the beginning:

In the 80 years from 1745 to 1825 Baltimore had developed from a sparsely-settled mud flat to an active seaport of the same rank as Philadelphia, New York and Boston. In an era when all of the Atlantic seaboard ports depended primarily on roads to reach inland, Baltimore had one important advantage—it was significantly closer to the hinterland than its more northern rivals (roughly 90 miles inland from Philadelphia and 140 miles from New York). Remembering that at this time it was an accomplishment to cover 40 miles in one day, and that the capacity of horse-drawn highway vehicles was extremely limited, Baltimore's location made a large difference in the cost and speed of moving goods east and west. The city got a further boost in 1818 when the government-sponsored National Road was completed from Cumberland to the Ohio River at Wheeling. Baltimore had direct access to the National Road through a string of roads and turnpikes stretching west to Cumberland; the National Road itself was hard-surfaced and, by the mud-bog highway standards of the time, an excellent road through the rugged Alleghenies.

But in 1825 the Erie Canal was opened across New York state, giving New York direct access to Lake Erie and much of the midwest over an improved waterway. The canal was certainly not fast, but it could carry large quantities of goods and people smoothly and very cheaply. In effect it was a notable technological innovation which immediately disrupted the competitive commercial relationships of the various eastern ports. Indeed, most historians credit the Erie Canal with making New York the dominant eastern seaboard port—a position it has held ever since. Acting for Philadelphia and Pittsburgh, the state of Pennsylvania promptly responded in kind by passing legislation (in February 1826) to create a canal system from the Susquehanna to Pittsburgh, reaching Philadelphia over the Union and Schuylkill canals. But Pennsylvania's Alleghenies were nothing like New York's level Mohawk valley and the system was doomed before it had even begun. Ultimately it developed into an unwieldy collection of connecting railroads, canals and inclined planes which was fascinating to behold but economically absurd. The smaller Potomac River ports of Georgetown and Alexandria, bordering Washington, also elected what had suddenly become the conventional competitive approach: Through the Patowmack Company and its later successor the Chesapeake & Ohio Canal Company, they were attempting to build a canal up the Potomac to Cumberland, then somehow over the Alleghenies to the Ohio River.

Baltimore was caught with no clear way to compete. Its only way of reaching west by canal also was up the Potomac. However, it was considerably inland from the river and the intervening country was too rough to build a satisfactory connecting canal. The best route for a connecting canal was south to Washington, 40 miles—hardly practical for Baltimore, since any trade would pass through Alexandria and Georgetown on the way. In addition, it was obvious that no canal over the Alleghenies could compete on equal terms with the Erie.

The merchants and bankers involved in overseas trade were well aware of the small English railways built in the early 1800's; in fact, some of the English iron they imported was moved part of the trip on rails. They were much more familiar with the potential of steam power, since steamships already were showing up in Baltimore and the other ports. Railroads—even steam railroads—had been discussed and planned in the U.S. beginning in the early 1820's. One of the earliest had been chartered in 1823 to run from Philadelphia to Columbia, Pa., but Philadelphia apparently hadn't recognized its implications; it was not until 1834 that the line was completed between these points. But the expense and primitive state of technology made railroads less attractive than the proven economies of waterways, particularly where natural water routes already existed. (Lest anyone now smirk at such shortsightedness, the basic principle is still true—under the right conditions, waterways are still cheaper than rail transportation.)

But being the odd port out, Baltimore had to explore means other than canals. No doubt the planners were swayed by the enormous improvement in transportation efficiency anticipated by the use of horsepower alone...a horse could pull about twelve times the weight of his peer on the best highways of the day when the load was borne by rails, and much faster to boot. Steam power would make the advantage even more sweeping and had the potential to completely change the economics of transportation, industry and agriculture...no longer would the commerce of man be tied to water movement.

The railroad was at least theoretically practical, and in truth there weren't many alternatives. So, some time in 1826, the Baltimore businessmen—notably Philip and Evan Thomas, George Brown and William Patterson—began talking and investigating. By February 1827 they were certain enough and organized enough to go after a Maryland charter; on February 28, 1827 the Baltimore & Ohio received its charter. The company itself was formally organized two months later, on April 24. Fourteen months of preliminary work then had to follow before anyone was ready for the gala sendoff.

IMPOSSIBLE CHALLENGE

CHAPTER 2

LEARN AS YOU GO: THE MAIN LINE, 1828-1836

The only appropriate followup for that spectacular Fourth of July sendoff would have been for an army of Wagnerian heroes to link arms and stride westward, felling trees and cleaving rocks with their swords. B&O, however, was an extremely human enterprise. Its policymaking management consisted of a collection of bankers, merchants, politicians and baronial landowners who knew vaguely what they wanted to accomplish but had no clear idea of the technicalities. The technicalities were in the hands of a disparate group of civil engineers and contractors who had built turnpikes, surveyed wagon roads and blazed trails beyond the frontier. Since no one in the United States then had any expertise in railroad location and construction, B&O's directors had gone to the next best source: the federal government, whose exploration and roadbuilding projects came closest to providing the skills needed for railroad surveying.

In July 1827 a rugged group of borrowed Army Topographical Engineers under Dr. William Howard, Lt. Col. Stephen H. Long and Capt. William Gibbs McNeill began surveying possible routes between Baltimore and the Ohio River. In April 1828 they were joined by a civilian government engineer, Jonathan Knight, who had laid out parts of the Pennsylvania state turnpike system and the Ohio portion of the National Road. Along with Knight came Caspar W. Wever, another Pennsylvanian who had been construction boss for the National Road between Wheeling and Zanesville. Howard soon was recalled by the Army, but Long, Knight and McNeill remained to form the railroad's senior professional management. Wever was appointed Superintendent of Construction, theoretically a subordinate position primarily charged with executing the engineers' plans.

Long, at 45, was by age and experience the senior of the group. He was, as one historian described him, "a plodding and honest soldier who

7

had gained considerable renown as an explorer of the Great West."
Knight, 41, was a combination of theoretical mathematician and politi-
cian; in fact his arrival in Baltimore had been delayed while he completed
his term in the Pennsylvania legislature. Wever was a freewheeling,
aggressive entrepreneur, allegedly unscrupulous but apparently quite
competent in masonry construction and in managing contractors.
McNeill was 28, the youngest of the lot, but quickly became adept at the
work and later took his surveying skills and B&O experience to several
other pioneering eastern and New England railroad projects.

The engineers' first and most critical quandry was how to set the
basic grade and curvature standards for building the railroad. On one
hand, the most essential ingredients to calculate these—that is, the characteristics and capabilities of motive power and cars and traffic volume—
were largely unknown. Although B&O's directors had intended to use
horses and light two-axle cars as an initial expediency, it was already
clear that steam eventually would power the line. But in 1827 and 1828
railroad steam power was mostly a promising hope and a very primitive
reality. Thus far the only practical experience had been with the over-
weight, underpowered and mechanically awkward English mine tramway locomotives—which even in 1828 were considered obsolete. Robert
Stephenson's *Rocket*, the first truly "modern" steam design, was still a
year away. Thus B&O's engineers could only guess how much a steam
locomotive would weigh, what it would pull, how steep a grade it would
conquer or around how sharp a curve it would move. Similarly, freight
and passenger car length and carrying capacity were conjectural.

On the other hand, the topography B&O had to cross was all too well
known. It was rough, ranging from rolling hills to high mountains, cut
through by rock-walled rivers. In this type of terrain, even small variations in grade and curvature standards would make enormous differences in construction costs. Long and Knight were thus faced with a
variation of the classic chicken-or-egg problem: Should they let the terrain dictate the alignment—meaning sharp curves and steep grades—
and try to develop locomotives and cars to fit? Or should they design the
railroad around the unknown capabilities and requirements of the vehicles?

They compromised: Apparently most concerned about the ability of
steam to haul tonnage on grades, they decided that the line had to be
level—not literally level, of course, but 0.6% was considered the maximum.
Grades beyond this would be treated as inclined planes, probably operated by steam hoisting machinery. Oddly, they were much less concerned
with curves and were content to allow 14°-18° curves around the rocks in
the river valleys. As it turned out, it was exactly the wrong compromise—
the grades could have been steeper, but the curves should have been
wider.

But at least the location work went ahead. B&O's most obvious path
was up the Potomac River valley, which offered a more or less easy route
to the base of the Alleghenies just beyond Cumberland. (The competitive

C&O Canal from Georgetown also planned to use the Potomac over much the same route, for the same reason.) The immediate problem was to get from Baltimore to the Potomac. Baltimore was anywhere from 40 to 65 miles inland from the river, depending on whether you went south or west from the city. No way was particularly easy. Baltimore lay in a small bowl around its harbor; beyond were rolling Piedmont hills erratically cut up by small streams and creeks. The chain of roads leading from Baltimore to the National Road at Cumberland simply rolled with the hills in a direct line, but the railroad had to be level as far as possible, which meant following some waterway.

The only waterway that offered anything resembling a direct route was the Patapsco River, which rose 40 miles west near Mt. Airy, Md. and flowed into the bay just south of Baltimore. A short distance west of the Patapsco was the Monocacy River basin leading directly to the Potomac. In all it was about 65 miles from Baltimore to the Potomac via the Patapsco-Monocacy route. The two watersheds were separated by a low but steep ridge—the only spot en route where it would be impossible to hold to the river grades.

Some sense of B&O's problems getting west from Baltimore can be felt in this present-day view of the Patapsco valley south of Hollofield, Md. It was good terrain for water-powered mills but poor for a railroad. Credit: H.H. Harwood, Jr.

The Patapsco was, to be blunt, not much of a route. Really more creek than river, it twists sharply through a deep, narrow rocky valley which in spots could be called a gorge. Not only was the little river full of wriggles and rocky spurs, but the constricted valley was ideally formed for flooding—as the railroad, valley communities and industries periodically learned. But it did provide a gentle grade through otherwise difficult terrain. So, although B&O surveyors explored many other routes out of Baltimore (including parts of the route later taken by the Western Maryland Railway), the Patapsco seemed to be the only clear choice—particularly in view of the engineers' grade limitations.

B&O's biggest initial problem, however, was the seemingly simple job of getting from Baltimore to the Patapsco. The river flows somewhat south of the city and empties into the harbor at what is now the Brooklyn section—about three miles south of the city's center. The easiest and cheapest way would have been simply to follow the flat shoreline around the harbor south from Baltimore, picking up the Patapsco somewhere near Brooklyn.

Between Baltimore and Relay the infant B&O had to build across hilly country, necessitating many curves, cuts and fills which remain today. In this March, 1969 photo, an eastbound freight negotiates the reverse curve between Relay and St. Denis. Credit: H.H. Harwood, Jr.

Unhappily this was not to be. Instead, the railroad's exit from Baltimore turned out to be extremely difficult, unnecessarily costly and—sadly—symbolic of the type of artificial problems B&O regularly seemed to face during its history. (Throughout the railroad's development, it seemed, political and competitive maneuverings would force it into expensive routes and awkward operations.) In this case the villain was the infamous "66-foot agreement," later written into the financial aid agreement with the city and also the city ordinances allowing the railroad to enter Baltimore. In essence, this specified that the railroad must enter the city at 66 feet above sea level. The reason for what seems to be such an absurdly arbitrary stipulation was quite selfishly practical: The city fathers feared—probably correctly—that the easy harbor-level route would take the railroad line past better natural harbor sites south of the city, which would then be developed to Baltimore's detriment. Given this objection, B&O's engineers then tried to match the most commercially practical point to enter Baltimore with the most favorable spot to meet the Patapsco and decided on the 66-foot elevation.

Whatever the logic, this meant that the unfortunate railroad had to build overland from Baltimore to the Patapsco. Its best route seemed to be to head directly southwest from the city, picking up the Patapsco on high ground at what is now Relay—about 7½ miles from Baltimore and also about 7½ miles upstream from the river's mouth at Brooklyn. It was hilly country, cut up by numerous streams of varying sizes, all of them running crosswise to the planned railroad line. Building such a line meant a continuous succession of cuts, fills and bridges—some of which had to be quite large. Railroad builders would soon consider such terrain routine, but for the pioneering B&O the job turned out to be a supreme effort—considerably aggravated by the engineers' insistence on "level" grades and the directors' sudden fixation with eternally enduring substructures. Ironically, the level route along the harbor lowlands was partly used years later by B&O's South Baltimore branch and by the Baltimore & Annapolis Short Line to get to other places. By then Baltimore's inner harbor had largely been supplanted by such terminals as Locust Point, Canton and Curtis Bay, and nobody cared.

Once into the Patapsco valley B&O's heavy grading problems ceased, but were traded for others. The valley had a natural grade of not much more than 0.3%-0.4%, and most tributary streams were small and could be crossed on culverts. However the river's twists and multiple rock spurs and outcroppings meant either sharp curves or extensive blasting and tunnelling. B&O's engineers picked the curves, of course. In addition, there were two points where the line was forced to cross the river to avoid sheer rock walls. At the end of the Patapsco was Parr's Ridge, the hills separating the Patapsco and the Monocacy, which was a general divide running across the entire state. Parr's Ridge was a different type of problem—its grades far exceeded the maximum established for normal train operation. More about that later.

On the west side of Parr's Ridge the projected line picked up Bush Creek, a tributary to the Monocacy, smaller but slightly less torturous and rocky than the Patapsco. The alignment followed Bush Creek to the Monocacy and crossed the Monocacy on what would have to be a large bridge—but from there to the Potomac the terrain was reasonably easy across the wide and easy undulating fields of Carrollton Manor.

Still another problem was getting into downtown Baltimore itself from the 66-foot entry point. The city was tightly clustered around the harbor area and—even by 1828—was heavily built up to the point where there was no open right-of-way into the center of town or the docks. An early proposal was to bring the line into town along approximately the present Mt. Clare branch alignment as far as Pratt and Parkin Streets, then continue northeast to a terminal at West Baltimore Street and Fremont Avenue (then called Cove Street). At this time that area was largely undeveloped and this terminal would have been quite remote from everything. To reach the city's center, the railroad had three alternatives, all of which were disagreeable: It could swing around the north of downtown to Jones Falls, then follow Jones Falls south again to the harbor and the City Dock. It could condemn and purchase property occupied by buildings and run in directly. Or it could build down the center of the streets, tramway-style. The first would have required tunnelling Lexington Hill, a wide and high rise immediately north of the downtown area, and would also have bypassed much of the city's commercial activity. Both the first and second alternatives would have been impossibly expensive for the young company, and the second would be disruptive to the city as well. The third was cheap but unpopular, since it would put railroad trains directly on the street in the middle of already heavy wagon, carriage and foot traffic. (And with steam power already vaguely being discussed, downtown residents were considerably less than enthusiastic.)

The question was hotly discussed and many variations of these proposals were made up. In the end, however, B&O had little choice but using the streets—which meant negotiating with the city and coping with the objections of property owners and draymen along the route. Eventually Pratt Street was selected as the route into town, but because of the opposition permission to use the street was not immediately forthcoming.

In the meantime the railroad decided to start construction in open country just southwest of Pratt Street on property already donated or sold to it by the Carrolls and other friendly landowners—then an area of farmlands and country estates. Temporarily at least, its first terminal would be at the spot where its own right-of-way met Pratt Street a mile west of the center of Baltimore—about half a block east of the present Mt. Clare station and B&O Museum complex.

On July 7, 1828 B&O announced that it had started its final route location work between Baltimore and the Potomac River at Point of Rocks. In August contracts were being let for the first section of this line, the 12 miles from Pratt Street to Ellicott's Mills in the Patapsco valley. By October, work was under way over most of this segment.

It was a fitful start. In many places construction proceeded slowly as the engineers and directors argued over the most practical methods of overcoming the natural obstacles and the contractors tried to carry out the ones selected. Already organizational weaknesses, personality clashes and fundamental differences in theory had begun to surface.

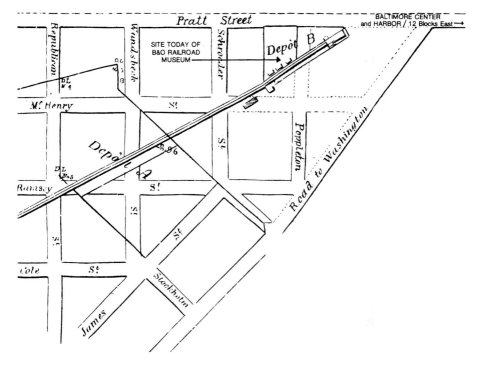

B&O's original Baltimore terminal, at Pratt and Poppleton Streets. The map dates to early 1831; later the "Road to Washington" (now Washington Boulevard) was relocated in this area, joining Pratt Street considerably farther east. The area labelled "Depot A" was the original Mt. Clare shop site. Note that the line appears to end in a shed at Pratt Street; only a small shed of some type shows on the site of the present Mt. Clare station which, according to the best evidence, was not built until 1851.

First, it was difficult to tell who was in charge. Having no real experience with the people making up the professional staff, and recognizing the primitive state of railroad location and construction knowledge, B&O's directors had decided to defer the establishment of a conventional management organization with clear lines of authority. Instead they created a three-man Board of Engineers which somehow was to be jointly responsible for making the day-to-day engineering decisions and supervising the construction work. The Board consisted of the two senior professionals, Long and Knight, plus B&O president Philip E. Thomas, a 52-year-old merchant and banker. (Later, McNeill was added to the Board.) This ambiguous organization with no single line of authority and no single responsibility forced the layman Thomas to resolve the inevitable differences in technical opinions—not to mention the personal conflicts among this rugged group of individualists.

To add to the confusion, just as full-scale construction was starting in October 1828, Thomas sent Knight and McNeill on a six-month trip to England to study railroad construction and mechanical experience there. The trip was unquestionably necessary, since England was then the only

13

Jonathan Knight was the dominant member of B&O's original Board of Engineers and its Chief Engineer from 1831 to 1842. Although greatly aided by his assistant, Benjamin Latrobe, Knight was ultimately responsible for the form of the original B&O. Credit: B&O Museum Archives.

source of such practical knowledge—but it came at a time when many quick, on-the-spot engineering decisions had to be made at home. Long was theoretically in charge, but almost immediately Wever—who was not a Board of Engineers member—began managing things his own way and working through Thomas and the directors. Thomas apparently trusted Wever more than Long and declared himself as Wever's immediate supervisor, cutting Long off from the subordinate who was supposed to be carrying out his policies.

While all this perhaps was an ordinary squabble over power and authority which periodically happens in any business, it was a poor start for the B&O at a critical time. Not only was its management disunited, but decisions were made which turned out to be unnecessarily costly and time-consuming to the company. This was particularly true on the crucial question of the design of bridges and other substructures. The pragmatic Army engineers preferred to follow the frontier theory of construction: build low-cost wood bridges and trestles and get the line into operation quickly, replacing them with heavier and more permanent structures when the traffic and finances built up to the point where they were justified. The directors, influenced by Wever, came to favor stone bridges and heavy earth fills to span the streams and other depressions en route to Relay and beyond—structures certainly suited to the heavy railroad traffic and power of the 1900's but hardly necessary for the 1830's. It promised to be a slow and very costly process, made more so by Wever's penchant for finely-dressed stone surfaces on his bridges. Similarly, the directors specified a double-track railroad the entire length, requiring wider cuts and fills than would be needed for some time. As already mentioned, the engineers were too conservative about maximum grades, requiring deeper cuts and higher fills than were really necessary.

In short, the railroad started off as a combination of commercial artery and eternal monument—an enormous burden for an under-financed enterprise which had to get through 380 miles of wilderness before it could produce a full return on its investment. In retrospect Wever was right about the durability, low maintenance and load carrying capabilities of his bridges—some of them still stand, carrying any present-day loads. And the B&O directors whose names those viaducts memorialized —Carroll, Patterson, Oliver and Thomas—perhaps were remembered longer by some. It might also be noted that two of B&O's engineering veterans—McNeill and Lt. George W. Whistler—went on to build stone bridges on their New England railroad projects, notably McNeill's spectacular Canton viaduct on the Boston & Providence. But at the time, this heavy work was a luxury B&O did not need and really could not afford.

Gwynns Falls, a minor stream on Baltimore's outskirts, was responsible for one of B&O's earliest and certainly one of its most spectacular stone bridges — the Carrollton Viaduct, shown here as it looked about 1926. Col. Long had wanted a wood trestle, but Caspar Wever persuaded the directors otherwise. The arch measures 80 feet across. It still stands, of course. Credit: B&O, H.H. Harwood Coll.

Nonetheless the contractors went bravely ahead on their first 12 miles. Just west of the Pratt Street starting point a fill had to be built over a gully at the present Carey Street. Immediately beyond, at what is now Monroe Street a cut had to be excavated 30 feet deep and 1,972 feet long. Then came Gwynns Run with another fill and small stone bridge— followed by Gwynns Falls, to be crossed on a massive stone viaduct 297 feet long, with a single 80-foot arch. The first viaduct, of course, had to be named to honor Charles Carroll of Carrollton.

Just beyond the viaduct was another hill, over which ran the Washington Road (now Washington Boulevard). At this point the directors favored the idea of a 100-foot tunnel under the ridge and road—

mostly, according to Long's testimony, because they wanted the first railroad tunnel in the country. Long proposed an open cut with a wood truss (of his own design) to carry the road over. Thomas and the directors finally agreed, apparently willing to compromise their heavy masonry standards for highway overpasses. Long built his 107.6-foot Jackson's Bridge, which became famous as an early long wood truss design; it lasted into the late 1800's. Long had named it—perhaps pointedly—in honor of the new President, Andrew Jackson, rather than a railroad officer.

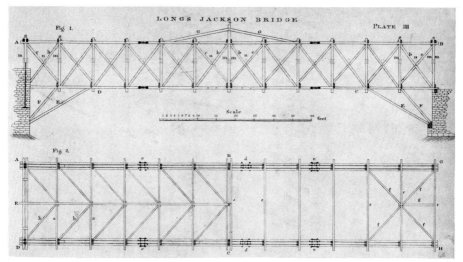

Long got one of his few chances to build a wood bridge for the cross-ing of the Washington Road (now Washington Boulevard) over B&O's tracks just west of Gwynns Falls. His Jackson Bridge, built in 1829, lasted at least 35 years. Credit: B&O Museum Archives.

Slightly less than two miles west of the Carrollton viaduct was a high ridge separating the Gwynns Falls and Patapsco drainage systems. This one required a large cut 68 feet deep and 3,000 feet long—so formidable that the railroad builders respectfully christened it the Great Cut, and later the Deep Cut. A mile and a half further, just west of present Lans-downe, the tracks had to cross Roberts Run on an earth fill about 50 feet high. Next came Gadsby's Run, west of what is now Halethorpe, and a longer, higher (57 foot) fill. Vinegar Hill, where U.S. Rt. 1 now crosses the railroad east of St. Denis, necessitated a cut 50 feet deep and 1,628 feet long. Between here and Relay two lesser fills had to be built.

In the Patapsco section beyond Relay, the work consisted mostly of grading a ledge alongside the river and building small stone arch bridges over several streams which came down the steep hillsides. The right-of-way followed the north side of the river for 3½ miles, dodging around rock cliffs. But at today's Ilchester a combination of sharp river bend and sheer rock wall forced the line to cross to the south side. Another substan-

No early views of the infamous Deep Cut survive, but this is how it looks today. It was widened for four tracks in the late 1870's (recently reduced to three because of drainage problems), but one has to imagine how it looked as a narrow two-track cut with steeper side slopes. The view looks west from Patapsco Avenue; the freight is eastbound. Credit: H.H. Harwood, Jr.

The valley of Gadsby's Run, west of Halethorpe (presently variously called Herbert or Hubbards Run) was another costly obstacle in 1828. The 57-foot high fill was one of the largest and most impressive on the original line. The little stone bridge below is the original 1828 structure, rebuilt in 1875 when the fill was widened. The train is eastbound in early 1979. Credit: H.H. Harwood, Jr.

17

tial stone viaduct had to be built—this one 360 feet long with four arches (two 55-foot arches over the river and a 20-foot arch at each end for county roads), to be named for director William Patterson. From the Patterson viaduct the line followed the somewhat easier south side of the Patapsco into Ellicott's Mills, already an active little grist milling and ironmaking town located where the Baltimore-Frederick turnpike crossed the river. At Ellicott's Mills the tracks had to be carried over the turnpike and a small adjacent stream on a triple-arch stone viaduct (each arch was 20 feet)—named for director Robert Oliver.

The Carrollton viaduct was put under contract in December 1828, although not much was accomplished until the following spring. The Patterson was begun in January 1829 and the cornerstone of the Oliver viaduct was laid on July 4, 1829. The engineers argued about crossing Gadsby's Run with a wood trestle or an embankment and it was not until early 1829 that the directors decided on an embankment and stone bridge.

By the end of 1829 the two big viaducts—Carrollton and Patterson— were finished and about three miles of track had been laid in three disconnected sections: a short portion near Ellicott's Mills, another piece at the Patterson viaduct to facilitate hauling its stone, and 1½ miles in Baltimore between Pratt Street and the Carrollton viaduct. The line was beginning to take shape, although Alexander Brown despaired in a letter written in December 1829 that "A vast amount of money has been expended. More than ought to by the ignorance of our engineers. We think it is likely the board will part with all of them shortly except Knight....One track of our road about 1½ miles is completely finished, which seems to meet our most sanguine expectations....It has however cost much more money than we calculated on; a great part of this arose from want of practical experience; many mistakes have been made which we hope will be guarded against in the future." Brown might also have put a slight bit of blame on his fellow directors, but perhaps that was too close to home.

But at least the directors were able to celebrate New Year's Day of 1830 with an inaugural ride from Pratt Street to the Carrollton viaduct and back in a horse-drawn car. A week later, on January 7, this short section was opened for public joyriding and on January 16 various members of Congress came up from Washington for a special trip. On this occasion a single horse reportedly pulled four carloads of people together. The trips were continued at least through January, partly as an early 19th Century form of public relations but more practically to get some working experience with the track structure.

Also in early 1830 the management organization was straightened out. On January 1 Jonathan Knight was named Chief Engineer, with sole responsibility for the design and construction work. Long went back to the Army and McNeill followed shortly afterwards. For better or worse, Wever remained, working under Knight.

Excavating the Deep Cut turned out to be the nastiest construction problem and the key barrier to getting the line open to Ellicott's Mills. During the summer of 1829 construction crews were worked through the night to finish it. The job eventually took 18 months—the longest of any single project on the line.

As the track went down the engineers continued to experiment. Following the philosophy of permanency over cost, Jonathan Knight decided that the "ideal" track structure should consist of longitudinal granite stringers laid in a trough in the ground, carrying an iron strap rail on their top inside surface. But the best sources of this stone were in the Patapsco valley and, with the railroad still unfinished, it was too slow and costly to get the material in to the Baltimore end. Also the numerous fills had to settle before placing the heavy stone roadbed on them. With these problems and the necessity to get the railroad into some semblance of operation after the construction delays, Knight made two expedient compromises: From Baltimore to Relay the line was laid with strap rail carried on longitudinal wood stringers, supported by wood ties. The "strap" rail consisted of thin (⅝ inch), narrow (2½ inches) flat strips of iron

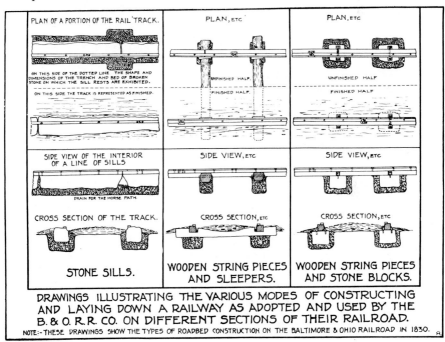

DRAWINGS ILLUSTRATING THE VARIOUS MODES OF CONSTRUCTING AND LAYING DOWN A RAILWAY AS ADOPTED AND USED BY THE B. & O. R.R. CO. ON DIFFERENT SECTIONS OF THEIR RAILROAD.

NOTE:- THESE DRAWINGS SHOW THE TYPES OF ROADBED CONSTRUCTION ON THE BALTIMORE & OHIO RAILROAD IN 1830.

B&O used all of these primitive track types on its original line: the wood stringer/strap rail combination between Baltimore and Relay, the stone block/wood stringer/strap rail on one track between Relay and Ellicott's Mills, and the stone stringer/strap rail on at least one track between Relay and Sykesville. Beyond Sykesville, economy and expediency fortunately dictated a "temporary" return to the wood stringer/strap rail system.

fastened to a flat surface. The rail weighed about 15 pounds per yard and generally was made in 15 foot lengths. The wood "ties" were hardly comparable to a modern railroad tie. Said one authority: "The stringers (carrying the strap rail) were let into notches in log cross ties, which were about seven inches in diameter. . . .As the ties were only four feet on

The floods from Tropical Storm Agnes allowed a rare firsthand look at B&O's original stone track bed 140 years later. In this section, looking east at Ilchester, two methods can be seen side by side. In the foreground is the north side of the original eastbound track, laid with longitudinal granite stringers and plainly bearing the marks where its strap rail was fastened. To the rear are scattered rectangular blocks which once carried wood stringers for the westbound track. Credit: H.H. Harwood, Jr.

center, and also heavily hewn away at their center to provide sufficient earth cover for a horse path, their function clearly was little more than to maintain the track gauge." From Relay to Ellicott's Mills Knight used granite, but still compromised both for the sake of speed and experimentation. This six-mile section was laid with a single track using the strap rails on wood stringers, but anchored to large rectangular granite blocks, a separate line of blocks for each rail. (The blocks were about 20 inches long, a foot wide and 8 inches to a foot deep, and were spaced on about 4½ foot centers. The wood stringer carrying the rail was anchored to the blocks by cast iron brackets fastened to the blocks by spikes driven into wood plugs set in drilled holes.) Once the line was open to Ellicott's Mills, Knight was able to go back and lay the second track from Relay with his longitudinal stone stringers. These stringers were simply long, narrow sections of stone laid end to end, with the strap rail fastened directly to the finished inner edge of the stone.

Pushed by the now-nervous directors, the engineers and contractors got a single track laid between the end of Pratt Street and Ellicott's Mills as quickly as possible, and on May 22, 1830 an official inaugural trip was run all the way. The following Monday, May 24, the railroad was opened for scheduled service, advertising three trips a day to Ellicott's Mills. Hauled by horses, of course, the cars took about 1½ hours to make the 13-mile run. But typical of many rushed "completions", the railroad was not really ready for full business for a while. It was not until late June that enough passenger cars were completed to handle the schedules and only by July 5 could service be expanded to four trips a day. Freight cars were not ready until fall. Double tracking also had to be completed, although for the moment it was scarcely needed.

But horses or not, and completed or not, that late May opening was the first regular railroad service in the United States.

It had taken 18 months to open the 13-mile section to Ellicott's Mills— not really bad by modern construction standards, but slow by the railroad building techniques which had developed by the mid-19th Century. One wonders how many of the directors privately calculated this rate of progress and arrived at the depressing conclusion that it would take another 40 years to reach the Ohio River.

The railroad was at least finally a revenue-producing enterprise. Since Ellicott's Mills was a junction with the Frederick turnpike, the major highway between Baltimore and the west, B&O could tap into through passenger and freight traffic for the eastern end of its journey Outbound passengers and inbound flour (from the local mills and elsewhere) flowed in reasonably heavy quantities by the end of the year.

The situation at the Baltimore end was equally temporary. The line into the city center was not yet open and in fact was stalled because opposition to using Pratt Street continued. So, for over a year after the Ellicott's Mills service opened, the terminal remained at the end of the railroad's right-of-way where it met West Pratt Street near Parkin. A temporary shed was built there along with a small ticket booth, stables,

The station at Ellicott's Mills (now Ellicott City), probably finished in early fall of 1831, was one of the first permanent structures on the railroad and, in somewhat altered form, still stands. This 1965 view shows it as it looked from the mid-1880's to the present. As built, the station had had a large doorway on the end nearest the camera; a track entered the building for freight loading/unloading and locomotive storage. Some of the wood trim and the multicolored glass windows were added about 1885. Credit: H.H. Harwood, Jr.

The Patterson Viaduct, at Ilchester, was the railroad's first multiple-arch stone bridge and its first crossing of the Patapsco. Three of its four arches were taken out by the great flood of 1868. The original alignment was bypassed in 1903, but one arch of the bridge remains. Credit: B&O Museum Archives.

and a car repair and storage depot. (The legendary brick Mt. Clare station which now stands near this site is exactly that—a legend; it was built 20 years later.) In 1830 this terminal area was largely in open undeveloped country—an area of country estates dominated by James Carroll's "Mount Clare." Pratt Street ended here and such cross streets as Parkin and Poppleton did not exist outside the surveyors' maps.

As the horses plodded between Pratt Street and Ellicott's Mills, the builders pushed west from the latter. To get the job done quickly it was decided not to open any more of the railroad for public use until it had been finished to Frederick, the first major way point. Generally the work was easier, although in some sections a ledge had to be carved out along the narrow river bank and supported with stone retaining walls. An awesome cliff immediately north of Ellicott's Mills, locally known as the Tarpean Rock, was blasted through, leaving a towering section of the spur remaining next to the track on the river side.

Immediately north of Ellicott's Mills station was the Tarpean Rock, definitely an untypical feature of the railroad. This 1831 view looks south toward the station. The spectacular rock remnant on the river side was finally blasted away in the late 1850's.

Buzzard's Rock, between Relay and Avalon, was an early scenic attraction and also a fairly typical sample of Patapsco valley topography. This 1831 lithograph shows both tracks laid with granite stringers, although actually the westbound track (at the right) consisted of wood stringers on granite blocks. Credit: B&O Museum Archives.

The track now became the chief drag on progress. Against Knight's better judgment, the company was now committed to laying both tracks with longitudinal granite sills rather than making any temporary compromises with wood. Getting the stone quarried, dressed and hauled to the sites was frustratingly slow. Knight had hoped to have at least a single track finished to the Forks of the Patapsco (between Woodstock and Marriottsville) by the fall of 1830, but was barely beyond there in June 1831. He got at least one stone track as far as Sykesville and then gave up, reverting to the wood stringer-wood tie system as a "temporary" expedient to move faster.

Another type of delay occurred in June 1831 at Sykesville, where some construction forces had been left marooned and unpaid by an absconding contractor. After some fruitless negotiations with railroad officials, the workers rioted. The problem was solved in typical 19th Century style by calling out the Baltimore militia and running it up to Sykesville in railroad cars, where one-third of the workers were arrested and the rest dispersed. The event had the melancholy honor of being the first troop movement by railroad.

The line west of Ellicott's Mills continued along the south side of the Patapsco for 12 miles, crossing many streams on small single-arch stone bridges. But less than a mile west of Marriottsville another combination of sharp river bend and sheer rock forced the line back over to the north side, where it remained until it reached the end of the river at Parr's Ridge. To get over the river at this point the tracks had to be twisted through a sharp "S" curve, cross the river on another stone arch bridge (a single 40-foot arch this time), then pass through a rock cut on the north side followed by another sharp curve. From here (the present Henryton) west to Parr's Ridge, the valley gradually opened out and the work was easier. The only other significant stream in this section was Gillies Falls, just west of Woodbine, which was crossed on a 25-foot stone arch.

The Parr's Ridge hump was solved by laying out a system of horse-operated inclined planes to take the tracks up out of the Patapsco watershed and down to Bush Creek—an inconvenient, expensive but (reasoned Knight) necessary evil which, he assumed, would also have to be used when the railroad eventually reached the Alleghenies. There were four planes—two on the east side of the ridge and two on the west—topping the ridge just south of Ridgeville, about a mile south of Mt. Airy. (A separate section tells the detailed story of these deservedly forgotten inclines.)

Bush Creek's twists and tributaries required four more small stone bridges, the largest a 25-foot arch about a mile east of Monrovia to carry the line over Bush Creek itself. The Monocacy River crossing forced the only compromise with B&O's stone bridge standard: The 37-foot elevation of the track level over the river and the 350-foot wide crossing at this point clearly would have required another long and costly delay if done with stone. The result was a three-span wood deck truss bridge, each span 110 feet long resting on stone piers and abutments, and eventually

25

weatherboarded on top and sides. It was built by the legendary German-born covered bridge builder Lewis Wernwag, who at that time was head-quartered in nearby Harpers Ferry.

At the west end of the Monocacy bridge the line divided: The main line swung southwest following the broad valley between the Monocacy River and Catoctin Mountain, heading toward the Potomac at Point of Rocks; a 3½ mile branch turned almost due north to Frederick. The Point of Rocks route ran through a broad valley and needed no heavy work other than the usual small stone arch bridges over such streams as Ballingers Creek and two branches of Tuscarora Creek. The short single-track Frederick branch was somewhat more rugged, requiring one long deep cut through limestone, and several smaller cuts.

Frederick, incidentally, had ended up as the country's first branch line city—much to its dismay. As one of Maryland's larger towns at the time, and an active milling and market community, it had fully expected to be on the main line and had invested in B&O accordingly. But in plotting the final line location, the engineers had decided to pass it a short distance south of Frederick to take advantage of the valley grade and avoid some of the rougher ground around the town.

By the middle of 1831 work was under way on virtually all of the railroad between Ellicott's Mills and Frederick/Point of Rocks. In the meantime, things were finally moving on the east end of the line. The ordinance allowing B&O to build down Pratt Street was passed in early April, 1831. Immediately a single track (laid with stone stringers and strap rail) was laid east on Pratt across the harbor front to President Street and south on President to the City Dock. Operations into down-town Baltimore and the City Dock began September 29, 1831, two months before the main line west of Ellicott's Mills could be opened. A permanent passenger and freight station was established on the south side of Pratt Street in the block bounded by Charles, Light and Camden. This eventu-ally developed as a little hodgepodge of reconverted and newly-build buildings serving as B&O's Baltimore terminal for the next 22 years. However, the local residents' fear of steam locomotives chugging by their doorsteps had produced a prohibition in the ordinance requiring the railroad to use animal power over any city streets. As B&O adopted steam power, the West Pratt depot (eventually called Mt. Clare depot) became the changeover point between horse and steam. Generally the horses hauled the passenger and freight cars singly over Pratt Street from the Charles Street Station and the City Dock to Mt. Clare, where they were assembled into trains to go west.

And steam power was a reality by mid-1831. Peter Cooper had bolted together little *Tom Thumb* and in August 1830 showed the directors that locomotives could indeed be designed to operate on B&O's hairpin Patapsco curves. Heartened by the demonstration, the railroad had adver-tised in January 1831 for new designs suitable for regular work on its kind of railroad. The response was limited and disappointing—only five entries appeared, only one of which had any real spark of promise. That entry, the

York, built by watchmaker Phineas Davis of York, Pa. was reworked and put into service in June 1831 hauling the Ellicott's Mills trains. Although it did manage as many as four cars over this relatively level section and could reach 30 m.p.h., its 3½-ton weight was too light for extended use and it was retired about a year later. However, Davis's principle of a short four-wheel upright boiler locomotive seemed ideal for B&O. By late 1832 he had built a 6½-ton successor, the *Atlantic*—the forerunner of a rugged fleet of geared four-wheel vertical-boiler locomotives which became B&O's backbone by the mid-1830's.

Ellicott's Mills in 1835. The Ellicott flour-mill complex and town are at the far right; in the foreground is the Frederick turnpike (present Frederick Road). Across the river a B&O Grasshopper heads a two-car train for Baltimore. Credit: Enoch Pratt Free Library.

With or without a practical steam locomotive, B&O was able to open the next sections of its railroad by the end of 1831. On October 31 a horse-drawn special car was run to the foot of Plane 1 at Parr's Ridge, followed by another in November. On December 1, 1831 the first ceremonial "train"—a succession of four horse-drawn cars—entered Frederick. In contrast to the sunny summer sendoff July 4, 1828, the arrival day was damp, grey and cold with a light snowfall on the ground—perhaps a more accurate symbol of B&O's early life. The train had left the temporary Baltimore terminal at the Three Tuns Tavern at Pratt and Paca Streets 7:15 a.m. and arrived in Federick between one and two o'clock, to the accompaniment of artillery and ringing church bells. On April 1, 1832 service was started with somewhat less ceremony to Point of Rocks.

In the meantime at least two permanent stations had also been completed. The first—and now the country's oldest—was finished at Ellicott's Mills some time late in 1831; in 1832 a larger one was built at Frederick, fronting on South Carroll Street and measuring 70 feet by 100 feet. Both were solid, stone structures primarily designed as combination freight houses and car (or locomotive) storage facilities. Passenger facilities were secondary and, in the case of Ellicott's Mills, apparently nonexistent—here passengers used the adjacent Patapsco Hotel, which had its own access to the platform. In addition to these way stations, terminal buildings began to appear in Baltimore: During 1831 and 1832 a brick car storage house was built at Mt. Clare as well as a brick freight warehouse downtown on Light Street near Pratt.

A.

The Frederick depot as it looked near the end of its life about 1910. Note the doorway and track at each end; freight cars were loaded and unloaded inside, much like at Ellicott's Mills. View A. shows the station's east end; B. is the west end, fronting on South Carroll Street. A new passenger station was built in 1854, but the 1832 structure served as a freight station until about 1910. Credit: (both photos): B&O Museum Archives.

B.

In mid-1832 the railroad's track was a mishmash of different types which, to anyone unfamiliar with B&O's construction problems, seemed to follow one another in no logical order. From Baltimore to Relay the two tracks were both still laid with the "temporary" system of strap rail on wood stringers and ties. Between Relay and Ellicott's Mills, the westbound track consisted of strap rails on wood stringers attached to stone blocks, while the eastbound track—laid later—was strap rail on longitudinal stone stringers. From Ellicott's Mills to the Forks of Patapsco, east of Marriottsville, both tracks were stone stringers—except for several short sections where wood stringers and ties were laid on yet-unsettled embankments. From the Forks to Sykesville, one track continued to be stone stringers, the other wood. West of Sykesville, to both Frederick and Point of Rocks, both tracks reverted to strap rail on wood stringers and ties. However, reports show that somewhere between the summit of Parr's Ridge and the Monocacy River, 1¾ miles of track was laid with logs—whether as expedient or experiment is not recorded.

Initial service was two "trains" a day between Baltimore and Frederick, and later to Point of Rocks. A passenger run left Baltimore at 5:30 a.m. and reached Frederick about 1 p.m. and an afternoon mail schedule left at 5 p.m. and arrived at Frederick at 1 a.m.—eight hours to cover the 58 miles counting meal stops, horse relays and the trip over the inclined planes. Depending on the time of day, trains stopped for meals at Ellicott's Mills, Marriottsville and Sykesville. Horses were changed at 12 points on the way to Frederick: at Relay, Ellicott's Mills, Dorsey's (west of present Daniels), Marriottsville, Sykesville, Shipley's, Zepp's, the foot of Plane 1, the top of Parr's Ridge (Ridgeville), the base of Plane 4, Smith's and Littlejohn's. Passenger trains mostly consisted of single cars, sometimes run in multiple sections—still hauled by horses at this time; freight trains were true trains in many cases, consisting of up to three cars carrying almost three tons each. Although the railroad had been in full operation only part of the period, during the 12 months from October 1, 1831 to September 30, 1832 it carried 89,000 passengers and 41,000 tons of freight. The freight consisted mostly of flour coming east from Ellicott's Mills, Frederick and Point of Rocks, plus granite and limestone from the Patapsco valley and Frederick.

In September 1832 the second steam locomotive arrived—the 6½-ton *Atlantic*. The *Atlantic* was another product of Phineas Davis, and like his little *York* had two axles, small wheels and a vertical boiler; it was heavier, however, and had a geared drive. Although still not ideal for B&O's needs it worked well enough to be regularly assigned to the Frederick passenger train between West Pratt Street and the base of Plane 1 on the east side of Parr's Ridge.

At Point of Rocks work had stopped abruptly. Waiting there for B&O—somewhat like the classic western gunfighter—was the Chesapeake & Ohio Canal out of Georgetown, also building west. Directly ahead of them both was Catoctin Mountain, the easternmost outpost of the Alleghenies. Anyone on the scene at Point of Rocks knew why the spot had been so named without being told: the east wall of the mountain came almost directly down to the river, creating a tight squeeze around the ledge for anyone building through. And immediately west, another spur of the same mountain also reached close to the Potomac. There were two similar tight spots further up the river—Millers Narrows, between Weverton and Sandy Hook, and Elk Hill (Maryland Heights) opposite Harpers Ferry. Unless B&O wanted to blast out these massive rock walls or tunnel them—which it definitely did not—the railroad and canal would be forced tightly together for a total of four miles in the 12-mile stretch between Point of Rocks and Harpers Ferry. There was probably room for both but the two carriers would be so close that the questions of how they would be aligned—and who would control the design and construction—were critical. Thus the managers of both companies saw the 12 miles as the key to their futures and dug in for a fight over control of the passages.

The confrontation at Point of Rocks was long expected by everyone. Furthermore, its implications went far beyond these 12 miles between Point of Rocks and Harpers Ferry. From the time each company started construction in 1828, they had both planned to follow the north side of the Potomac all the way to Cumberland—well aware that the other intended to do the same. Each felt that it had a prior legal right to the route, but the issue had not been clearly resolved in the courts when they began building. So to protect themselves in the meantime, both companies had thrown injunctions at one another in 1828, preventing either from building west of Point of Rocks. In January 1832—shortly before B&O could begin service—the canal finally got a favorable court decision and tried to start work west through the narrows as quickly as it could. But property acquisition problems, B&O-inspired legal harassment and a devastating cholera epidemic in early fall slowed work. (Interestingly, Caspar Wever had bought a large piece of riverfront property in this area with the idea of establishing a mill complex and community. Presented with a unique opportunity to combine company loyalty with personal greed, Wever held out for the highest possible dollar and let the canal company take him to court.) The canal lost the initiative and in the meantime B&O was able to force the issue back into the state legislature, which was helping to finance both companies.

The story of the subsequent legal tangle has been told often—in fact overtold and perhaps overdramatized. Nonetheless it is deservedly considered a classic episode in transportation history: two rival modes of transportation representing two rival economic areas, supported by shifting and conflicting political interests—all forced into a legal shootout against a mountain wall.

To nobody's surprise the fight took time—over a year from the date B&O completed its rails to Point of Rocks. The outcome was a complicated compromise in which the canal technically won, but both lines went ahead. B&O was allowed to share the right-of-way between Point of Rocks and Harpers Ferry, including a 20-foot minimum width and 14° minimum curve around the mountain spurs. The C&O Canal would be responsible for actually building both the railroad and canal through the three most critical areas—for about a mile west of Point of Rocks, another mile through the upper Catoctin spurs, and two miles between Millers

A.

B.

This rare view from the mid-1860's graphically illustrates the problem at Point of Rocks, even more evident in the 1978 photo. In both cases the camera looks west from approximately the same location. In the intervening years B&O tunnelled the rock spur, but in the early 1960's it relaid its eastbound main track on the old alignment to provide better clearances in the tunnel. By then the tangle of trees on the left marked the C&O Canal bed, which was partly filled in here to allow a wider curve. Credits: A-John P. Hankey collection — B-H.H. Harwood, Jr.

Narrows and Harpers Ferry. (Part of this last section also had to accommodate the Frederick-Harpers Ferry turnpike.) B&O would buy canal company stock as part of its contribution to the joint construction cost. Most important, however, B&O had to back away from its original plan to follow the north side of the Potomac to Cumberland, leaving it in both a political and engineering quandary over where to go from Harpers Ferry.

It is difficult to tell which company had been hurt the worst by the litigation: The C&O Canal lost over two years time and came close to forfeiting its charter; B&O not only lost a year in reaching Harpers Ferry, but the necessity to find another route west—and the tangled political ramifications it produced—cost it an additional five years.

In any event, both companies had agreed to the compromise by early May 1833 and work went ahead soon after. B&O had to accept a single track over much of the route, but otherwise held to its high standards: Grades were negligible and stone bridges spanned the various streams along the way. A large twin-arch stone bridge (containing 50-foot arches) was built over Catoctin Creek and a smaller 25-foot single arch took the tracks over Israel Creek at Weverton. The line was finished to the Maryland side of the Potomac opposite Harpers Ferry on December 1, 1834.

31

The track ended by the wood covered highway bridge over the river (locally known as Wager's Bridge), built by Lewis Wernwag in 1824-25 to replace the historic ferry dating back before 1747. For the time being, railroad cars were hauled by horses between Point of Rocks and Harpers Ferry—another product of the compromise agreement with the C&O Canal. The canal apparently feared the frightening effect of steam locomotives on its horses and mules (and perhaps feared more the speed of its competition) and had included a stipulation requiring B&O to put up a high, solid board fence between tracks and canal at the points where the two adjoined. The fence idea was impractical for several reasons, not the least of which was drainage; B&O chose simply to ignore it and use horses until it could work out a better agreement.

Late in 1836 it got such an agreement (the canal took a payoff instead) and started steam operation all the way from Baltimore to Harpers Ferry—except, of course, for the inclined planes at Parr's Ridge. By mid-1834 the railroad had begun to receive the first "improved" versions of Phineas Davis's locomotive— much like the *Atlantic*, but a little heavier and designed to drive both axles. These were B&O's first truly practical main line locomotives and quickly became the company's standard steam power. They also became the first in a long line of picturesquely nicknamed B&O steamers: their long vertical rods moving up and down gave them an unmistakable grasshopper look, and so they became. In addition to the Grasshoppers, B&O's later roster would include Crabs, Camels, Muddiggers, Jersey Greenbacks, One-Armed Billys, Dutch Wagons and Snappers.

The next problem was getting across the wide and sometimes highly unpredictable Potomac into Harpers Ferry itself. Principal Assistant Engineer Benjamin H. Latrobe took on the design job, aided by Lewis Wernwag, the builder of the Monocacy bridge. In this case stone also seemed clearly out of the question and, in fact, Harpers Ferry became the dividing point between the original solid "stone railroad" of the early 1830's and the much more practical wood trestles and bridges of the western extensions.

At this time B&O had no clear idea how it was going to get its main line west to Cumberland. In fact, for political reasons it was ostensibly considering an inland route on the Maryland side of the river which would leave the existing main line at Weverton, three miles east of Harpers Ferry, and head off in the direction of Hagerstown. Thus Latrobe was not primarily concerned with a western route when he aligned his Harpers Ferry bridge. His immediate objective was an end-on connection with the Winchester & Potomac Railroad, which was then completing a line from Harpers Ferry down the Shenandoah Valley to Winchester, Va. (The W&P had been organized in 1831 and had begun building in 1833 after the canal controversy was resolved and it was clear that B&O would make it to Harpers Ferry.) B&O had somewhat fuzzy hopes that the W&P would eventually develop into a through route into the deeper south, but for the moment it was valuable enough as a traffic feeder from the heavily agricultural upper Shenandoah region. The

W&P's terminal was close to the point where the Potomac and Shenandoah joined at the far east end of town, slightly downstream from the Wager highway bridge, so Latrobe aimed his bridge there. Because of a curve in the river and extremely confined quarters on the Maryland side and the location of the W&P terminal on the other side, Latrobe was forced to design still another sharp curve at the bridge's east end.

This somewhat inaccurate scene shows the original layout of bridges at Harpers Ferry. The nearest of the two wood bridges is the Wager highway bridge, built by Lewis Wernwag in the mid-1820's; B&O's bridge, shown here as unsheathed, is immediately behind. The Wager bridge was dismantled in 1839 when the railroad bridge was rebuilt. Credit: Smithsonian Institution.

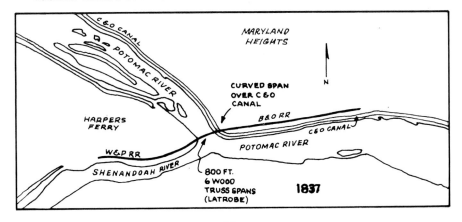

With Wernwag's close collaboration, Latrobe developed a wood truss design about 800 feet long overall, using six spans to cross the river (their lengths varied from 77 ft. to 135 ft. each; most were 134½ feet) plus a span carrying a curved track over the canal at the Maryland end. It accommodated a single railroad track and wagon roadway side by side, the track on the east side and the highway on the west. Typical of most wood bridges, it was covered with wood roof and siding to protect it from deterioration.

Work on the bridge began in the fall of 1835 under Wernwag's direction and by January 1837 it was complete enough to carry its first locomotive. The Winchester & Potomac had already been opened in March 1836 and in the interim freight and passengers were transferred across on the Wager bridge. Unfortunately B&O discovered that the piers and abutments of its new bridge had to be rebuilt immediately afterwards, so horses had to pull the railroad cars over the bridge for several months more until it could be strengthened for locomotives.

As an aside, the junction with the W&P was the first between two separate railroads in the country, and a freight car interchange agreement in 1841 was one of the earliest cases of two railroads using one another's cars to handle through shipments.

IMPOSSIBLE CHALLENGE

CHAPTER 3

MAKING THE MAIN LINE INTO A RAILROAD: 1836-1860

While the carpenters and masons were strung across the Potomac trying to finish the Harpers Ferry bridge, the company itself was undergoing a significant management transition. B&O's first president, Philip E. Thomas, had resigned at the end of June 1836. Joseph Patterson, son of one of the directors, temporarily took charge pending a permanent successor and by summer 1837 Louis McLane was active as president. He took office facing a mass of problems. The grand parade of that Fourth of July 1828 had long since gone by. Now, nine years later, B&O had spent large amounts of money but was still very far from its goal — in fact, far from any significant traffic generating point that would help cover such an investment. And much of this money represented the price of pioneering; it had been wasted on what, in hindsight, had turned out to be engineering mistakes and managerial misjudgments. As a result, McLane was in the unhappy position of having to get the railroad west and at the same time go back and correct some of the worst problems in the east — all in an unhealthy financial atmosphere and a confused political situation.

The east end needed immediate attention. Despite its impressive stone viaducts, deep cuts, level grades and steam power, B&O was essentially a tramway. The Parr's Ridge inclined planes were obviously impractical. The stone roadbed was impossible. And it was clear that some Patapsco valley curves were too sharp even for the small locomotives and short cars of the mid-'30's.

McLane's first major project was a bypass for the Parr's Ridge planes, the railroad's most unfortunate early engineering miscalculation. Surveys for a new route over the hill suitable for locomotives had already begun in 1836. McLane pushed the job hard and finished it in 1838. A 5½-mile double track line was built north of the planes route, departing from the original line about a mile east of Plane 1 and following a little branch of the Patapsco northwest toward the summit of the ridge at Mt. Airy. At the

35

Benjamin H. Latrobe, son of the notable American architect, joined B&O as an assistant engineer in the early 1830's and became its Chief Engineer after Jonathan Knight's resignation in 1842. Among his earlier accomplishments were the wood bridge over the Monocacy, the Harpers Ferry bridge and the pair of covered bridges over the Patapsco at Elysville. Latrobe also surveyed the Washington branch (Chapter 10) and supervised the surveying and building of the B&O between Harpers Ferry and Wheeling. Credit: B&O Museum Archives.

top of the hill construction crews had to blast out a substantial rock cut 50 feet deep east of the present Ridge Road crossing. The line then angled south down the west slope, picking up a branch of Bush Creek and following it to the base of Plane 4 where it rejoined the old line. Considering costs and the technology of the time, it was probably the best alignment that could be found over the troublesome ridge — but almost the entire line was on a brutal 1.58% grade, either up or down. The grade did, however, have the virtue of being relatively short. The small horse/steam transfer depot at the base of Plane 4 was retained as an engine house and water station, and over the next 60 years became an increasingly active terminal for the helper engines needed to push the loaded eastbound freights up to Mt. Airy.

Elsewhere McLane had a total of about six miles of line in the Patapsco Valley realigned to eliminate the worst hairpin curves. Most of this work was relatively modest, merely straightening scattered kinks where the tracks twisted around rock ledges or swung sharply inland to avoid building fills or retaining walls. But bold rebuilding was required just west of Elysville (now Daniels), where the river makes a right-angle turn in front of a steep rock hillside. The line had clung to the south bank of the river around the curve as best it could, but the characteristics of the site made it impossible to ease the curve or protect the track from flood damage. The engineers decided that their only solution was to slice off the curve by crossing to the north bank, running through the flat hook of land bordering the river bend, then recrossing the river to meet the old line upstream. The Elysville "cutoff" totalled about half a mile of new railroad and, because of the angle of the two river crossings, required two long skew bridges. Again Latrobe picked wood. His truss design for the upstream ("upper") bridge consisted of an odd collection of diagonal struts based on a Swiss bridge over the Rhine at Schaffhausen; it was a two-span structure about 300 feet long in total and, of course, covered with weatherboarding. The downstream ("lower") bridge presumably was the same design, although no plans or drawings of it seem to survive; however, it was a three-span design about 330 feet long. All was completed in 1838.

When the relocations were finished, the "worst" curves were eliminated. However, at least one 323 ft. (18°) curve remained, plus several in the area of 14°. And between Baltimore and Point of Rocks, half the line was curved to one degree or another, including 6½ miles of curves ranging between 12° and 14°—almost 10% of the total distance. Thus in 1838 the Main Line in parts was not too different from Maryland's beloved "Ma & Pa" Railroad, nationally known for its tortured alignment. But at least B&O's grades were excellent — except for the Mt. Airy hill, most of the line was 0.7% or less.

Finally there was the track. In 1836 the entire line from Baltimore to Harpers Ferry was still laid with iron strap rail — most of it on wood stringers and ties, although the stone stringers and blocks still staunchly supported the rail between Relay and Sykesville. Unhappily, the rapid changes in locomotive, car and rail technology had made this type of rail obsolete at almost precisely the same time that B&O had completed its line. As steam locomotives began regular operation over the railroad in 1834, it became quickly clear that strap rail was the wrong choice. Although adequate enough for light horse-drawn cars, locomotives and heavier cars acted like rollers on the thin iron strips, bending them upward and forcing them to separate from whatever they were attached to. Much worse, the uneven, unyielding granite roadbed, so painfully put down in 1830-31, was absolutely unsuited for steam locomotives whose weight and power required resiliency and smoothness.

In late 1837 McLane dispatched Knight and Latrobe to several northeastern railroads to study their track experiences — probably well aware what they would bring back. Not surprisingly, their report strongly recommended replacing one track of the Baltimore-Harpers Ferry main

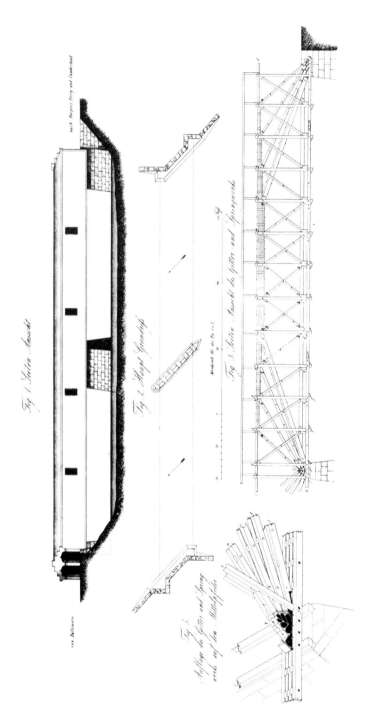

Latrobe designed this two-span wood truss bridge for the 1838 Elysville relocation. A second bridge, presumably the same design but three spans, was located a short distance downstream. The bridge shown here was replaced by an iron Bollman truss in 1852. Credit: B&O Museum Archives.

line with rolled iron T rail as soon as possible. (They really already knew this anyway; when they had built the Washington branch in 1834-35, they used a variety of T rail for the entire line.) Yet the massive money demands for building the railroad west of Harpers Ferry caught McLane with not enough to do everything. Rolled iron rail was imported and very expensive — one of the major reasons B&O had chosen the strap rail in the first place. McLane's first priority was to get the railroad to Cumberland, and he had to use rolled rail for that line too; re-laying the 82 miles between Baltimore and Harpers Ferry was just too much.

He was thus forced into another unhappy patchwork compromise. The stone track structure had to go at all costs. But even this was an expensive job if the full 40 existing track miles laid on stone (17½ miles of double track and 5 miles of single) were replaced in kind. On the other hand, the reality of actual traffic volume had overtaken the original lofty ideal of a double track railroad. McLane and the engineers swallowed hard and did what they could to achieve at least a passable railroad with minimal money. New iron T rail was laid on only 19 track miles. This included two tracks of the new 5½ mile line over Parr's Ridge at Mt. Airy and probably a single track between Mt. Clare and Relay, by now also used by Washington branch trains. Much of the rest of the main line was reduced to single track and apparently the excess track was cannibalized to provide at least a complete single track of strap iron on wood to replace the long stretch of stone. When the project was finished, the railroad was still largely laid with strap rail and was now double track only between Mt. Clare and Ellicott's Mills and between Parr's Ridge and Monocacy station (Frederick Junction). In short it was still mostly an obsolete railroad, although at least the stone roadbed was gone. Incredibly, all of this strap rail lasted on the line until 1846 and was not completely replaced on the main running tracks until 1852 — by then carrying loads four and five times greater than it was built for. Possibly part of its longevity was owed to the light little Grasshoppers with their small wheels and geared drive, which were as easy on track as any locomotive could be.

And in the early McLane days, B&O was almost entirely Grasshopper-powered. In 1838 a total of 14 of these peculiar creatures handled the railroad's business west and south of Mt. Clare, augmented by two newly-delivered Grasshopper-derivatives called Crabs. (Four or five Grasshoppers were assigned to the Washington branch; the rest ran between Mt. Clare and Harpers Ferry. Horses continued to haul the cars in and out of downtown Baltimore.) With their vertical boilers, flailing vertical rods and geared drive, they were unique to B&O and ideally suited to its light, torturous track. Most weighed between 7½ and 8 ½ tons, had either 35″ or 36″ wheels and, when pushed, could get up to about 30 m.p.h. The later models could pull as much as 220 tons on level track, a very respectable performance for anything of that size and weight. However their basic design elements—particularly the upright boiler—made it impossible to develop larger and faster Grasshoppers or Crabs. McLane decided to stop the production of such home-grown designs and buy the more conventional products of the commercial manufacturers who were now becoming established in the railroad business. So the McLane era marked a motive power turnabout too. Beginning in 1837, horizontal-boilered Norris 4-2-0's began to arrive — the first three for the passenger-oriented Washington branch, followed by five more in 1838-39 for the main line. (These were promptly nicknamed "One Armed Billys", for their single drivers and their builder, William Norris.) And following them between 1839 and the late 1840's came a collection of light 4-4-0's from Norris, New Castle, East-wick & Harrison and Ross Winans. But the Grasshoppers remained in daily service, now largely demoted to freight duties.

Sykes's tavern and hotel served also as the original station for Sykes-ville. Built at the time the railroad came through, it was originally a meal stop for the horse-powered trains. It was situated between the railroad and river — ultimately its undoing, as it was wiped out in the 1868 flood. The photo dates to 1858 and looks west from the station platform. Credit: Maryland Historical Society.

Incidentally, although this is not a locomotive history, a special word has to be said for these remarkable little Grasshoppers. The pioneering American locomotives certainly were not noted for longevity. Their experimental design, sometimes questionable construction materials and limited performance capabilities doomed them to a very rapid obsolescence — indeed, their useful life often was measured in months. Yet most of the Grasshoppers worked for at least 30 years; five survived in service for 50 years and four were still active in 1892 — 56 years after they were built. They had outlived all of their successors as well as some locomotives built 20 years after them. Fifty-six years service is an outstanding record even

Through the 1830's a small fleet of these compact but amazingly effective little 0-4-0's powered virtually all of B&O's main line trains. Built by Phineas Davis and later by Ross Winans, they quickly acquired an obvious nickname — the Grasshoppers. Credit: Janice Harwood.

This hackneyed publicity pose from about 1926 at least helps to relate the early Grasshoppers to the scale of 20th Century railroading. Although labelled as the *Atlantic*, this engine was actually the 1836 *Andrew Jackson*, a more typical example of B&O's Grasshopper roster. Credit: Baltimore & Ohio; H.H. Harwood collection.

Also powering B&O trains were two 1838 Ross Winans Crabs, basically Grasshoppers with horizontal cylinders. This photo shows how they looked in the mid-1860's. Credit: Baltimore & Ohio; H.H. Harwood collection.

for sophisticated 20th Century locomotives. Considering the state of the art in the mid-1830's, it is astounding. Their secret seems to have been a combination of high power with small size and low weight. Although eventually evicted as main line engines, they proved extremely practical at points where light rail, sharp curves or close quarters were problems. In effect they became the 19th Century equivalent of the durable General Electric 44-ton diesel. Phineas Davis got his due credit as a pioneer, but his designs have been dismissed as dead ends in locomotive development. That they were, but the most meaningful tribute to any mechanical designer is the continuing utility of his creations and in that, Davis's odd locomotives were superb testimonials.

While coping with his track, alignments, inclined planes and locomotives, McLane also had to get the railroad started west again. After losing its fight to build along the north side of the Potomac B&O had sent Latrobe and his surveyors back out to find a reasonable alternative — preferably all or mostly in Maryland. The engineers dutifully followed orders, but it was obvious that there was no easy way to stay in Maryland and still keep clear of the canal. Immediately north of the river, the topography was a continuing series of ridges and mountains running crosswise to the railroad route. The south side of the river was preferable, but was entirely in Virginia — creating a new problem in obtaining rights and financing, and hence new delays.

Between political and financial negotiations, new surveys and company management changes, the process took five years from the time B&O first arrived opposite Harpers Ferry. But by 1839 the railroad was cleared to build west along the south bank of the Potomac toward Cumberland.

The first problem, however, was how to get out of Harpers Ferry. Once again B&O had found itself in an all too familiar box: The high Harpers Ferry bluffs created an extremely constricted site for everything there — town, federal armory, arsenal buildings and railroads were all jammed together on the tiny bits of level land by the river. There were only two clear ways out: south along the Shenandoah a short distance and then inland or directly west along the Potomac shore from the bridge. The Shenandoah route would have to use the existing Winchester & Potomac track; the Potomac river shore was largely occupied by the large federal armory. The W&P was the easier exit of the two. By following its line about 8 miles southwest to a spot between Halltown and Charles Town, B&O could get a clear and easy shot west to Martinsburg. But somewhat oddly the W&P would not agree to trackage rights (which was also ultimately ironic, since after the Civil War B&O bought control of the W&P and made it its present Valley branch.)

So B&O again ended with the worst alternative. To get out of town the tracks had to be carried on a trestle sandwiched between the armory and the south river bank. Worse, the alignment along the river was such that it intersected the south end of B&O's bridge at an almost precise right angle, with no space to lay anything resembling a gradual connecting curve. (Remember, the bridge originally had been aligned to connect head-on with the W&P, not to lead upriver.)

Latrobe's only answer was to begin his curve out on the bridge. He thus inserted his junction switch at a point 265 feet out from the south shore and designed a 138-foot "Y" span to take the westward track around the curve and onto the trestle alongside the armory. It was an inventive solution and the best that could be done at such a site, but it promised to be an operating nightmare — and it certainly was. Not only was the curve sharp, but right at the midriver junction the new track had to cross over the highway which shared the bridge. Furthermore, the junction, roadway and curve were all inside the smoky gloom of the wood covered bridge. Unhappily, this layout proved very durable. Even after the repeated destruction and rebuildings during the Civil War and the abandonment of the armory afterward, successive generations of bridges faithfully followed the awkward alignment. It was only in 1894, long after the necessity for the layout was gone, that a new double-track railroad bridge was put across the river on an easier (but still less than ideal) alignment.

But at least the railroad was moving west again. Construction west of Harpers Ferry began in September 1839 (including the bridge rebuilding) and, compared to its progress before that, moved rapidly. By November 1842 trains were operating into Cumberland. Initial service consisted of one passenger and one scheduled freight a day between Baltimore and Cumberland. The passenger run took five hours to cover the 82 miles from Baltimore to Harpers Ferry, counting the horse-powered segment on Pratt Street and the locomotive transfer at Mt. Clare; the freight got there in $8\frac{1}{2}$ hours.

Although still far from the Ohio River (which it would not reach for 10 more years), B&O finally had a source of heavy traffic at hand—coal. Coal began moving east in a trickle in 1843 but slowly swelled as mines west of Cumberland were opened and B&O was able to improve its Baltimore port terminals to handle the flow. By 1848, over 66,000 tons of coal were rolling into Baltimore — 42% of B&O's entire eastbound freight tonnage. In 1850 this had doubled to 132,000 tons — now 57.5% of the eastbound tonnage.

This gush of new business was indeed welcome, but it meant that suddenly the primitive state of the main line between Baltimore and Harpers Ferry was a worse worry than ever. Not only was true tonnage now beginning to pound over the railroad, but B&O once again shifted its motive power policy to handle it. Beginning in 1844, heavy eight-drivered locomotives appeared and were rapidly augmented by more in the late 1840's and '50's. First came the $23\frac{1}{2}$-ton Winans "Muddiggers" — 12 of them built between 1844 and 1847 — followed by Baldwin, New Castle and company-built 0-8-0's in 1848 and 1849. (One of these, the *Memnon,* still survives at the B&O Museum). Also in 1848 came the first of the highly distinctive Winans Camels — a powerful if controversial breed that eventually would number 119 engines weighing from $22\frac{1}{2}$ to 24 tons.

With motive power and tonnage of this type, the already serious problems of track, bridges and general alignment became impossible. Plainly a main line laid largely with strap rail dating to 1830-34 had to be replaced immediately before it collapsed completely. (B&O's newer 4-4-0's of the mid-1840's averaged 11-13 tons, which already was heavy enough for

A.

B

Latrobe's rebuilt Harpers Ferry bridge, as it looked between 1840 and 1861. A. a slightly distorted view from the Maryland side; the federal arsenal is at the right of the bridge in the picture's center. The railroad had to skirt these buildings by a trestle on the river side. B. looks east from the arsenal trestle. The diagram C. shows the midstream railroad junction and highway section (outlined by stringers on the north side), but by all available evidence the bridge carried only one track. Credits: B-National Parks Service –C-Smithsonian Institution

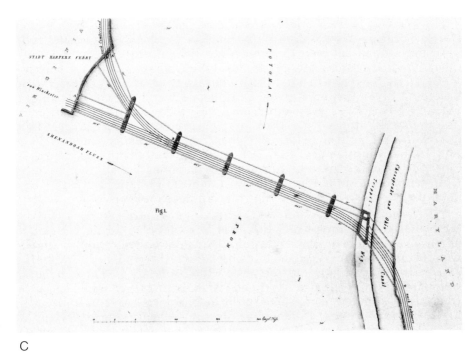

C

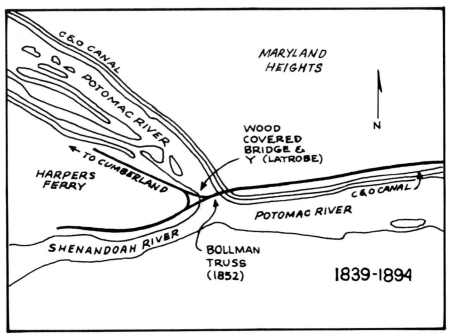

strap rail designed for a five-ton load; the new eight-coupled freight engines would weigh double that.) The bridge situation was better, thanks to Casper Wever's farsighted but expensive tastes. The beautifully overbuilt section between Baltimore and Relay hardly needed improvement, nor did the stone bridges at most other spots on the way to Harpers Ferry. However, it had to be admitted that the two Latrobe-designed wood bridges at Elysville were already getting shaky and the wooden mongrel at Harpers Ferry was worrisome. And finally the constantly curving main line along the Patapsco and Bush Creek was a continuing irritation which only worsened as locomotive wheelbases and trains lengthened. Thus McLane's realignments of 1837-38 turned out to be only the beginning. In fact, straightening the main line would be an almost constant occupation for over 65 years, until finally at the turn of the century the railroad gave up on half-measures and built virtually a completely new railroad.

The track reconstruction was frighteningly overdue. In late 1845 Benjamin Latrobe (by now Chief Engineer) was detailed to study the track situation and make recommendations. Diplomatically grumbling that he was documenting the obvious, Latrobe said: "...I cannot but reiterate the expression of my fears that this track will *absolutely go down* under the weight of this increased trade. Already it is carrying three or four times the trade of any similarly constructed track in the country, and the iron, which has borne up well under 15 years hard use, is now beginning to break up.... The velocity with which trains are obliged to pass over it also creates risks which, although happily productive thus far of few disasters, are not a little to be dreaded...without such reconstruction, it will hardly be possible, at any expense, to maintain the road under this augmented trade."

With money still short and the railroad from Cumberland to Wheeling yet to be built, the company could not follow Latrobe's strong urging to rebuild the entire Baltimore-Harpers Ferry line within a year. Instead the job was spread out over the next five or six years, taking the most critical sections first — notably the eastbound approach up Bush Creek to Parr's Ridge and the tortuous sections along the Potomac where the track and canal were sandwiched together. By late 1848 one track between Mt. Clare and Harpers Ferry was almost fully laid with rolled iron rail of one type or another, some of it a "T" rail variety put down in the 1838 project and the rest an inverted "U" design rolled in Wales. But strap rail on the two sections of second track (Mt. Clare to Ellicott's Mills and from the west side of Parr's Ridge to the Monocacy) was not fully replaced until about 1852. Even then, the ancient and obsolete rail was frugally re-used on secondary trackage — an 1853 report shows the equivalent of 18½ track miles of strap rail in various yards, sidings and spurs between Baltimore and Harpers Ferry, including large amounts at the Mt. Clare and Locust Point yards in Baltimore. The Frederick branch remained laid with strap rail and wood stringers until the first year of the Civil War, when it was hastily replaced.

As the track rebuilding proceeded, so did more line straightening — some of it fairly substantial. Included was work at an especially serpentine section east of Sykesville, a short cutoff at the Patapsco forks east of Marriottsville and miscellaneous kinks at many points between Avalon and the

A   The first and for fifty years the only tunnel on the east end of the main
line was Marriottsville tunnel, actually at present-day Henryton.
Originally built as a single-track bore about 1850, it was enlarged for
two tracks immediately after the Civil War and rebuilt again in 1903. A.
shows Marriottsville tunnel in 1870 following its double tracking,
looking west toward Henryton; B. looks east in 1979 as a westbound
freight emerges. The original line skirted the hillside to the right.
B   Credits: A-B&O Museum Archives — B-H.H. Harwood, Jr.

Monocacy River. But the biggest and most difficult project was west of Marriottsville, where a narrow and tight twist in the river had forced the original line into a long and sharp "S" curve immediately followed by a river crossing on a stone arch bridge. Latrobe decided to cut directly across the bow in the river by building a new bridge downstream and tunnelling the offending hill. As designed, the tunnel was single track and only 430 feet long, but the hill was granite and turned out to be difficult. The project was started in late 1847 but was not completed until about 1850. Originally called the Marriottsville tunnel, it was the first east of Harpers Ferry; after two rebuildings and one name change (to Henryton tunnel) it still exists. The new bridge leading to the tunnel was a 48'9" iron truss, one of B&O's first iron bridges and also one of the earliest of Wendel Bollman's unique spiderweb design.

Bollman, a onetime carpenter, had become B&O's Master of Road, a position under Latrobe responsible for track, structures and maintenance. Coincident with the need to replace the short-lived and sometimes ill-designed wood bridges, Bollman had designed a pioneering iron truss which became virtually a standard on B&O over the next 20 years. In 1851 the so-called "Winchester span" of the Harpers Ferry bridge — the single span at the west end carrying the W&P connection and the highway — was rebuilt with iron Bollman trusses supported by granite towers. The "upper" Elysville bridge was Bollmanized in 1852 and its downstream "lower" companion was similarly replaced in 1856. Finally, the high three-span 1831 wood bridge over the Monocacy was rebuilt with three Bollman deck trusses after the wood bridge burned in mid-March 1854. By the end of the project in 1856, all B&O's bridges between Baltimore and Harpers Ferry were either stone (mostly original) or iron (mostly Bollman). Wendel Bollman desperately wanted to replace the entire Harpers Ferry bridge with iron trusses, but other projects kept taking precedence.

This 1856 Bollman truss bridge carried the line across the Patapsco at Elysville (now Daniels), which can be seen dimly in the background. The present alignment crosses immediately behind the spot where this 1857 photo was taken. Credit: Smithsonian Institution.

The original wood covered bridge over the Monocacy at Frederick Junction was replaced by Bollman trusses in 1854. This 1870 scene shows it as rebuilt after the Civil War. Credit: B&O Museum Archives.

The tinkering and patching job on the main line track alignment plugged on through the 1850's. Between 1852 and 1954 a second main track was laid between Monocacy station (Frederick Junction) and Point of Rocks, once again giving a double track line all the way from the east side of Parr's Ridge to Point of Rocks. About three years later work started on re-double tracking the line west of Ellicott's Mills, including still more re-alignment. By 1858 double track on the east end of the railroad reached as far west as Marriottsville; it remained single from here to the Plane 1 station on the east side of Parr's Ridge until after the Civil War. One notable casualty of this project was the spectacular Tarpean Rock at Ellicott's Mills, a landmark for all early railroad travellers. The tall rock shaft towering over the track had to be blasted away to provide clearance for the new second track. Curves were also eased over the five miles of line between Ellicott's Mills and Elysville, including particularly troublesome spots at Rock Point and Union Dam. (Considering that the new "eased" curve at Union Dam was 13°, one wonders what the old one must have been like.) A short section of double track was also built around Millers Point on the Potomac, between Weverton and Sandy Hook.

But whatever it might do to make the winding Patapsco-Mt. Airy-Bush Creek route more operable, B&O knew its best solution really was to start all over again somewhere else. In 1856 the directors dispatched Latrobe's surveying forces out to look at a new route which would run some distance south of the existing line. They investigated two alternate lines which would use the Washington branch to Laurel, then would strike out west toward Point of Rocks — one route passing north of Sugar Loaf mountain and one passing south. Latrobe reported that either line was feasible, with better ruling grades than the Mt. Airy hump and certainly better curves. The idea was deferred, of course, but did not completely die. When the Metropolitan branch was built between Point of Rocks and Washington in the early 1870's, it partly followed some of these surveys. With much of the route thus built, a connecting line between Laurel and the Metropolitan branch at Gaithersburg would have been relatively short and easy; it was seriously considered as late as 1876 but afterwards ended in the overstuffed wastebasket for unbuilt lines.

B&O paid less attention to way station buildings during this convulsive growing and rebuilding period. The records show that aside from the early masonry buildings at Ellicott's Mills, Frederick and one at Harpers Ferry, there were no more than wood buildings along the line — in many cases little more than sheds and platforms. There was one major exception: A company director from Frederick managed to persuade the board to spend $5,500 on a new passenger station there. The stone 1832 station was and always had been mostly a freight warehouse with minimal passenger facilities. The station was built in 1854 on a new site at the corner of Market and All Saints Streets, and the track extended a block west on All Saints Street to reach it. Although relatively small, it was a fashionable Italianate three-story stuccoed brick building somewhat similar to B&O's larger stations completed earlier at Wheeling and Washington, D.C. The "new" station, with additions and alterations, still stands; the 1832 station lived on as a freight house until 1911.

On January 1, 1853 B&O was at last able to celebrate its entry into Wheeling, theoretically the fulfillment of its Ohio River dream. Coming when it did, it was almost an anticlimax. But at least B&O was now a trunk line and had begun to look like one.

Curves like this at Sykesville could be eased somewhat but never removed; some remain uncomfortably sharp today. Some realigning can be seen in this 1979 view looking east from Maryland Rt. 32: The original line made a sharp hook to the left of the first car of the train, then ran to the right of the track in the foreground. Credit: H.H. Harwood, Jr.

Frederick stations old and new, both as they were around the turn of the century. By this time the "new" 1854 passenger station had been expanded with a single-story addition on its rear. Credit (both): Gary Schlerf collection.

B. & O. Station, Frederick, Md.

IMPOSSIBLE CHALLENGE

CHAPTER 4

NEW BALTIMORE TERMINALS: 1848-1863

Meanwhile, at the Baltimore end B&O practically had to start all over again. In the mid-1840's all Baltimore traffic—including the Washington branch—was still funneled down the horse-powered single track laid in the center of Pratt Street. This track (which, incidentally, was still strap rail) also carried any through movements to Philadelphia via the Philadelphia, Wilmington & Baltimore. B&O's terminal consisted of the rabbit-warren of warehouses and passenger facilities in the Pratt-Charles-Light-Camden block, some of them built by the railroad in the early 1830's and some simply adapted for the purpose. Elsewhere along Pratt Street were various warehouses and piers as far as the City dock at the foot of President Street. Mt. Clare yard was a feverishly active spot as the yard handling the assembly and breakup of all trains and as a rapidly developing locomotive and car shop.

Not only was the railroad terminal itself congested, slow and awkward, but the harbor facilities left much to be desired—especially for handling the newly-developing coal business. Even in the late 1840's Baltimore's inner harbor was becoming too shallow for deep-draft ocean vessels and the piers and railroad tracks serving them simply were not designed for volume bulk traffic.

New passenger and freight terminals were critical needs—coal piers the most critical. A terminal site was needed which was accessible to deep water and away from the congested downtown area. In 1845 B&O picked Locust Point, a flat expanse of land on the north side of the peninsula held down by Fort McHenry. To reach it, and at the same time avoid street running through built-up areas, a new branch had to be snaked through the marshy flats of south Baltimore. It left the main line at Gwynns run, just west of the present Monroe Street bridge, turned southeast, skirted around the north end of the Middle Branch on a large inverted "U" shaped route, then ran east across the peninsula to a loop track and pier at Locust Point. More time was spent in getting the needed

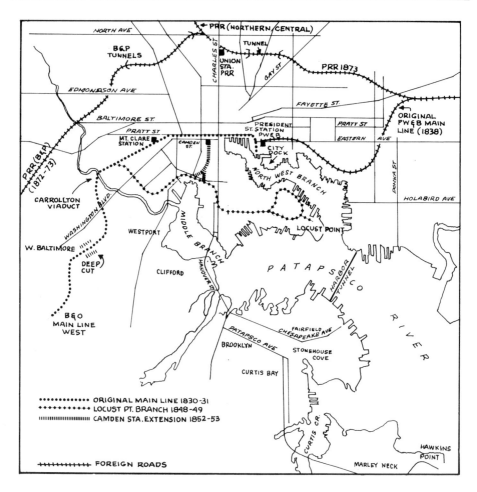

city ordinances, and work was not begun on the Locust Point branch until April 1848. It was opened in 1849. Initially Locust Point was designed strictly for coal traffic and, in fact, was legally limited to bulk minerals. (At the time, Baltimore was still anxious to protect its inner harbor area.) But eventually Locust Point also became a large grain export terminal, a passenger immigration point and finally a general merchandise export and import terminal. The massively growing coal traffic was relocated to a still larger terminal at Curtis Bay in 1884, leaving Locust Point as a grain and merchandise facility; it continued to expand down to the present, although now largely owned by the Maryland Port Administration.

Shortly afterwards B&O also faced up to the glaring inadequacies of its downtown passenger and merchandise freight terminal. On the first day of 1853 the railroad at last officially reached Wheeling and was already at work on a line to Parkersburg, Va. which would connect with railroads to Cincinnati and St. Louis. B&O was becoming a long-distance passenger trunk line and obviously needed something better than its obsolete streetside Pratt Street station. Its competitors and connections in Baltimore already had built elaborate new combination passenger and freight terminals which distinctly outshone B&O's. In early 1850 the Philadelphia, Wilmington & Baltimore completed its classical-style President Street terminal and in the same year the Baltimore & Susquehanna opened its large Italianate Calvert Station.

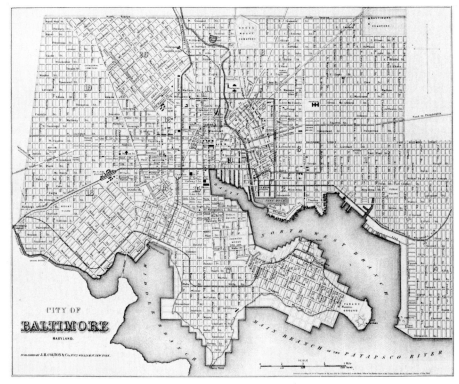

Baltimore in 1855. B&O's main line enters the city at the left. Its original route proceeds across the center of the map, passing Mt. Clare and following Pratt Street and President Street to the City Dock in about the center. The new Locust Point branch leaves the line at the left side of the map and heads in the direction of Fort McHenry. The Philadelphia, Wilmington & Baltimore enters at the far right and the Northern Central comes in at the top center. Credit: Smithsonian Institution.

But for B&O, finding an adequate station site—not to mention a clear off-street access line—was a severe problem. Needless to say, downtown Baltimore was even more tightly built up by the early 1850's than it was in 1831. In June 1852 a large tract was finally purchased in a section slightly southwest of the city's center—a four-block area fronting on

Camden Street and bounded by Howard on the east, Eutaw on the west and Lee Street on the south. The site lay about seven blocks north of the Locust Point branch track and could be reached fairly easily by running a spur north from the Locust Point line near Ostend and Eutaw Streets. This access avoided all street running, but since it was a branch of a branch it certainly was not the most direct way of reaching the new station. Entering Baltimore from the west, passenger trains would follow the original main line on a wide swing north over the Carrollton viaduct, then south over the Locust Point branch, then north again over the Camden Street station spur. This corkscrew routing would last until 1868 when the Camden cutoff was completed.

Although the new terminal and its access line was somewhat away from the most heavily developed sections of town, property acquisition nonetheless was very expensive. Among other things, 49 houses had to be condemned and removed. In addition, there apparently was some management dissension over the size and cost of the station building itself. Between the expense and uncertainty, the railroad found itself resorting to still another expedient makeshift. Construction of the permanent passenger station was deferred and a collection of temporary wood sheds built at the south end of the plot between Barre and Lee Streets for both passenger and freight business. A small five-stall circular brick engine house was also built on the southeast corner of the station property at Howard and Lee Streets—the first really permanent building in the area. As soon as the sheds and the new double track access line were completed, the old Pratt Street station was vacated and all B&O passenger trains taken off the Mt. Clare-Pratt Street route. The Pratt & Charles terminal buildings were sold in August 1853.

As an aside, the Pratt Street line was hardly abandoned. It continued to flourish as a freight line and also a connection to the PW&B and the Baltimore & Susquehanna (Northern Central)—intensely so, judging by the statistics. In 1856, for example, horses pulled a total of 25,945 loaded freight cars over the street during the year. Assuming that an equal number of empties were hauled back, this means that over 150 cars a day were dragged over this single track line. One wonders how passenger trains were ever fitted in in the first place. In addition, through passenger cars between New York, Philadelphia and Washington continued to be transferred over the part of the Pratt Street route from President Street to Camden until 1880. Although its freight traffic gradually tapered off as inner harbor commercial activity diminished in the mid-20th Century, the hardy Pratt Street line survived until 1972 when it was finally evicted by the harborfront renewal program.

In 1856 work finally began on the permanent Camden station building—or rather what was to be the first part of a grandly sprawling permanent building. This consisted of a three-story brick station and office structure with a three-arch colonaded central entrance and a soaring three-tiered tower. Architecturally, the building was a variation of the "railroad Italianate" style popular on B&O and other eastern rail-

Locust Point terminal as it looked in the early 1880's. Credit: B&O Museum Archives.

Another view of Locust Point, probably also dating to the Eighties. The large structures in the rear are grain elevators; the peculiar "pot" hoppers in the foreground carry coal. Credit: B&O Museum Archives.

Camden Station as it appeared in 1871, soon after it was fully completed. The central portion was opened in 1857; the two wings were added between 1863 and 1865. At this time the company's headquarters offices were also located here. Over the years, the station was substantially altered; compare this view with others in later chapters.
Credit: B&O Museum Archives.

roads in the early 1850's; the tower defied analysis, but came closest to something from Christopher Wren. Like the B&S's nearby Calvert Station, Camden was designed as both a passenger and freight terminal and would also house the company's headquarters offices. However, it outranked Calvert in size and architectural pretense—perhaps intentionally.

Camden was first occupied for a directors' meeting in February 1857; presumably passengers followed soon after. But it was not until eight years later, in the midst of Civil War turmoil, that the building was completed to its full planned extent. In 1863, work started on the balance of the station plan—a pair of two-story brick wings, each of which terminated in a three-story Italianate tower topped by a cupola. The additions were finished in early 1865. Behind the station was a very long wood trainshed extending south to Lee Street but broken in the center by Barre Street which crossed the tracks at grade a block south of the station.

The question of who designed Camden has generated a mild amount of heat among Baltimore architectural historians, mostly because of the delays in completing the full plan and the confused history of the architectural firm which did the initial work. Although specific documentation is vague, it seems certain that the Baltimore architectural firm of Niernsee & Nielsen drew up the original plans for the passenger terminal in 1854. (This, incidentally, was the same firm which designed Calvert station. Niernsee also had worked for B&O as an engineer and architect under Latrobe in the early 1840's.) When Camden was finally built, the railroad apparently followed the basic Niernsee & Nielsen design, completing it in the two separate stages mentioned. In the meantime, however, Niernsee had left Baltimore to work on the South Carolina state capitol building and had severed his connection with B&O. The actual construction of the building was put under the supervision of Joseph Kemp, a B&O draftsman and possibly a former Niernsee & Nielsen associate, who has sometimes been given full credit for its design.

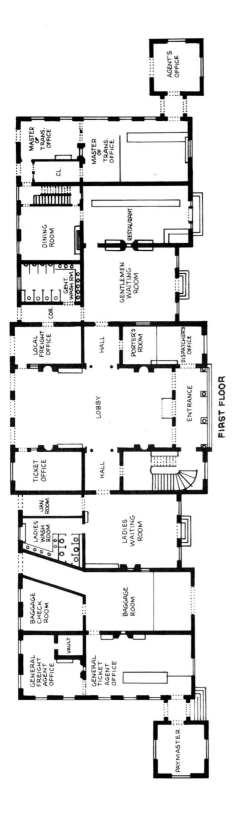

FIRST FLOOR

Camden's original floor plan as it was in 1880, before the headquarters offices were moved "uptown" to B&O's new Central Building at Baltimore and Calvert Streets. In the early 1890's the ground floor layout was rearranged when the central trainshed was converted for freight and a new passenger trainshed added on the east (left) end. Credit: Adapted from drawings in collection of Frank A. Wrabel.

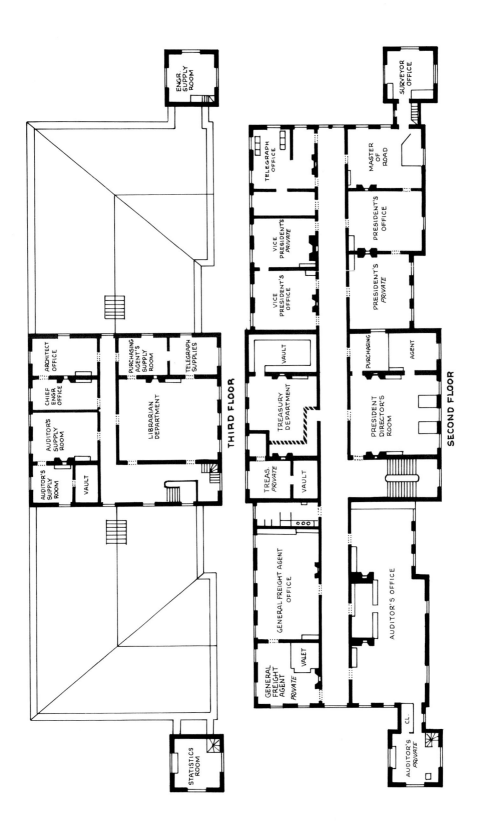

THIRD FLOOR

ENGR. SUPPLY ROOM

ARCHITECT OFFICE

CHIEF ENGR OFFICE

AUDITOR'S SUPPLY ROOM

AUDITOR'S SUPPLY ROOM

VAULT

PURCHASING AGENT'S SUPPLY ROOM

TELEGRAPH SUPPLIES

LIBRARIAN DEPARTMENT

STATISTICS ROOM

SECOND FLOOR

SURVEYOR OFFICE

TELEGRAPH OFFICE

VICE PRESIDENT'S PRIVATE

VICE PRESIDENT'S OFFICE

MASTER OF ROAD

PRESIDENT'S OFFICE

PRESIDENT'S PRIVATE

VAULT

TREASURY DEPARTMENT

TREAS. PRIVATE

VAULT

PURCHASING

AGENT

PRESIDENT DIRECTOR'S ROOM

GENERAL FREIGHT AGENT OFFICE

GENERAL FREIGHT AGENT PRIVATE

VALET

AUDITOR'S OFFICE

AUDITOR'S PRIVATE

CL.

IMPOSSIBLE CHALLENGE

CHAPTER 5

RUNNING AN 1850's RAILROAD

With B&O now at last at the Ohio River and equipped with passably comfortable Baltimore terminals, perhaps we should pause and look at the railroad itself — what it looked like, what it was hauling, what was doing the hauling and how.

Despite the fulfillment of the Ohio River dream and the beginning of the long hoped-for flow of merchandise and people between Baltimore and the midwest, the railroad really was turning into a bulk carrier funneling Allegheny coal into Baltimore. And later, as it extended further into the midwest, it would also perform the same function for bulk grain. By 1857 coal had climbed to 68% of the railroad's total freight tonnage into Baltimore and 57% of all freight both in and out of the city. The only other significant eastbound commodity was flour, mostly from the Wheeling and Parkersburg gateways, but also substantial amounts from Maryland and the Shenandoah valley region. Freight from Baltimore to the west was only one-fifth the volume of the eastbound business and consisted mostly of dry goods, groceries and coffee.

It is thus not surprising that B&O was a pioneer in eight-coupled locomotive designs to haul heavy volumes at low speeds — or that the main line was heavily populated by such engines by the 1850's. Altogether, between 45 and 50 freight locomotives were regularly assigned between Baltimore and Martinsburg in the mid- to late 1850's, most of which were heavy 0-8-0's of one variety or another. In early 1859, for example, there were 46 "tonnage" locomotives assigned to the division — 26 of which were Winans Camels, plus 10 0-8-0's of older designs, 5 Denmeade-built Hayes ten-wheelers and 3 light 4-4-0's (which presumably were used for way freight work). In addition, the sturdy Grasshoppers and Crabs switched yards at such points as Frederick and Mt. Clare and handled work trains along the line. Typical of mid-19th Century practice, road crews were assigned to specific locomotives.

Before the Civil War, 0-8-0's hauled B&O freights over the main line. These two varieties were typical: No. 32, shown at Weverton about 1870, was built at Mt. Clare shop in the mid-1850's. No 123 was one of the massive fleet (massive at least by the standards of the time) of Winans Camels. This sample was built by Ross Winans in 1853. Credits (both): B&O Museum Archives.

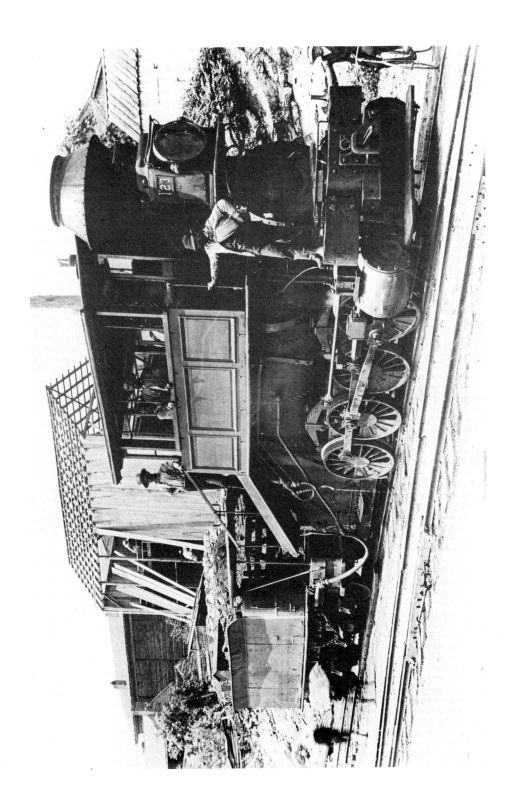

Also represented were several Hayes-designed ten-wheelers built by Denmeade. No. 159 dates also to 1853, the photo to the early 1860's. Credit: Baltimore & Ohio; H.H. Harwood collection.

The freight was moved according to timetable, although the printed schedule gave little indication of the true number of trains actually moving. Operating timetables of the mid-1850's showed three scheduled freights each way between Baltimore and the next division point at Martinsburg, Va.: one coal train, one livestock and one "tonnage" (general merchandise) train. But in most cases, each of these trains ran in multiple sections called "convoys", each section about ten minutes apart. The convoys could be quite large — dispatching reports of the period show as many as 11 locomotives handling one "train" with up to 280 cars. Each section would average 22-26 cars. Their scheduled speed was extremely slow in deference to the heavy eight-wheeled locomotives, serpentine curves and — for that time — heavy trains equipped only with hand brakes and link-and-pin couplers. Timetables speeds for all classes of freight averaged a glacial 10-11 m.p.h. over the entire line east of Harpers Ferry. Through freights were scheduled to cover the 98 miles between Mt. Clare yard and Martinsburg in anywhere from 8½ hours (for westbound coal empties) to 12 hours (for westbound merchandise trains). Obviously, a crew's day could be long.

But crews then apparently were just as resourceful with their time as crews now, as evidenced by this 1859 memorandum from Master of Transportation W.P. Smith to one of his supervisors:

> "I have learned most reliably that the men in charge of the stock trains east on 1st Division, are in the habit of seriously disregarding our rules with reference to regular running and slow speed. This is particularly the case at Gaither Siding, where, arriving on prompt time, or ahead of it perhaps, they stop for an hour or more to play ten-pins. They then, although starting so much behind time, reach Ellicott's Mills according to the book, or as in the case of Engine 167 yesterday, five minutes ahead of it. I learned that the whole convoy practised this thing yesterday, and I have sent Mr. Synder to get their names, with an order that they shall not go out again until the matter is fully investigated."

It might be mentioned that freights were scheduled to cover the 18 miles between Gaither and Ellicott's Mills in one hour and 45 minutes. By running at 25-30 m.p.h. instead of the specified 10, the crews could easily get in their game and make the schedule.

Passenger service had begun to grow as through traffic developed, although at this time B&O's passenger business was more locally-oriented than its freight. In 1855 five trains a day each way were scheduled in and out of Baltimore: a Baltimore-Wheeling express, a Wheeling mail train, a Frederick accomodation (local) and two Ellicott's Mills locals which also handled way freight. They moved considerably faster than the freights — the Wheeling express was timed for 30-35 m.p.h. along the curving Patapsco section, although locals plugged along at 20-25. But whether local or express, their loads were mostly short-haul. B&O's largest single passenger generating point between Baltimore and Wheeling was Ellicott's Mills. Washington Junction (Relay) was second, since at that time it was the transfer point between Washington and anywhere west. Frederick was third in passenger volume.

Frederick Junction (then called Monocacy station) in 1858. The train is heading west. All the facilities shown here were destroyed during the Civil War. Credit: Maryland Historical Society.

Graphically reflecting the difference in freight and passenger traffic volumes, only 8 passenger locomotives regularly ran in the area between Baltimore and Martinsburg in 1859. They did cover a wide range, however — from four newly-delivered William Mason 4-4-0's built in 1857-58 to two Norris 4-2-0 "One Armed Billys" assigned to the Frederick accommodation train. (On occasion, these little single-driver teakettles had to be doubleheaded up the Mt. Airy hill with one of the hulking Winans Camels normally stationed there to help freights.)

The railroad itself was now (and belatedly) laid entirely with rolled iron rail, and the T design was already replacing most of the inverted "U" type laid in the late 1840's. The "U" in turn had been put into spurs and sidings to replace the last of the strap rail, which by the mid '50's was at last almost entirely gone. A telegraph line had been strung along the main line in 1854-55 and by 1858 there were telegraph stations at Camden and Mt. Clare in Baltimore, Relay House, Ellicott's Mills, Marriottsville, Plane No. 1 station, Plane No. 4 (the east and west sides of the Parr's Ridge hill), Monocacy station (Frederick Junction), Point of Rocks, Harpers Ferry and Martinsburg. However, it would be another 10 years before the telegraph was used for regular transmission of train orders to crews.

Train crews from Baltimore normally worked to Martinsburg, 100 miles west. All Baltimore freights began or ended their runs at Mt. Clare yard, where trains were broken up and hauled to Locust Point or Camden freight terminals by switchers. Their locomotives were also based at Mt. Clare — after 1855 kept in the odd sawtooth-shaped string of single-stall engine houses at the far west end of Mt. Clare, collectively called "Rus-

Although shot in 1977, this view at Relay conveys an almost timeless sense of B&O's Patapsco Valley terrain. Credit: H.H. Harwood, Jr.

sia". Passenger runs, of course, terminated at Camden after 1853 and all passenger power was turned and serviced at the little Camden engine house at Howard and Lee Streets. On the Martinsburg end, locomotives were serviced and shopped at the large new roundhouse-shop complex built in 1853-54. In between were small engine terminals at Plane No. 4 and at Sandy Hook, opposite Harpers Ferry on the Maryland side of the Potomac. Plane 4 engine house was located at the onetime base of inclined Plane 4, at the bottom of the stiff Mt. Airy grade. In the late '50's two Winans Camels were normally based here as pushers, primarily for the heavily-loaded eastbound freights but available for work on either side of the ridge. According to one account, the first regularly assigned helper here was the 0-8-0 geared "Muddigger" *Mt. Clare*, built in 1847. Its long rigid wheelbase caused constant derailment problems, even on the relatively gradual curves of the hill. Sandy Hook engine house handled Harpers Ferry layovers and the small yard there was the setoff and pickup point for any Harpers Ferry and Shenandoah Valley (Winchester & Potomac) freight. After the Civil War, Sandy Hook terminal would also handle locomotives from the Washington County (Hagerstown) branch.

Had you been a B&O passenger west of Baltimore in the 1850's, most typically you would have passed coal trains pulled by Winans Camels. But you would also have seen a string of thriving small industries as you coiled up the Patapsco Valley, loading freight cars with flour, cotton goods, iron products, stone and various manufactured goods. In fact, the Patapsco Valley already was a busy manufacturing center when the railroad arrived in 1830 — the river's water power was enough of an advantage to overcome the distance and hilly, rutted roads into Baltimore. At Avalon, just west of Relay, was the Avalon Nail & Iron Works, first established about 1800 and rebuilt in 1854 — based on locally-mined iron ore. Three miles beyond began a string of mills stretching from Ilchester to Elysville: Ellicott's Ilchester flour mill, dating to 1831; the Thistle cotton mill, built in 1821, almost directly across the river from Ilchester; Gray's Patapsco Factory (1820), another cotton mill on the other side of the river. Next was the Ellicott brothers' complex of flour mills and iron works at Ellicott's Mills —the pioneer industry in the valley, first operated in 1774. A mile upriver came the Union Manufacturing Co. cotton mill at what is now Oella, over the river from the tracks; it had been opened in 1810 and rebuilt after an 1815 fire. Marking the upper limit of the Patapsco's milling was one of the handsomest of all — the new Alberton mill at what used to be Elysville, a stone and belfried factory built in 1845 and surrounded by its own neat company town of uniform brick row houses. Being a company town, Elysville adapted its name to its owner of the moment — first it became Alberton and, when the property was sold to the C.R. Daniels Co. in the 1940's, it was renamed Daniels. Stone quarries also dotted the route, notably east of Ellicott's Mills and at Granite (Putney & Swope) and Marriottsville.

Elsewhere on the way to Harpers Ferry were scattered mills and quarries. The little town of Mt. Airy had a flour mill. Frederick was a

An eastbound freight crosses Catoctin Creek, just east of present Brunswick, in April 1978. The bridge dates to the original construction to Harpers Ferry, although it was enlarged following the contour of the original in 1902. The onetime C&O Canal crossed the creek on another stone viaduct at the point of the photo. Credit: H.H. Harwood, Jr.

Once a busy on-line industry in the lower Patapsco valley, the Avalon Nail & Iron Works was wiped out by the flood of 1868 and never rebuilt. Some remnants of it still stand. Credit: Maryland Historical Society.

major milling and fertilizer manufacturing center and also quarried limestone. Ijamsville had a slate quarry. Weverton, near Israel Creek between Point of Rocks and Harpers Ferry was perhaps the strangest "industry" along B&O lines or anywhere else. The site was picked by the enterprising Caspar Wever about 1832. During his B&O construction and location work he had decided that the characteristics of the land and the drop of the Potomac River level here were ideal for the establishment of a milling complex. Ultimately three large mill buildings were completed; plans were made for a fourth mill, a hotel and housing for the workers. But the complex never caught on, reputedly because Wever's rents were as lofty as his dreams. When he died about 1847, the complex was largely vacant. A cotton mill was finally started in one of the buildings shortly before the Civil War, but the war's outbreak shortstopped any further development. After brief use during the war as Union barracks, the buildings were again abandoned but, battered by floods and disintegrating from natural decay, stood well into the 20th Century. Now the name is all that remains of what was supposed to be a rival of the great Lowell, Mass. mills.

And finally there was Harpers Ferry, an early version of a government town. Although the town was always a junction point for the Potomac and Shenandoah valley trade routes, its only local industry consisted of the federal armory, arsenal and the Hall's rifle works — none of them large railroad shippers. Militarily, however, it was considered a strategic and sensitive spot, as B&O discovered to its horror in the fall of 1859.

Typical of the Patapsco cotton mills and their company towns was Alberton, first called Elysville and later renamed Daniels. The town is now gone and the mill is in ruins. Credit: B&O Museum Archives.

IMPOSSIBLE CHALLENGE

CHAPTER 6

ORDEAL BY FIRE, FLOOD AND BLOOD: 1859-1865

With Cumberland coal and midwestern flour and grain finally rolling in quantity over its iron rails, B&O seemed at last on its way to becoming a respectable railroad. Perhaps symbolic of its new stature, it had acquired an appropriate new president in November 1858: John W. Garrett. Garrett, a physically large, commanding and ambitious man, was determined to make B&O a powerful and profitable enterprise after too many years of what he viewed—somewhat correctly—as aimless management and lost commercial and political opportunities.

But at the same time a new, unanticipated kind of problem was beginning to take form—and one that no railroad manager, however able or aggressive, could do much about. In sum, B&O's main line across central Maryland and up the Potomac valley was becoming the informal border in the increasingly tense and bitter sectional split developing in the late 1850's. As the southernmost east-west trunk line, it was in the process of commercially anchoring its service territory to the North, regardless of state lines or personal emotions. Yet the line also lay inside the somewhat tenuous political, economic and cultural boundary of the South.

Thus as Garrett was beginning to think about new markets to conquer his railroad was interrupted by a brief but frightening bit of violence. On the night of October 16, 1859 a small group of heavily armed revolutionaries surprised the federal arsenal at Harpers Ferry and took control of both it and the town. Shortly before dawn the next morning they ambushed B&O's eastbound passenger train from Wheeling as it rolled into the station, shooting and mortally wounding the black station porter in the confusion. The train was held a while and then allowed to continue to Baltimore, although in the interim the railroad telegraph wires—the only communication with the outside—were cut and the B&O station master shot dead.

73

The leader turned out to be an intense, bearded fanatic named John Brown; his aim was to begin a slave rebellion in the South, supplied by arms from Harpers Ferry. But Brown was overoptimistic about both his strategy and his support, and Harpers Ferry was ridiculously indefensible. By this time everyone had become adept at moving troops around quickly by rail. Once the railroad and government confirmed what was happening, a small company of federal marines was loaded on a train in Washington and dispatched to Harpers Ferry. Arriving that evening and joined by local militia from Maryland and Virginia, they made short work of the troublemakers, killing at least half and capturing the wounded Brown. After a day's interruption the railroad went back to its routine; Brown was hustled off to nearby Charles Town where he was quickly tried and executed.

But of course his soul went marching on. Eighteen months of political turmoil followed Brown's raid, then on April 12, 1861 the "irrepressible conflict" began. Almost instantly B&O was caught up in it. A week after Fort Sumter the railroad's "border" status was again brutally dramatized. This time it was the horse-powered Pratt Street line in Baltimore, still the only direct rail link between the east coast cities and Washington. On April 19 Federal troops from Massachusetts being rushed to Washington were moving between the PW&B's President Street station and Camden when they were attacked by a hostile pro-Southern mob. In the ensuing melee at least 16 soldiers and civilians were killed, and the enraged Union military officials immediately sealed off both the city and B&O's lines to the west and south. Garrett had committed his railroad to the Union and managed to get it back into operation quickly, but the worst was ahead.

Its main line up the Potomac valley was both strategic and exposed. Despite the ebb and flow of the war elsewhere, it suffered from an almost continuous Confederate presence in one form or another, and at one place or another, during virtually the entire four years. In addition, the Confederate campaigns culminating in the battles of Antietam (in September 1862), Gettysburg (June and July 1863) and Monocacy (July 1864) swept directly across the railroad. The area around Harpers Ferry and Martinsburg was a favorite corridor for the armies of both sides as well as smaller groups of raiders, and Frederick also seemed to be a favorite stopping off point on the way to somewhere.

As a result, from mid-1861 to early 1863 (except for a brief two-month period in mid-1862) the Baltimore-Wheeling main line was cut in one place or another, and parts were intermittently out of service at many times afterwards. During these periods the unhappy railroad was again reduced to a local carrier, often able to operate only to the Maryland side of Harpers Ferry. (Ironically, during these times it was dependent on the C&O Canal for freight connections to the parts of its railroad beyond Cumberland.)

And, although neutral in the war but seemingly hostile to the railroad, Nature joined in and battered the B&O further. Throughout the war, Potomac floods periodically knocked down what the railroad had tried to rebuild in between the military devastation. A key problem was the early destruction of the original Harpers Ferry bridge on June 14, 1861. The temporary trestlework erected afterwards to keep the line open was spectacularly vulnerable to the notorious floods which have constantly ravaged this spot. The substitution of four iron Bollman spans in 1863 helped, but the remaining trestle sections still regularly collapsed.

The enormous new wartime traffic also tended to flow in directions different from B&O's route layout, causing irritating delays and unwieldy operations. With no direct rail route west from Washington, everything between Washington and any western points had to go to Relay and reverse direction. A wye track at the Relay junction finally eliminated the reversing problem in 1862, but the roundabout routing was still frustrating when hours were critical.

Worse were the interline railroad connections in Baltimore: Anything going between Washington and the northeast rolled slowly down single tracks in city streets behind plodding horses. Pratt Street remained the sole connection with the Philadelphia, Wilmington & Baltimore's route to Philadelphia. The Northern Central to Harrisburg was reached by an equally tedious mile-long track laid in Howard Street between Camden and NC's Bolton station (near the present Mt. Royal station). The military authorities pressed Garrett to build a direct rail connection between Relay and the PW&B at Back River (near present Essex), bypassing the street transfers; they also pushed for another route around the west side of Baltimore from Relay to the Northern Central at Hollins (Lake Roland). Garrett did neither—ultimately a correct judgment in the second case but a mistake in the first. Soon after the war, the Pennsylvania Railroad made a similar connection with the PW&B and started on its way to locking up the Philadelphia route for itself.

B&O's role in the Civil War permeates the history of the conflict; it thus shows up constantly in the overwhelming amount of literature on the subject. We won't attempt to rehash it or reinterpret it here. But less has been written from the viewpoint of the pragmatic railroaders struggling to maintain some semblance of operation through it all. The following doleful diary, recorded in the railroad's annual reports by Master of Road John L. Wilson, gives some feeling of what they had to cope with and how they did. It is reproduced here largely verbatim, edited only to confine the narrative to the area covered by this book. Although seemingly overlengthy, it conveys beautifully the atmosphere of constant struggle under the worst conditions. And, unmentioned anywhere but clear in every line, is the bravery and persistence of the railroaders running trains between and around the fighting, rebuilding bridges as gunfire still sounded in the background and fighting across the swollen Potomac on a suspension wire:

JUNE 14, 1861

Harpers Ferry covered wooden bridge, 7 spans.....also flooring, rail-joist, cross-ties, double track and iron hand railing on iron trestling through arsenal yard, destroyed.

JUNE 20, 1861

Winchester iron span at Harpers Ferry (wood work) burned, and engine 165 ran through the bridge into the Potomac River.

Destruction of the Harpers Ferry bridge in June 1861 broke B&O's main line and began a four-year-long ordeal to keep traffic moving over the Potomac. Credit: B&O Museum Archives.

AUGUST, 1861

The trestling of the Potomac at Harpers Ferry was commenced, but progressed with difficulty, owing to the high stage of water. The work was stopped on the 19th on account of withdrawal of the United States forces from the vicinity.

AUG. & SEPT. 1861

Thirty-six and a half miles track torn up between Harpers Ferry and Paxton's Cut (west of Martinsburg), and the iron and several thousand ties and track fixtures were being transported by animal power to Southern roads.

SEPT. 29, 1861

All the trestling of Potomac river (bridge) at Harpers Ferry (which had been) erected up to August 19th, was carried away by a freshet, with the exception of two trestles adjoining the Maryland shore.

SEPTEMBER, 1861

Two derricks, to work by horse power, were erected on bank of Canal at Sandy Hook to transfer coal from canal boats to our cars. Other derricks were being put up sufficient to load fifty cars per day. This had become necessary, owing to the continued closing of our line between Harpers Ferry and the coal regions, and the great demand for Cumberland coal, also for the gas coal from Newburg and Fairmont.

FEB. 7, 1862

United States forces under Col Geary crossed over into Harpers Ferry and burned the Company's hotel, warehouse, ticket office and water station; also, 38 panels, 570 feet in length, of wood work on the double track iron trestling through the arsenal yard and boatway bridge. This was the remainder of the Company's property in Harpers Ferry not destroyed by the enemy.

MARCH 4, 1862

(A work force) repaired to Harpers Ferry on the 4th to commence working westward. Owing to the great depth of water and the swiftness of the current, it was found impossible to raise the trestles in the Potomac River. A dangerous and difficult task was performed. Large cables were stretched across the river, by means of which the heavy timbers to restore the line of wood work 1620 feet in length upon the original iron trestling through the arsenal yard in Harpers Ferry, and to trestle the Tilt Hammer bridge, also the iron rails, track fixtures and cross ties, were rafted over the river and hoisted to their position. Frequent efforts were made by lashing boats to the cables and to the masonry, to raise the trestles in the river. On the 5th one was placed in position, but in consequence of the excessive cold, the ropes becoming stiffened with ice, the work force was again sent to the work through the arsenal yard and upon the Tilt Hammer bridge. This bridge was completed on the 6th. On the 9th, the work forces were put upon four of the river spans, but their most energetic efforts were unequal to the power of the elements. On the 10th, heavy rain all day, but trestling in the river progressed. From the rain of the 10th the river continued too full, and the current too swift, to accomplish much at the main bridge on the 11th.

MARCH 12, 1862

On the 12th, work was resumed on the main bridge, and pressed with all possible energy until the night of the 18th, when the first locomotive for nine months went over into Harpers Ferry.

MARCH 19, 1862

On the 19th, the track was completed on the iron trestling through the arsenal yard.

All this work in Harpers Ferry, including the Tilt Hammer bridge, would have been done in much less time if the main bridge could have been completed first; but the time saved fully repaid all the disadvantages in getting the materials for it across the river, for the additional labor required to accomplish the work.

APRIL 13-16, 1862

Water again very high. It was necessary to stand loaded cars upon the Potomac trestling at Harpers Ferry to weight it down.

APRIL 22, 1862

River again very high.... At 11:30 a.m. the curved span of Harpers Ferry trestling, adjoining the Maryland shore, and two contiguous spans, were swept out, and fourteen loaded coal cars went into the river. At 3:15 p.m. a canal boat having floated over the tow path came against the next span and swept it out with ten loaded cars, and at 7:45 p.m. one-half of the wide span with 12 cars went out. The water continued at such great height that trestling could not be commenced until April 28th. Passengers and baggage were transferred by boats.

MAY 4, 1862

On the 4th of May it was finished and 400 loaded cars passed over it.

JUNE 7, 1862

Remainder of Potomac River trestling at Harpers Ferry, from shore to shore, carried out by high water.

JUNE 9, 1862

Work forces from east and west commenced re-trestling Potomac River at Harpers Ferry, and completed it on the 15th.

JUNE 24, 1862

Commenced raising iron bridge at Harpers Ferry with No. 4 span. In consequence of the frequent delays at this point by trestling washing out, it was determined to risk (building) the iron bridge.

AUGUST 21, 1862

Two iron spans, No. 3 and 4 of the magnificient Harpers Ferry bridge completed during the month, and preparations made to erect span No. 5.

The cars lost in the river at the time the trestling was swept away, were also taken out during this month and sent to Baltimore and Piedmont for repairs.

AUGUST 21, 1862

United States troops left Berlin (now Brunswick), cut 26 telegraph poles and destroyed the wire.

(Lee's Antietam campaign was beginning)

SEPT. 8, 1862

The splendid iron suspension bridge at Monocacy (actually a Bollman truss) blown up by the enemy....The water station at Monocacy, including pump house and engine, also burned.

SEPT. 15, 1862

Commenced removing debris of Monocacy bridge. This vicinity was the camping ground of the Confederate army, and before operations could be commenced at the bridge, dead men, horses and cattle had to be buried.

SEPT. 17, 1862

Government Canal bridge at Harpers Ferry destroyed. This was a covered wooden bridge, 148 feet span, and the only one between Monocacy and Cumberland that had remained intact up to this period.

SEPT. 17, 1862

Monocacy trestling commenced; crossed trains over at 11 a.m. September 21.

SEPT. 24, 1862

Reconstruction train went to Harpers Ferry. The iron spans Nos. 3 and 4, also Winchester iron span, blown up and laying in confused masses in the river. The trestling in all other spans destroyed, also 24 spans of wood work on iron trestling, Boatway bridge, Wasteway 12 spans, two bridges of 13½ spans at Beck's Quarry, and carpenter shop at Harpers Ferry, tool house and blacksmith shop burned. Also, ten house cars (box cars) burned in Harpers Ferry, and 14 in Quarry Siding, 3 gondola cars run into the river, 4 house (box) and 2 crane cars thrown into the C&O Canal. Engine No. 30 burned and hanging in trestlework at west end of bridge, and engine No. 166 burned in Harpers Ferry tunnel (just west of Harpers Ferry).

SEPT. 25, 1862

Workmen commenced removal of wrecks of cars, engines and iron bridge at Harpers Ferry; also, restoring damage to iron trestling, Boatway bridge, Wasteway; also retrestling the Main and Government Canal bridges.

The water station at Monocacy was rebuilt during the month.

The transfer of coal from canal boats into B&O cars at Sandy Hook continued...Additional derricks were erected, and by this means the supply of coal for the Company's use east of Harpers Ferry was fully maintained.

Large quantities of gas coal from Newburg were also transferred. 14,425 crossties, and the lumber for relaying the Howard Street track (in Baltimore), were also brought from the western portion of the road via canal from Cumberland to Sandy Hook.

OCT. 2, 1862

The trestling in the Potomac River at Harpers Ferry completed.

OCT. 7, 1862

Finished trestling Government Canal span, also Wasteway bridge and bridge at Beck's Quarry.

On an apparently rainy October 1, 1862 B&O's Frederick station was the scene of a visit by President Lincoln to inspect the Antietam battlefield. Credit: B&O Museum Archives.

OCT. 8, 1862

>Completed trestling the curve spans at Harpers Ferry; also the Boatway bridge.

>Main line restored as far west as United States troops had possession.

JAN. 6, 1863

>Freight and coal trains commenced running through, and passenger trains on the 7th.

FEB. 9, 1863

>Commenced the erection of No. 6 iron span of Harpers Ferry bridge, and completed it on the 14th; commenced No. 4 iron span, but had to stop it on account of severity of the weather and high stage of the water.

FEB. 28, 1863

>High water at Harpers Ferry; had to stand loaded cars iron trestling at 5 p.m., and transferred passengers of express trains east and west over Pontoon Bridge at daylight on the 1st of March, and at 12 midnight passed six delayed freight trains over the

trestling, but in consequence of one trestle leg becoming loosened from the force of the current, and the wind blowing with such power until dark that the men could not stand upon the trestling to repair it, trains were further delayed until 9 p.m.

The key junction at Relay was guarded throughout the war — both against organized rebel raiders and also Southern sympathizers in Maryland. Credit: B&O Museum Archives.

MARCH 11, 1863

Commenced erecting iron span No. 4, Harpers Ferry bridge, and completed it on the 18th.

APRIL 13, 1863

Commenced erecting iron span No. 3, Harpers Ferry iron bridge, and completed it on the 22nd. Four spans of this magnificent structure completed.

APRIL 24, 1863

Monocacy River higher than for many years, also the Potomac River and Bush Creek; passengers and baggage transferred between Monrovia and Monocacy (Frederick Jct.) in stages; express train did not leave Baltimore at night. Monocacy River fell eleven feet on the 25th but trains were further delayed by a large slip near Point of Rocks, and again at Harpers Ferry by a flat boat lodged against the trestle spans. Mail trains passed slip at 7:30 p.m. and Harpers Ferry at 11:30 p.m.

APRIL 26, 1863

All trains on good time between Baltimore and Cumberland, but not so favorable west of Cumberland.....

JUNE 3, 1863

Rumors of an advance of the enemy; no freight trains ran west of Monocacy until night.

(Thus was the railroad's first touch with Lee's last push north and the events ending at Gettysburg.)

JUNE 3, 1863

Enemy reported crossing at Point of Rocks, but trains were worked through cautiously.

JUNE 13, 1863

Rumors of the past week assume a tangible form. The threatened northward movement of Lee's army commenced. Engines and cars all sent east from Martinsburg.

JUNE 15, 1863

Mail train running only to Sandy Hook.

JUNE 16-17

Passenger trains running between Baltimore and Monocacy; military trains to Sandy Hook.

JUNE 17, 1863

Enemy crossed the Potomac near Point of Rocks and captured and burned engine 108 and train, consisting of 17 cars. This wreck was all cleared up and road reopened from Baltimore to Sandy Hook on the 20th, and all engines and cars sent from Sandy Hook to Baltimore....Until the advance of the United States army after Lee's retreating columns (following the battle of Gettysburg July 1-3), the line of our road was occupied by the enemy, at intervals, from Sykesville, 30 miles from Baltimore, to Rawling's water station, a distance of 160 miles.

JUNE 18, 1863

All the engines and cars sent from Frederick to Baltimore. Frederick train went into Frederick and returned to Plane No. 1 for safety, and went again to Frederick on morning of 19th for passengers.

JUNE 20, 1963

Frederick train went only to Mt. Airy; the enemy in Frederick.

Relay station looked like this during the Civil War period. The junction was Washington's only safe transportation link with the west. The Relay House, catering to passengers transferring between trains, stands at the right. Credit: B&O Museum Archives.

JUNE 21, 1863

The enemy at Mt. Airy. Track torn up at Mt. Airy and telegraph wires cut at midnight and repaired next morning.

JUNE 22, 1863

Mail train run only to Mt. Airy. Train of government supplies went to Mt. Airy and held there until 6 p.m., and moved cautiously to Sandy Hook, and returned on the 23rd.

JUNE 23, 1863

Mail train went to Frederick.

JUNE 24-25

Mail train went to Sandy Hook; Frederick train to Frederick.

JUNE 29, 1863

Mail train went only to Marriottsville, 27 miles from Baltimore. Stewart's cavalry (actually J.E.B. Stuart) crossed the railroad at Hood's Mill, going toward Westminster.

JUNE 30, 1863
> Harpers Ferry occupied by the enemy; mail train went to Monocacy.

JULY 2, 1863
> Trains running to Frederick.

> (Gettysburg was then raging to the north)

JULY 3, 1863
> Enemy at Sandy Hook and Berlin (Brunswick).

JULY 5, 1863
> The trestle work over the C&O Canal and all the wood work upon the four iron spans at Harpers Ferry bridge burned by Maj. Henry A. Cole's United States cavalry.

JULY 7, 1863
> Troop trains running to Sandy Hook and passenger trains to Frederick.

JULY 9, 1863
> Mail train went to Sandy Hook and construction party proceeded to repair Harpers Ferry bridge, but enemy held the Virginia side and fired upon them. Heavy troop movement to Frederick.

JULY 18, 1863
> The erection of trestling in canal span of Harpers Ferry bridge commenced, also the removal of burned wood work and track upon the four iron spans of said bridge; the work was completed at 9 a.m. on the 20th. Several army corps were crossing over into Harpers Ferry during the progress of this work, occupying the railroad and county road so that it was almost impossible to get the necessary materials to the bridge.

JULY 23, 1863
> Iron-clad train went from Harpers Ferry (west) to Opequon. The road found to be in order to that point.

SEPTEMBER, 1863
> During this month the middle span of the Monocacy iron bridge was erected.

> The transfer of coal from canal boats into B&O cars at Sandy Hook continued until the close of navigation in December 1863.

JANUARY 13, 1864
> West span of the Monocacy iron bridge was completed.

JAN. 21, 1864
> Commenced the erection of the east span of the Monocacy iron bridge and completed it on the 25th.

APRIL 10, 1864
> The Potomac River at Harpers Ferry became very high, with

much heavy drift running. The trestled spans were weighted by standing loaded cars upon them. At 11:40 p.m. the wide span, including the Winchester track thereupon, was swept out, carrying along 12 of the cars.

The river continued to rise on the 11th, and the current was so swift that it was evident that it would be impossible to cross in boats for several days. Large bodies of troops being upon the line en route for Washington, extraordinary measures were determined upon to ensure prompt transportation. Wire cables were ordered from Baltimore by special train, which reached its destination at 9 a.m. on the 12th. Previous to its arrival a small line, with weight attached, had been thrown across the opening, by means of which larger lines increasing in size, were passed and repassed, until a five inch cable was secured, upon which the wire ropes were taken over. At 5 p.m. on the same day, all passengers from delayed trains were passed safely over a suspension bridge. The mails and baggage were also thus transferred. Regiments of troops then passed over. Several carloads of ammunition were also transferred by means of this suspension bridge.

On the 14th, by securely lashing boats to the piers, a commencement was made to renew the trestling, and on the 15th at 11:15 a.m. the straight, or Winchester span was completed. The mail train west crossed over on time and all delayed trains then moved forward. The suspension bridge was taken down and the renewal of the trestling in the curved span commenced (this was the main line west, as distinguished from the "Winchester" span directly to the former W&P at Harpers Ferry); but this work was suspended on the 16th by heavy rains, which again raised the waters. The curved span was completed on the 18th. A melancholy accident occurred during its construction. One of the foremen of carpenters, John McLaughlin, fell into the river, and notwithstanding every effort to save his life, was drowned. By this sad event the Company lost a faithful employee, and his fellow workmen an esteemed friend.

MAY 16, 1864

The Potomac River at Harpers Ferry was much higher than April. The pontoon bridge at Falling Waters was carried off, also the pontoon at Harpers Ferry.... Several boats from these bridges lodged against the trestles at Harpers Ferry, upon which loaded cars had been previously placed. In consequence of the heavy weight upon the top, and the immense accumulation of drift, combined with the wreck of the pontoon bridges, the sixth trestle in the wide span broke off and fell at 2 p.m. The second trestle in the same span broke shortly after, followed by four trestles going out from the curved and four from the Winchester span, carrying also two cars into the river. The loss of these supports so weakened the structure that at 3:30 p.m. the wide span entire, the

The much-battered Harpers Ferry bridge as it looked at the war's end. Four of the Bollman spans built in 1862 and 1863 had survived, but temporary trestling supported the rails and roadway at the Harpers Ferry end. Credit (both views): Smithsonian Institution.

Winchester span, and all of the curved span, except six trestles near the Virginia shore were swept out, and 14 (more) cars went into the river.

On the 18th an attempt was made, by use of the life boat, to get a cable across the river to establish a ferry. The men in charge of the boat were compelled, from the condition of the current, to throw the cable into the river to save themselves. Another cable was sent from Baltimore by special train, which reached the bridge at 7 a.m. This was successfully placed, and the ferry thus established. All passengers, baggage and mails from delayed trains were transferred by 9:40 a.m. Several regiments of Ohio 100-day troops were also brought safely over the river in a large boat, which had been built on the previous day for the purpose.

The trestling was commenced on the 19th and finished on the 21st, when the mail train east passed, also all delayed troop and tonnage trains.

(The next entries follow Jubal Early's brief foray toward Washington with 14,000 men. Lew Wallace moved a greatly outnumbered 2,500 Union troops to the Monocacy where the final major battle in B&O's eastern territory was fought. The Confederates won and got as far east as the outskirts of Washington, but by then had lost the initiative and retreated.)

JULY 2, 1864

Advance of the enemy in force. Engines and cars moved east from Martinsburg by 11 a.m. on the 3rd. Gen. Sigel's troops left Martinsburg at 1 p.m. and joined Col. Mulligan, who had been forced back through Kearneysville to the Maryland side of the Potomac River. They reached Maryland Heights on the evening of the 4th.....Harpers Ferry was evacuated on the evening of the 4th by Gen. Max Weber's forces. After crossing the bridge into Maryland, these government troops destroyed the two trestle spans. The pontoon bridge was also taken up.

On the 6th the enemy destroyed the canal span, and all the wood connected with the iron spans of the main bridge; also all the timber, track and platforms on 16 spans of the trestling on the iron columns in Harpers Ferry.

JULY 4, 1864

The mail train east was attacked near Point of Rocks. The fireman was shot, but the engineman promptly reversed his engine and ran the train back to Sandy Hook. This train reached Baltimore on the evening of the 5th. The telegraph line, which had been cut in many places, was promptly repaired. On the 8th trains were run to Sandy Hook and Frederick.

Harpers Ferry was evacuated on the 8th by the enemy, and reoccupied by a brigade of Gen. Sigel's forces. Frederick was evacuated by the U.S. forces and on the 9th the battle of Monocacy was fought. The Federal forces, after a gallant struggle, were compelled to retreat, and trains were sent to points on the line to transport the wounded, as well as retreating and exhausted troops.

The line west of Ellicott's Mills was speedily visited by detachments of Confederate cavalry....After the success of the enemy at Monocacy they moved toward Washington, while detachments of their cavalry made their appearance at many points in the vicinity of Baltimore. On the 11th Baltimore was cut off from the north by the destruction of bridges on the Philadelphia, Wilmington & Baltimore and the Northern Central railroads. The Confederate cavalry reached the line of the Washington Road on the 12th. On the 14th the main body of the enemy were retreating, but roving bands of cavalry still visited various portions of our line.

In addition to the destruction previously mentioned, the following property of the company was destroyed, viz.: one-fourth of a mile of track near Plane No. 4; the siding at Monrovia, and one house car loaded with hay; the water stations at Hartman's (on Bush Creek) and Monocacy; all the buildings at Monocacy, viz: agent's and passenger house, telegraph office, coal bins, sand houses, platforms, etc.; three spans of the iron bridge at Monocacy were much damaged by cannon shot; the turnpike bridge crossing the railroad at Monocacy (present Urbana Pike) burned..

(A large amount of damage was also done in the vicinity of Martinsburg, and the line cut again.)

JULY 14, 1864

A reconnoitering train with military guard moved to Monocacy. The telegraph line was repaired from Baltimore to Harpers Ferry. On the 15th the construction corps went to Monocacy and commenced operations. It was necessary to trestle under the iron bridge entire for the east and west spans, and for a portion of the center span, as three of the towers, many of the castings, and 17 of the suspension rods were broken by solid shot. The construction train crossed the bridge on the 17th at 3 p.m. and moved on to Harpers Ferry and commenced trestling and repairs there on the 18th.

JULY 21, 1864

New (water) tubs were completed at Hartman's water station.

JULY 25, 1864

....a few days after the opening of the road, hostile movements again commenced. The enemy advanced upon Martinsburg, the Federal forces falling back to the river and crossing into Maryland. Fighting was in progress in Martinsburg as the express west passed that point. All engines and cars were moved from Martinsburg without loss and trains held at Sandy Hook and Cumberland.

Another postwar view of Harpers Ferry. By this time the railroad bridge had been rebuilt, but the burned-out and abandoned arsenal buildings remained. The railroad continued to follow its original alignment along the trestle to the right of the old arsenal site. Credit: William F. Smith collection.

JULY 26, 1864

Mail train west run only to Sandy Hook. The U.S. military ordered one span of the Harpers Ferry trestling to be disconnected, so that trains could not cross. It was repaired on the 29th.

Mail train run to Sandy Hook and return daily until the 30th, when Confederate cavalry were at Adamstown and cut the telegraph line. It was repaired on the same day. On the 31st, the mail train of the day previous came to Baltimore from Sandy Hook.

(At this point the line was still badly damaged east and west of Martinsburg; repair operations continued through August and September, interrupted by new Confederate raids.)

SEPT. 28, 1864

Line again re-opened.

OCT. 14, 1864

The enemy crossed the Potomac at Edward's Ferry (east of Point of Rocks) and threatened the road at Buckeystown and Catoctin;

but trains were moved with great caution through the night, and military guards sent with passenger trains beyond said points. The enemy were attacked and compelled to re-cross the river.

NOV. 14-15, 1864

Attacks expected at Duffield's and Catoctin; passenger trains were run under strong military guards.

DEC. 4, 1864

Enemy appeared opposite Point of Rocks; trains uninterrupted.

DEC. 5, 1864

Three miles west of Harpers Ferry the track was torn up; engine, tender and baggage cars thrown off; fireman slightly hurt.

In consequence of the frequency of these raids, it was deemed judicious to establish a cordon of silent watchmen who, whilst they could not prevent these incursions through the military lines, might prevent injury to passengers and damage to trains.

JAN. 18, 1865

Watchman captured and rail taken up 1½ miles east of Duffield's; engine, tender and one car thrown off the track; the contents of three cars carried off. The train following, promptly notified, returned to Sandy Hook and remained until the track was clear, on the morning of the 19th.

FEB. 13, 1865

One of the watchmen captured three miles west of Harpers Ferry. Another went back and notified approaching trains and they returned to Sandy Hook and remained until daylight.

And finally:

APRIL 15, 1865

President Lincoln's assassination caused all trains on the Main Stem and Washington branch to be held at Relay House until noon, by military orders.

So it was over, right down to the tragic postscript. At least the fighting was over. But the rivers hadn't completely finished with the railroad. On May 22, 1865 the Potomac took another swipe at the battered Harpers Ferry trestling and took out most of both the curved (main line) span and the Winchester span. Another rapid patching job put the Winchester span back in service May 25 and the curved span May 27.

IMPOSSIBLE CHALLENGE

CHAPTER 7

THE VICTORIAN MAIN LINE: 1865-1890

When the war ended, John W. Garrett had a dishevelled railroad but a commanding position. Over the next 19 years he proceeded to rebuild and expand "his" railroad to match his aims and ego. Although his abilities were not really up to his ambitions — particularly when compared to the Pennsylvania Railroad's J. Edgar Thompson and Thomas Scott, or the New York Central's Vanderbilts — he did manage to spread B&O across the midwest and greatly build up the port of Baltimore. Garrett moved quickly: In 1871 B&O reached Pittsburgh, one of its original goals which its early promoters had lost. By late 1874 it had established a line — albeit rather roundabout — into Chicago. B&O's connection from Cincinnati to St. Louis, the Ohio & Mississippi, had been standard gauged in 1871. Also in 1871 B&O completed its bridge over the Ohio River at Parkersburg so that for the first time it could offer a genuine through all-rail service between Baltimore and Cincinnati and St. Louis. The coal business increased spectacularly as mines in West Virginia and Pennsylvania began to open, and export grain from Ohio, Indiana and Illinois added to the heavy eastbound bulk traffic flow. Through all of this, B&O remained mostly a bulk railroad.

The other side of Garrett's accomplishments were less discussed. He was consistently outmaneuvered by his large rivals, particularly the Pennsylvania; he missed several excellent competitive opportunities and sunk too much money into bad ones. He paid less attention to the railroad's physical plant than he should have, perpetuating the sharp curves, steep grades and tight tunnels that eventually made B&O the most obsolete and operationally expensive of all the eastern trunk lines. Shortly after the end of the Garrett father-son reign, B&O was in both financial and commercial trouble; although it eventually recovered, some of the shortcomings spawned or left unresolved during the Garrett era continue to curse the railroad today.

All of the foregoing is background for what happened on the main line during this critical pair of decades. To return to 1865: Several major improvements had to be made immediately, either to rebuild war damage or to allow the railroad to handle the heavy tonnages which were again flowing. Most obvious was the Harpers Ferry bridge, half of which was still precariously trestled. Even more necessary — and expensive — were the two remaining stretches of single track: thirteen miles between Marriottsville and Plane No. 1 station at the east side of Parr's Ridge and the short but torturous line around the mountain spurs west of Point of Rocks. The railroad got to work on all of these almost simultaneously.

The four 1862 Bollman truss spans on the Maryland side at Harpers Ferry had survived the war and similar sets of trusses were re-erected over the balance of the bridge, including the complex junction span in mid-river and the sharply curved section leading the main line west along the river shore. By this time the original reason for this awkward alignment — the federal armory buildings — was gone. The buildings had been destroyed during the war and the government had learned that the Harpers Ferry location was strategically unwise; the property had thus been abandoned afterwards. But expediency and probably overstretched finances dictated using the old piers and existing spans despite the single track, curve and joint highway use. By 1868 the "new" Harpers Ferry bridge was completed. With eight complex spans of differing lengths and alignments — including the oversized birdcage-like junction span — it was the most magnificent of Bollman truss bridges and the ideal engineering companion to the ornate Victorian house architecture.

Its alignment and increasing obsolescence notwithstanding, the Harpers Ferry bridge carried all B&O trains, and the highway, for 26 years after. When the railroad finally realigned its river crossing in 1894, the old bridge was retained for exclusive highway use. It remained the primary road access to Harpers Ferry until the great 1936 flood finally took it away. Its stone piers, still following the alignment of the original 1836 wood bridge, remain in the river.

Double-tracking the Marriottsville-Plane No. 1 section was an easy job, since the line had been doubled-tracked before 1838 and many of the structures, cuts and fills needed little additional work. Most of the job was completed in 1865; the single-track Marriottsville (now Henryton) tunnel turned out to be more difficult than expected and took another year to finish.

The 2½ miles along the Potomac between Point of Rocks and Catoctin station were a legacy of the 1832 C&O Canal battle and the worst problem of all. Here the single track coiled cautiously around three massive mountain spurs, hemmed in by the canal on one side and rock walls on the other. The railroad had no choice but to do what it couldn't afford to do in 1832: tunnel the rocks. After the countless tunnels B&O had been forced to drill through the Alleghenies in the 1850's on the way to Wheeling and Parkersburg, Point of Rocks was not the impossible obstacle it once was.

Three tunnels were necessary — an 800-ft. bore at Point of Rocks and

A.

This superlatively complex collection of Bollman truss spans at Harpers Ferry was at least the aesthetic epitome of Victorian bridge design. Note that the truss members and towers were colorfully painted. At this time the railroad still followed the C&O Canal around the rock spur of Maryland Heights. A short freight spur continued west on the Maryland side. Credits: A-B&O Museum Archives—B-Smithsonian Institution.

B.

two shorter tunnels at "upper Point of Rocks", or Williams Point, near Catoctin. Work started in 1866 and was finished in 1868; for the first time, B&O now had a double track line all the way from Baltimore to Martinsburg — except, of course, for the Harpers Ferry bridge.

Finally, a short but almost too obvious improvement had to be made in the Baltimore terminal layout. The passenger approach route to Camden station consisted mostly of a patched-together combination of a main line originally aligned to meet West Pratt Street and the freight branch to Locust Point. As a result, passenger trains circled around a giant and useless "S" curve, taking twice the distance necessary and, incidentally, adding to the increasing congestion of freight transfers between Mt. Clare and Locust Point. A direct double-track line was laid from West Baltimore station (east of present Patapsco Avenue) to Carroll's switch (near Monroe Street), cutting across one loop of the "S". The Camden cutoff, as it was called, was 1½ miles long and crossed Gwynns Falls on a twin-span Bollman through truss bridge — a distinct contrast to the hulking Carrollton viaduct upstream on the old line. It was opened in April 1868; afterwards, scheduled passenger trains disappeared from the oldest part of the B&O, although the original line remained a heavy freight route as well as the access to Mt. Clare shop.

Unfortunately, 1868 is also celebrated as the year of one of the most devastating floods in the Patapsco Valley's history. On July 24, 1868 a freak rainstorm dumped 18 inches within half an hour in the upper part of the valley; according to contemporary accounts the river rose five feet in ten minutes at Ellicott's Mills. Thirty-six people died and many houses and factories were destroyed or badly damaged. The little town of Sykesville was almost completely wiped out. For B&O, the destruction was fully as much as anything suffered during the war. All four of its bridges over the Patapsco itself were swept out, along with several which crossed tributary streams: Three of the four stone arches of the original Patterson viaduct at Ilchester were removed plus the two long Bollman truss bridges at Elysville, the iron truss just east of Marriottsville tunnel, the original stone arch over Gillie's Falls at Woodbine, an iron bridge over Bush Creek and several stone culverts.

Despite B&O's recently-acquired skills in putting a damaged railroad back into service quickly, the destruction was such that it took a full two weeks before temporary trestlework, fills and new track could be completed for limited operations. Permanent rebuilding took two years. Between 1869 and 1870 new Bollman trusses were built at the two Elysville locations, Marriottsville tunnel and Woodbine (Gillie's Falls). The 1829 Patterson viaduct was much too battered to replace in stone; the remains of its two river spans and eastern roadway span were dismantled and replaced by a long single-span Bollman through truss bridge; the small western roadway span escaped the flood and was retained as the abutment for the new bridge. It still remains today, now the only remnant of either bridge.

B&O may have survived the 1868 flood and perhaps was even

An immediate post-Civil War project was the elimination of the tight twist around the mountain at Point of Rocks. This 1871 view looks east at the new double track tunnel. The original line followed the poles. The tunnel still exists, although enlarged and now single tracked; the eastbound main track now skirts the rock again, occupying part of the old canal bed. Credit: B&O Museum Archives.

improved by it, but some Patapsco Valley industries did not. Many of the riverside mills and factories were wiped out or damaged beyond economical repair; some gave up and closed forever, including the large Avalon Nail and Iron Works.

Another postwar accomplishment was a general speedup of the leisurely freight schedules, partly permitted by faster power but more so by a different operating management philosophy. About 1871 Thomas R. Sharp took charge of operations, first as Assistant Master of Transportation and shortly afterwards (following W.P. Smith's death) as Master of Transportation. Interestingly, Sharp was the Confederate officer who engineered Stonewall Jackson's famous abduction of B&O locomotives at Martinsburg in 1861. John E. Spurrier, a B&O operating officer at the time, later reminisced that "before Sharp's time the freight trains were not allowed to exceed 10 or 12 miles an hour, being so slow the enginemen could scarcely keep awake; they were continually falling asleep, allowing water to get low in the boiler, or too much in the boiler, or bumping into the train ahead".

This brightly-painted Bollman truss replaced the stone Patterson Viaduct at Ilchester after the 1868 flood. The arch on the right is all that remains of the 1829 bridge. It still stands, now buried in trees and underbrush. The photo was taken from the approximate location of the present railroad bridge and looks downstream. Credit: Smithsonian Institution.

Spurrier continues: "Mr. Sharp lost no time in seeing the trouble and in quickening the speed of everything and everybody on the road. He made a schedule for the empty coal hoppers, so that the coal cars unloaded at Locust Point up to 10:30 or 11:00 a.m. would be at the mines for the next day's loading. The name of this schedule was Coal No. 1 West. He thought it too fast for the 43″ wheeled Winans Camels and the Jersey Greenbacks (0-8-0's also), and ordered that the 50″ wheeled Camel ten-wheelers should run on No. 1."

At this point it should be mentioned that, under today's operations, such an order is merely a routine power reassignment with little effect on the train crews. But remember that in those days crews were still assigned to specific locomotives; if a locomotive was not used for a run, the crew did not work. Says Spurrier: "This gave the ten-wheel engine crews so much more time and money that the Winans Camel and Jersey Greenback men called on Mr. Sharp and explained the matter; (they) claimed they could make the time with safety just as well as the ten-wheelers — all they asked for was a trial. Mr. Sharp agreed to give them the show, and ordered that all engines would run their turns regardless of class. It became a race as to who could make the best time, there being no speed limit. It turned out that

96

the Winans Camels and Jerseys made the best time to Mt. Airy, and could make the time just as well as the ten-wheelers on the whole run from Mt. Clare to Martinsburg. They were kept on No. 1. Strange as it may seem, there were fewer accidents than at the slow speed, which was no doubt accounted for by every trainman being on the alert and wide awake, and knowing each train would be doing its best."

With no signals or automatic air brakes, the primary method of avoiding collisions was a strict rule that trains should run no less than six minutes apart. If Spurrier's account is to be believed — and it probably should be — the "primitive" railroading of over a hundred years ago seems considerably advanced over the present. (Of course accidents did happen — sometimes bad ones. On June 12, 1877, for instance, a 13-car Frederick-Washington excursion collided head-on with an eastbound train of deadhead passenger cars half a mile from Point of Rocks on the Old Main Line. Two excursion cars were smashed and five people killed.)

The year 1870 was just about the last year of the "old" B&O with its western terminals at Wheeling and Parkersburg. During the next five years through passenger and freight services would begin to points such as Cincinnati, St. Louis, Pittsburgh and Chicago; in addition the new Metropolitan branch (to be studied later) would change passenger routing patterns in and out of Baltimore. So passenger schedules in 1870 were still simple and straightforward: Three through trains a day each way operated between Baltimore and Wheeling, with Parkersburg connections. Depending on the specific train, these stopped at such way points as Ellicott's Mills, Elysville, Marriottsville, Sykesville, Frederick Junction, Point of Rocks, Sandy Hook and Harpers Ferry. In addition, an all-stops accommodation train was scheduled between Baltimore and Harpers Ferry, plus three Baltimore-Ellicott's Mills locals each way.

But in 1873 a fundamental change came to the east end of the main line. Giving in to pressures for a direct rail line west from Washington, Garrett finally built the Metropolitan branch extending between Washington and a junction with the main line at Point of Rocks. After several years of stop-and-start construction during the late 1860's and early '70's, the "Met" was officially opened May 25, 1873. Chapter 12 describes the background and life of this "branch" which became more than just a branch. Immediately the form, operations and general life style of the main began to change.

All through passenger trains between Baltimore and the rapidly expanding list of western cities (Chicago, Cincinnati, St. Louis, Pittsburgh, Wheeling) were taken off the original Patapsco Valley line and routed through Washington, following the Washington branch between Relay and Washington and the Metropolitan branch from Washington to Point of Rocks. Any local Washington or Alexandria freight to or from the west (meaning mostly coal and food products) also used the Metropolitan, rather than the circuitous routing through Relay and Baltimore. The Patapsco valley route continued to carry any freight directly in or out of Baltimore — which meant most of the coal, all of the grain and large amounts of general merchandise — plus a still-considerable volume of local passenger traffic oriented primarily to Frederick and Ellicott's Mills.

In short, B&O's eastern end became permanently subdivided and forever afterwards the railroad was never quite sure where its main line was. The original Patapsco Valley route between Baltimore and Point of Rocks was first informally designated the "old line" in timetables; later it was officially christened the Old Main Line, capitalized and all. However the Metropolitan branch was never formally designated as the main line and, in fact, it did not fully function as a main line until after World War II.

In any event the line east of Harpers Ferry was now a two-pronged system, splitting at Point of Rocks. East of Point of Rocks, the Old Main Line, shorn of its prestigious through passenger business, settled back into the status of a drudge route — albeit usually an active one. West of there, the main line became an increasingly busy and congested funnel for all of B&O's passenger and freight business regardless of what it was or where it was going.

As usual, stations got secondary attention along the main line to Harpers Ferry, at least until the early 1870's. Probably the largest way station built in the immediate post-Civil War years was a long two-story frame structure at Monocacy (soon afterwards renamed Frederick Junction), put up in 1865 to replace the facilities burned the year before during the battle of Monocacy. This station got a two-story addition on its rear in 1871 and another addition in 1893; it stood, progressively sagging, until replaced by an austere little train order station in 1943. Another large frame station was built at Weverton in 1868 to serve passengers transferring to and from the newly-built branch to Hagerstown, which had opened in December 1867. (Chapter 16 covers this delightfully rural line). Mt. Airy got a small new station in 1869 and an oddly-designed single-story wood way station went up at Adamstown in 1871 — the latter identical to stations built on the Washington branch at Beltsville and Bladensburg (Hyattsville). Their basic layouts were conventional, but all had heavy, flat overhanging roofs unlike anything else on B&O before or since. The Adamstown structure survived World War II, far outliving its Washington branch brothers.

By the early 1870's B&O began to pay more attention to station design. John W. Garrett may not have cared much about such prosaic operating matters as poor grades, curves or yards, but apparently he did understand the status value of a handsome and expensive building. Through the 1870's and '80's an extraordinarily fine collection of stations appeared on all the lines in Maryland, as well as many other locations on the system. Garrett had a particular affection for hotels and combination hotel-stations, a type of building never popular in the United States and already becoming obsolete by the growing use of railroad sleeping cars. During the early and mid-'70's he built large resort hotels in the western Maryland mountains at Deer Park (1873) and Oakland (1875), as well as the large and ornate Queen City station-hotel at Cumberland (1872) and smaller brick station-hotels in 1875 on his newly-built Chicago line at Newark, Ohio and Chicago Junction (later Willard), Ohio.

After 1873 B&O's Patapsco Valley main line became the "Old Line", still well-travelled by freights but stripped of through passenger trains. This eastbound local, shown pausing at Woodstock about 1885, was typical of passenger runs afterwards. The station behind the first car was newly-built to serve the Jesuit seminary across the river. Credit: Enoch Pratt Free Library.

The facilities at Frederick Junction (then called variously Monocacy station and Monocacy Junction) were casualties of the Civil War. Immediately afterwards B&O built this rambling board-and-batten building at the junction, shown here in 1871 looking fresh and new at age six. The camera looks west; the branch to Frederick curves off sharply to the right. Clearly, ballasting and track maintenance were not top priority needs on B&O at this time. Credit: Smithsonian Institution.

Looking east at Adamstown in July 1947. The picturesque wood station was built in 1870 and was similar to contemporary stations at Beltsville and Bladensburg on the Washington branch. Credit: E.L. Thompson.

For reasons which now seem somewhat irrational, Relay was picked as the site of what was to be one of B&O's showcase station-hotels. In July of 1872 work started on the Viaduct Hotel, a combination of a three-story hotel and two-story station building, located in the center of the Y formed by the junction of the main line and the Washington branch adjacent to the Thomas viaduct. At the time, the site was partially broken up by rock cuts where the two lines had been put through a large granite spur; the Civil War-inspired connecting Y track also occupied the property. These were cleared away and the magnificent stone Gothic-style building rose on the ledge overlooking the Patapsco valley. It opened for guests and passengers late in 1873.

It was indeed a sumptuous building, looking larger than it actually was. The three-story hotel section measured 55 by 70 feet; the station at the east end, facing the junction, was 43 by 52 feet. A two-story rear porch looked down on the river valley and stone railroad viaduct; inside the hotel was a 25 ft. by 50 ft. dining room. The entire structure was heated by steam and lighted by gas "generated on the premises". As recently described by industrial historian Dianne Newell, the Viaduct Hotel-Station was constructed of blue Patapsco granite which, although supplied locally, "was an unusually extravagant material. The whole was generously trimmed with red Seneca stone and the roof was patterned with multicolored slate. The interior was finished with hardwood and the dining room, like those of other station-hotels, was quite spacious. The small but exquisite fenced garden to the west was laid out in the English Romantic style, 'more beautiful than nature itself.' The focus of the garden with its fountains, gravelled walks, flowers and hedges, was the stately marble monument honoring the Thomas viaduct." In 1883 a large greenhouse was added on the property to supply plants for this garden as well as the company's other resort hotels.

The reasoning behind a hotel and station at this location is less clear. Although Relay traditionally had been an important transfer station for passengers travelling between Washington and western points, it had lost this function before the station was opened. Only 7 miles from Baltimore, it made little sense as a stopover point for travellers going anywhere else. The site was certainly scenic, and being close to both Baltimore and Washington it was advertised as a convenient escape from the summer heat. But its appeal as a resort must have been limited by its rather confined grounds and its location in the center of a busy railroad junction. One justification given by a contemporary railroad official was that Relay was intended as a meal stop and transfer point for passengers travelling between western points and Philadelphia or New York. At that time B&O's western trains terminated at Baltimore; the Philadelphia and New York services (jointly operated with the PW&B) operated from Washington and were transferred over the streets in Baltimore (or, after 1880, across the harbor). Thus Relay was a convenient spot to catch the through cars which did not stop at Camden. It probably served this function to one degree or another at least through the early 1880's.

A.

B.

The new Viaduct Hotel-station, fore and aft. The "fore" view (with a new 2-8-0 and a surviving Grasshopper) was made immediately after the building was finished. (For locomotive purists, the 2-8-0 was mis-numbered; according to legend, it was rushed out for the photo and Mt. Clare shop slapped the number on it too quickly.) Note the colored, patterned roof slates. The rear view dates slightly later (ivy has grown up the walls) but shows the "English romantic garden" overlooking the valley and viaduct. Credits: A-Harry C. Eck — B-C.S. Roberts Collection.

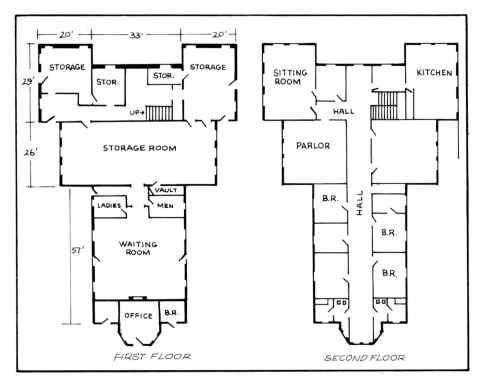

FIRST FLOOR   SECOND FLOOR

Despite its seemingly superfluous function, the Viaduct Hotel-station building survived quite long. Although long since closed, it stood until 1950, perhaps largely for the sake of sentiment. A bronze plaque buried in a tangle of weeds marks its site today.

Progressively more elaborate stations also began to appear at small way points. Beginning in the mid-1870's, Garrett employed E. Francis Baldwin, a locally notable Baltimore architect, to design many of B&O's stations and other buildings, including Garrett's ostentatious new head-quarters office building at Baltimore and Calvert Streets in 1881. The designs of Baldwin and other B&O architects of the time were distinctive and picturesque, and despite similar floor plans and basic functions, usually no two were exactly alike.

The Old Main Line, having been demoted to secondary passenger ser-vices and freight, did not receive as full a quota of such stations as other points. But some notable structures appeared, the most prominent of which was the large, spired "gateway" station at Point of Rocks at the junction of the Old Main and the new Metropolitan branch; designed by Baldwin, it was completed in 1875 and is described more fully elsewhere in this narrative. Mt. Airy received a brick freight house in 1876 which was expanded with passenger facilities in 1882; although of a fairly conven-tional single-story layout, the station had rather ornate brickwork and wood roof brackets, all which may still be seen and studied. A fine little brick combination freight-passenger station was built in 1879 for the little river town of Berlin, between Point of Rocks and Harpers Ferry. Also conventional in basic design, it was handsomely trimmed with a light granite band around its center and windows. Berlin was renamed Brunswick in 1890 and the station replaced by a newer building moved from a nearby location sometime afterwards; however, it survived as an express station at least until the late 1930's.

This typical brick way station was built for Berlin, Md. in 1879. Berlin was then a popular Potomac River crossing and a small C&O Canal town. In 1890 it was literally bought by B&O, renamed Brunswick, and converted into a railroad yard and shop town. The photographer here is facing west and is standing close to the site of the present Brunswick station. Credit: Brunswick Museum.

Considerably more picturesque stations — all of them designed by Baldwin — appeared in the mid-1880's at Woodstock, Sykesville and Ilchester. The first two were brick and although different from each other and from all other B&O stations, were the same charmingly distinctive Queen Anne style used by Baldwin for such locations as Gaithersburg, Hyattsville, Laurel and Oakland, Md. Both were built in 1883-84. Ilchester, finished in 1885, was wood and slightly more subdued, but had the characteristic high gabled roof and colored window glass. Woodstock station disappeared long ago; Ilchester was slightly relocated in 1903 when the line was realigned and survived until 1964; Sykesville still stands. Weverton also got a new station slightly later (in 1888) to replace its 1868 original — a non-Baldwin product with a squat tower and rounded windows forming an arch around its main door.

Even more than station architecture, Garrett was interested in building up Baltimore and expanding the railroad's port facilities there.

Sykesville received this new Francis Baldwin-designed station in 1884. It has survived floods and the abandonment of passenger service, and is still a regular stopping place for occasional enthusiast excursions. This one passed through in May, 1970. Credit: H.H. Harwood, Jr.

Somewhat similar to Sykesville station was Woodstock, also built in 1884 by the same architect. Unfortunately, it is not only gone but scarcely recorded; this crumpled postcard was the best view of it which could be found. Credit: R.W. Janssen collection.

Through the 1870's and '80's B&O tracks and terminals began spreading all over the city, particularly its waterfront. In fact, during these two decades construction was constantly going on at one place or another — so much that it can only be briefly summarized here.

Some tentative expansion had already begun before the Civil War when B&O built a short piece of track in Fell Street at Fells Point in 1860. The little Fells Point "branch" was horse-powered and isolated from B&O tracks; freight cars were floated to it from Locust Point, directly across the harbor. It served waterside warehouses and small manufacturers in what was then Baltimore's primary merchandise port section — Locust Point at that time was confined strictly to bulk coal and grain shipping. Another carfloat terminal was established at nearby Chase's Wharf warehouse in 1867.

By the late 1860's the bulk business was beginning to overwhelm Locust Point and between 1871 and 1874 land was filled around the peninsula, extensive new trackage laid and two grain elevators built.

And in mid-1880 Locust Point began getting passenger trains and interline transfer freight to add to its congestion. To bypass the increasingly irritating Pratt Street transfer between B&O and the Philadelphia, Wilmington & Baltimore Railroad, the through traffic to Philadelphia and New York was rerouted into Locust Point and floated across the harbor to the PW&B's carferry terminal off Boston Street near Canton. B&O bought a large new sidewheel ferry, the "Canton", to shuttle cars between the two railroads. Powered by two beam engines and measuring 324 feet long with a 36 ft. beam, the "Canton" could carry 10 passenger cars or 27 freight cars. While this operation lasted, solid through passenger trains were run between Washington and Philadelphia/New York, bypassing Camden by running directly into Locust Point. However, many schedules dropped or picked up local Baltimore cars at Bailey's, which were switched in and out of Camden. But it didn't last too long. In one of Garrett's more humiliating defeats, the Pennsylvania bought control of the PW&B in 1881, and cut off the through B&O passenger traffic in October 1884. By this time the PRR had its own competitive line to Washington. Garrett had already started his own railroad to Philadelphia; when it was opened in late 1886, B&O continued the carferry from Locust Point to its new Philadelphia line terminal in Canton. This operation continued another 10 years until the Howard Street tunnel and the Baltimore Belt Line were opened.

While Locust Point yard was expanding, work also began on rebuilding the main line into Baltimore. The old double-track route between Relay (where the Washington branch joined) and West Baltimore (where the Mt. Clare freight line diverged) was rapidly bogging down as increasing numbers of slow freights from the Old Main Line and fast passenger trains for Washington tried to keep out of each others way. Beginning in 1875 this key four-mile bottleneck was rebuilt for four tracks. The job involved heavy cut and fill work, since it meant going back over many of the obstacles so unpleasantly familiar to B&O's original builders — Vinegar Hill, Gadsbys Run, Roberts Run and the Deep Cut. The project was completed in 1879.

A sampling of Locust Point in the 1880's. By this time B&O not only operated extensive coal, grain and general merchandise export piers, but had developed an active "navy" of tugs, carfloats and lighters. The tug *Convoy* shown here was also used for B&O's Potomac River carfloat service at Alexandria, Va. Credit (both): B&O Museum Archives.

At the same time the Baltimore engine terminals were relocated and greatly expanded. In 1875 two large new roundhouses were built — one for passenger power and one for freight. The cramped little Camden station engine house at Howard and Lee Streets was replaced with a brick 24-stall roundhouse located eight blocks south at Bailey's (Ostend Street) in the center of the Y formed by the junction of the Camden and Locust Point branches. Since most of the freight traffic had gravitated to Locust Point, the primary freight locomotive facility — a large 44-stall roundhouse measuring 305 ft. across — was built at Riverside on the Locust Point peninsula, close to the piers and yards. Riverside largely replaced Mt. Clare as a freight terminal, with road locomotives and trains operating directly to Locust Point rather than being switched at Mt. Clare.

By the early 1880's it was clear that even Locust Point could not handle all the coal, grain and interchange traffic being squeezed through it. In 1880 inbound commercial coal into Baltimore totalled 1.6 million tons alone. In addition, B&O needed more space for the general merchandise export-import business, which had outgrown Fells Point and the inner harbor, and also wanted to establish facilities for a new phenomenon — European immigrants now flooding into the U.S. It was decided to shift the export coal traffic to a completely new section of the harbor at Curtis Bay, about six miles directly south of the city center. In 1883 a 5-mile branch was built from the Old Main at Curtis Bay Junction (near West Baltimore)

The old "Deep Cut" looked much less formidable after being widened for four tracks in the late 1870's. Here P-7 Pacific No. 5300 (now preserved in the B&O Museum) leads the "Fort Pitt Limited" through the cut in May, 1931. Credit: Smithsonian Institution, C.B. Chaney collection.

passing around Brooklyn and ending at the large wood coal trestle loading piers on Curtis Bay. A sub-branch was extended from Brooklyn to Fairfield in 1885. With the Curtis Bay branch in operation in 1884, Locust Point was turned over largely to grain, general merchandise and immigrants.

A.

Bailey's roundhouse was one of a pair of new engine terminals built in 1875 to service B&O's expanding Baltimore business. Bailey's handled passenger power for Camden station, eight-tenths of a mile north. Both of these views look approximately east. The train scene dates to September 1946, in the last years of the roundhouse; Ostend St. bridge may be seen directly behind. Credits: A-B&O Museum Archives — B-C.T. Mahan, Jr.

B.

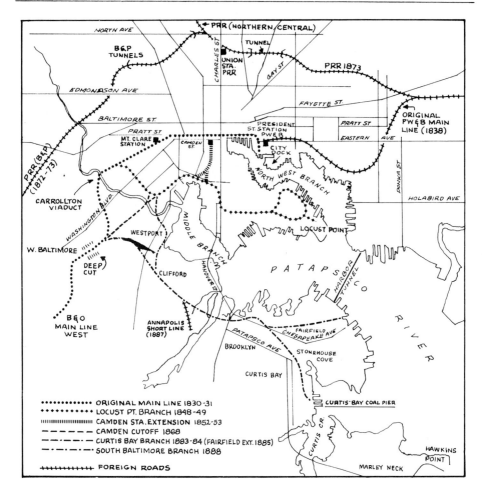

Camden station also embarked on its long life of rebuildings and facility expansion. In 1880-81 a 600-foot long freight delivery shed and brick and stone freight office were built on the east border of the property along Howard Street, the area now occupied by the approach track to the Howard Street tunnel. A grain elevator was built at Camden in 1883 to handle oats and feed for local delivery. And in 1886 the original wood trainshed was dismantled and replaced by a shorter iron shed, which extended only as far as the Barre Street grade crossing.

Shortly afterward, Camden got a tenant. In 1880 a company called the Annapolis & Baltimore Short Line had been organized to provide a direct rail route between Baltimore and the state capital. Since 1840, anyone going by rail between Baltimore and Annapolis followed a two-hour roundabout route over the B&O's Washington branch to Annapolis Junction and the onetime Annapolis & Elk Ridge from there to Annapolis—

Mt. Clare shop at its height, about 1885, as seen from the roof of the passenger car shop (now the B&O Museum roundhouse). The round building to the left is the freight car shop; directly behind it is the machine shop. Obviously, wood was the major ingredient in car construction. Today only the long building at right center remains. Credit: B&O Museum Archives.

hence the new railroad's pointed "Short Line" title. The Short Line was independently promoted and slow in getting started, but finally opened on March 9, 1887. Its 22-mile route from Annapolis joined B&O's Curtis Bay branch at a spot called Clifford's, about 1½ miles west of Brooklyn; from here Short Line trains used B&O tracks into Camden. The original operation apparently was rather awkward, since the Curtis Bay branch ran west to the main line near West Baltimore. In 1888, however, B&O completed its South Baltimore branch from Carroll's (near Monroe Street) to a junction with the Curtis Bay line south of Westport — partly built to provide a direct freight connection between Curtis Bay and Camden-Locust Point, and partly built specifically for the Short Line's Baltimore entrance.

For 33 years, and under various names — the Annapolis & Baltimore Short Line, the Baltimore & Annapolis Short Line (1894), and the Maryland Electric Railways (1906) — the little railroad continued to use Camden. A short-lived merger with the Washington, Baltimore & Annapolis interurban system removed Short Line trains from the B&O in 1921, but they were back after the WB&A's demise in 1935 and lasted until February 1950. Traditionally, Annapolis trains were assigned tracks at the west side of the Camden trainshed and, except for a period in the early 1900's, used B&O's main line as far as Carroll tower, where they switched onto the South Baltimore branch. Annapolis freight was usually interchanged at the old Clifford's junction.

While the Baltimore terminals were expanding, the Old Main Line was plodding. Typical of its post-Metropolitan branch passenger services were the schedules of June 1875; one Baltimore-Grafton local each way,

113

A Baltimore-bound Old Main Line local eases into Ellicott City in the 1890's. Credit: B&O Museum Archives.

And from the other direction, another local chuffs upgrade into the station about ten years later. At the right is the Patapsco Hotel, which served B&O passengers in the days when the present station was used as a freight depot. Credit: Gary Schlerf collection.

one Harpers Ferry local (connecting with Valley branch service to Winchester), one Frederick local, and one Ellicott's Mills accommodation train. In addition, connecting trains shuttled between Frederick and Frederick Junction to meet any trains not running directly to Frederick and two round trips were scheduled between Frederick and Point of Rocks to meet main line trains. For a small branch-line city, Frederick saw a lot of trains in the 1870's and '80's. In 1884, for example, 8 passenger trains were scheduled into Frederick and another 8 out, plus two freights each way. Admittedly these were either locals or connecting trains, but Fredericktonians nonetheless had a wide choice of schedules. The through run to Baltimore was fairly typical of train speeds on the Old Main — it took two hours and 50 minutes to make the 6½ miles.

Five through freights each way were also scheduled over the Old Main, although these undoubtedly ran in multiple sections. With the heavy freight traffic and local workhorse passenger trains, it was common practice to keep the line fluid by running trains around one another on the opposing track of the double-track line. In fact, operating timetables of the late 1870's and '80's provided for regular left-hand operation of specific trains over specific sections.

By this time, too, motive power was beginning to look more conventional. Beginning in 1873 B&O had standardized on 2-8-0's for its tonnage trains. Gradually the strange conglomeration of Winans Camels, Jersey Greenbacks, home-built 0-8-0's and Hayes Camels that had set B&O apart

115

from other railroads began to disappear. Heavier and handsome 4-4-0's had long since taken over passenger runs from the One Armed Billys and primitive eight-wheelers of earlier years; the 4-4-0 in various sizes and shapes powered virtually all B&O passenger trains on the eastern lines until after the turn of the century.

By the mid-1880's, 4-4-0's like this were B&O's almost universal passenger motive power. No. 775 sits in the Washington, D.C. station yard about 1887. Credit: Smithsonian Institution.

But the infamous Old Main Line curves and the Mt. Airy grade still were very much in existence. The rebuilding work done immediately after the Civil War was the last major investment Garrett or his successors had made on the line. Basically the Old Main remained a patched and adjusted version of the original railroad — bad enough during the days of light engines and short trains, but increasingly impossible as the Consolidations got longer and heavier and the tonnage kept building. B&O's arch-competitor, the Pennsylvania, had made a fetish of low-grade bypasses and grade and curve reduction during the 1870's and '80's; by the 1890's it had embarked on a massive program of realignments, multiple tracking and replacement of iron bridges with stone viaducts. But — thanks in part to the Garrett legacy — B&O was slipping into financial problems at the same time, aggravated by its slow and expensively obsolete railroad.

Oddly, its major savior was to be the Pennsylvania Railroad.

This ramshackle pair of structures of indeterminate age served as B&O's Knoxville station in the 19th Century. Shortly after this turn of the century photo, they were replaced by a smaller single-story building on the same site. Credit: Smithsonian Institution.

Mt. Winans, a suburban stop in Baltimore, about 1900. The station dates to 1876. Credit: Smithsonian Institution.

Before Brunswick yard was opened in 1890, the railroad operated a small yard and engine terminal at Sandy Hook, near Harpers Ferry. Sandy Hook's combination station and operating office looked like this about 1900. Credit: Smithsonian Institution.

IMPOSSIBLE CHALLENGE

CHAPTER 8

A NEW "OLD MAIN": 1890-1910

By the late 1880's B&O had two severe operating problems at its east end. First was the crooked Patapsco and Bush Creek section of the Old Main Line, with its Mt. Airy hump—all of which have been described. Everyone fully recognized that something had to be done about this route, but the only satisfactory solution was either a ground-up rebuilding or a completely new line at some other location—neither of which the railroad could afford.

Also serious but easier to solve was the freight yard situation. Up through the 1880's B&O had no freight classification or storage yards between Baltimore and Cumberland, and not really much at Cumberland. Martinsburg, 100 miles west of Baltimore, was the intermediate operating division point between Baltimore and Cumberland, but it was primarily a crew and locomotive terminal; its yard track capacity consisted of two long sidings and some shorter yard tracks, with little room for expansion on its existing site near the center of town. Baltimore had no single yard capable of classifying all the freight in and out of the city. Instead, a collection of more limited, scattered specialized yards had begun to appear to serve specific areas of the city or port facilities, such as Mt. Clare, Camden, Locust Point and Curtis Bay. This pattern, incidentally, still exists today; if anything, the Baltimore yard problem has become more complex and disjointed. At that time, Washington had no freight yard whatever except for the confined and congested freight house block near the New Jersey Avenue station. Shipments which could not be handled in Washington usually had to be held at Martinsburg, Point of Rocks or some intermediate sidings.

In the meantime, not only was the total freight volume growing dramatically but its nature was changing. Traditionally B&O had been predominantly a bulk coal and grain carrier, funnelling solid trainloads into Locust Point and Curtis Bay. These needed little or no intermediate switching and Martinsburg's minimal yard was reasonably adequate simply to change power and crews and move the trains out. But as the railroad expanded into new territories and as new industries built along its tracks, the flow of general merchandise and less-than-carload shipments became much heavier and more diffuse. In addition, Baltimore was no longer B&O's sole eastern freight terminal. The opening of the Baltimore-Philadelphia line in 1886 had added a new dimension to the freight traffic flow, since the cars for Baltimore and Philadelphia had to be separated somewhere.

In brief, B&O needed a large new yard somewhere near its east end—but preferably some place west of Point of Rocks where traffic for all of B&O's major eastern points such as Philadelphia, Washington and the various scattered Baltimore terminals could be switched and, if necessary, held until the Baltimore terminals could accommodate it. As an established crew base, engine terminal and shop location, Martinsburg was the obvious choice. Instead B&O picked the tiny town of Berlin, located in the Potomac valley six miles east of Harpers Ferry and 72 miles west of Baltimore. Berlin was chosen partly because of the wide and cheap riverside bottomland available there and partly because it sat in between three more-or-less strategic junctions—the Metropolitan branch/Old Main Line junction at Point of Rocks (7 miles east), the Hagerstown branch at Weverton (3 miles west) and the Shenandoah Valley line at Harpers Ferry. Fully as important, Berlin was in Maryland, and B&O was exempted from paying property taxes in Maryland. The only workable alternate sites, such as Martinsburg, were in West Virginia.

Land was bought, sometimes secretively, in the late 1880's; soon B&O came to own not only the land for the new yard but much of the town, which would soon evolve into a classic railroad town. Work on the yard began in 1890 and, though incomplete, was opened in May. At the same time, with the railroad's blessings, Berlin's name was changed to keep company mail from straying to another Berlin, Md. located on the Eastern Shore. Berlin's new name became Brunswick.

And indeed Brunswick had almost no relationship to Berlin. As the original part of the yard opened about 1893, the community had already begun to change its form. A onetime canal town and river crossing point, the old Berlin had hit its population peak of about 500 after the Civil War; by 1890 it was down to 200. In 1900, 2,471 people lived there and by 1910 population was estimated at 5,000. Railroad workers' homes, stores, churches, meeting halls and schools all appeared at once, along with grids of paved streets running up and down the hills bordering the river. In true "company town" style, B&O donated land for churches, public buildings and parks and in 1907 built the large wood YMCA building to serve as a crew "hotel" and general community center—a function it still performs.

In 1891 the railroad real estate development company also built an attractive wood station (designed by the familiar E. Francis Baldwin or his firm, Baldwin & Pennington) on the eastern edge of town at 7th

The original section of Brunswick yard, seen about 50 years later but essentially the same. The engine house and town are at the top of the photo (west); the remains of the C&O Canal are at the left. Credit: B&O Museum Archives.

Brunswick's heart is its Railroad YMCA, at left, WB tower at right, and engine house directly behind. In this 1966 photo, a mixed set of C&O and B&O F-7 diesels has just uncoupled from a westbound empty hopper train. Credit: H.H. Harwood, Jr.

According to local historians, Brunswick's present station was originally built at the east end of town in 1890 to attract buyers to a railroad-promoted residential development; it was moved into the center of town a short time later. Designed by Baldwin & Pennington, it is basically a straightforward structure but its tacked-on gables with their Palladian windows seem to be an attempt to give it suburban respectability. October, 1966. Credit: H.H. Harwood, Jr.

The 1894 Harpers Ferry bridge and alignment still were not entirely ideal, but a vast improvement on the old. The eastbound all-Pullman "National Limited" poses about 1926. Immediately to the left are the vestiges of the Civil War-vintage Bollman spans, now used only by the highway. The two nearest spans had just been replaced. Credit: B&O Museum Archives.

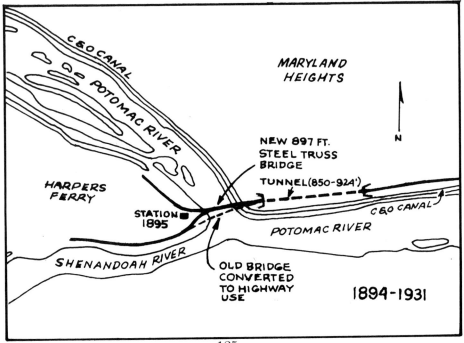

The older bridge as it looked after 1894, with most of the railroad spans removed. The portal of B&O's original Maryland Heights tunnel, also drilled in 1894, is at the far right; it was considerably altered in 1930-31. Credit: Baltimore & Ohio; H.H. Harwood collection.

Avenue as a "suburban" station for new company-sponsored houses in the area; the slightly smaller 1879 brick station remained at the center of the city. The location generated little business and several years later the new station was moved to a spot a block east of the old station where it became the city's primary passenger stop. When the yard was greatly expanded in the early 1900's, track changes made it necessary to build a second station a block south to serve eastbound trains only. Finished in 1908, this structure was smaller and considerably more austere. The original brick station—by now one of the few reminders of old Berlin—was kept as an express station and lasted in this use until the 1950's.

As it existed in the mid-1890's, Brunswick yard spread slightly less than two miles eastward from the center of town and had a designed capacity of 4,000 cars.

As Brunswick was rising, the railroad also was finally doing something about its 1836 alignment over the Potomac at Harpers Ferry. The obsolete single-track Bollman bridge with its two sharp approach curves and shared highway, the sharp swing around the mountain spur at Maryland Heights and the long trestle along the river bank on the West Virginia side were all replaced by a completely new railroad in 1894. B&O tried its best to lay out a straight line through the rock wall and across the river, but had to compromise in order to provide for the junction with its Valley branch (the onetime Winchester & Potomac) on the Harpers Ferry side. The result was still an "S" curve crossing, but far gentler than the old one. Starting on the Maryland side, a 850-ft. tunnel was blasted through the rock spur...this was soon extended to 924 feet to protect against falling rocks. A mild curve at the tunnel's west end led directly onto a new 896½ foot double track steel bridge slightly upstream from the old Bollman. The bridge was a sturdy seven-span structure, consisting of three through truss spans and four girders. On the Harpers Ferry side the old armory site was covered by fill for another curve leading the main line west. The Valley branch was also put up on a fill and twisted slightly west to meet the main line at the west end of the bridge. The highway portion of the old Bollman bridge stayed where it was, although most of the railroad spans were later dismantled.

The three-story frame tavern-hotel which had served as the railroad's Harpers Ferry station since the Civil War (the passenger platform was on the trestle behind the building at the second-floor level) was torn down and its site buried in the fill. Its replacement, built some time in the 1892-94 period, was an unusual combination of a long single-story frame station with a two-story interlocking tower incorporated in its east end to control the Valley branch junction. Like the new Brunswick station, Harpers Ferry was designed by Francis Baldwin, although by this time the increasingly poverty-stricken railroad was losing its interest in decorative embellishments on its way stations. It was handsome and, with its high peaked tower, picturesque—but otherwise rather plain.

In fact, B&O's new stations of the 1890's began to reflect its growing struggle to stay solvent. Several were put up along the main line during

127

An adjunct of the new bridge project was this combination station-interlocking tower at the west end of the bridge. At left is the Shenandoah Valley branch. In 1931 this station was moved west to the new alignment where it still stands. The tower was removed in the 1950's. Credit: B&O Museum Archives.

the decade, but rather than the two-story brick beauties of the late Garrett era, they were frugal smaller single-story wood structures. Francis Baldwin was nothing if not flexible and continued to design most of them. He developed a rather attractive standardized pattern which could be repeated with minor variations at many different rural and suburban spots. Both the Washington and Metropolitan branches received several samples in the '90's; on the main line two were built at Baltimore suburban stops—one at Lansdowne in 1892 and one at St. Denis in 1896—plus a similar station and small frame freight house at Morgan, east of Woodbine in the upper Patapsco valley, in 1891. The 1854 Frederick passenger station was expanded in 1892 with a Baldwin-designed plain single-story brick addition at its east (rear) end.

By this time whatever financial resources B&O could find were being channelled primarily into one of its most difficult, costly, but important projects: the Baltimore Belt Line. B&O had rushed its Baltimore-Philadelphia line to completion in 1886, but it was isolated from the rest of the railroad on the far east side of the city. In trying to connect the Philadelphia route with the main line terminals in downtown Baltimore, the railroad faced much the same problem as it did when it first entered the city in 1831: the hills immediately surrounding the downtown area and the heavily built-up waterfront left no easy and cheap way to get across town. Temporarily, the Philadelphia line ended at a carferry terminal in Canton and both freight and passenger cars were ferried across from Locust Point. For over four years B&O and the city jointly agonized over how to connect the routes with the least disruption. The final route chosen was an extremely difficult one: Starting at Camden Station, it immediately dove into a 1.4-mile-long tunnel running directly under the length of Howard Street, emerging at the site of Mt. Royal Station. It then climbed torturously up the hillside along Jones Falls to Huntingdon Avenue and swung directly east across the north side of Baltimore through a continuous series of short tunnels and cuts. Not only was the work expensive, but the combination of the long Howard Street tunnel and steady upgrade from Camden to the north side of Baltimore dictated electrification of the line—the first main line electric installation in the United States. The Baltimore Belt Line and the Philadelphia route—the fondly-remembered Royal Blue Line—properly belong to another book; indeed, the tunnel, the electrification and Mt. Royal station could support a full-length study alone. We won't and can't describe them here, but will at least mention their effect on the Camden station end of the project.

Typical of B&O's suburban and way stations of the Nineties was this one at Lansdowne just west of Baltimore. It was built in 1892, as attested by the elaborate date on its little gable. Credit: Smithsonian Institution.

The Howard Street tunnel work began in September 1891 and lasted until early 1895. During that time the Camden station facilities had to be rebuilt and reorganized to accommodate the tunnel approach on the east side of the station building. Since the depressed ramp to the tunnel followed the line of Howard Street, the almost-new 1881 freight shed and office fronting on Howard had to be torn down and the freight facilities relocated. They were moved into what was then the central part of the station, in what had been the passenger train shed. At the same time a new passenger shed was built directly adjacent to the older one on the east side, abutting the tunnel approach. The station interior was redesigned so that the waiting room and concourse were oriented to the east end of the building rather than the center. The job was completed in 1892 in order to clear the property for the tunnel work.

Camden station at its height in the mid-1920's. Note the many changes made since the 1871 photo shown in Chapter 4. Still more would come. Credit: Enoch Pratt Free Library.

When through train operations began in 1895, Philadelphia passenger trains using the tunnel had to back in and out of Camden's trainshed, now on the "upper level" of the station. But in 1897 a lower-level platform was built in the tunnel approach cut to serve through trains. It was reached by an overpass off the east side of the new trainshed. At the same time a single-story brick baggage room was added at the east side of the station.

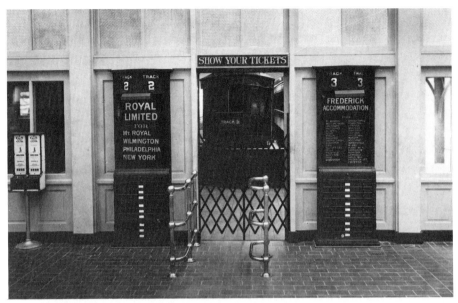

Camden's concourse about 1900. Beauty and the beast apparently are ready to load side by side: The luxurious "Royal Limited", the premiere Royal Blue Line limited, and the Old Main Line local making 34 stops (and probably more) on the way to Frederick. Included on the list are such long-forgotten stations as Warfield and Plane No. 4. Credit: B&O Museum Archives.

A lower-level platform for Philadelphia trains was built in 1897. The westbound "Royal Blue" accelerates away toward Washington in September 1937. The older upper-level tracks are directly above the "Blue's" P-7 Pacific. Credit: Smithsonian Institution; C.B. Chaney collection.

Although the Belt Line and Howard Street tunnel were opened almost 11 years after John W. Garrett's death, his hand could be seen making a last gesture in the project. A year later, in March 1896, one more gesture came: B&O went into receivership. As railroad receiverships go, B&O's was not long or particularly traumatic—it ended in late 1899, with essentially the same management and corporate structure. But if nothing else it was an emotional blow to the railroad, to Baltimore and to much of Maryland. To those sentimental or historically-minded enough to remember that Fourth of July celebration in 1828, it perhaps seemed the last step down the ladder—the end of the spirit of innovation and adventure which had launched the railroad. In a more practical sense it was a clear statement that, despite B&O's early start and long record of "firsts", it had come out in third place in commercial competition—well

The scene at Camden's south end was considerably bleaker by 1970, but this view from the now-razed Lee Street bridge gives an excellent idea of the station's basic layout. The freight roars over the site of the lower-level passenger platform; the Howard Street tunnel portal can be spotted at the upper right, and the fence in the right foreground follows the line of Howard Street, seen in the distance. The truncated stubs of the two train sheds protrude from the rear of the much-altered station at the upper center — the 1886 shed at left, the 1892 on the right. Credit: Bill Rettberg.

behind the Pennsylvania and New York Central. And this in turn implied a repudiation of the Maryland-based banking-political-mercantile management which had dominated the railroad and, indeed, the entire state. Frustratingly, too, the financial problems of the receivership meant that B&O's powerful rivals could continue to spend money to build up their facilities and become more powerful while B&O was tied down to its inadequate and obsolete plant. Indeed, the Pennsylvania, now under the aggressive and expansionistic A.J. Cassatt, was then in the process of building the most magnificent railroad plant in the world.

Just as the company was struggling out of its receivership, it decided to go hunting for its long-buried cornerstone. Maintenance crews finally found it in August 1898—buried six feet below the ground surface.

A romantic might say that the unearthing of the First Stone was some sort of mystical sign signalling the rebirth of the now-tattered B&O. Perhaps, or perhaps not. But there is no question that the turn of the century brought a significant turn in both its fortunes and physical condition. Strangely, though, it was not the businessmen of Baltimore who accomplished it this time. It was the Pennsylvania Railroad.

The southern approach to Camden station about 1910. The little wood tower on the right protects the Hamburg Street grade crossing, later replaced by a bridge. Annapolis Short Line trains ran under the electric catenary line. Credit: Baltimore & Ohio; H.H. Harwood collection.

It happened this way: By the late 1890's the large New York financial institutions and the major railroads—notably the Pennsylvania and New York Central—had realized that the brutal free-for-all railroad competition of the past three decades was jeopardizing some very large investments. They also well knew that once a railroad is built, the investment is largely sunk—it can't be transferred somewhere else. Thus almost any railroad, no matter how weak or unnecessary, tended to stay in business and do its best to survive; its investors and managers had few other choices. To do this they cut rates, tried to build new competitive routes, or both—all of which simply made the problem worse. In this unstable atmosphere the large, strong railroads couldn't earn an attractive return on their own enormous investments and were having problems in finding money to finance improvements to handle their ever-growing traffic. So, for better or worse, someone had to take the disorganized, overbuilt and overcompetitive railroad system as it existed and somehow get the competition under control and the facilities rebuilt for efficient operation.

The method for accomplishing this end was the much-reviled "community of interest" system, primarily hatched and executed by J.P. Morgan and the Pennsy's A.J. Cassatt. The idea simply was that the strong railroads—again the PRR and NYC—would buy control of the weaker

This 1898 photo is doubly significant: It typifies B&O power and operations just before the turn of the century and it memorializes the uncovering of the First Stone. The camera looks east toward Mt. Clare at Gwynns Run in Baltimore; the pile of ties in the foreground cover the excavation where the stone was found six feet below. It was raised and fenced on the site. Credit: B&O Museum Archives.

troublemakers in their territory to keep them from cutting rates or building more lines. Competition would continue, but would be more closely controlled and organized. With all railroad traffic rising rapidly, a more coherently organized and less competitive railroad industry could generate enough investment money to rebuild the facilities that needed it, wherever they were, creating a sort of self-perpetuating stability.

B&O was one of these "troublemakers"—its shaky financial condition had made it more prone to risk extremes to get business. The receivership had given Cassatt his opportunity, and beginning in November 1899 the Penn quietly bought up working control. During the same period, Pennsy and New York Central also bought into lines like the Chesapeake & Ohio, Norfolk & Western, Hocking Valley and Reading, while Morgan and other large New York investment bankers took over policymaking on great masses of other eastern, southern and western railroads.

For the railroads in general and B&O in particular, the community of interest system turned out to be much more positive than it might seem. The building of duplicating lines was largely stopped and more cooperative terminal and line projects were launched. And with the promise of stability, large amounts of money were invested to modernize the railroads. In fact, many of the major present-day railroad facilities were the products of this last great era of railroad building.

This was certainly true of B&O's life during and immediately after Pennsy control, and its main lines in Maryland were outstanding examples. Among other things, it was community of interest control that created Potomac Yard and Washington Union Station, both treated elsewhere in this book; it also allowed the rebuilding of the Old Main Line, the doubling of Brunswick yard, tunnel enlargements on the main line, stone viaducts on the Metropolitan branch, new roundhouses and countless other improvements.

First off, the Pennsylvania installed one of their own men as B&O's president in May 1901. The choice was perhaps better than Pennsy had intended—youngish (42) Leonor F. Loree, a brilliant engineer and operating man who had already worked his way up to a junior vice president position on the PRR. Loree's background alone was a refreshing change from B&O's long tradition of presidents who were primarily politicians or financiers—aside from the short, unhappy reign of Samuel Spencer, he was the first B&O president skilled in building and running railroads.

As it turned out, Loree did not stay long—he left in January 1904 as Pennsy was forced to back away from B&O—but his administration must have been a whirlwind and the effects lingered long after. He promptly picked up some improvement projects B&O had planned or begun after its receivership, added many of his own, and proceeded to rebuild the railroad Pennsy-style. Emulating Cassatt, Loree built low grade cutoff lines, multiple tracks, stone viaducts and heavy steel bridges, new yards and began installing heavy locomotives and high-capacity cars.

One of his first projects—in fact an inherited one just begun by the doomed management of John Cowen — was the rebuilding of the Old Main Line. Building a wholly new railroad is almost more accurate. Undoubtedly Cowen and his operating managers had debated long over what to do about this impossible piece of railroad. Nothing short of a complete realignment would be adequate for 20th Century tonnage trains; yet even so, there was only so much the engineers could accomplish within the rocky confines of the Patapsco. It promised to be expensive, but the end product would still be far from ideal. By then the Metropolitan branch existed as a possible alternate route, although at the time two-thirds of it was still single track and several large bridges required rebuilding. And it was also possible to revive some of the old plans to run a new cutoff line between the Metropolitan branch and Washington branch, allowing a far better route than the Old Main Line without the excess mileage involved in using the full length of the Metropolitan through Washington. A projected line called the Hanover cutoff was apparently a product of some of this debate—it was planned to leave the Metropolitan west of Gaithersburg and join the Washington branch near what is now Fort Meade Junction.

But when the discussions were over, it had been decided to put the money into the Old Main Line. The project had started in 1900 and was well along when Loree arrived in Baltimore.

This time it was not just a matter of easing some curves. Virtually the entire railroad between Relay and Point of Rocks had to be redesigned in

Frederick Junction in 1910. An eastbound freight powered by a 2-8-0 camelback (B&O crews called them Snappers) pulls away from a water stop heading for the Monocacy bridge. The station has changed little from the view in Chapter 7, but the track has come a long way up. Credit: B&O Museum Archives.

one way or another. Ultimately the project took eight years and cost over three million uninflated dollars; when it was completed, over 25 miles of entirely new railroad had been built, eight new tunnels drilled and one existing tunnel completely rebuilt, seven heavy steel bridges built over the Patapsco plus several over Bush Creek and many tributaries, the Monocacy bridge replaced at Frederick Junction, an entirely new locomotive helper station installed at Reels Mill, and, as a by-product, eight new stations built. The sharpest curve was now 11° and most were 8° or less (the old line still had several in the 13°-15° range), the Parr's Ridge grade had been cut down from 1.6% to 0.85%, and the total route shortened by 1.6 miles. During the same period, the Point of Rocks and Catoctin tunnels were rebuilt and enlarged and Brunswick yard doubled in size.

Loree's aim was to operate 2,500-ton coal trains behind a single heavy 2-8-0 over most of the Old Main, with a single additional 2-8-0 helper for the Parr's Ridge grade at Mt. Airy. Between 1902 and 1904 Loree also installed a fleet of heavy E-24 class Consolidations built to the PRR's current standard design; these were followed up in 1905-06 by a larger group of essentially similar E-27's to replace the conglomeration of lighter 2-8-0's of the late 19th Century. The line was also engineered— theoretically, at least—to keep helper locomotive mileage to a minimum.

Going west, the first section of the reconstruction began at Orange Grove, 2½ miles west of Relay, and stretched for a short but spectacular

An example of the heavy engineering work needed to straighten the Old Main — the 1904 bridge-tunnel combination at Ilchester. Originally the track curled around this hill and crossed the river downstream. The train heads east in May, 1979. Credit: H.H. Harwood, Jr.

seven-eighths of a mile to Ilchester. Here the old line had twisted around a high rock spur, crossed the Patapsco on an 1869 Bollman truss bridge (the successor of the Patterson viaduct), then negotiated another reverse curve on the south side of the river. The new route blasted straight through the rock in a 1,404-foot double-track tunnel and emerged into a heavy two-span bridge over the river. The sight of the 263-foot long combination deck girder and through truss bridge leading into the sheer rock wall is still an impressive one today; it may be seen directly from River Road in Ilchester. The picturesque 1885 frame station at Ilchester was frugally saved and moved several hundred feet to the new alignment, where it survived until 1964.

From Ilchester to Ellicott City (the onetime Ellicott's Mills) the line was left essentially on its original alignment, but several wriggles were ironed out. At about the same time, an interesting skewed truss bridge was built across the river to carry a short spur into the flour mill on the north bank. At Union Dam, about two miles beyond Ellicott City, the line cut across another rock spur in a curved tunnel, shortcutting a particularly tortured section where the old line crawled around the spur on a 13° curve. Midway between Union Dam and Hollofield station a pair of sidings and an interlocking tower were installed to allow trains to pass one another in either direction.

Starting at Hollofield, a wholly new 3½-mile line was laid out to Davis. This long section was begun after most of the other Old Main Line work was finished and was not completed until late 1907. It crossed the river at Elysville—by now called Alberton—on a long four-span deck girder bridge, then followed the north bank of the river for almost two miles, tunnelling another rock hillside on the way. It then recrossed the river, dove into another tunnel east of Davis, and rejoined the old line which had clung to the south bank all the way. The historic pair of Elysville bridges were bypassed in the process; only their stone piers remain now.

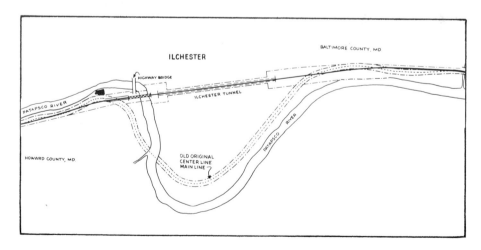

The next 8½ miles from Davis to Sykesville stuck mostly to the original alignment, tempered by many straightenings of minor curves. The old Marriottsville tunnel was enlarged, arched with brick and re-christened Henryton tunnel; the picturesque Bollman truss over the Patapsco at its east end was replaced by a sturdy and very utilitarian concrete span. Between Sykesville and Gaither a new alignment sliced straight through a hill and river bend, tunnelling the hill and crossing the river twice.

The tiny community of Gaither, 1-1/3 miles west of Sykesville, was a pleasant open area, and by Patapsco valley standards, wide and flat. Here B&O built another pair of long passing sidings, an interlocking tower and new water facilities, making it a major stop for westbound

Upriver from Alberton (Daniels) an entirely new line was built on the north side of the river. The alignment differences can be seen graphically in this view looking northeast from the roadbed of the curving original line to the straight replacement across the river. The location: midway between Daniels and Davis in November 1978. Credit: H.H. Harwood, Jr.

freights before they took on the Mt. Airy grade. From Gaither to Wood-bine the new line again stuck close to the old except for boring through another rock spur just east of Woodbine.

For the third time in B&O's history, the problem of cutting down the Parr's Ridge grade was the most formidable engineering challenge. At the point where the railroad crossed, Parr's Ridge was a high but some-what narrow hump. Thus the old line had approached both sides of the ridge on relatively mild river grades, then rose abruptly to climb over the top at Mt. Airy. As the engineers studied Parr's Ridge in 1900, they decided to begin the grades several miles farther back on either side in order to make the climb more gradual, and tunnel the ridge about 135 feet underneath its peak near Ridgeville. To accomplish this they built 10 miles of entirely new railroad, leaving the old line about a mile west of Woodbine and heading directly for the ridge on an alignment close to the route of the long-abandoned inclined planes. The Mt. Airy tunnel (which more properly should have been called the Ridgeville tunnel) was the longest on the Old Main—almost exactly half a mile—and crossed the ridge almost exactly underneath the summit of the planes. The new line then dropped gradually down the west side on a heavy fill. The new

An eastbound coal drag rolls over the relocated line at Davis in late 1978. The photographer was standing on the portal of Davis tunnel; the original alignment circled the rock from the lower right, crossed the present line behind the lead diesel unit and made a small loop to the left in the center of the photo. Credit: H. H. Harwood, Jr.

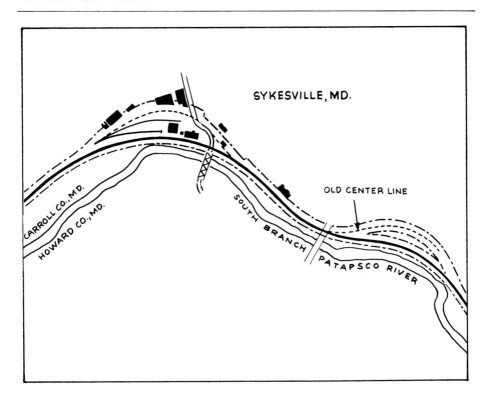

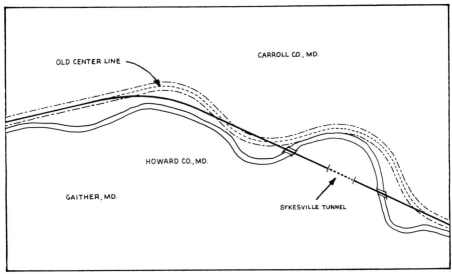

This stretch east and west of Sykesville was fairly typical of the dekinking work done on the Old Main Line.

Gaither was a major water stop on the Old Main just west of Sykesville. A westbound way freight pauses about 1948. Credit: Baltimore & Ohio; H. H. Harwood collection.

The largest single part of the rebuilding project was the 10-mile Mt. Airy cutoff, piercing Parr's Ridge with a 2,758-foot tunnel. Here a westbound drops downhill at Mt. Airy Junction, near the west portal, in 1945. The old inclined planes went over the top of the ridge to the right of the train. Credit: C. T. Mahan, Jr.

grade, substantially higher than the old line at the point it passed the site of the base of Plane 4, did not reach the level of the original line until Monrovia, 5½ miles west of the tunnel.

The 1838 line over the hill at Mt. Airy was kept to serve the small collection of industry and the passenger business in the town. This route became a "loop" branch, realigned at each end to join the new cutoff line. On the east side of the ridge it left the new route at an unpopulated spot called Watersville Junction; it rejoined on the west side about midway down the hill at Mt. Airy Junction, a short distance west of the tunnel. The balance of the old line down the ridge to Bush Creek was abandoned along with the Plane 4 helper station, now 55 feet below the grade level and partly buried by the fill. The helper terminal was moved 10½ miles farther west to a flagstop called Reels Mill, slightly east of Frederick Junction.

The Mt. Airy cutoff produced a longer but much milder grade than the earlier line—0.89% as opposed to the steady 1.58% and curves of the old route over the top. In fact, the new grade allowed higher tonnages than on the Metropolitan branch—which has helped to guarantee the Old Main Line's existence ever since.

The 1838 route over the ridge via Mt. Airy was tied into the new cutoff at Mt. Airy Junction on the west slope. In this 1948 view the Mt. Airy branch, now single-tracked, climbs uphill to the left. This point was also once the base of inclined Plane no. 3 which came down from the right of the westbound wayfreight. Credit: B&O Museum Archives.

West of Monrovia, a total of 2.3 miles of new line was laid in the twisting Bush Creek valley between Ijamsville and Reels Mill, including five steel girder bridges over the creek and a short tunnel. Reels Mill, a tiny community a mile east of the Monocacy River, was the last stop along Bush Creek before Frederick Junction. For eastbound tonnage trains, it marked the beginning of the grade toward Parr's Ridge. Lacking adequate space at Frederick Junction, B&O decided to locate the eastbound helper terminal in the flat woodsy area west of the little station here. Reels Mill thus quickly blossomed into an impressive, albeit sadly short-lived, yard consisting of two long passing sidings, a coaling trestle, interlocking tower, water tank and helper engine tracks. Since the helpers actually were based at Brunswick, there was no engine house at Reels Mill nor were there any turning facilities—any engines which had to be turned used the wyes at either Frederick Junction or Mt. Airy Junction.

The ill-fated facilities at Reels Mill. The Bush Creek hamlet was intended as the primary helper station for eastbound tonnage assaulting Parr's Ridge. The location was a mistake and by 1925 it had been closed. Credit (both): B&O Museum Archives.

The Monocacy River, once crossed successively by wood and iron trusses, got this austere but sturdy deck girder bridge during the rebuilding project. A westbound merchandise freight drifts into Frederick Junction in 1944. Credit: E. L. Thompson.

An eastbound pulls through Doub, north of Point of Rocks in the broad lower Monocacy valley. This area, still known as Carrollton Manor, was once owned by Charles Carroll of Carrollton. The railroad line through here was largely untouched by Loree. The date is July 1947. Credit: E. L. Thompson.

At Frederick Junction, the 1864 Bollman truss spans over the Monocacy gave way to an ordinary four-span deck girder bridge. From here west the railroad was always reasonably tolerable and only some minor realignment was done near Buckeystown to reduce the eastbound grade slightly.

The last, least successful but probably most interesting section of the Old Main Line project was the Adamstown cutoff, a completely new bypass route between Adamstown station and Point of Rocks which supplemented but did not replace the original line. The theory was thus: For about two miles between Point of Rocks and Doub, eastbound Old Main Line tonnage trains must climb a grade of 0.58%, with a short stretch of 0.71% as the land rises north of the Potomac valley. The grade is neither long nor steep, but the moderate climb meant that full-tonnage eastbounds often needed a helper to make it. But once beyond this grade, one engine could get the train to Reels Mill at the base of the Bush Creek-Mt. Airy grade. The Adamstown cutoff was designed to provide a lower grade line for eastbound traffic, eliminating the need for pushers to be put on at Brunswick or Point of Rocks. All Old Main Line helpers thus would work out of the new Reels Mill terminal over the Mt. Airy grade—theoretically a much more concentrated and efficient operation.

The Adamstown line, built in the 1901-02 period, swung in a wide arc to the east of the original line, generally following Tuscarora Creek north to Adamstown. Trains followed the Metropolitan branch route through the Point of Rocks junction to a switch about a third of a mile east of the junction where the cutoff began. The cutoff paralleled the Metropolitan another mile, then gradually veered north as it approached Tuscarora Creek. The distance from Point of Rocks to Adamstown Junction was 4.2 miles over the original line and 6.3 miles via the cutoff, but the grade was only 0.3%. Since the cutoff was meant to handle only eastbound tonnage trains, it was single track with no passing sidings. But like the other products of the reconstruction project, it was substantially built with heavy cuts and fills through the winding little stream valley and several small stone arch bridges.

In addition to the enormous track and grading work along the Old Main, many way stations were replaced. As a practical engineer—and a Pennsylvania Railroad man—Loree was a passionate advocate of standardization. His stations were plain, single-story frame structures designed by the railroad engineering department which varied little or not at all from location to location; they were meant strictly to shelter passengers, handle l.c.l freight and transact railroad business rather than to reflect a personality. Such buildings were put up at Hoods Mills (1907), Woodbine (1906), Bartholow (1902), Monrovia (1903), Ijamsville (1906), Lime Kiln (1903), Buckeystown (1906), and Doub (1906). The Woodbine station subsequently succumbed to fire and was again replaced by a standardized structure in 1917. At about the same time, smaller shelter stations were built at Marriottsville, Gorsuch, Gaither and Reels Mill.

Catoctin tunnel west of Point of Rocks was one of many enlarged and lined during Loree's reign. This rock wall was one of the critical squeezes for B&O and the canal in 1832; the railroad first ran around it, then tunneled it in 1868. Credit: H. H. Harwood, Jr.

Woodbine's ultra-plain 1917 frame station was at least the third to serve this little upper-Patapsco valley town. The freight heads east in 1943. Credit: E. L. Thompson.

West of Point of Rocks, Loree enlarged and lined the post-Civil War tunnels at Point of Rocks and Catoctin, eliminating one small tunnel in the process.

The final major accomplishment of this hectic and memorable decade was the doubling of Brunswick yard, done mostly in the 1906-1907 period. A new 4,250-car yard was built at the west end of town to classify and hold eastbound traffic and to do heavy car repair work. At the same time, the main line was widened to four tracks from the west end of Brunswick yard to Weverton to keep traffic moving in this congested section. The original frame-and-iron 1891 roundhouse was replaced in 1910 with a 12-stall brick engine house which in turn was expanded to 19 stalls in 1917.

Camden warehouse—only half of which is seen here—was unquestionably one of the most monumental of its breed anywhere. This view shows the original section, built in 1899. Credit: H. H. Harwood,

Improvements in Baltimore were much less extensive or visible, with two notable exceptions: the Camden warehouse and Riverside roundhouses. At Camden, the western border of the station property fronting on Eutaw Street was cleared in 1899 and work started on a merchandise storage warehouse which by anyone's measurements was mammoth. The structure was built in three stages between 1899 and 1905; when completed it consisted of a 1,116-foot long eight-story warehouse together with an eight-story office building. The warehouse was advertised as having 430,000 sq. ft. of floor area in six separated sections—enough space, the railroad said, to hold a thousand carloads of merchandise.

The motive power equivalent of Camden warehouse was built at Riverside, in the Locust Point-Fort McHenry area. By 1905 both the 1875 Bailey's passenger roundhouse and its bigger freight brother at Riverside had become too small for the size and quantity of locomotives now steaming in. Heavy Consolidations had become plentiful by 1906, and in the same year B&O bought its first passenger Pacifics. By 1911 new 2-8-2's would also begin to appear. The railroad decided to consolidate all its Baltimore locomotive servicing and light repair work at Riverside, which was about as close to a central location as any place in the scattered terminal area, and establish a high-capacity facility capable of handling any present or future locomotive types. Although it was built after his reign, the idea smacks strongly of Loree's thinking. In 1907 it was completed—a sprawling set of twin roundhouses totalling 50 stalls, with an adjoining machine shop and large nearby coaling trestle. Unfortunately, Riverside's 80-ft. turntable length limited its later use to 2-8-2's and Pacifics. As B&O's steam power roster expanded into 2-10-2's, Mallets and 4-8-2's over the following years, the east end of the Baltimore division was unable to take any practical advantage of larger locomotive designs and had to fight its way through until the end of steam in 1953 pulling its tonnage freights with single and doubleheaded Mikados. With the opening of Riverside, Bailey's was abandoned as an operating engine house, although it managed to survive until the early 1950's as a storage facility—housing, among other things, the B&O Museum locomotive collection between 1935 and 1953.

In the same period B&O built an interesting piece of track in the south Baltimore area which it had no intention of using itself. Since 1887 the light 4-4-0's of the Annapolis Short Line had been hauling their trains into Camden over the South Baltimore branch through Westport, joining the main line at Carroll tower. The Short Line also maintained its own small freight house and yard southwest of Camden at the corner of West and Ridgely Streets, reached by a short spur off the B&O main. But in 1908 the Short Line had begun to electrify its line, using a 6,600-volt a.c. overhead catenary system. B&O had qualms about stringing a line of that voltage over its main tracks and made an agreement to build a new double-track approach line into Camden for the Short Line's exclusive use. This "branch" left the South Baltimore branch about midway between Westport and Carroll tower and followed the line of Russell Street (the present highway approach to the Baltimore-Washington Parkway) to the point where it crossed the B&O main line just south of Camden. Here it crossed the main and joined track no. 5 leading directly into the Camden train shed. This operation continued until early 1921, when the Short Line was merged with the Washington, Baltimore & Annapolis Electric Railway and moved its trains into the WB&A's downtown Baltimore terminal. Afterward the Russell Street track was abandoned piecemeal, the northern end in 1921 and the southern stub in the early 1930's. As an aside, when the Annapolis Short Line electrified in 1908, it also built a new line of its own from the old B&O Cliffords interchange into Westport in order to avoid running over the South

Baltimore branch as much as possible. Camden Station was kept busy enough with Short Line trains alone—during mid-day hours, Annapolis limiteds and locals alternated departures every half hour.

The WB&A, incidentally, had become a close neighbor to B&O's main line outside Camden. The interurban line's Baltimore entrance—also completed in 1908—approached the city from the south, passing just west of Westport and crossing B&O's South Baltimore branch on a steel bridge; it then paralleled B&O's main tracks on a steel trestle for four blocks between Bush Street and Stockholm Street before swinging over the railroad at Scott Street and descending to street level on a ramp.

An interesting albeit irritating neighbor of B&O was the Washington, Baltimore & Annapolis electric line, whose steel trestle paralleled B&O's main line for several blocks in south Baltimore. This 1929 photo looks east near Scott Street; the interurban train is bound for downtown Baltimore. Credit: B&O Museum Archives.

In the midst of the reconstruction frenzy, the Old Main Line's passenger services reached what was probably their peak. In late 1904, for example, six locals were scheduled each way over the line: Two trains each way covered the entire line from Baltimore to Point of Rocks, with Frederick connections. One of these then continued to Martinsburg; the other ran down the Valley branch from Harpers Ferry to Winchester, Va. In addition, two locals ran each way between Baltimore and Frederick, plus two more between Baltimore and Mt. Airy. Six additional locals shuttled between Frederick and Point of Rocks. By this time the long-hallowed Ellicott City local service had dried up, a victim of the streetcar line from Catonsville.

By 1908 most of the great reconstruction projects were finished, Loree was gone and B&O was back in the hands of local management—albeit with more financial strings pulled from New York. But the work had put the railroad at a physical peak which it would not reach again. In fact, almost everything built afterwards in the area amounted merely to improvements and adjustments to the basic facilities created in the 1890-1908 period. The generous-sized tunnels have been adapted to modern high-clearance equipment with little trouble and virtually all the bridges are still carrying their loads after almost 80 years of service. Leonor Loree went on to gain a formidable reputation as a creative, colorful and controversial railroad industry leader. He lived long (to 82) and accomplished much. But the modern B&O is still probably his most enduring legacy.

IMPOSSIBLE CHALLENGE

CHAPTER 9

THE ERRATIC 20th CENTURY: 1910-1979

For a quarter of a century, the Old Main Line and Q-4 Mikados were synonymous. The location of this 1940's photo is unknown, but the power and scenery could not be more typical. Credit: I.V. Kopp; C.T. Mahan, Jr. collection.

When the construction forces finally left the Old Main Line in 1908, most of Jonathan Knight's original railroad was gone. In its place was an infinitely improved — albeit still curvy — line designed strictly for moving the swelling volume of freight while tolerating a few passenger locals and way freights. The Old Main was thus in sort of a railroad no-man's land between a genuine main line and a secondary branch — a situation which made its fortunes gyrate up and down between intense activity and near-abandonment over the next 70 years.

It went into the early 20th Century with a surge. By 1912 B&O's total system coal traffic had climbed to 30 million tons, much of which was hauled east to Baltimore, Philadelphia and the New York area over the Old Main. Grain (now totalling 1½ million tons systemwide) and general merchandise also flooded the line.

Frederick Junction was still a key Old Main point, seen here in the early 1900's. Note the large wood finial on the roof next to the train order signal. The station was finally dismantled in 1943. Credit: Smithsonian Institution.

Busy, double tracked (but unsignalled), the Old Main relied heavily on lots of manpower to keep the traffic fluid. As in the 19th Century, it was normal practice to switch trains back and forth on the two main tracks to pass one another, but now controlled by manned interlockings spaced an average of 5½ miles apart. These "towers" (some were merely small single-story frame offices) were located at Grays (east of Ellicott City), Hollofield (HS tower), Marriottsville, Gaither (G tower), Watersville Jct. (WX), Mt. Airy Jct. (MA), Monrovia (RO), Reels Mill (RS), Adamstown Jct. (AX), and Point of Rocks (KG). Long double passing tracks had been installed at Hollofield, Gaither and Reels Mill for additional flexibility, particularly in allowing merchandise and passenger trains to get around the long drags of hopper cars. In addition, telegraph offices at many other way stations handled train orders to keep the traffic moving.

Those hopper cars were by now flooding the 1884-89 timber coal trestle at Curtis Bay. By the early 1900's new designs of bulk materials transfer machinery had revolutionized the traditional 19th Century technique of pushing the coal cars out onto a trestle and dumping their loads into pockets which in turn unloaded into ships below. In 1916 work started on an entirely new coal terminal, consisting of twin inland rotary car dumpers feeding a series of conveyor belts which carried the coal onto the concrete pier where it was dropped into four large movable steel loading towers. The new Curtis Bay pier, which opened in 1917, had a theoretical capacity of 6,000 tons an hour. In actual operation it initially averaged about 500 tons an hour, but was brought up to 1,400 tons an hour in 1920 by the addition of a mechanical ship trimming system. As both ship and freight car capacity increased, the terminal's performance continued to rise and it remained B&O's primary east coast coal export facility until rebuilt in 1969. Even today, with new dumpers and machinery, essentially the same system operates.

The new Curtis Bay coal pier shortly after its completion in 1917. A remarkably modern design for its day, it worked virtually unaltered until the late 1960's. Credit: B&O Museum Archives.

Sadly, the same cannot be said for the expensively-rebuilt western end of the Old Main Line. By the early 1920's it had become embarrassingly clear that the Adamstown cutoff and the location of the Reels Mill helper station were not working according to theory. Locomotive engineers on the eastbound coal drags found that the speed restrictions necessary to negotiate the crossovers at Point of Rocks prevented them from working up enough momentum to overcome a curve-grade combination at a spot about two miles beyond called Red Cut, where the line swung abruptly north along Tuscarora Creek. Here — particularly in wet weather — they usually stalled and had to get a pusher from Point of Rocks or Brunswick to get moving again. This effectively nullified the purpose of the cutoff, which had been built solely to eliminate helpers at this point. It also made Reels Mill superfluous, since it was pointless to keep helpers further up the line when they usually were needed at Point of Rocks anyway.

So in March 1925 Reels Mill was taken out of service and the helper base moved back to Point of Rocks and Brunswick. The pushers would couple on at either point, depending on train tonnage and traffic needs. The same helpers were also used on eastbound Metropolitan branch freights as far as Barnesville or Gaithersburg. Everything remaining at Reels Mill (the coaling trestle had already burned down in 1919) was removed and the little hamlet lapsed back into its 19th Century torpor. Today the site is still clearly marked by a wide area between the two main line tracks and one can feel some of the old grittiness, although it takes some imagining to see the coal trestle, bunk house, tower, water tank, waiting coal trains and smoking 2-8-2's moving in and out. About three years after the retirement of Reels Mill, through trains ceased using the Adamstown cutoff, now less than useless since it took two miles extra to accomplish nothing. But having already sunk its investment in the line, B&O kept it intact "just in case". During the grim 1930's it became a six mile-long storage track for the surplus and unrepaired freight cars now clogging the railroad. With the onset of World War II it was rehabilitated as a standby route in case of derailments or line congestion, but as best anyone can remember now it never handled a through road train. The abortive and now scarcely-remembered cutoff finally was retired in January 1952 and dismantled. But its cuts, fills and stone bridges still may be easily found in the underbrush along Tuscarora Creek north of present Maryland Route 28.

The mid-1920's also marked what was pretty much the height of steam power development on the Old Main — or, for that matter, on any of the B&O lines radiating out of Baltimore. Limited by the short turntable at the big Riverside twin roundhouse complex and various clearance problems in the Baltimore terminal area, Mikados and Pacifics were the largest locomotives which could be regularly used in the area. Bigger power could and did operate into Baltimore — primarily to move in or out of Mt. Clare locomotive shop — but these had to be turned on one of the several Y tracks in the Baltimore terminal, an expensive nuisance to do on a regular basis. The major exception was the Metropolitan branch, which did run a few 4-8-2's regularly during the 1930's and 1940's. These were turned at Washington Terminal's large Ivy City roundhouse, whose twin 100-foot turntables could accommodate 4-8-4's.

A pair of Q-4's head west out of Baltimore at Hammonds Ferry Road near Lansdowne. Two 2-8-2's were often necessary to get heavy westbounds as far as Mt. Airy Junction. The photo was made about 1949. Credit: H.H. Harwood collection.

Another Q-4 works empty hoppers west through Relay in June, 1950. Credit: E.L. Thompson.

For the Old Main Line, this meant that the ultimate motive power was the rugged and practical fleet of Q-4's delivered between 1921 and 1923. For 30 years afterwards, the Old Main and the Q-4 were virtually synonymous — coal drags, merchandise manifests, way freights, helpers, whatever. A single Q-4 was rated at 2,750 tons in either direction over the ruling Mt. Airy grade. Typically, 8,000-ton coal trains of up to 100 cars would be hoisted up Bush Creek and over Parr's Ridge by one wide-open Q-4 at the head and two more pushing. Shorter drags and merchandisers normally got one Q-4 at each end. It was common practice to doublehead the empty hoppers westbound. Helpers usually were turned on the Y at Mt. Airy Junction and run back light. During the hectic World War II years, however, some eastbound full-tonnage trains running through to Philadelphia would carry the helper all the way...these would push as far as the Mt. Airy tunnel then drift downhill behind their train as far as Hoods Mill, where they would run around the train as it took water at Gaither and couple onto the head end for the rest of the trip. This practice lasted until the end of steam in 1953.

Old Main Line passenger power was generally less impressive, except for special occasions. The light local trains got along with a variety of castoff 4-4-0's, and, in later years, some A-2 and A-3 Atlantics and B-18 ten-wheelers. Railroad enthusiast excursions (which first appeared in 1938), detours, and wartime troop trains brought out Pacifics and — reputedly — newly shopped "President"-class Pacifics fresh out of Mt. Clare occasionally would be assigned to an Old Main Line local to break them in.

There were no such limitations west of Brunswick; its turntable could take anything, including Mallets. So, what the 2-8-2 was to the Baltimore division, the 2-10-2 was to the east end of the Cumberland division. Hefty S-class Santa Fe's first appeared in 1914, but the true "standard" power between Brunswick and Cumberland were the heavy, impressive and (for a 2-10-2) fast S-1 "Big Sixes" built between 1923 and 1926. One "Big Six" usually sufficed for anything that two Q-4's would bring in or out to the east — up to 4,750 tons alone or 9,500 tons with a helper out of Martinsburg. A diverse collection of ten-wheelers, Consolidations and light 2-8-2's was also based at Brunswick for branch runs down the Shenandoah valley, up to Hagerstown and main line way freights in three directions.

Passenger services on the Old Main Line through the first third of the 20th Century followed the mold set in 1873 when the through trains were moved over to the Metropolitan branch. This was a slightly complex three-way flow of accommodation trains: locals running between Baltimore and Frederick or Point of Rocks, shuttles between Frederick and Frederick Junction to connect with these, and Frederick-Point of Rocks runs to meet mainline trains. As with local passenger service everywhere, these slowly withered away during the 1920's as roads were paved and more autos appeared — and as some of the little Patapsco and Bush Creek Valley communities lost their mills or quarries and shrank. And as the trains were trimmed back, attempts were made to utilize crews and equipment more efficiently by combining the scattershot array of branch line services in the area — particularly the various runs radiating from Brunswick.

A two-car Frederick local simmers at Frederick Junction about 1910. The view looks east. Credit: Smithsonian Institution.

Brutish S-1 2-10-2's hauled most freights between Brunswick and Cumberland from the 1920's through the 40's. No. 6200 briefly but memorably dominates the scene at Harpers Ferry in the early 1930's as it gets a roll on a westbound. Credit: B&O Museum Archives.

In May 1916, for example, five weekday trains each way covered the length of the Old Main: three between Baltimore and Point of Rocks (then called Washington Junction), one terminating in Frederick and one to Mt. Airy — the latter leaving Baltimore in early evening and returning in early morning. One of these westbound runs actually ran all the way from Baltimore to Hagerstown via Point of Rocks, but did not return and was not advertised as a through run. Any Baltimore-Hagerstown through passengers could get there 40 minutes faster by catching a later main line express via Washington and transferring to the local at Weverton. Four round trips also shuttled between Frederick and Washington Junction, one of which also ran through to Hagerstown westbound only.

By 1928 the shrinking process could now be seen: Only three trips ran each way from Baltimore — one between Baltimore and Hagerstown (now running both ways), one to Frederick and one to Point of Rocks. Again, the Baltimore-Hagerstown train carried little or no through riders; passengers could still catch the express and make the connection at Weverton. The Frederick-Point of Rocks services still consisted of four trips each way, but had been rearranged so that two of the trains were consolidated with

162

Valley branch schedules and ran through between Frederick and Strasburg Junction, Va. A Frederick-Washington steam run still operated. One thing which had not changed was the leisurely running time — the direct Baltimore-Frederick trains took 2 hours and 40 minutes to make the trip.

In early 1930, even before the brutal effects of the Depression were felt, Old Main Line service had been cut down to only two weekday trips each way — one Baltimore-Hagerstown train and the Baltimore-Frederick schedule, which westbound ran also to Point of Rocks. Inexplicably, an eastbound-only early morning Ellicott City-Baltimore run had appeared in the timetables. From Frederick west, gas-electric cars had appeared in 1929 and now handled two of the three surviving Frederick-Point of Rocks trips. Both of these gas-electrics continued down the Valley branch to Strasburg.

The on-line freight business had heavily gravitated toward the west end of the Old Main. By 1928 the Patapsco Valley was still relatively active, but between the ravages of old floods and new manufacturing techniques and products many of the old mills had closed. The old Thistle mill near Ilchester still operated and Ellicott City continued as a major flour milling center — the old Ellicott complex now replaced by a large eight-story concrete mill operated by the C.A. Gambrill Co. Upriver at Oella the historic Union cotton mill had been torn down and rebuilt in 1919 as a big woolen mill of the W.J. Dickey company. Both the Ellicott City and Oella mills, incidentally, were on the opposite side of the river, reached by short spurs which were almost completely on bridges. Slightly less than a mile east of Woodstock at a remote spot called Putney's Bridge, another spur crossed the river and ran up a little gully to the quarry at Granite, now owned by the Guilford & Waltersville Granite Co. The branch was owned and operated by the quarry, which used its own switcher. The handsome cotton mill at Alberton (Elysville) also still prospered and over the years had added new buildings around the original stone mill.

Elsewhere east of Mt. Airy were a scattering of typically rural industries — milling companies at Sykesville and Hoods Mill, a canning company and a farming supply company at Woodbine, another supply company at Gorsuch. Probably most fascinating was the Springfield State Hospital at Sykesville, situated high on a hillside overlooking the valley and reached by a privately-owned spur climbing a long and harrowing grade up the valley wall. The hospital's little switcher picked up its cars — usually inbound coal — from an interchange half a mile west of the station, then wrestled them uphill along a route which circled around the outside of town and ended on a high bluff northeast of the station. Mt. Airy, nestled in a tight little notch on Parr's Ridge along the 1838 railroad line, had grown up into an active small town with a group of feed mills and lumber, fertilizer and canning companies huddled around the old brick B&O station.

Aside from a brick company at Monrovia, Bush Creek was now devoid of any significant freight customers — but west of Frederick Junction the freight activity picked up noticeably. A succession of quarries busily blasted out limestone from the large deposits along the Monocacy valley — one on the east side of Frederick, others at Lime Kiln, Keller and Buckeystown station. Buckeystown proper was reached by a short branch running east from Lime Kiln. Frederick had reached its peak as a manufacturing and milling center and B&O's yard and spurs around the east side of town served various fertilizer, brick, milk and milling plants — plus the slaughterhouse. Sorrowfully, the package freight business had outgrown the ancient 1831 stone depot; in fact, box cars no longer could fit into the building and one side had to be torn off to accommodate them. It was replaced about 1911 with a larger frame freight house. B&O also connected in Frederick with the Hagerstown & Frederick electric line, a locally-built trolley company which switched many industries on the south and east ends of the city.

Gas-electric cars began taking over many of the branch line passenger runs by 1929. The early morning sun catches No. 6045 and an express trailer at the Frederick station in March 1947. Credit: H.H. Harwood, Jr.

Financially and operationally exhausted from its turn-of-the-century rebuilding program, B&O did little else to the Old Main—or anywhere else on its system, for that matter—during the Twenties. The last major reconstruction project was the Magnolia Cutoff east of Cumberland, completed in 1914. The important but much less extensive job of finishing the double tracking of the Metropolitan branch was done in 1927-28. But just before the Depression stopped even the minor projects, B&O managed to complete two more improvements—one at each end of its lines in Maryland.

Most important was the final realignment of the perenially irritating Potomac crossing at Harpers Ferry. The 1894 reconstruction had turned an impossible operation into a marginally tolerable one, but the sweeping

A westbound string of loaded steel gondolas and empty coal hoppers digs out of Frederick Junction after a water stop in July 1947. Credit: E.L. Thompson.

The original Frederick depot in its last days, about 1910 or 1911. Note that its entire left side has been removed in order to clear freight cars now too large to fit in the doors. (Compare with the photos in Chapter 2.) The street in front is South Carroll Street and both the track crossing and dinky single-truck freight cars at the left belong to the Hagerstown & Frederick interurban line. Credit: B&O Museum Archives.

This 1942 scene gives a graphic idea of B&O's three generations of alignments at Harpers Ferry. By this time the original line (at far left) was gone, but its bridge piers remained—and still do. The early railroad line through town is marked approximately by the wall between the two newer bridges. The 1894 main line trackage was still intact through Harpers Ferry, retained as an emergency bypass. Note the relocated station. Credit: B&O Museum Archives.

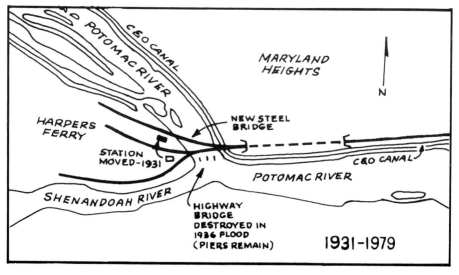

An eastbound coal train gets a straight shot at Harpers Ferry tunnel, just below the camera, in August 1977. Credit: H.H. Harwood, Jr.

When the 1936 flood swept out the old highway (and ex-railroad) bridge at Harpers Ferry, B&O's 1894 main line bridge was decked over for joint use by motor traffic and Valley branch trains. In July 1948 Pacific 5168 cautiously takes a Winchester local over. Credit: C.T. Mahan, Jr.

"S" curve remained a serious operating impediment. By the late 1920's passenger train speed had become more critical—particularly with the new all-Pullman "Capitol" and "National" Limiteds—and it was difficult and expensive to brake the heavy fast freights through the curves. In 1930 the railroad finally faced up to the only possible solution and threw a new alignment across the river on a straight line from the Maryland side. The solution was perhaps obvious, but it required a complete redesign of the Valley branch junction (which had been the cause of the twisted 1894 route) and the tunnel at Maryland Heights.

The west end of the tunnel was "belled out" to accommodate the new direct alignment, which emerged onto a 14-span 1,362-foot long deck girder bridge which cut across the Potomac on a considerable skew, landing on the Harpers Ferry side some distance upstream from the older bridge. The Shenandoah Valley branch junction was then relocated on the Maryland side, inside the west end of the tunnel on the old main line alignment; the branch was carried across the river on the 1894 bridge, which was kept as it was but reduced to single track. The 1894 station—complete with interlocking tower—was picked up and moved west to the new alignment where it still stands. (The tower was later removed.) A single track of the old line was left in place to connect the two bridges on the Harpers Ferry side as an emergency detour route. The new bridge was put in service June 1, 1931; for five years afterwards it was possible to see all three generations of B&O crossings at Harpers Ferry—the Civil War-era Bollman truss (used by the highway), the "new" 1894 main line bridge (for the Valley branch) and the 1931 crossing. A flood took out the venerable Bollman spans in March 1936, cutting the direct highway connection between Harpers Ferry and the Maryland side. In a flashback to the 19th Century days, the Valley branch bridge was then decked over and used jointly by road traffic until the present U.S. Rt. 340 bridge was built downstream in 1947. Today the two bridges remain in railroad service, along with the odd Valley branch junction—one of the few main line junctions located inside a tunnel.

The second project was less interesting but probably just as costly. In Baltimore the Locust Point freight line—which also carried all locomotive movements to and from Riverside engine terminal—followed the line of Wells Street at ground level across part of the Locust Point peninsula. This included a bad grade crossing at Hanover Street, by now an extremely busy main route between downtown Baltimore and the industrial areas of Brooklyn, Curtis Bay and Fairfield. To eliminate the crossing and also provide more room for yard expansion, the entire line was relocated a block to the south, passing Riverside roundhouses on the south side instead of the north, with a bridge and new yard leads over Key Highway. The new line—the route used today—was finished by early 1930.

And just in time. The Depression hit B&O even harder than most large railroads. Still in third place among the big eastern lines and overdependent on coal and steel, it found itself rapidly heading back to 1896. This time loans from the government-sponsored Reconstruction Finance Corporation helped avert another receivership, but for the next several years the railroad suffered severely. By 1932 its total freight tonnage was exactly half what it had been in 1929; systemwide coal traffic plunged 41% in the same period.

As a tonnage freight route, the Old Main Line reflected the worst of what was happening. According to one account, traffic on the line dropped as low as only about six trains a day. Gradually the profusion of towers and agencies were closed and some of the passing sidings disconnected or taken up. By 1941 only two 24-hour telegraph offices were open on the line—Mt. Airy Junction and Frederick Junction—supplemented by part-time offices at Gaither, Woodbine and Monrovia. All other towers had been closed, and the switches to the cutoff at Adamstown were removed. The line had never been signalled, so the cutback of interlocking towers, telegraph offices and passing sidings drastically reduced its carrying capacity—meaning that even the fewer number of trains sometimes clogged the line. As a result, for the first time B&O began regularly rerouting some of its fast merchandise freights—notably *New York 94* and *New York 97*—over the Metropolitan and Washington branches to keep them on time. It was done quietly and not always consistently, but nonetheless it marked the beginning of the Old Main's secondary status even for through freight movements.

Depression-era passenger service on the Old Main Line continued the slide started in the 1920's, now greatly accelerated. The combination of automobiles and decaying industry along much of the line left little for the locals to serve. By 1936 there was only one train left over most of the route—a commuter schedule between Baltimore and Frederick, leaving Baltimore in the late afternoon and returning from Frederick early in the morning. However, the mysterious one-way Ellicott City-Baltimore morning run also lived on. Two schedules still ran each way between the old Italianate Frederick station and Point of Rocks—one of them a steam train, the other a gas electric operating through to Brunswick, Weverton and Hagerstown. Four years later, in 1940, the single Baltimore-Frederick train still struggled back and forth, the Ellicott City train was gone and only the Frederick-Brunswick-Hagerstown gas-electric ran over the western end of the line. Shortly afterwards the Frederick commuter run was cut back to Mt. Airy and a gas-electric car substituted for the steam train. For the first time in 110 years—and forever after—Frederick had no rail passenger service to Baltimore.

The normally boring Mt. Airy commuter run was occasionally enlivened when the gas-electric car was disabled or needed shopping and some available steam locomotive was called to fill in. One such substitute was the onetime "Lord Baltimore", the light English-styled 4-6-4 built for the original lightweight "Royal Blue" streamliner. Now anonymously numbered 5340, it had been relegated to plug runs and worked to Mt. Airy for about a month.

So, by World War II the once extensive Old Main Line passenger timetables had shrunk down to a minimal two gas-electric motor trains—one between Baltimore and Mount Airy and one making a daily round trip over two branches from Frederick to Hagerstown. By then anyone riding on

Two 2-8-2's bang out of Ilchester tunnel with westbound hoppers in May 1951. Credit: Howard N. Barr

public transportation between Frederick and Baltimore or Frederick and Hagerstown used the buses of the Blue Ridge Transportation Company, a subsidiary of the Potomac Edison Company and an outgrowth of the Hagerstown & Frederick trolley line.

Back in Baltimore the Depression brought the old Annapolis Short Line home again to Camden station under a new name. The superbly-built but commercially luckless Washington, Baltimore & Annapolis, badly battered by railroad competition, new highways and increasing auto use, finally expired on August 20, 1935. But the old Short Line's direct Baltimore-Annapolis route appeared viable enough to operate on its own and B&O was anxious to keep what was then an important passenger connection to the state capital and Naval Academy. The Short Line bond-holders were able to reclaim most of their property and buy a short section of the north end of the WB&A's main line. With B&O financial and management aid, they reorganized the line as the Baltimore & Annapolis Railroad. The old WB&A Baltimore terminal at Howard and Lombard Streets was sold and a contract made with B&O to use Camden. The WB&A terminal later became a bus terminal, then was razed to make way for the Downtown Holiday Inn which now occupies the site.

Unlike the old Short Line days, the B&A did not join the B&O at Cliffords; instead it used what had been the WB&A main line through Westport as far as the point where the WB&A had bridged B&O's South

Baltimore branch close to Carroll tower. A new connection was built here and catenary for B&A's electric cars strung over one track of the B&O main line from Carroll to Camden, locally called "south siding." The old Cliffords junction remained as the B&O-B&A freight interchange, as it had through the WB&A era. B&O also helped B&A upgrade its line—notably the long wood trestle over the Severn River outside Annapolis—so that B&O steam power and passenger equipment could operate into Annapolis on special occasions.

B&A's heavy tuscan red interurban cars first entered Camden September 15, 1935. For 14½ years after, they ran hourly to Annapolis and served the Anne Arundel county suburbs on the way. B&A buses for Fort Meade also connected with B&O trains at Camden. And residents of spots like Severna Park and Glen Burnie were occasionally surprised by the sight of a B&O Pacific trailing a full-length passenger train under the wires, running to or from some football game or special ceremony at the Naval Academy.

From the 1932 low, B&O's freight business crept slowly back upward throught the rest of the Thirties, although neither the traffic, number of trains or manpower level came close to the peak of 1929. But World War II

B.

A. Stations were closed and torn down during the grim Thirties. Ilchester was one of the last survivors, shown in 1964 just before it too disappeared from the east and in a happier state of repair from the west. Credit: A-B&O Museum Archives—B-W.A. Barringer.

The Baltimore & Annapolis brought some variety and a bit of excitement to Camden station. In mid-1946 a two-car Annapolis train and B&O Washington local roll out simultaneously. The "race" won't last for long—the steam train will pull ahead and the electric will wait and cross over behind it near Ostend Street. Credit: H.H. Harwood, Jr.

St. Mary's College on a hilltop at Ilchester had a superb view of the Patapsco valley as well as a worldly procession of B&O coal trains. This one is eastbound in May 1951; it is crossing the river and about to dive into Ilchester tunnel. Credit: Howard N. Barr.

suddenly brought the depressed Old Main Line back to life. Coal use—both domestic and export—picked up enormously; so did export merchandise, military supplies and troop movements through Baltimore and other east coast ports. And the appearance of German U-boats along the Atlantic coast shut down oil tanker movements from the Gulf Coast to the east, diverting the crude oil into solid tank car trains for points like Marcus Hook, Pa., Philadelphia, and the New Jersey refineries. In addition to the rapidly multiplying freight trains, passenger business was ballooning on the Washington branch and Metropolitan, make it necessary to re-divert as much freight as possible onto the Old Main. From an average of about 20 trains a day in 1940, its traffic rose to 42 in late 1942. The Mt. Airy gas-electric, whose size and status apparently nothing could alter, fought its way through as best it could, seldom reaching home on time.

B&O scrambled to bring the Old Main Line back to its old operating capacity and hopefully more. Gaither tower was reinstated as a 24-hour office and telegraph operators added at Gray (east of Ellicott City) and Alberton. Semaphore-type automatic block signals were installed over the entire line by March 1944; also in 1944 a new 200-ton over-track concrete coaling station was built at Lees, just west of Ilchester. One of the major motivations for the latter was to enable trains from Philadelphia to run through Baltimore without stopping for coal in the congested terminal area. Finally, new General Motors / Electro-Motive FT road diesels appeared in 1942 to supplement the overworked Q's; in 5,400-h.p. four unit sets they could haul twice the merchandise tonnage of a Q-4 and triple the coal drag tonnage. Initially the diesels did not put much of a dent in the mass of Mikados—one set a day usually operated over the line each way on a heroically long run between Philadelphia and Willard, Ohio.

The concrete coaling tower at Lees, east of Ellicott City, was a wartime installation designed to save time by coaling road trains outside the Baltimore terminal district. It was used less than ten years, but its remains may still be found alongside the right of way. Credit: E.L. Thompson.

Peacetime produced the now-familiar succession of service abandonments, traffic decline, physical facility reductions, dieselization and partial rebirth—but with some unique B&O variations and punctuated by one spectacular Act of God. Old Main Line passenger service, probably overdue for extinction, ended in late 1949—the Frederick-Brunswick-Hagerstown run on November 1 and the Baltimore-Mt. Airy motor train on the last day of the year.

As financial pressure tightened during the 1950's, B&O began retiring whatever physical facilities it felt were unneeded, including some that were still there simply because nobody had the heart to tear them down. A pathetically proud example was the Relay Station-hotel, long since boarded up after erratic use as employee living quarters. The railroad got up its nerve in 1950 and knocked down the formidable stone structure—but as if to quiet Garrett's ghost it left a small bronze plaque on the site commemorating the building. The 1854 Frederick passenger station became a food market and virtually all of the frame way stations and passenger shelters along the Old Main line were dismantled. The long-dormant Adamstown cutoff was retired in January 1952 and the eastern portion of the old Mt. Airy line between Mt. Airy and Watersville Junction was taken off the books August 15, 1957. The west leg of this branch from Mt. Airy Junction to Mt. Airy still remains; although its future has been intermittently dim, it seems secure at the moment.

Another step down the ladder for the Old Main Line came in 1959 and 1960 when the entire line between the junction crossovers at Halethorpe and Point of Rocks was reduced to single track and converted to Central-

A set of B&O's first road freight diesels drums west through Weverton in 1947. They performed beautifully, but B&O's policy of spreading them thin throughout the system made them minority members of the Baltimore division locomotive roster. Credit: E.L. Thompson.

More common and certainly more spectacular were the handsome EM-1 2-8-8-4's, also bought during the war. They regularly operated west of Brunswick to relieve the now-overburdened 2-10-2's. Weverton, 1947. Credit: E.L. Thompson.

John Garrett's Viaduct Hotel-Station looked bleak and forlorn in its last days. The photo looks east on the Old Main shortly before the building was razed in 1950. Credit: H.C. Eck collection.

ized Traffic Control. Portions of the former second track were retained as long passing sidings at six points: at Avalon (just west of Relay), Davis, Hoods Mill, the west side of Parr's Ridge between Mt. Airy Junction and Plane No. 4, Reels Mill, and 2.7 miles at the west end of the line between Doub and Point of Rocks. All remaining lineside operators were removed and train movement governed by signals and switches set by a dispatcher in Camden station.

The single tracking was justified because many manifest freights were now being run through Washington over the Metropolitan and Washington branches, partly because of the higher speeds permitted but also because it was necessary to set off or pick up cars at Washington. The establishment of the automobile terminal at Jessup in the late 1960's and the subsequent development of plants and warehouses in the Jessup-Fort Meade Junction area required more setoff work on the Washington branch, which diverted even more freights around this route.

In the meantime, diesels had fully taken over the Baltimore division. Actually, they had first appeared rather inconspicuously in the fall of 1940 in the form of a group of 600 h.p. EMD SW-1 switchers working various yards in the Baltimore terminal. Passenger diesels were something else; more will be said about them in the chapters covering the Washington branch and the Metropolitan branch. As mentioned earlier, road freight units were first delivered in 1942, but it was not until the late 1940's and early '50's that they arrived in any quantity. As they did, B&O tried to concentrate them on specific divisions so that it could completely eliminate the expense of operating duplicate steam servicing and maintenance facilities. The Baltimore division was one of the first to go. All

A Q-4-powered local freight westbound at the little local stop at Marriottsville about 1948. Credit: B&O Museum Archives.

remaining steam power was rapidly phased out in late 1953; the official "last steam" was Pacific 5306 which pulled passenger train No. 22 into Camden on November 2, 1953. At about the same time, Riverside lost the easternmost of its twin roundhouses.

Camden itself had also suffered some trimming down. During a 1951 renovation project that was both beneficial and destructive, the old terminal received an exterior restoration and interior remodeling—but at the same time lost its two iron trainsheds, the third floor of its one remaining end wing and the single surviving decorative cupola. Ten years later, following the closing of Mt. Royal station, its lower level platform was also dismantled.

Socially far more disturbing was what was happening to Brunswick yard. Traditionally, B&O had split its major eastern freight classification work between Brunswick and Cumberland (with additional coal work at nearby Keyser, W.Va.). Through the 1920's, Brunswick had developed into the classic sociology and economics textbook example of a one-industry town. Anything affecting the railroad immediately affected Brunswick and a closedown of the yard would destroy it. B&O thus found itself in a continuing three-way struggle between operating economics, politics and pure humanity. Although increasingly uncomfortable with doing the same type of work at two locations, B&O had left Brunswick alone during the Depression and the late 1940's. But in the early '50's B&O decided to try to consolidate all eastern classification at Cumberland and

A westbound mail and express run roars over Harpers Ferry bridge in 1948. Credit: R.E. Tobey.

in 1952 embarked on a major yard expansion project there.

The Cumberland project lurched spasmodically along, periodically suspended as B&O's finances once again wavered, but the new westbound classification yard was finally opened in 1960 and all westbound work transferred from Brunswick. Fortunately for Brunswick the load turned out to be beyond Cumberland's capabilities and switching work gradually filtered back. And with the resurgence of the coal business in the 1970's, Brunswick even underwent an expansion of its own in 1978-79 to enable it to hold export coal destined for Curtis Bay.

By the late 1960's local freight business along the east end of the Old Main Line had virtually vaporized. Most of the surviving Patapsco Valley mills—notably those at Thistle, Oella and Daniels (ex-Alberton/Elysville)—had gone to truck and by late 1972 Oella and Daniels were out of business. Only some industry at Sykesville and the large onetime Patapsco Flouring Mill at Ellicott City, now operated by the Doughnut Corporation of America, generated any rail business. But west of the Monocacy River several substantial plants and warehouses

A special photo run of the new lightweight Washington-Chicago "Columbian" poses westbound at Sandy Hook just east of the Harpers Ferry tunnel in 1949. B&O's old Sandy Hook engine house was just around the curve to the rear of the train. Credit: B&O Museum Archives.

A merchandiser for the Old Main has just cleared the crossovers at Halethorpe and accelerates west through the little suburban station at St. Denis in 1967. Credit: H.H. Harwood, Jr.

Ellicott City's ancient stone station witnesses a westbound freight passage in 1970. The station has now been preserved and restored, but a safety fence unfortunately blocks the track view. Credit: H.H. Harwood, Jr.

appeared in the open Frederick County countryside. Largest was the Eastalco aluminum plant near Buckeystown, opened in mid-1970 and located there partly to receive its aluminum ore by rail from an import pier near Curtis Bay.

Although freight traffic was relatively good and the railroad surprisingly healthy, corporate policy changes in the Sixties brought the end of two long-hallowed B&O institutions in Baltimore. A disastrous 1962 fire destroyed the Mt. Clare locomotive erecting shop, the direct descendent of the country's earliest railroad locomotive building shop. Since the end of steam, the shop had handled heavy diesel repairs, and it was decided to consolidate this work in Cumberland rather than rebuild—leaving Mt. Clare to do only car repairs. This function was not particularly long-lived either; with the 1963 affiliation with C&O and the subsequent general consolidation of shops on both railroads, Mt. Clare was completely closed as a shop on March 15, 1974. In 1976 most of the now-derelict buildings— some of them built in the 1860's—were torn down after several fires and some storm damage. A victim of the same demolition spree was a brick building on the shop property which had been used over the years for various purposes including a shop superintendent's residence; reputedly it dated to 1754 and once served as an outbuilding for the Mount Clare estate.

Westbound grain empties on the Old Main Line at Sykesville in January 1979. Where possible, the derailment-prone high center of gravity grain hoppers are routed over the gentler curves of the Washington and Metropolitan branches. Credit: Bill Rettberg.

When Mt. Clare shops were torn down, these were among some of the
sadder losses. The brick buildings bordering Carey Street dated to
the 1860's and were some of the oldest on the property. The three-
story house was a survivor of the 18th Century Mt. Clare estate complex. Credits: A-H.H. Harwood, Jr.—B-B&O Museum Archives.

A.

B.

The second institution certainly did not end; it merely changed ownership and form. What ended in this case was a tradition. On January 1, 1964, B&O sold its somewhat dilapidated Locust Point pier complex to the Maryland Port Authority, which gradually replaced all the old railroad piers. B&O continued to serve them, of course, and also briefly retained its large 1923 grain elevator and its carfloat terminal. The float bridge was kept to reach the isolated Fells Point track directly across the harbor; by then the once-extensive Baltimore harbor lighterage and carfloat operations had been closed down. The Fells Point float ceased in 1969 when B&O made an agreement with Penn Central to handle the traffic by rail over PC's Fells Point trackage. The grain elevator was sold in 1967, leaving no railroad-owned pier facilities at the terminal which John W. Garrett had made into the center of Baltimore's port.

While no longer really in the category of an "institution", another historically important B&O facility quietly disappeared in early 1972—the Pratt Street line. This had been B&O's original Baltimore entry, so hard fought over in the late 1820's; it had been laid in 1831 to reach the downtown passenger and freight depots and the City Dock at President Street. Although the passenger and freight stations had been abandoned in favor of Camden in 1853, the street trackage remained to serve the disorganized tangle of piers, warehouses, wholesalers and manufacturing companies strung out along Pratt and President Streets. In the earlier years it had also carried interchange cars between B&O and the Philadelphia, Wilmington & Baltimore, and also the Northern Central.

The nature of the Pratt Street line changed drastically over the years as the port activity shifted to other areas and as the railroad interchanges were moved elsewhere. But a healthy scattering of industry remained and expanded along the street, and a daily late-night (to avoid tangling with auto traffic) switching run traditionally covered the route from Mt. Clare to the foot of President Street. From the 1920's to the '40's this work was usually handled by one of the legendary "Little Joe" (or, in its HO gauge incarnation, the "Dockside") 0-4-0 oil-fired saddletankers, specifically designed for the tight curves reaching into the streetside plants and warehouses. Originally there were four of these locomotives, later reduced to two. The run was later taken over by short wheelbase diesels—SW-1's and, most recently, Alco S-1's. But by the 1960's most Pratt Street industries had closed or gone to truck; when the city embarked on its inner harbor redevelopment program, almost all the remaining customers were forced out. In early 1972 the rail line itself became an urban renewal casualty, abandoned to allow the widening and repaving of Pratt Street. A short isolated section of track on President Street at the far eastern end of the line was kept (and survives today), switched by Penn Central/Conrail under an agreement.

Historical tradition was also suddenly left dangling in the Patapsco Valley soon afterward. In mid-1972 a near-repetition of the never-forgotten 1868 flood smashed through the valley, removing large chunks of the railroad. Between June 21 and June 23 the residue of Tropical Storm Agnes, which had veered inland through central Maryland and Pennsylvania, dumped heavy rains into the already-waterlogged drainage systems. The Patapsco behaved as usual, cresting at over 31 feet at Hollofield. Most of the Old Main went under water—so quickly that an eastbound coal train was caught at Woodstock and marooned; its head-end crew managed to abandon safely, but the two crew members in the caboose had to be taken out by state police helicopter. When the river dropped, the fine old Daniels/Alberton mill had been gutted, the 18th Century Ellicott brothers' houses at Ellicott City destroyed or badly damaged, the Thistle mill also seriously damaged and bridges all through the valley taken out. Unlike their predecessors in 1868, all of Loree's sturdy railroad bridges stayed, but many embankments were undercut, leaving long sections of track dangling in the air. Some of the worst damage was just east of Sykesville, east of Marriottsville at the Patapsco Forks, Davis and both sides of the river at

Typical of what Agnes wrought was this scene east of Sykesville. The tangled mass of steel under the trees on the opposite bank is the Sykesville highway bridge, carried half a mile downstream. Credit: H.H. Harwood, Jr.

Ilchester. Even more bothersome, poles, communication lines, signals and signal circuits and traffic control lines were destroyed.

Under normal circumstances the railroad would have been rebuilt with reasonable dispatch. In 1868, after all, the line was back in operation within two weeks—after much worse devastation. But the Agnes flood happened to coincide with another critical point in the company's history. B&O and C&O had recently emerged from a financially damaging coal strike and had also undergone some changes in management philosophy. The company was under pressure to eliminate anything that seemed surplus or redundant. By this time most merchandise freights were running via Washington anyway, and the virtual elimination of through passenger service on both the Metropolitan and Washington branches technically had given the lines more freight capacity. Rebuilding the Old Main Line not only required heavy earthwork, but the replacement of the signal and traffic control lines promised to be even more costly.

The wounded railroad thus was left to lie there while the company debated its future. The relatively undamaged west end eventually was restored as far east as Mt. Airy for local freight customers. On the east, temporary repairs were made between Relay and Woodstock to extract the stranded coal train, but otherwise the line remained out of service. The company finally concluded that the Old Main was necessary as a relief route—particularly for coal traffic—but it compromised on how it would be rebuilt. The line was to be restored, but without the expensive signal and traffic control systems—reducing its capacity considerably. At present the Old Main has automatic block signals (but no train control) between Mt. Airy Junction and Point of Rocks, and is unsignalled east of Mt. Airy Junction.

That settled, Chessie obtained the necessary regulatory authority to operate the line without signals and proceeded to rebuild. On April 2, 1974—close to two years after Agnes—the first train ran through between Baltimore and Point of Rocks again. Today the twisting, tenacious old railroad still carries the coal into Baltimore and ore out, plus whatever other odd freights B&O may choose to route over the line. It will probably become busier as the hoped-for increases in coal traffic materialize and as coordinations are completed to route more Western Maryland Railway traffic into Baltimore over B&O lines. Perhaps the Old Main Line is not what it once was, but it remains a remarkable example of how a railroad has adapted and survived from the most primitive early days to the uncertainties of the 1970's and '80's.

Longer and higher freight cars required more rebuilding around the old obstructions at Point of Rocks and Catoctin. To provide room, the tunnels were single tracked and the eastbound main track relocated around the outside of the tunnel, partly occupying the old canal bed. The view looks west in 1978. Credit: H.H. Harwood, Jr.

Empty hoppers head back to the mines through Harpers Ferry in September 1977. Credit: H.H. Harwood, Jr.

On a quiet winter Saturday in 1967, a Washington-bound RDC car pauses for passengers at St. Denis. The station and schedule are now gone. Credit: H.H. Harwood, Jr.

IMPOSSIBLE CHALLENGE

SWITCHING OVER STREETS AND WATER

Tight urbanization started early in Baltimore, often leaving B&O no clear right-of-way but the streets to reach its freight customers. During most of the 19th Century, horses switched the cars—but when mechanical power was finally permitted, Baltimore's railroads found that they needed special power to negotiate the streetcar curves and limited track layouts. In addition, the broken-up collection of small bays around the harbor gradually spawned a set of disjointed piers and marine terminals as the port expanded. Thus the railroads often had to float freight to ships they could not reach with their own tracks and ferry freight cars to unconnected branches. So at one time Baltimore offered a fascinating and sometimes unique assortment of street switchers, tugs, float bridges, carfloats and lighters. Little is left now. B&O's marine operations were completely gone by 1969 and most street trackage has been abandoned.

B&O's best-known street operation, and possibly one of the world's most famous, was the Pratt Street run, using the original main line first laid in 1831. Originally, 0-4-0 "dummy" engines were used, enshrouded in a streetcar-like body to reassure the omnipresent horses. In 1912 four specially-designed 0-4-0 oil-fired saddletankers were built for this and other street runs, although two were later rebuilt as conventional coal-fired tender engines. Here, in 1940, "Dockside" No. 98 chuffs carefully down Pratt Street. Credit: B&O Museum Archives.

In its later years the Pratt Street jobs normally operated at night to minimize accidents and traffic disruption. The stocky saddletanker pulls an empty newsprint car from the Baltimore News-American building, still standing. Credit: B&O Museum Archives.

Even more odd was the two-block-long disconnected track in Fell Street at Fells Point. Originally built in 1860, it was reached by a carfloat from Locust Point and switched by horses. In 1895 it was electrified, tapping into a nearby streetcar line and equipped with a tiny single-truck GE locomotive numbered 9. The 9 was replaced in 1910 by this equally diminutive steel GE motor which performed all the Fells Point work until 1954. (It may be seen today in the B&O Museum.) It poses here at the Fell Street float bridge in November, 1931. Credit: B&O Museum Archives.

B&O's largest customer at Fells Point was its own Henderson's Wharf warehouse, shown in 1931. The float bridge and electric switcher are to the right of the building. Track and warehouse still remain, although the warehouse is now empty and the track may be abandoned soon. Credit: B&O Museum Archives.

The electric was replaced by this trucklike rubber-tired tractor in 1954, shown on Thames Street at Ann Street in July 1976. It has just picked up two loaded cement cars left by Conrail, which operates somewhat similar tractors in the same area. Credit: H.H. Harwood, Jr.

Several large customers were once located along South Eutaw Street near Camden station, reached by a street-center spur from Bailey's. Fairbanks-Morse switcher 9719 jockeys cars at the Maryland Baking Co. plant near Ostend Street. The cupolaed building in the rear was one of the early industries in the Camden area. Built in 1869, it once housed the Knabe piano factory. This scene dates to 1967. Credit: Bill Rettberg.

Several blocks farther north, the Eutaw Street spur ran in the shadow of B&O's heroic Camden warehouse. SW-1 No. 206 attempts to cope with the motor traffic about 1949. Credit: B&O Museum Archives.

The *Hugh L. Bond, Jr.* typified B&O's Baltimore harbor tugs. It was built in 1906 and also worked New York Harbor during its career. B&O's Baltimore "navy" was much less extensive than in New York, but in 1946 two tugs, 12 car floats, 20 covered barges (lighters) and five deck scows were kept active in the harbor. Credit: B&O Museum Archives.

Lighters were covered barges used to deliver freight directly to shipside. Freight cars were unloaded into the lighters, which were then floated to ships tied up at piers not reached by B&O tracks. These are at Locust Point in 1974. Credit: H.H. Harwood, Jr.

Locust Point was B&O's primary carfloat terminal. Freight cars were switched over this float bridge (there were two here) onto steel carfloats, such as those seen in the distance. Carfloats were used to transfer loaded cars to waterside warehouses and switching spurs not directly reached by B&O rails over land. Credit: H.H. Harwood, Jr.

IMPOSSIBLE CHALLENGE

CHAPTER 10

WASHINGTON'S FIRST RAILROAD:
THE WASHINGTON BRANCH, 1835-1865

B&O had barely begun laying its rails up the Patapsco in 1830 when it started serious planning for a branch to Washington. Even by then, the idea was not new. The country's government officials and their hangers-on perhaps were resigned to living briefly in the small, swampy, steamy and crude new capital city. But they were not anxious to endure the long, jolting carriage or stagecoach rides necessary to get there from almost any place else. As early as May, 1828—before the railroad had even laid its cornerstone—an act of Congress authorized it to enter Washington. With Baltimore and Washington only about 35 miles apart and B&O planning to build southwest out of town to reach the Patapsco, it was probably inevitable that it was considered the obvious agency to bring a railroad to Washington. B&O was only mildly enthusiastic, however. Its basic orientation was westward, from Baltimore to the Ohio River. Washington was another eastern city and did not fit into B&O's purpose or projected traffic pattern. Most of the traffic to and from Washington— and it was virtually all passengers—flowed along the east coast, to cities like Baltimore, Philadelphia, New York and Boston. Thus a Baltimore-Washington route would have little value as a B&O feeder.

On the other hand, B&O's directors probably were shrewd enough to recognize several things: First, although Washington was adjacent to the small seaports of Alexandria and Georgetown, it could well become a market for Baltimore. More important, the branch would bring B&O both economic benefits and political prestige. By 1830, the seed of a new east coast transportation system was beginning to sprout. That year Camden & Amboy Railroad was incorporated to connect New York harbor with the Delaware River near Philadelphia; the year before, another "portage" railroad, the New Castle and Frenchtown, had been organized to build a line between the Delaware River and Chesapeake Bay. Taken together, these two lines formed parts of a water-rail-water-rail-water transportation chain between New York and Baltimore—a bit awkward, perhaps, but a considerable improvement over the very slow and dirty all-road route or the roundabout all-water route. Plainly a rail line from Baltimore to Washington would complete the chain and equally plainly it would be built soon by someone else if B&O did not act first. B&O's politically-minded management saw the public relations value in providing that link and thereby becoming a physical presence in the capital. Finally, it is entirely possible that they saw the branch's potential purely as a moneymaker—something they needed, since it had become obvious that the main line to the Ohio would not be a going business for many years.

But money was also a problem. With B&O's already thin finances being gobbled up by the "stone railroad" up the Patapsco and the clear prospect of massive amounts of new capital needed to get over Alleghenies, the company felt it could not fully finance the branch itself. In December 1830 it applied to the Maryland legislature for aid, and also attempted to negotiate with the federal government. The inevitable political arguments ensued and in the end the federal government backed away completely and Maryland waffled. It passed an authorization in February 1831, but avoided a firm financial commitment. The following year B&O brought the question up again, but still did not get the type of commitment it wanted; by this time preoccupied with the more important political showdown with the C&O Canal at Point of Rocks, it let the Washington branch ride.

In the meantime chief engineer Jonathan Knight and one of his principal assistants, Benjamin Latrobe, reconnoitered a route. Their work was made easier by a survey made in 1827 by William Howard, one of the senior Army engineers, for a Baltimore-Washington canal. In 1832 Latrobe began preliminary surveys, investigating several alternative alignments but basically following the projected canal route. Generally, the topography was a welcome relief from the Patapsco valley, Parr's Ridge and Point of Rocks. Although there was no direct water-level route between the two cities, and the terrain tended to be hilly, there were no serious obstacles either. The hills were low and the drainage pattern was diverse enough so that streams could be followed for at least parts of the line. The principal rivers—primarily two branches of the Patuxent—did flow crosswise to the route, but they were relatively small and crossed in areas where there were no deep ravines or valleys. Knight kept to his high engineering standards and, in fact, the prestige value of this branch made B&O's managers insist on the 1830's equivalent of a super-railroad. As he emphasized both to Latrobe and president Philip E. Thomas, "The railroad under consideration will have a national character, and should be planned in a manner worthy of its highly important position and functions." Knight felt confident that a line with gentle curves and mild

0.4% grades could be laid around the hills and over the streams at reasonable cost.

By the end of 1832 Latrobe had explored 12 alternate routes—actually two basic routes, with five minor variations on each. One route would leave B&O's main line somewhere between present-day Halethorpe and St. Denis, cross the Patapsco slightly downstream from the present Washington Boulevard (U.S. Route 1) bridge at Elkridge and follow a generally easterly path through nondescript farming country to Washington. The other would branch off the main line where it entered the Patapsco valley near Relay...the specific spot was then identified as Hockley's Mill, a riverside mill and dam near Elk Ridge Landing. It would then follow higher ground, more or less paralleling the Washington turnpike.

After laborious analysis, the minutest details of which were reproduced in the company's 1833 annual report, Knight picked one of the Relay/Hockley's Mill routes, generally following the old canal survey (but at a higher level) slightly east of the Washington turnpike. Knight based his choice primarily on the best theoretical blend of low construction cost, high speed and tonnage capabilities and low future operating and maintenance expenses. Probably its decisive advantage was a saving in new construction; the Relay route would use the existing main line out of Baltimore as far as possible—7½ miles, or one-fifth of the total distance between Baltimore and Washington. Less important but helpful in the future, this alignment crossed the major streams farther inland and at a somewhat higher elevation—thus offering better potential sites for on-line water-powered mills. In fact, large textile mills were already active slightly west of the projected line at Savage, on the Little Patuxent and Laurel Factory on the Big Patuxent. The route's primary drawback was the difficult terrain where it would have to cross the Patapsco near Relay. Here the line from Baltimore came into the valley 66 feet above the mid-tide level; the valley itself was wide and hemmed in by high, rocky ridges on either side. As a result the crossing would require the largest viaduct B&O had attempted so far—which also had to be curved to get the line onto a favorable footing on the south side of the valley.

But all things considered, the line was indeed well located. Grades were held to a maximum of 0.48% and that only for a short stretch northbound between Laurel and Savage; most were under 0.4%. By Patapsco valley standards, the curves were practically tangent—except for the Patapsco Viaduct and the hillsides around Elk Ridge immediately south of it, all curves on the route were in the 1°-2° range. The worst spot was just north of the viaduct itself, which demanded an 8°50' curve; the bridge was on a 4° curve and another 4° twist was necessary at Elk Ridge.

Beyond the Patapsco the route had no outstanding topographic features and no significant summits—at least none of the Parr's Ridge variety. Rather, it was a succession of gentle ups and downs as it crossed

three low ridges dividing the major east-west stream valleys in the area—
Merrills Ridge (at present Jessup) between the Patapsco and Little
Patuxent, Patuxent Ridge dividing the Little and Big Patuxents and
Snowdens Ridge near Contee, between the Big Patuxent and the
Potomac River drainage system. From the south side of the Patapsco at
Elk Ridge the line picked up a Patapsco tributary called Deep Run and
followed it gradually uphill to the first ridge at Jessup, where the track
cut through the top of the hill. South of the cut it levelled off through what
is now Fort Meade Junction then dropped down to the Little Patuxent
east of Savage. From Savage it climbed again through a cut at Patuxent
Ridge, crossed the Patuxent at Laurel, climbed to Contee—then sloped
gently downgrade toward Washington, following Piney Branch and the
Northeast Branch and passing just west of the crossroads settlement of
Bladensburg. At Bladensburg it crossed the Northwest Branch and
veered away from the Potomac tributaries, heading straight across
choppy countryside into Washington. The precise entry route into the
capital was left until last, since there were some difficulties finding the
best straight line across the terrain and also in settling on how the line
would pick its way through Washington's planned (but mostly unbuilt)
street system. Latrobe eventually located the line through present
Brentwood, with a long deep cut through Duel Ridge between Brentwood
and what is now Langdon. After some weaving through city streets south
of Boundary Street (Florida Avenue) the branch ended in the Tiber Creek

The countryside along the Washington branch was not particularly
rugged, but several deep cuts were necessary through the low ridges
separating streams in the area. This one near Savage shows the line's
high engineering standards. The train is No. 32, an east (north)
bound Cumberland-Baltimore local about 1931. Credit: Smithsonian Institution; C.B. Chaney collection.

lowland just northwest of Bullfinch's new Capitol building.

Once across the Patapsco, it was a visually unexciting line—mostly a succession of sweeping curves and tangents through woods and farms, interspersed with several cuts and low bridges. But what was dull to the eye was dear to the construction engineer and operating manager. Afterwards the Washington branch fulfilled the company's hope for a high-speed, high-capacity railroad that was "worthy of its highly important position and functions." In fact, alone among all of B&O's main lines in the area, it was never realigned or rebuilt—probably the ultimate tribute to Latrobe's work. It is admittedly ironic that the Pennsylvania Railroad's competitive Washington branch—built 37 years later—was straighter, faster (albeit hillier) and eventually carried more traffic. But Latrobe's line nonetheless remains an excellent piece of railroad with no apologies due.

The state financing impasse was finally resolved in February 1833—perhaps not coincidentally also about the time the legislature resolved the deadlock with the C&O Canal at Point of Rocks. Maryland agreed to put up $500,000 for the Washington branch—as much as one-third of the total initial capital—in the form of common stock. But the terms were strangely stiff considering the "national" nature of the branch and its political sensitivities. First, and worst, the state specified that it was to receive a 20% dividend on all *gross* passenger receipts—income "taken off the top", so to speak. This 20% "bonus," as the legislation somewhat whimsically called it, applied only to passenger fares; nobody paid much attention to freight, which was expected to be minimal anyway. This meant that rates had to be substantially above the anticipated operating costs in order to cover this arbitrary payment and still provide a normal financial return for the railroad. To accomplish this the law set the one-way passenger fare—originally intended to be $1.50—at $2.50, an extremely high rate in 1833 when an average worker's wage was about a dollar a day.

Second, in order to protect the state's investment and allow it to get additional "normal" dividends from the line's operation, the branch was to be financed by a separate stock issue. This put it in a strange sort of corporate twilight world: It was not a subsidiary company in the strict sense, since it had no separate corporate structure; however, its securities and financial accounts were kept separate from the B&O "Main Stem," and it was expected to pay its own dividends based on its own financial performance. As a result, in the early days it was operated virtually as a separate railroad, although fully managed by B&O and using B&O equipment and facilities. The equipment, although owned by B&O, was kept on a separate roster also. Before the Civil War, this peculiar structure was more an accounting nuisance than anything else, since the branch's operations and traffic flow had little relationship to B&O's main line anyway. But as it became an integral part of the large system, carrying through trains and requiring large new mainline facilities (not the least of which was Washington Union Station in the early 1900's), the separate bookkeeping system became an impossible anachronism.

Finally, the Washington branch financing legislation allowed the state to appoint two additional directors to the B&O—not the Washington branch, but the entire B&O. Since the Washington branch stock was to be separate "forever", the state-appointed directorships were also "forever." Although B&O's corporate structure and its political problems are not part of this book, it should be mentioned that this arrangement merely added to the railroad's woes later in the century.

But there was at least one overwhelming compensation for all of this: Although not specifically mentioned in any of the Washington branch legislation, the state's 20% "bonus" and its normal dividends from the line's operation carried with them the implied agreement that Maryland would not grant a charter to any other Baltimore-Washington railroad. B&O was thus guaranteed a monopoly, which somewhat eased its conscience about the high fare.

With financing assured, work started quickly. The most difficult part of the job—the Patapsco Viaduct and the section as far south as Merrills Ridge—were put under contract early in July, 1833.

By this time B&O had learned a lot about railroad construction and the characteristics of track and motive power. Almost none of the mistakes of the main line were repeated on the Washington branch. Even though the railroad was still in the process of laying strap rail toward Harpers Ferry it did not even consider such track for the new line—and certainly not any form of stone roadbed. Instead the branch was to be laid with a surprisingly modern form of iron "T" rail, using wood ties. (The rail, of course, had to be rolled in England). Typical of early track everywhere, the rail was light—40 lb. to the yard—and, like the strap rail, was laid on a longitudinal wood stringer which in turn was fastened to the ties. The stringers were usually six inches square, although in some spots roughly finished logs were so used. The ties tended to be light and sometimes casual, too; they were laid three feet apart (an improvement on the original main line's four-foot centers) and held in place by longitudinal wood sills set in the roadbed underneath them.

One characteristic of the main line was emphatically carried over to the Washington branch: the use of stone for bridges. The branch was to be completely a "stone railroad", including the wide and deep Patapsco valley crossing between Relay and Elk Ridge. Large single arch stone bridges were built over the two Patuxents and the Northwest Branch west of Bladensburg and smaller single arches and stone culverts spanned the minor streams. But getting across the Patapsco was hardly a routine problem. Had Knight and Latrobe intentionally chosen some spot strictly to produce B&O's most monumental structure, they could not have done better. Latrobe's alignment called for a 612 foot long bridge carrying the track 60 feet above the stream—on a curve. A timber trestle of these dimensions would be impressive enough; in stone, it would be the largest such structure ever attempted in the United States.

Latrobe handled the design and the durable Caspar Wever supervised its building, employing his friend John McCartney of Ohio as the contractor. The viaduct was built of Patapsco granite and had eight arches, each varying slightly in size but averaging 58 feet across, with wedge-shaped piers fitted to the curve line. Between its length, height and the massive stone abutments at each end, it consumed 24,475 cubic yards of masonry. B&O had already established a tradition of naming its important stone viaducts after company directors; this most magnificent and best known of B&O bridges was chosen to memorialize president Philip E. Thomas. Although the railroad's stone bridges and their names exhibit perhaps at least a touch of corporate megalomania, this one was at least appropriate. More than any other single individual, Thomas was responsible for forming both the dream and the tangible shape of the Baltimore & Ohio. At the time he resigned the B&O presidency in 1836, tired and somewhat saddened, the dream had dissipated into a tangle of physical, financial and political problems. Although he was alive when the line was completed to Wheeling—in fact he died in 1861 at the very ripe age of 85—he was only a bystander. And the big granite obelisk placed at the Thomas Viaduct when it was finished in 1835 was really put there to commemorate the bridge's builder rather than Thomas. But thanks to "his" viaduct's high historic status—as well as its awesome size and its engineering aesthetics—Thomas's name has endured, even if few remember what he did to deserve it.

As the viaduct painfully rose over the Patapsco, work proceeded quickly on other parts of the Washington branch through late 1833 and 1834. The bridge was completed July 4, 1835, allowing at least partial services south of there—but delivery delays on the English rails and several riots among the immigrant laborers (including a bad one near Bladensburg in June) slowed completion at the Washington end. A semblance of service started July 20 as far as Bladensburg (the railroad station was actually at present-day Hyattsville), with stagecoaches from Washington meeting the trains there.

In the meantime, Phineas Davis had turned out four new Grasshopper locomotives for the line in June 1835 at Mt. Clare shop. Being meant for the Washington branch, they were given appropriate Washington names: "Thomas Jefferson", "James Madison", "James Monroe" and "J.Q. Adams"..."George Washington" had already been built in 1834. It had been estimated that the branch would need four engines for regular service—three for passenger trains and one for freight—but power was exchanged between the branch and the "Main Stem" as needed for peaks and valleys in traffic.

With its already-established flair for staging celebrations, B&O had originally hoped to run its first train into Washington on July 4 as sort of a seventh anniversary of the 1828 Baltimore sendoff. The various delays pushed that back almost two months, but on August 25, 1835 the gala was finally held. In Baltimore a select crowd estimated at 800 people climbed into about 18 new double-truck passenger cars at the Pratt & Charles station and were hauled by horses out to Mt. Clare where they were assembled into four full trains. Included in the party were the standard

A.

The Thomas Viaduct became B&O's most famous landmark forever after its completion in 1835. (A) It's best known angle was looking south from Relay; here P-7 Pacific 5311 heads a heavy Washington-

New York train about 1936. (B) The view north from the site of Hockley's Mill in 1974. Credits: A-H.W. Pontin; H.H. Harwood collection—B-H.H. Harwood, Jr.

B.

collection of city and state dignitaries—the Governor, state legislature members, Baltimore's Mayor, City Council members, railroad officers and directors, plus wives and friends. With four or five cars behind each of them, four Grasshoppers chuffed off in a "brigade" to Bladensburg; there they were met by a two-car train of city officials from Washington, Alexandria and Georgetown, accompanied by the Marine band. The whole armada went on to a temporary station in Washington two blocks from the railroad's 2nd Street and Pennsylvania Avenue terminal, which was not yet ready. According to a later account, several thousand Washingtonians turned out to meet the trains, but—a revealing indication of what downtown Washington was like then—"there was no crowding, for few houses were nearby."

The branch itself, measured from the main line junction at Relay to Washington, was 32 miles long; the total rail distance from B&O's Pratt Street station in Baltimore was 40 miles. Over the years this mileage gradually diminished as a result of realignments at the Baltimore end and terminal location changes in both cities. At present it is 36.8 miles between Camden station in Baltimore and Washington Union Station.

As built, the Washington branch had been fully graded for two tracks—including all cuts and stone bridges—but only a single track was laid between Relay and Washington. A total of 2½ miles of second track had been built in the form of extended passing sidings at the three major cuts on the line. The longest of these was a pair of sidings totalling a mile and a half at what was called Watson's Cut at the summit ridge separating the two Patuxents between Laurel and Savage—roughly the halfway point between Baltimore and Washington. Other long sidings were located at Jessup's Cut (Merrills Ridge) and at what was called Bladensburg Cut, actually at Duel Ridge inside the District Line. Although the branch's main track and several of the long second-track sidings had been laid with "T" rail, Washington trains rolled over B&O's original strap rail between Baltimore and the Relay junction. As secondary sidings were built along the branch they were also laid with the cheaper strap rail, some of it salvaged from the main line. As best as can be deduced from comments in early reports, the Washington branch may have been well engineered and solidly built, but it was bare of any formal way stations. As late as 1847, an annual report states that the Washington terminal (actually a rebuilt boarding house) and its accessorial buildings were the only structures on the line.

The branch was scarcely a month old when a sobering tragedy occurred. On Sept. 27 Phineas Davis was joyriding to Washington and back with some of his shop workmen on a newly-built Grasshopper when it derailed. Davis, who was riding in the tender, was thrown into the locomotive and killed instantly.

Getting down to business, B&O scheduled two trains a day each way between Baltimore and Washington. Their overall average speed was 18 m.p.h.—including local stops and the horse transfer down Pratt Street at Baltimore—making the total running time two hours. Business was hearteningly healthy, particularly in comparison with B&O's main line at the time; an average of over 200 passengers a day rode the two daily trains during 1836. Not surprisingly, passenger business far outweighed freight—it made up 94% of the total branch revenues in 1836—although Washington slowly developed its unvarying pattern of receiving food, supplies and building materials (in those days, lumber and Patapsco granite) by rail. Washington branch trains also began carrying mail in 1836, which was temporarily lost to stagecoaches a year later. And thanks to the outlandish fare structure, the branch proved instantly profitable. Even after deducting the 20% state "bonus" (which everyone realistically called a tax) B&O made close to a 50% operating profit.

The Washington branch quickly settled down to a basic operating pattern which varied little over the next 25 years, except for the infrequent addition of a new train schedule. But whatever the line lacked in scenic excitement or operational interest, it made up in the erratic but fascinating variety of its passenger traffic—both in quantity and quality. Almost by definition, Washington's only railroad was a different kind of animal from ordinary railroads. Thus although its normal operations tended to be routine, it was subjected to wild gyrations in traffic loads for inaugurations, celebrations and all sorts of special events. Its clientele also tended to be something more than the usual run of railroad passenger. One of the earliest samples of what would occasionally

This idyllic rural scene is now the center of downtown Washington. The view looks northeast from the Capitol at the approximate present location of Union Station Plaza, as it was seen by a contemporary artist in 1839. The train is crossing Tiber Creek on its way to the little house which served as B&O's Washington Terminal. Credit: Library of Congress.

happen to the line came on September 12, 1836. To help several companies of Baltimore militia celebrate an anniversary of the battle of North Point, B&O hauled over a thousand of the "citizen soldiers" with arms and associated baggage to Washington and back. Four Grasshoppers handled the movement, one of which hauled over 300 people and their paraphenalia. Another "typical" Washington branch passenger was the doomed William Henry Harrison, who arrived at the B&O station for his inauguration during a snowstorm in February 1841.

One part of Washington branch operations which did soon change was its motive power. With their short wheelbases and small geared drivers, the little grasshoppers were well suited to digging in and hauling loads around the tight turns of the main line. But these same qualities were liabilities on the fast and easy Washington line, which hardly needed a gutty, slow, switcher-type of engine. In April 1837 B&O received its first Norris 4-2-0, a conventional horizontal-boiler design with a single pair of 48-inch drivers. Named the "Lafayette," it was heavier (at 10 tons), faster than the Grasshoppers and more stable at speed, although its single driving axle limited its hauling capacity. The "Lafayette" was far more suited to the Washington branch, and in mid and late 1838 three more similar "One Armed Billys" arrived from Norris to displace the Grasshoppers. Afterwards Washington trains were usually hauled by the "Billys" supplemented later by light 4-4-0's.

"One Armed Billys" such as this were far better suited to the easy grades and wide curves of the Washington branch than the little Grasshoppers.

As expected, the east coast rail network developed quickly, if not completely, with the Washington branch as its southern leg. In 1838 the Philadelphia, Wilmington & Baltimore started service between Baltimore and Philadelphia, initially using B&O's Pratt Street station in Baltimore. By 1840 an all-rail route had been completed from Philadelphia to Jersey City, opposite New York. With a river ferry at the Susquehanna and over-street transfers at Baltimore and Philadelphia, it was hardly a true through route—but at least it was now possible to get between Washington and New York by rail.

With the Washington branch open, Annapolis saw its chance to get a railroad, too. Despite B&O's relationship with the state of Maryland, it had justifiably little interest in reaching the state capital itself. But in 1837 local interests organized a company called the Annapolis & Elk Ridge Rail Road to connect the small city with the Washington branch. Although its name implied a terminal at Elk Ridge—just south of the Thomas viaduct and, at that time, head of navigation on the Patapsco— the railroad ended up picking a site eight miles farther south for its junction with B&O. The location, called Annapolis Junction (now Fort Meade Junction), was on a level section of the Washington branch between Jessup's Cut and the Little Patuxent at Savage; essentially it was a classic "middle of nowhere" spot. Presumably Annapolis Junction was chosen since it allowed the Annapolis & Elk Ridge to build the shortest and most topographically favorable route to Annapolis; it also put the railroad almost midway between Baltimore and Washington, making it equally convenient to reach from either city. Unfortunately, it also made it equally inconvenient, since it offered a direct route to neither place.

Be that as it may, the A&ER began building in the early summer of 1838 and started operations on Christmas Day, 1840. Two eight-ton woodburners, four passenger cars, two baggage cars and some freight cars constituted its entire roster. The 20-mile line met B&O trains at Annapolis Junction and, in later years, B&O operated through passenger schedules between Baltimore and Annapolis with connecting runs from Washington. Basically a plodding rural railroad, the Annapolis & Elk Ridge led a marginal life; after a costly and unproductive dalliance with a long extension toward Drum Point it was reorganized in 1886 as the Annapolis, Washington & Baltimore Railroad. A year later the new competitive Annapolis & Baltimore Short Line was opened over a direct route between Baltimore and Annapolis, using B&O's Camden station and B&O track to reach it. Afterwards, B&O's traffic relations with the AW&B soured and through runs ceased. However, the railroad did remain as a connection for Washington and an alternate, albeit circuitous, route from Baltimore. By that time the AW&B also connected with the Pennsylvania's Washington line at Odenton.

Through the 1840's the Washington branch's problems were less operational than political. The high state-set fare began causing competitive problems, not the least of which was the stimulation of lower-cost steamship services between Baltimore and southern points. One important southern railroad, the Richmond, Fredericksburg & Potomac—which at that time operated a combination rail-steamboat service between Richmond and Washington—attempted to work through a Baltimore-Washington stagecoach line in order to offer a fare which would allow it to compete with the Baltimore steamboats. Through this and other pressures, the Baltimore-Washington railroad fare was gradually whittled down to something more reasonable, although the state still took its full 20% off the top.

Besides handling crowds, soldiers and various types of dignitaries, the Washington branch occasionally found itself in another unusual role. Because of its nearness and visibility to legislators and government officials, it was used to show off hopeful new inventions in communications and transportation. The first and most famous of these was arranged in 1844, when Samuel F.B. Morse approached J.H.B. Latrobe, Benjamin's brother, with the idea of stringing a wire along the railroad between Baltimore and Washington to demonstrate his new telegraph. Both Latrobes were enthusiastic about the idea and agreed to help. Using an appropriation from Congress, Morse laid his line—partly in a trench, partly on poles—and on May 24, 1844, "What hath God wrought" was received at B&O's Pratt Street station.

After 1840 Annapolis Junction blossomed into a major station. By the 1860's, when this photo was made, two hotels had been established to take care of passengers transferring between Baltimore, Washington and Annapolis. Credit: B&O Museum Archives.

Considerably less successful—in fact not successful at all—was another demonstration seven years later by Dr. Charles G. Page, senior patent examiner for the Patent Office, professor of chemistry and pharmacy and scientific generalist. Page had become fascinated by the possibilities of applying electricity to motive power and, through Sen. Thomas Hart Benton of Missouri, had managed to get a $20,000 Congressional appropriation in much the same manner as Morse. With it he developed a motor and system of batteries which were put into an experimental locomotive. The locomotive looked deceptively conventional: Its running gear was basically an ordinary 4-2-0 steam layout and its superstructure consisted of a truncated coach body, giving it the look of a later 19th Century inspection engine. But inside the coach/cab body was a massive (and very fragile) set of batteries and the electric motor.

By that point Page had used up his appropriation and then some—and had also lost his political support. Unready but left with little choice, Page arranged a demonstration trip of his electric locomotive from Washington to Baltimore in the hope of convincing the government to put up more money for his work.

As it was, poor Page almost didn't make it that far. Reported the Washington *National Intelligencer* on April 3, 1851:

"The eleven o'clock train from Baltimore yesterday got on the wrong track and drove into the house occupied by Prof. Page's electro-magnetic locomotive. How much damage was done is not ascertained, but the conflict and crash was tremendous. Fortunately no person was injured, though fences, doors and timbers flew in all directions. One curious freak was performed; the box or casing of a carboy of acid was entirely stripped off without breaking the carboy."

Apparently the engine escaped this act of mechanical aggression along with the carboy. Three weeks later, on April 29, 1851 the Page locomotive pulled out of Washington heading for Baltimore. Onlookers were undoubtedly impressed by the lack of smoke and steam—but unfortunately there was little performance either. The effects of the track and motion of the running gear began to disintegrate the batteries; between this and other mechanical problems, Page took 39 minutes to cover the five miles to Bladensburg, reaching a top speed of 19 m.p.h. At Bladensburg the rapidly deteriorating batteries forced him to abort the trip and he headed back to Washington. By that time the batteries were so weakened that it took two hours to make it.

The demonstration was not just a mechanical failure. Even assuming the batteries could be made more rugged and the power transmission more workable, everyone was convinced—correctly in this case—that battery-generated electric motive power simply was too costly and too limited in its power output. And even now, almost 130 years later and in a era of satellites and space probes, the commercial economics of heavy-output battery power remain elusive. The Page locomotive disappeared and it was not until the development of centrally-generated power transmitted through overhead wires or third rail that electric motive power became practical. But be that as it may, the disasterous demonstration at least gave B&O another "first"—the first electric locomotive to operate on an American railroad.

One physical disaster did occur to the Washington branch which began the slow process of turning the original "stone railroad" into an "iron railroad." On October 7, 1847 a severe flood washed out the 50-foot single arch stone bridges over the Little Patuxent at Savage and over the Northwest Branch of the Potomac at Bladensburg, as well as several stone culverts. The two bridges were temporarily patched with timber trestling; in 1850 both had been replaced by the first examples of a new iron truss design invented by Wendel Bollman, B&O's Master of Road. These two single-span Bollman trusses (the Savage bridge measured 76 feet; Bladensburg's length is unknown, but about the same size) were the forerunners of a unique breed of bridge which multiplied across the B&O system over the next 25 years. Each had granite towers at the ends, supporting the mass of iron rods; their cost averaged $20,000 each.

B&O's Washington terminal at New Jersey Avenue and C Street as it originally looked before an 1873 street regrading and an 1889 addition to the building. This handsome Italianate station was built in 1850-52 to replace a boardinghouse at 2nd and Pennsylvania Avenue which served as B&O's first station in the city. Credit: William F. Smith collection.

By 1849 three passenger trains a day were running each way over the branch. Despite the faster 4-2-0's and 4-4-0's they still took two hours to make the trip—because of the Pratt Street transfer in Baltimore, a slow route in and out of Washington and many local stops along the way. In addition, one freight was scheduled each way between Mt. Clare yard and Washington, plus an additional freight running only between Mt. Clare and White Oak Bottom (near Muirkirk) to serve several textile mills and iron furnaces on the northern section of the line. By then there were two cotton mills at Laurel—the Laurel Factory and Avondale Mill—plus the nearby Savage mill. The Patuxent Iron Works near Annapolis Junction received limestone by rail from the north and shipped its iron back out north. Another ironworks had been established near Muirkirk. Through the late 1840's, five locomotives took care of all normal Washington branch service—three Norris "One Armed Billys" dating to 1837-38 and two early New Castle 4-4-0's, the "Arrow" of 1840 and the "New Castle" built in 1846.

With the completion of the New Jersey Avenue station in Washington in 1851-52 (Chapter 15 covers it in detail) service was again increased. On March 1, 1852 a new round trip was added, giving the branch four passenger trains each way, now including an early morning express. Thanks to the new Washington station, the establishment of the temporary Camden station in Baltimore in 1853 and the addition of the express schedule, it was possible by 1854 to get between Baltimore and Washing-

Relay in 1858. The train at right is westbound on the main line. Credit: Maryland Historical Society.

ton in an hour and a half. Unfortunately, that particular schedule required leaving Baltimore at 4:15 a.m., but the other trains covered the distance in anywhere from an hour and 45 minutes to an hour and 55 minutes.

And by the mid 1850's these trains were carrying greater numbers of people travelling through to Philadelphia or New York and to southern points. Going north they used the PW&B connection in Baltimore; south, the Orange & Alexandria from Alexandria or a boat connection with the Richmond, Fredericksburg & Potomac through Aquia Creek, Va., south of Quantico. During 1856, for example, B&O carried almost 50,000 Philadelphia and New York passengers to and from Washington—15% of the line's total passenger load. Close to 33,000 others—another 10%—went between Baltimore and cities south of Washington. Not surprisingly, the number of passengers travelling strictly between Baltimore and Washington was large—119,000, or 36% of the branch's business. But not so obviously, a heavy proportion of traffic was purely local, getting off or on the trains at way points between the two cities. Over 121,000 passengers during the year fell into this category, 37% of the total. Some of them, incidentally, were regularly riding to work in Baltimore and Washington with reduced fare tickets—the dawn of commuter travel on B&O. A paltry 3,237 passengers (1%) rode between Washington and western points on B&O's main line—evidence enough of the lack of relationship between B&O's two lines out of Baltimore. Most of these passengers rode the Washington branch as far as Relay House, transferring there to and from the western trains. Those with the stamina could catch the 6:00 a.m. train from Washington, have breakfast at Relay House and climb onto the morning Baltimore-Wheeling train. Others preferred to take the late afternoon train up the previous day and spend the night at Relay House.

Bladensburg station about 1870. The little station on the left was built in 1869. The stop is now Hyattsville. Credit: B&O Museum Archives.

So by the eve of the Civil War the Washington branch was a well-built but not overburdened single-track line carrying about a 60%-40% mixture of through and local passenger business on its four daily trains. By 1859 its locomotive roster had expanded to a grand total of seven engines—two for freight and five for passenger—most of which were new, fast and handsome. The passenger roster consisted of three William Mason eight-wheelers built between 1856 and 1859, including No. 25—the engine now on display at the B&O Museum as the "William Mason"; there was also an 1859 Taunton 4-4-0 and an 1854 Norris "Dutch Wagon" in passenger service. Freights were hauled by a new Tyson ten-wheeler and an 1852 New Castle 4-4-0. Altogether, it was an attractive little self-contained railroad.

As an interesting sidelight, about 1860 B&O's president John W. Garrett became involved in what was a fairly routine situation for someone in his position: a plea for financial aid in building a locally-promoted feeder line. In this case it was a projected railroad running considerably east of the Washington branch into the tobacco-growing country of southern Maryland. Back in 1853 a group of plantation owners had incorporated a company called the Baltimore & Potomac Railroad with the hope of building from Baltimore to Pope's Creek, Md., a small

The south end of the Thomas Viaduct looked like this in 1905 when company photographers were doing a publicity series on the Washington-New York "Royal Blue Line" trains. The white-gowned ladies wave from an eastbound which has just cleared the old Lawyers Hill Road grade crossing. Credit: Smithsonian Institution.

Potomac River port in southern Charles county about 32 miles to the southeast of Washington. Lacking much financial support or any substantial traffic prospects from the thinly-populated rural reaches of Prince George's and Charles counties, the B&P could not even start surveying its line until 1859. In 1860 it managed to get a ten-year extension of its charter and approached B&O for help. Garrett was hardly impressed either; the B&P's passenger potential was marginal at best and the major freight commodity, tobacco, moved out mostly by water from river ports such as Pope's Creek. So B&O declined to buy any stock and the B&P continued to languish unbuilt and largely unmourned—but its charter remained active. Garrett was certainly correct about the commercial potential of any railroad between Baltimore and Pope's Creek, as was amply proved later. Unfortunately, however, his lawyers did not check that charter carefully. The oversight proved monumentally costly to B&O, later setting off a chain of events that would alter the entire railroad geography of the east.

The Washington branch's semi-stepchild status suddenly ended in April 1861. As the only railroad between the Federal capital and any place in the north—and with Washington right on the frontier of the fighting—the line was instantly deluged with military traffic, plus the inevitable loads of civilians scurrying in and out of Washington for

The New Jersey Avenue station looks like the horn of plenty in this slightly exaggerated Civil War scene, but the crowds that were crammed through the terminal were very real. Note the single-stall brick engine house on the far left. Credit: B&O Museum Archives.

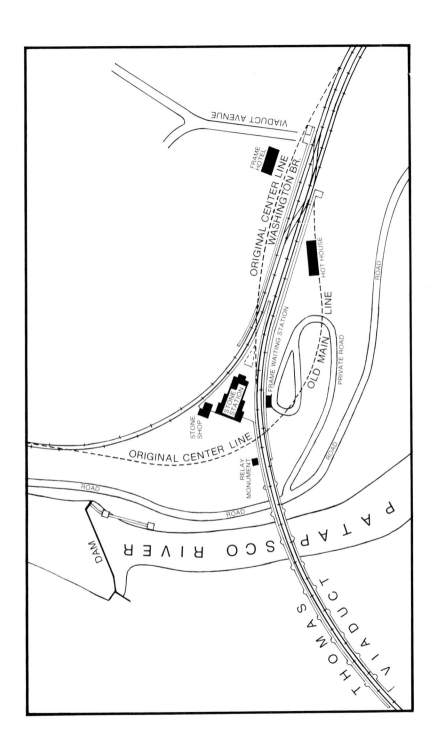

A.

Concurrent with the double-tracking of the Washington branch in 1864, the junction with the main line at Relay was completely realigned and rebuilt. The map shows the original layout in dashed lines. Note that the original main line swung to the southeast of the present line in order to avoid the large hillside. When the Washington branch was built in 1835, if left the main line on the northwest side, near the Relay House, and crossed over it onto the Thomas Viaduct. (A) The photo looks south after the reconstruction, with the Washington branch and the viaduct on the left and main line on the right. Part of the hillside had been cut away to accommodate the main line, which originally was located on the far side. In the early 1870's the rocks in the center and at the left were blasted away to provide the site for the new Viaduct Hotel-station. Credit: Enoch Pratt Free Library.

various reasons. During the period when Washington's only other life-line, the Potomac River, was blockaded, inbound freight shipments surged from a prewar average of 6-10 cars a day to 450. Fortunately, unlike the main line, the Washington branch physically was only mildly molested during the war—mostly in July 1864 during Jubal Early's abortive encirclement of Washington. During the four years of the Civil War, essentially it was the Washington branch that carried the loads while the main line got battered.

Carrying these loads was an immense problem for a line which had not been built either for the traffic volume or some of the directional flows. Not only was it still single track, but that track still consisted mostly of the original 40 lb. iron rail laid on wood stringers. The immediate priority was to replace the track structure; between 1862 and 1863 the old rail was pulled out and the track entirely relaid with 60 lb. iron rail resting directly on heavy ties. Double-tracking was started shortly afterwards, often interrupted by the necessity to move the work forces to Harpers Ferry and other main line points to rebuild the damage there. Erratically during 1864 double tracking was completed all the way from Relay to Washington; at the same time the rock ledge at Relay was blasted out, the main line realigned, the junction trackwork rearranged to eliminate an awkward crossing and a Y track installed to allow trains to move directly between the western main line and the Washington branch.

In the middle of the reconstruction project, another flood swept out the last remaining large stone arch bridge on the branch. On July 13, 1863 the single span over the Big Patuxent at Laurel was destroyed. Like the previous flood victims at Savage and Bladensburg, it was replaced with a single-span Bollman truss in 1864. After this all the large bridges on the branch were iron Bollmans, some of them twin spans to carry the double track; a few smaller stone arches and culverts survived from the original line and two of these may still be seen in something close to their original form.

223

TIME TABLE

For WASHINGTON BRANCH PASSENGER & TONNAGE TRAIN

TO TAKE EFFECT MONDAY, APRIL 23, 1855.

TRAINS FROM BALTIMORE.

LEAVE	Miles.	Passenger TRAIN No. 1.	Passenger TRAIN No. 2.	Passenger TRAIN No. 3.	Passenger TRAIN No. 4.	Tonnag
Camden Station, . .	0	4 15 A. M.	9 15 A. M.	3 00 P. M.	5 15 P. M.	
Mount Clare Junction,	1	4 25 "	9 25 "	3 10 "	5 25 "	4 30 A.
Relay H. (Wash. Junc.)	8	4 40 "	9 40 " P	3 25 "	5 40 " P	5 25 "
Jessop's Cut, East End,	15	4 50 ".	9 50 "	3 35 "	5 56 "	
Annapolis Junction, .	17	5 00 "	10 05 "	3 50 " P	6 05 "	6 55 "
Watson's Cut, E. End,	20					
W. Oak Pottom, E. End,	23½	....	10 20 "	4 05 "		
Beltsville, ...	26	....	10 28 "	4 13 "		7 45 "
Paint Branch, . .	30					8 05 "
Bladensburg, . . .	33	....	10 45 "	4 30 " P	....	8 25 "
Washington City, .	38	5 45 "	11 05 "	4 55 "	6 55 "	9 00 "

TRAINS TOWARDS BALTIMORE

LEAVE	Miles.	Passenger TRAIN No 1.	Passenger TRAIN No. 2.	Passenger TRAIN No. 3.	Passenger TRAIN No. 4.	Tonnage
Washington City, . .	0	6 00 A. M.	8 30 A. M.	3 00 P. M.	4 30 P. M.	11 00 A.
Bladensburg, ...	5	....	8 40 " T	3 10 "	4 40 " P	
Paint Branch, . . .	8		8 47 "	--.....	4 47 "	11 45 "
Beltsville, . . .	12	....	8 55 "	3 25 "	4 55 "	12 10 P. M
W. Oak Bottom, W. End	14½					
Watson's Cut, W. End,	18					
Watson's Cut, E. End,	19½					
Annapolis Junction, .	21	6 55 " T	9 20 "	3 50 " P	5 15 "	1 05 "
Jessop's Cut, East End,	24	....	9 26 "	4 05 "		
Relay H. (Wash. Junc.)	30	7 20 "	9 40 " P	4 10 "	5 35 ")	2 00 "
Mount Clare Junction,	37	7 35 "	9 55 "	4 25 "	5 50 " } P	2 40 "
Camden Station, . .	38	7 45 "	10 05 "	4 40 "	6 00 "	

Passenger Train No. 1 from Washington and Tonnage Train from Baltimore, will meet at Annapolis Junction at 6 55 A. M.

Passenger Train No. 2 from Washington and Tonnage No. 1 from Baltimore, will pass at Bladensburg, at 8 40 A. M.

Passenger Train No. 2 from Baltimore and No. 2 from Washington, meet at Washington Junction at 9 40 A. M.

Passenger Train No. 3 from Baltimore and No. 3 from Washington, will meet at Annapolis Junction at 3 50 P. M.

Passenger Train No. 4 from Washington, will pass No. 3. from Baltimore at Bladensburg, at 4 40 P. M. No. 3 from Baltimore keeping out of the way of No. 4, which is Express, stopping only at Annapolis Junction and Washington Junction.

No. 4 will not wait the 15 minutes for No. 3 at Bladensburg.

☞ *Conductors will notice this Exception particularly.*

Passenger Train No. 4 from Baltimore and No. 4 from Washington, will meet at Washington Junction at 5 40 P. M.

Tonnage from Washington must *stop* before reaching *Mount Clare Junction,* to see that the Coal Trains are all out of the way, and the switches all right. The Tonnage will arrive and depart from Mount Clare as usual.

Tonnage from Baltimore must cross the Main Stem at the Relay House, (Washington Junction,) with extreme care.

Between Trains of the same class going in opposite directions the following rule will be observed, viz: A Train arriving duly at a regular meeting place, shall wait *fifteen minutes* beyond its own time of leaving; in case of the non-arrival of the train expected to be met, it may then proceed carefully, provided it keep fifteen minutes beyond card time, and approach each siding very carefully, the delayed train keeping out of the way. [See Exception between No. 3 and 4.]

For Trains arranged to meet on the double track, the south-west end of that track shall be regarded as the waiting place of the Train bound to Washington.

All Trains will leave Baltimore and Washington promptly, and proceed by card time, though Trains of the same class then due, have not arrived, and the delayed Trains must avoid them. [See Exception below.]

On reaching Washington Junction, (Relay House,) from Washington, be sure to learn what Trains have preceded you, and how long they have been gone, before you proceed—mark and observe the Time Book Rules—the thirteenth in particular.

☞ In case the 4 15 A. M. Train from Baltimore does not arrive in Washington by 6 A. M., the 6 A. M. Train from Washington shall hold back until 6 15 A. M.

Scenery, industry, opulence and spectacular engineering all coex-
isted at Relay for many years. In this late 1870's scene looking north
from Elkridge, Hockley's grist mill is in the foreground and, at the
opposite end of the Thomas Viaduct, the Viaduct Hotel-Station with
its small but carefully landscaped grounds. Note the siding, box
cars, and loading chute serving the mill and the long-abandoned
road crossing in the foreground. The mill is now gone but the
adjoining house still stands. Credit: C.S. Roberts collection

IMPOSSIBLE CHALLENGE

CHAPTER 11

THE WASHINGTON BRANCH IN A NEW WORLD: 1865-1979

By the time the Washington branch had emerged from the war it had grown up considerably. Although its wartime traffic quickly vaporized (passenger volume in 1866 was half what it was in 1865), the city and the territory had matured; in addition, genuine through interline services were being operated. Beginning in December 1863 through passenger cars were run between Washington and Jersey City, although still slowed by the Susquehanna River ferry and the horse-operated Baltimore and Philadelphia street trackage. Garrett had also begun to develop ambitions of controlling a southern railroad system and started buying control of the Orange & Alexandria Railroad in 1866. A year later the O&A had merged with the Manassas Gap Railroad to form the Orange, Alexandria & Manassas; it then reached from Alexandria, Va. (five miles south of Washington) to Harrisonburg and Lynchburg, Va. Connections at Lynchburg extended deeper south to Bristol, Knoxville, Chattanooga and Memphis. After the war B&O had been given rights to operate the government-built Long Bridge over the Potomac at Washington, giving Garrett the ability to schedule through passenger cars from Baltimore to Lynchburg.

Also in 1866 Garrett had started work on the long-debated Metropolitan branch between Washington and B&O's western main line at Point of Rocks. This line would give the capital a direct route west and would also enable B&O to route its main-line passenger trains through Washington by running them around the triangle legs formed by the Washington branch and the Metropolitan branch. (Chapter 12 tells the Metropolitan branch's story.) At the same time B&O's expansive president was planning B&O extensions to Pittsburg (as it was then spelled) and to Chicago.

All of these projects took time to accomplish, but one thing was immediately clear: The post Civil War life of the Washington branch promised to be radically different from the uncluttered and somewhat isolated prewar days. In the truest sense the war was the Washington branch's watershed. In the ten years after 1865 its traffic flow would change, its volumes would dramatically increase, its relationship to B&O's main line would be altered, and — unhappily — its competitive situation would completely turn about.

Indeed, it was a different world for the entire B&O system. All things considered, the 30 years following the Civil War were not especially happy ones for the railroad. Business increased, to be sure, and the railroad did expand to many strategic terminals in the midwest. But the competition expanded too. And in B&O's case, the major competition was among the smartest, toughest and most aggressive in the business — the Pennsylvania Railroad. Under the shy but shrewd and brilliant J. Edgar Thomson and the aggressive, freewheeling Thomas A. Scott — president and senior vice president, respectively — the PRR was moving quickly and decisively to make itself the largest and strongest railroad in the country. The virtues and shortcomings of John W. Garrett, who headed B&O through the most critical of these years (he was president from 1858 to his death in 1884), are beyond our scope here. But judging strictly by the end results, he simply was not in the same league as Thomson, Scott and one of their rising young lieutenants, Alexander J. Cassatt.

B&O's Baltimore-Washington territory provided a perfect example of how the hapless railroad was outmaneuvered. Back in 1860 Thomson had begun buying control of the Northern Central Railway, the successor of

A 4-4-0 and new ten-wheeler roll a heavy Washington express at an unknown location in 1910. Credit: Smithsonian Institution.

the Baltimore & Susquehanna, which connected Baltimore with the Pennsylvania's main line at Harrisburg, Pa. (Amazingly, in the process Thomson picked up a large amount of NC stock formerly owned by Garrett.) By 1861 the Northern Central was controlled by the Penn, although not fully owned. Working through the NC, Pennsy could now directly challenge B&O for western traffic right in B&O's home town.

The Pennsylvania may have settled into Baltimore, but from Baltimore to Washington B&O was assured a comfortable monopoly by virtue of the 1833 state aid legislation. Maryland would not grant a charter to any other Baltimore-Washington line. In addition, the company operating the Baltimore-Philadelphia rail line, the PW&B, was independent and worked closely with B&O on through passenger and freight traffic between Washington and the large eastern seaboard cities to the north. Secure in its position but sensing trouble, B&O determined that it would not help the Pennsylvania get any Washington business through Baltimore and the Northern Central. It refused to sell through passenger tickets or interchange freight between Washington and PRR points.

Allegedly it was this rebuff that, after the war, prompted the Pennsylvania to look for ways of building its own line from Baltimore to Washington. Perhaps so, but unquestionably it would have gone ahead anyway. Scott, especially, also had his eyes on expanding into the south and Washington was the obvious gateway. The problem, of course, was Maryland's implied pledge not to grant a charter to a competitive railroad. How it was solved — and what happened afterwards — clearly showed how the Pennsylvania became the powerful company that it did.

Thomson's lawyers quickly picked up what Garrett had missed six years before: The already-existing charter of the unbuilt Baltimore & Potomac — spurned by B&O in 1860 — contained a provision allowing it to build branches up to 20 miles long *at any point and in any direction*. The B&P's projected route between Baltimore and Pope's Creek passed through Prince Georges county to the east of Washington. By building the line by way of present-day Bowie, a branch could be run into Washington in less than 20 miles. At that point, unlike Garrett, the Pennsylvania was positively delighted to help the tobacco farmers build their railroad. In 1866 a group of ostensibly private individuals made a contract to finance and build the Baltimore & Potomac and in 1867 they obtained rights to build their "branch" into the District of Columbia. Also in 1867 the Pennsylvania Railroad officially took over the B&P financing and construction contract and began building.

The Pennsy had its own problems with its Washington line. B&O was able to stir up enough local opposition at least to slow the process of property acquisition and construction, if not stop it. It also had a serious engineering problem in Baltimore: Again, the city's built-up downtown area and hilly environs precluded any cheap and easy connection between the Northern Central's line, which followed Jones Falls valley into the city from the north, and the B&P/Washington branch running out to the southwest. Pennsy was finally forced to dig around Baltimore's northwest

John W. Garrett's Viaduct Hotel-Station at Relay forms an atmospheric backdrop for handsome A-3 Atlantic 1436 with a Washington-bound local about 1935. A deadhead diner, probably just shopped, is cut in ahead of the usual combine. Credit: H. W. Pontin; H. H. Harwood collection.

outskirts with a string of three closely-connected tunnels and deep cuts — which turned out to be difficult to build and, afterwards, even worse to operate.

Between one obstruction and another the B&P/PRR Washington line was not opened until July 2, 1872. Even then it operated only from Washington to a temporary terminal on the far west side of Baltimore with no operable rail connection into town. (The B&P's "main line" to Pope's Creek, built only because it had to be built, opened in January 1873.) It was exactly one year more — July 1, 1873 — before Pennsy's Washington trains could come all the way into the new Baltimore union station on Charles Street south of North Ave. By this time Pennsy had also built a new line — which included another long tunnel — around the northeast side of Baltimore to reach the Philadelphia, Wilmington & Baltimore's Philadelphia line near present-day Highlandtown. Although the PW&B still remained independent, this connecting line allowed the Pennsylvania to offer a direct service between Washington, Philadelphia and New York — as pointedly distinguished from B&O's horse-hauled Pratt Street transfer to the PW&B. Pennsy's new east side connection also enabled it to reach the Canton waterfront on the east side of Baltimore harbor, where it could develop a large export-import terminal to compete with B&O's Locust Point.

On its way south from Baltimore, Pennsy's Washington branch passed under the B&O main line at Halethorpe, then paralleled B&O's Washington branch several miles to the east. Its route passed through an undeveloped area that for a century after would be less populated and less industrialized than B&O's territory to the west. On the other hand, it lay east of the low hills which gave the B&O line its many graceful curves, making it straighter and potentially faster. Entering Washington it followed the Eastern Branch (Anacostia River) through Bennings, then swung across the river into southeast Washington. As a gesture of both its power and political influence, it laid its line straight across the Mall, ending at a large, towered brick terminal and trainshed at 6th and B Sts., N.W.

The Pennsylvania's entry into Washington meant more than just the intrusion of a competitor into what had been a B&O monopoly. As soon as Thomson and Scott had legally cleared their route into Washington, they moved quickly to control the strategic gateway to the southern railroad network — such as it was. Working through their staunch ally, Senator Simon Cameron of Pennsylvania, they managed to get Congress to evict B&O from the Long Bridge over the Potomac — the only direct rail link to the Virginia railroads — and give Pennsy the rights instead. Pennsy also bought the short Alexandria & Washington Railroad and in 1872 extended it south to Quantico, Va. to join the Richmond, Fredericksburg & Potomac. This not only gave the Pennsylvania direct rail connections with most of the south but at the same time deftly cut B&O off from its own Virginia affiliate, the Orange, Alexandria & Manassas. Ironically, in 1872 — the same year Pennsy completed its coup — Garrett was able to announce that he had completed obtaining stock control of the OA&M.

John Garrett raged helplessly, but Thomson and Scott had plainly scored a major and permanent victory. They had not only broken B&O's Washington monopoly, but had pre-empted B&O at the only eastern gateway to the south. Given the economic state of the south after the Civil War and the volume of north-south traffic at the time, Pennsy's victory was more moral than immediately profitable. But as the years went on it dominated a growing business, a position which continues today under Conrail and Amtrak, even if in diminished circumstances. Afterwards B&O did the best it could to find alternatives — first with the semi-successful Alexandria branch in 1874 (Chapter 13), then an extension of the Shenandoah Valley branch, the abortive Quantico extension (Chapter 14) and various other interline arrangements. But it was not until it was allowed to participate in Potomac Yard in 1906 under Pennsy's sufferance (and dependent on Pennsy for trackage rights) that it was back in a competitive position. But by then the PRR had absorbed the PW&B and made itself dominant in the entire area from New York to Washington. It operated all of the through passenger services between the east coast and the south, and thanks to the strategic industrial position of its east coast lines, it had a large part of the freight business. Of course, by then B&O also had its own line to Philadelphia and an excellent working route to Jersey City through the Reading and Central Railroad of New Jersey, but B&O's line was commercially weaker.

Operationally, however, B&O's Washington branch was never busier and it would get more so. The completion of the Metropolitan branch on May 25, 1873 not only added another line into B&O's Washington terminal but, as planned, it changed the main line passenger routings. Afterwards all through passenger trains between Baltimore and Cincinnati, St. Louis, Chicago, Pittsburgh and Wheeling were added in between the growing number of Baltimore-Washington runs.

Between these new main line services and the general growth of Washington as a city, the branch simply kept adding passenger trains. In June 1868, seven round trips operated between Washington and Baltimore, plus two more between Washington and Annapolis Junction. Less than ten years later service had more than doubled. In May 1876, 16 Baltimore-Washington trains were scheduled each way, which included three through western trains. In addition, several odd short-turn trains shuttled between specific points: one round trip operated the six miles between Washington and Alexandria Junction (Hyattsville), where the new Alexandria branch joined the line. An early morning accommodation train (most likely a milk run) ran northbound-only from Laurel to Baltimore. And one southbound-only schedule took passenger cars from Baltimore to Shepherd's Landing on the Alexandria branch. Northbound the cars were picked up at Alexandria Junction by a local out of Washington. In addition, a short-lived direct Virginia Midland Ry. connection was also operating over the Alexandria branch in 1876 (see Chapter 13 again); cars to and from this train were dropped and picked up at Alexandria Junction by one of the through trains each way. Two scheduled freights also ran each way between Baltimore and Washington.

Passenger running times had also improved over the casual pre-Civil War days: Expresses now made the trip in an hour and ten minutes; all-stops locals took, at worst, an hour and 40 minutes.

To handle this traffic and some of the special intermediate work that had to be done at junctions, some offbeat operating moves had to be made. For example, the 1876 operating timetable had this sampling of special instructions for certain southbound trains:

> "Train 74 will use south (i.e., northbound) track from Alexandria Junction to Washington to let 76 pass."

> "Train 98 will use south track from Hanover to Annapolis Junction to let 60 (another southbound) pass."

> "Train 10 will take Shepherd cars to Relay and give them to 50."

> "Train 50 will get Shepherd cars from 10 at Relay and use south track from Relay to Hockley's Mill (south end of Thomas viaduct)."

There were several others, and northbound trains had similar complications. Crews on many specific trains were admonished to watch out for an opposing movement on their track.

An immediate casualty of the Civil War was the cosy practice of keeping Washington branch locomotives and cars on their own roster — wartime traffic demanded anything that would move, regardless of where it came from. After the war the complications merely increased. Through passenger car operations fanned out north, west and south; locomotives were interchanged between the Washington branch, Metropolitan branch and main line as needed.

Another relic of the older days — in this case the bad old days — had died with the Pennsylvania's successful invasion of Washington. After a legal struggle, B&O managed to remove the now-hated 20% passenger receipts tax taken by the state. The court case dragged on several years, but the relief was made retroactive to July 1872 when Pennsy trains first started running. However, the Washington branch remained a separate financial entity under the terms of the original law. The state may have reluctantly given up its 20%, but it still held its stock and expected normal operating dividends. So B&O continued to keep separate income and capital investments accounts for the line and make dividend payments based on the branch's earnings.

Passenger schedules were in a turmoil through much of the 1870's and '80's as competitive conditions changed and B&O floundered around with various through routes to off-line points. Early in 1874 the Alexandria branch had been completed from a spot called Alexandria Junction, just north of Hyattsville station, to Shepherd's Landing, opposite Alexandria on the east side of the Potomac. As more fully explained in Chapter 13, the branch was a desperation attempt to keep a rail connection with the Orange, Alexandria & Manassas (later to become the Virginia Midland); although primarily built as a freight route, B&O tried to operate through passenger cars over the line briefly during 1875 and 1876, and possibly afterwards. But in 1881, overextended and blocked by his competition anyway, Garrett sold B&O's control of the railroad and gave up any more attempts at a through passenger service over that route. By then the Pennsylvania was handling all through southern runs directly through its Washington station and over the Long Bridge.

Similarly, the long-traditional through passenger route between Washington and Philadelphia and New York began to wobble as the Pennsylvania moved to tie down that service, too. Although the PW&B was very much an independent company during the 1870's, Pennsy had persuaded it to set up a competitive Washington-Philadelphia-New York service in 1873, operating through Pennsy's direct Baltimore connection. To keep its own PW&B connection competitive, B&O had to overcome the liability of the tedious Pratt Street transfer. In 1880 it rerouted the Washington-Philadelphia trains through its Locust Point (Baltimore) marine terminal, floating the cars across the harbor to the PW&B. This necessitated splitting the Washington branch passenger schedules, since the Philadelphia runs now bypassed Camden station and could not serve downtown Baltimore passengers. Some Philadelphia schedules carried a Camden dropoff (or pickup) car which would be switched off and on at the Bailey's junction in Baltimore. But in another deft coup (this one partially engineered by A.J. Cassatt), the Pennsylvania snatched the PW&B out from Garrett's grasp in 1881. Afterwards, the end of any B&O-operated through Washington-Philadelphia-New York services was simply a matter of time. The time came in October 1884, and for several years B&O was back to just a Baltimore railroad. It completed its own Philadelphia line in late 1886 and again could offer a more-or-less competitive service, which was greatly improved in 1895 with the inauguration of the deluxe "Royal Blue Line" trains to Jersey City.

But although the timetables may have varied, visibly there was little change in Washington branch operations — except for the inevitable increases in the number of trains. Many physical improvements also appeared during the last quarter of the century. By all accounts the line was still largely bare of wayside buildings before and immediately after the Civil War, but as the little communities developed and more money became available, a group of picturesque little stations began to dot the branch. Perhaps because most of the spots were tiny rural communities, B&O was less inclined to invest much in Washington branch structures. Although Garrett had begun B&O on a brick station binge in the mid-1870's, most stations on this line were modest wood structures — typically a little single-story building for passengers and agent, with an even smaller freight house adjoining.

One early brick station was built in 1865 at Paint Branch, an important water station south of present Berwyn. In 1867 wood combination station-dwelling houses were put up at Laurel and College station (College Park). Jessup got a large board-and-batten Gothic-cottage station in 1870; Sunnyside (between Beltsville and Branchville) also had a station built for it that year. A pair of twin single-story stations of an unusual flat-roofed design with a heavy overhang were put up at Bladensburg (Hyattsville) in 1869 and at Beltsville in 1871. And throughout the 1870's a series of attrac-

This unusual station design was built at Beltsville in 1871; similar structures once stood at Bladensburg (Hyattsville) and at Adamstown, Md. on the Old Main Line. Beltsville station was replaced by a much more ordinary standard wood station in 1905. Credit: Smithsonian Institution.

A pot pourri of 1870-era stations along the Washington branch: (A) Muirkirk and its picturesque little freight house. Present U.S. Route 1 now occupies the field behind. (B) College station, now College Park. This 1867 station was replaced in the early 1900's. Note the gingerbreaded outhouse at the end of the platform. (C & D) Hanover and Brentwood were identical designs built in 1872. (E) This somewhat austere station at Annapolis Junction succeeded the collection of hotels and outbuildings shown in Chapter 10. It was built in 1877 and itself replaced in 1917. (F) Elk Ridge station, dating to 1875. The view looks north at the old Washington road crossing. All these photos date to about 1905. Credit (all photos): Smithsonian Institution.

A.

B.

C.

D.

E.

F.

tive little frame "country depots" appeared at such points as Elk Ridge (1875), Hanover (1872), Dorsey (1876), Savage (1875), Annapolis Junction (1877) and Muirkirk (date unknown, but probably mid-1870's). All were simple single story structures of varying sizes (Annapolis Junction was the longest; some others were tiny); some were plain, others had scrollsaw bargeboards and other Victorian decorative touches.

There were two exceptions to the generally run-of-the-mill Washington branch stations, both built slightly later during the memorable outpouring of unique brick buildings designed by Francis Baldwin during the last days of the Garrett administration. In 1884 Baldwin built stations at Hyattsville and Laurel. Both were his typically creative brick variations on Queen Anne style. Hyattsville's had a capped tower and was the larger of the two; Laurel was less lumpily ornate and more original and charming. The two towns were the largest way points on the branch, and the stations replaced small facilities built in the late 1860's. Happily, Laurel still survives to serve commuters — the only station of any type on the line now standing.

B&O also worked with various camp meeting groups in this period to promote picnic and meeting areas along the branch. Although the topography lacked the summer resort appeal of, say, the higher ground west of Washington on the Metropolitan branch, it was pleasant, rolling open countryside — and easily reached from both Baltimore and Washington. In 1881 the railroad built a dancing pavilion at a spot called Irving Park, half a mile north of Annapolis Junction; in 1882 an apparently similar pavilion was put up at Harman's, near Dorsey, for use by the Wayman Grove Camp Meeting Association. Lakeland, a picnic spot on Paint Branch between Berwyn and College Park, also briefly flourished.

But B&O's most unusual venture in promoting resorts in the area involved building a railroad separated from the Washington branch by almost 20 miles. In 1886 the railroad somehow became involved in building a large beach resort on Chesapeake Bay at Bay Ridge, a point of land about four miles south of Annapolis. To reach the resort B&O financed and built a short 4½ mile connecting railroad running from a junction with the Annapolis & Elk Ridge just west of Annapolis to Bay Ridge. (The A&ER had just reorganized as the Annapolis, Washington & Baltimore.) At the same junction outside Annapolis the line also joined the Annapolis Short Line, then under construction. Corporately called the Bay Ridge & Annapolis, the strange little railroad had no equipment of its own; it acted strictly as a route to get excursion trains from Baltimore and Washington into B&O's Bay Ridge resort. The line was opened in August 1886 and flourished at least for a short while — on occasion, over 9,000 people a day came to Bay Ridge on the Bay steamboats and on excursion trains routed over the AW&B and the Annapolis Short Line. But like many Chesapeake Bay resorts, Bay Ridge's popularity was brief. Railroad operation ceased in October 1903 although the line was left intact almost 15 years more. It was finally dismantled for wartime scrap in 1918.

A. Two views of the 1884 Hyattsville station, one of the largest and most ornate on the Washington branch. The track directly in front of the station was used by Chesapeake Beach Railway trains between 1898 and 1913. Credits: A-Smithsonian Institution—B-B&O Museum
B. Archives.

Laurel station was built at the same time as Hyattsville, 1884, and also designed by E. Francis Baldwin. It was still highly active in April 1979 when this photo was made and is the last survivor on the Washington branch—but one of the best anywhere on B&O. Credit: H.H. Harwood, Jr.

A more practical type of branch was built off the Washington line in 1888 to reach the old Savage mill, 1-1/3 miles up the Little Patuxent from the point B&O crossed the river. Since the Washington branch opened in 1835, the mill's output and supplies had to be hauled by wagon between the railroad's Savage station and the little mill town. The branch followed the south side of the river, crossing it next to the mill and immediately dead-ending at the mill's rear. To take the single-track branch over the river, an obsolete 1869 double-track two-span Bollman truss bridge was moved from some main line point and set up at Savage. (The bridge's exact origin has never been documented and may never be. Even its installation date at Savage is open to speculation, since it is possible that the bridge may have come later to replace a temporary trestle.) Because of its backwash location this bridge managed to survive long past the time when B&O had pulled out all the Bollmans on its main line and branches. And as locomotives got heavier, they were banned from the bridge — but because the branch ended on the other side, crews simply used strings of idler freight cars to reach across it to pull or place cars at the mill. Thanks to this operation the railroad never felt the need to replace the bridge and it stands today, the last Bollman truss anywhere and a remarkable engineering relic.

Fourteen years later the Savage branch was extended three miles farther up the Little Patuxent to several granite quarries at Guilford. At the Guilford end it bridged the Little Patuxent again, this time with an ordinary little single-span Pratt through truss (which also still stands there, long bereft of track). This line was completed in 1902, but was not so long-lived; it ceased operation in 1928, although technically kept in service many years after.

For better or worse, by the early 1890's Washington branch passenger service had settled down to the basic patterns which, allowing for improvements in equipment and changes in running times, remained essentially the same through the 1940's. It was a dense pattern. Mid-1893 timetables show a total of 31 passenger trains running each way between Baltimore and Washington — 10 locals, 19 expresses and semi-expresses (which included "Royal Blue Line" trains and western mainliners) and two Washington-Annapolis Junction runs. By this time the expresses needed only 45 to 55 minutes to make the run while the locals, serving some commuters and a rural clientele, took 1½ hours. Scheduled freights still consisted of two a day each way to Washington and an unknown number to Alexandria over the branch. Although the railroad had been routing its western passenger runs over the Washington branch for 20 years by now, normal freight trains between Baltimore or Philadelphia and the west used the Old Main Line and would do so at least for the first 40 years of the 20th Century. Incidentally, to help cope with this mass of trains, B&O had installed an automatic block signal system in 1890-91.

By the beginning of the century the southern end of the Washington line had begun to flower into suburbs, stimulated partly by the frequent B&O steam trains and partly by new trolley lines creeping out from Washington. Attractive wood suburban stations were built during the 1890's at such locations as Langdon (1891), Riverdale (1891) and Branchville (1890). Beginning in 1899, an extension of Washington's Rhode Island Avenue streetcar line worked its way north paralleling the B&O line. It had reached Hyattsville in May 1899 and Berwyn by the fall of 1900; in a burst of overoptimism, it was built through Beltsville to Laurel in 1902 — not so much for the traffic potential in Laurel as a hope of establishing a trolley route to Baltimore. That particular plan went glimmering at Laurel, although the Cleveland-financed Washington, Baltimore & Annapolis did build a fine high-speed Baltimore-Washington line in 1908. The WB&A followed a route to the east of both B&O and Pennsy's Washington branches. Although well-engineered and very fast for an interurban line, it suffered from a long stretch of slow street running in Washington and a shorter one in Baltimore; it thus ended up being more competitive in price than speed.

The last and certainly the largest change to the Washington branch's physical face was the Washington Union Station project of 1903-07, requiring complete realignment of most of the line inside the District. Some of the physical side of this enormous undertaking is told in Chapter 15. Financially, the Union Station project finally triggered the end of the

The new Patuxent, or Savage, branch crossed the Little Patuxent on this recycled Bollman truss, originally built in 1869 and moved here in 1887. The old Savage mill stands behind it at the end of the branch. The mill dates to about 1815—at least 20 years before any railroad was even nearby. March 1969 is the date of the photo, but the scene is the same now. Credit: H.H. Harwood, Jr.

Washington branch as a separate entity. The massive capital requirements for the relocation work and property acquisition, plus B&O's increasing casualness about paying dividends on the Washington branch stock over the previous decade, led the state to launch a formal investigation of the entire arrangement. The outcome was a welcome decision to sell the state's stock in the branch to B&O. This was done in 1906 and at the same time B&O picked up the remaining Washington branch stock in private hands. Thus the unique "subsidiary that wasn't a subsidiary" disappeared and the Washington branch legally became what it had long since operationally become — an integral part of the B&O system.

Another realignment project at the north end of the branch had intermittently started and stopped around the turn of the century. Despite the visual splendor of the Thomas viaduct, the railroad was increasingly unhappy with the alignment of its route over the bridge. The line describes an almost perfect horseshoe curve between Halethorpe and Elkridge, and inside of this is a reverse curve between St. Denis and Relay. The alignment was an 1830's engineering expediency, but once the Washington branch began carrying speeded-up main line passenger traffic in the early

A.

B.

Three suburban stations of the 'Nineties: (A) Langdon, (B) Branch- C.
ville, and (C) Riverdale. The photos were all taken about 1905. Credit
(all): Smithsonian Institution.

1870's this curvy, roundabout alignment became a steadily increasing
operating nuisance. Beginning in 1876 and running through the 1880's
and '90's the railroad quietly picked up property for a direct cutoff line
between Halethorpe and Elkridge, bypassing the viaduct and the series of
curves on either side of it. Interestingly, this would have partly followed
one of Latrobe's alternate alignments of 1832. The complete right of way
was eventually acquired and some grading started in the mid-1890's. But
receivership stopped the project in 1896, and although it remained an
active plan through the early 1900's too many other critical rebuilding projects took precedence. The property and partial grading continued to be a
tantalizing hope through the 1920's, Depression and World War II — but
always deferred. Even as late as the 1960's the Relay cutoff was at least
partly alive. By that time the large Seagram (Calvert) distillery had been
built along the west side of the cutoff property line. Seagram needed part of
the projected right-of-way for its own expansion and forced B&O into a
final soul-searching. The railroad finally concluded that the savings in
operating costs and running times could not justify the cost of building the
new line. In June of 1972 it sold a part of the land to Seagram and closed its
books on the cutoff forever.   245

Two 4-4-0's take an eight-car Washington train past Washington Terminal's Ivy City engine terminal about 1910. Credit: Smithsonian Institution; C.B. Chaney collection.

Passenger traffic continued heavy but slowly falling in the early 1900's as local traffic began to drop a bit, siphoned off by the closely parallel trolley line through Hyattsville, Riverdale and Branchville — and by the autos beginning to appear. But a big new traffic source also appeared: In 1910 the Laurel racetrack was built and over the years developed into one of the country's more prestigious tracks. The track lay immediately adjacent to the railroad tracks just north of town and B&O built sidings and special platforms along its main tracks to accommodate special race trains from both directions.

With the onset of World War I the Washington branch got even more than its normal share of government and military traffic — thanks largely to a surprise package produced through the efforts of the struggling Washington, Baltimore & Annapolis interurban line. Back in 1907-1908 when the WB&A was formed and built, it had also acquired the old Annapolis, Washington & Baltimore as its Annapolis branch. Whatever passenger interchange with B&O that had remained through Annapolis Junction disappeared as the WB&A started its own Washington-Annapolis and Baltimore-Annapolis services, although the junction remained in use for freight movements. Because of its terminal handicaps and its thin intermediate territory, the interurban's early life had been unpromising. But its opportunistic and politically well-connected Cleveland promoters found hope for a traffic bonanza when the Army began looking for an east coast site to train troops on their way to Europe. WB&A had property along its old AW&B branch at its Admiral station, a flagstop located in between the B&O and Pennsylvania lines about four miles east of Annapolis Junction. It managed to persuade the military to establish its new camp here, with WB&A providing most of the passenger service. Camp Meade, as it was called, was built rapidly in mid-1917; when completed it spread over 8,000 acres, had 1,200 wood buildings and could accommodate, if that is the word, 40,000 soldiers. As part of the project, both B&O and PRR were given access to the camp over the AW&B right-of-way, the Pennsy building west from Odenton and B&O east from Annapolis Junction. B&O realigned the AW&B line slightly, relaid it with heavier rail and shortly afterwards built some paralleling sections. A new frame station and a pair of single-story interlocking towers were built at the once-moribund Annapolis Junction, which was rechristened Camp Meade Junction.

Train No. 4, the St. Louis—New York "Diplomat" passes the World War I station at Fort Meade Junction in August 1946. Credit: E.L. Thompson

Camp Meade's boom was short-lived, of course, but following the war it was continued as a permanent military installation and eventually expanded, providing some semblance of a continuing freight business for B&O. With the base's change from "Camp" to "Fort" about 1929, the junction point was renamed again, now to the mouth-filling Fort George G. Meade Junction. When the unhappy WB&A finally expired in August 1935, B&O bought about five miles of the old WB&A/AW&B right of way into the base. (It had previously operated the branch under a trackage rights agreement with WB&A, which had been cancelled in 1931.) With the end of WB&A passenger service, Fort Meade soldiers were carried on buses of B&O's subsidiary West Virginia Transportation Company from train connections at Jessup and Laurel. Also, the newly-formed Baltimore & Annapolis Railroad ran direct Baltimore-Camp Meade bus service from Camden station.

During the Twenties the Washington branch's automatic semaphore signals were still kept well-exercised. Twenty-nine passenger trains each way were scheduled over the line in 1928; between the locals, Baltimore-Washington expresses and the New York (Jersey City) runs, anyone rid-

Clean-lined Pacifics first appeared on the Washington branch in 1906 and quickly became regular power on through trains. Probably on one of its first trips, 2107 poses at Halethorpe with a short westbound Royal Blue Line train. Credit: Smithsonian Institution.

President Garfield wheels through Relay on its way to Washington about 1935. Credit: H.W. Pontin; H.H. Harwood collection.

ing between Baltimore and Washington had at least one train an hour to choose from. Typically he would ride in olive green heavyweight (and of course un-air conditioned) coaches or parlor cars hauled by a variety of P-class Pacifics or perhaps an Atlantic. Most frequently seen on the line—and most impressive—was the handsome fleet of gold-striped olive green P-7 "President" class Pacifics, built in 1927 exclusively for the Washington-New York trains. Freights—still primarily merchandise trains between Baltimore or Philadelphia and Washington/Potomac Yard—were in the hands of Q-class 2-8-2's, where they steadfastly and somewhat dully remained until the early 1950's. Typical freight power of the early '20's was Q-1 or USRA Q-3 classes; beginning in 1921, the heavier Vanderbilt-tendered Q-4's began showing up and eventually became the next thing to universal.

But the branch did get at least one bit of variety and excitement in 1923. In May of that year a large portion of the roof in one of the Pennsylvania's Baltimore B&P tunnels collapsed, blocking the Pennsy Washington line for about 12 days. During this period everything Pennsy could move in or out of Washington and Potomac Yard rolled over B&O's Washington branch, hauled mostly by Pennsy's Belpaire-boilered K-4 Pacifics, L-1 2-8-2's and H-10 Consolidations.

While schedules and basic train operations of the Depression years stuck to the traditional (although by now diminishing) pattern of earlier years, some of the equipment turned surprisingly exotic. Reflecting the uncomfortable blend of conservatism and innovation that characterized the later years of President Daniel Willard's reign, motive power and passenger cars went through a breathtaking series of one-shot experiments.

Typical of happier and better-manicured days on the Washington branch, P-3 No. 5128 and a three-car local chuff past Riverdale's lawn and hedges in November 1949. Credit: L.W. Rice collection.

In the end they resulted in very little that lasted, but while they were there the Washington branch became one of the most interesting and innovative pieces of railroad anywhere.

It became so largely because of the competitive pressures and prestige of its geographic position. After its victories over Garrett and the 1910 completion of A.J. Cassatt's Pennsylvania station in New York, the Pennsylvania Railroad had permanently put B&O in second-place in the heavily-travelled Washington-Philadelphia-New York market. With a more favorably located railroad and a direct rail entrance to Manhattan, Pennsy had clearly become the primary passenger hauler in the territory; electrification of its line in 1935 merely sealed its dominance. Ever since the short-lived "Royal Blue Line" days of the 1890's, B&O had to depend on its creativity to carve out some piece of the market. Yet the prestige and passenger potential of the route made it worth fighting for and Willard wanted to fight with whatever new ideas the railroad could muster.

It all began at least partly conservatively in 1931 when the standard heavyweight "Columbian", the premiere Washington-New York express, was fully air conditioned—the first completely air-conditioned train in regular service in the United States. The next step was more radical: In June 1935 the original "Royal Blue" appeared—a lightweight fully streamlined train with wide vestibules and a rounded glassed-in observation car. Painted in a deep blue as a harkback to the trains of the Nineties, it was one of the country's earliest lightweight streamliners and also a harbinger of the return of color to the olive-green railroads. The "Royal Blue's" locomotive was equally eye-catching: a light, exceptionally clean-lined 4-6-4 named the "Lord Baltimore", built from the ground up by Mt. Clare shop as a B&O translation of English locomotive design.

The Viaduct Hotel's gardens were still well-kept in June 1931 despite the deepening Depression. P-7 No. 5307 eases past with Baltimore-Washington train 149. Credit: Smithsonian Institution; C.B. Chaney collection.

After 1911, Mikados hauled most of the through freights on the Washington branch and most other B&O lines in Maryland. In their earlier days they looked like this. Q-1 4097 charges through Laurel in 1923 with a freight for Potomac Yard. The two locomotives in the consist probably are bound from the Baldwin Works outside Philadelphia to some southern railroad. Credit: Smithsonian Institution; C.B. Chaney collection.

On the other hand, the rural territory between Washington and Relay produced only light local freight—enough for hand-down 2-8-0's and ten-wheelers to handle. Here an 1890-built B-7 trundles through Laurel in June 1923. Credit: Smithsonian Institution; C.B. Chaney collection.

The "Lord" lasted only two months on the new "Royal Blue" when it was replaced by something much different—locomotive No. 50, the country's first main-line passenger diesel. This rectangular apparition basically followed the utilitarian lines of the successful diesel switchers built in the mid and late 1920's; it was hardly as handsome as the trim "Lord Baltimore" but it worked much more competently than the slippery and vibration-prone "Lord". The 50 not only signalled the ultimate end of steam power on main-line trains, but it proved remarkably hardy itself— although transferred to the Alton Railroad and rebuilt twice, it survived in operation until 1957. It can be seen today at the St. Louis Museum of Transport.

However, it was not seen long on the Washington branch. Willard took a dislike to the lightweight "Royal Blue"—properly so, perhaps, since it turned out to be a rough rider on the curving Washington-Philadelphia part of the route. Along with its diesel the train was transferred to B&O's midwestern subsidiary, the Alton Railroad, in 1937. In its place B&O built its own "Royal Blue", a train of 1920-era heavyweight cars completely re-

From the mid-1920's on to the end of steam, the Q-4 Mikado was the freight mainstay of all lines out of Baltimore and Washington. Essentially ordinary engines, they nonetheless could put on an awesome show when pushed. Here 4611 pounds west through Relay on a bitter midwinter day about 1943. Credit: B&O Museum Archives.

fitted and streamlined by Mt. Clare shop. Power reverted to steam in the form of a specially streamlined P-7 Pacific, given a bullet-nosed shrouding by industrial designer Otto Kuhler. Kuhler, who had an excellent sensitivity to color combinations, gave the train a new color scheme also—the conservative yet highly attractive combination of "royal" blue, grey and gold which quickly became standard on B&O "streamliners" and diesel locomotives. The second incarnation of the "Royal Blue" began regular runs in April 1937. For whatever distinction it is, the new "Blue" was one of the few cases—and undoubtedly the earliest—where a heavyweight train was substituted for a lightweight and a steam locomotive regularly took the place of a diesel.

The Washington branch was also a convenient place for B&O's creative, if not always popular, motive power superintendent George H. Emerson to carry on his own experiments with water tube fireboxes and a duplex steam locomotive design. Certainly the most spectacular product of the Emerson era was the duplex 4-4-4-4, appropriately named the "George H. Emerson", turned out by Mt. Clare in 1937 and occasionally run on the "Royal Blue" and other Washington trains. But after all the dust had settled, conventional 1920-era Pacifics were still hauling heavyweight, mostly conventional cars over the railroad. In 1937 the diesels again appeared on the Washington branch after a one-year absence, this time regal streamlined General Motors production units painted the new standard blue-black-grey-gold. First assigned to the "Royal Blue", the hand-

The *Lord Baltimore* shines proudly in Washington Union Station with the new lightweight "Royal Blue" in May 1936. Credit: Bruce D. Fales; H.H. Harwood collection.

The *Lord* has the eastbound "Royal Blue" rolling out of Washington in September 1936. The lightweight ACF-built train rode poorly on the curving Washington-Philadelphia route and was eventually exiled to the B&O-controlled Alton Railroad. The truck at right is on what is now New York Avenue. Credit: W.R. Osborne; H.H. Harwood collection.

some EA's and later E-6's and E-7's gradually took over many of the Washington-New York runs, particularly the through "Capitol Limited" and "National Limited" connections.

Afterwards it was mostly anticlimax, although World War II again swelled the service and added almost regular VIP and Presidential movements. President Franklin Roosevelt was a particularly active train rider, making numerous (at times almost weekly) trips to his home at Hyde Park, N.Y. Although the PRR got a few of these moves, the bulk were given to B&O—a result, it was rumored, of Roosevelt's old admiration for Daniel Willard and perhaps a political distaste for the Pennsylvania's Republican executive management. Whatever the reasons, B&O was extremely adept at catering to the whims of the Presidential entourage; to those riding the trains, the well-stocked B&O diner was usually the highlight of the trip. The Hyde Park trains usually followed the "Royal Blue Line" route between Washington and Jersey City, where they were hauled over a freight connecting line to the New York Central's West Shore division at Weehawken; the NYC then took them up the Hudson to Highland, N.Y. opposite Poughkeepsie where automobiles met the train and drove the President to Hyde Park.

The "Royal Blue" remembered by most was this set of rebuilt heavy-weight cars first operated in 1937. It stands here in Union Station before its last run in April 1958. Credit: Ara Mesrobian.

B&O's motive power enlivened the late-Depression scene in Washington. The unsuccessful 4-4-4-4 duplex *George H. Emerson* backs a train into Union Station alongside one of the pioneering streamlined Electro-Motive EA passenger diesels. The date was September 1939—a time when engines like the *Emerson* seemed perhaps to have promise as the power of the future. Credit: L.W. Rice; H.H. Harwood collection.

But unfortunately there really was no contest; that blue, black and grey diesel mumbling to itself alongside the *Emerson* won hands down. A pair of EA's were assigned to the Royal Blue in 1937 and as the years went on the E's multiplied. No. 52, one of the original fleet, opens up with the "Royal Blue" through Relay on a late afternoon in 1940. Credit: E.L. Thompson.

While diesels took over the Washington-Jersey City trains, handfired Pacifics still stepped lively with the locals. P-17 No. 5141, inherited from the Buffalo, Rochester & Pittsburgh, storms through Savage in September 1945 with train 157 for Washington. Credit: E.L. Thompson.

The nature of Presidential train operation and Roosevelt's own personal whims could create some problems on the heavily-travelled Washington branch: All opposing trains had to be stopped before the special passed and the President insisted on a 50 m.p.h. maximum speed. But since the Hyde Park trains usually left Washington in early afternoon or late evening—most of them at 10:30 p.m.—the line was not badly tied up. Interestingly, wartime security caused some problems in finding an appropriate loading and unloading point in Washington. Although Union Station's special VIP section was sometimes used, both the station itself and the terminal trackage were considered poor because of the crowds and heavy traffic. Experiments were made in loading the train at Silver Spring, University station and Benning on B&O as well as the Pentagon on the Virginia side of the river, reached by the Pennsylvania's Rosslyn branch. The final favored spot, however, was an unobtrusive underground siding into the Bureau of Engraving near the foot of 14th Street S.W. This could hold two cars and had a high-level loading platform ideal for the wheelchair-bound President. The train was then put together on the PRR's Long Bridge freight line and taken out over B&O's Alexandria branch to Alexandria Junction (Hyattsville) where it joined the Washington branch north.

Washington branch traffic remained respectably heavy immediately after the war, mostly because the railroad was still the quickest and most comfortable way of getting between Washington, Baltimore and the other eastern seaboard cities. And by that time the Washington branch was indeed a fast railroad: Passenger trains took full advantage of the 80 m.p.h. official speed limit, and sometimes then some. (One regular rider, a member of B&O's passenger department, timed speeds as high as 102-103 m.p.h. on occasion.) Nonstop Washington-Baltimore runs were regularly scheduled to cover the 36.8 miles between Union Station and Camden in 38 minutes—a start-to-stop average of 59 m.p.h., including terminal speed restrictions at both ends. Baltimore-Washington trains needed an extra five minutes to negotiate the Washington wye and back in. Even the locals moved sharply—many northbound runs covered the distance in 50-55 minutes, making three to four stops along the way.

In short, it was challenging work for engine crews. Said Harry Eck, then a locomotive engineer and later Chessie's General Supervisor Locomotive Operations: "Washington branch passenger service was a great training ground for engineers and firemen before qualifying to Cumberland and Jersey City. Passenger locals were mostly hauled by hand-fired 5100's (1913-vintage P-3 Pacifics) up to the end of steam. Smoke ordinance in Washington prohibited *any* smoke, which made firing tough until you reached Langdon. Most important of all, those branch trains were *fast!*"

Fast or not, the business began dropping severely in the 1950's. The Baltimore-Washington Parkway greatly eased the agonies of driving U.S. Route 1 between the two cities. B&O also was finally forced to recognize the realities of its competitive position for the Washington-New York business

Considerably less inspiring but much more efficient Budd RDC cars began taking over local passenger runs in 1951. Here a single eastbound RDC-2 is no match for the Thomas Viaduct's magnificence. Credit: Bill Rettberg.

The last true through B&O passenger train—a ceremonial pre-Amtrak run of the "Capitol Limited" —heads for Baltimore from Chicago the morning of May 1, 1971. Matched B&O and C&O E-8's head a mixed consist of coaches and sleepers which includes both ex-"Columbian" strata-domes. Credit: H.H. Harwood, Jr.

Name trains have been gone from the Washington branch for over 10 years, but heavy passenger loads are still carried. Indeed, the Baltimore-Washington commuter business recently increased 20% in one year, necessitating stopgap extra equipment. A Washington-bound crowd of commuters at Laurel waits to scramble on board five well-filled coaches in April 1979. Credit: H.H. Harwood, Jr.

and on April 26, 1958 it ended all "Royal Blue Line" passenger service north of Baltimore in a single sweep.

In the meantime the railroad had also begun converting the remaining runs to diesel or self-propelled cars. Beginning with two cars in 1951, B&O substituted Budd RDC motor cars for its locomotive-hauled local and commuter trains (again, it was one of the first railroads to use this type of equipment); by 1956 the Budds had displaced most of the heavyweight commuter equipment. And besides being cheaper to operate than a hand-fired Pacific hauling two to four heavyweights, the double-ended RDCs could bypass the bugbear of B&O's Washington operations—the Ivy City wye track. On November 2, 1953, P-7 Pacific 5306 took the last steam-powered train over the line. The last regularly-scheduled through western train, a truncated version of the "National Limited", came off in 1967 and the last through train of any type — a ceremonial last run of the "Capitol Limited" — crossed the Thomas viaduct on the morning of May 1, 1971 on its way in from Chicago.

Passenger trains continue to run between Baltimore and Washington and probably will indefinitely, although for all practical purposes they are no longer really B&O trains. The line is still a popular commuter route in both directions, but particularly for the string of Washington suburbs from Laurel south. In 1979 four state-subsidized morning and evening round trips shuttled between Union Station and Camden using an increasingly diverse assortment of former B&O RDC cars, other RDC's picked up by the state from Amtrak, Chessie diesels and conventional passenger cars from several sources. The state transportation department presently plans to acquire more of its own locomotives and cars for the growing traffic load and eventually B&O's name will disappear from both the time-tables and the trains.

But what started life as a passenger railroad has now become a heavy freight carrier. As passenger service diminished and more track space became available, B&O routed more of its western merchandise manifests over the Metropolitan branch-Washington branch circuit to Baltimore and Philadelphia. This was done partly to take advantage of the faster, higher capacity onetime passenger main line, but it was also necessary to set off freight (particularly perishables and piggyback trailers) at Washington. With the traditional Potomac Yard traffic and Baltimore-Washington freight, the Washington branch carries a heavy load. In late 1974, for example, a grand total of 23 east and westbound manifests a day were scheduled over the line, not counting frequent grain extras and regular local freights.

In addition, as both Washington and Baltimore oozed outwards, the territory along the Washington branch has turned from a nondescript string of farms and woods into a goods distribution center for the merging metropolitan areas. In the mid-1960's B&O began promoting the area around Jessup and Fort Meade Junction as an ideal midway point to reach both cities. In March 1967 it opened a large unloading and preparation terminal for new automobiles just south of Jessup. This was followed by the development of a food warehousing center and fresh produce market in the same area, opened in sections between 1973 and 1976. During the same period it managed to persuade General Electric to locate a large new appliance manufacturing plant at Columbia, which began operations in March 1971. The GE Appliance Park East plant, incidentally, is reached by a long spur which roughly follows the route of the long-abandoned Patuxent branch to Guilford, although it is intentionally located on higher ground. Other warehouses and consumer product manufacturing plants have sprung up in centers such as Muirkirk and Dorsey. As a result, local freight traffic along the branch is heavy and several mainline manifest trains make setoffs and pickups at the newly-built (in 1967, soon to be expanded) yard at Fort Meade Junction.

Thus like Washington itself, Washington's first railroad has become inundated in urbanization. But running between all those industrial parks, housing developments and expressways is a genuine 1835 railroad, its alignment essentially untouched, still able to carry 70 m.p.h. passenger trains and 55 m.p.h. freights.

Washington branch curves were many but gentle, and the track fast. This is a typical stretch looking north at Muirkirk about 1920. The road at left is now U.S. Route 1. Credit: B&O Museum Archives.

The Washington branch was fast and busy. On a July morning in 1950 westbound and eastbound expresses pass at Relay. The old hotel gardens were still more or less intact, but the hotel itself was being demolished. Credit: W.P. Ellis; H.H. Harwood collection.

College Park's frame suburban station watches the Baltimore-Cleveland "Washingtonian" swing past in 1946. Credit: E.L. Thompson.

Alexandria Junction, just north of Hyattsville station was (and still is) a key operating point on the Washington branch. JD tower, still standing, controls the switches to the Alexandria (Potomac Yard) branch which joins the Washington line behind the camera. The westbound "Washingtonian" for Cleveland roars past on a cold November morning in 1947. Credit: E.L. Thompson.

IMPOSSIBLE CHALLENGE

CHAPTER 12

WASHINGTON FINALLY GETS WEST:
THE METROPOLITAN BRANCH

It was the Metropolitan branch that gave B&O its Capitol dome symbol. It was the Metropolitan branch that eventually became B&O's real main line west, turning the pioneering original main line into a secondary route and — at one point — almost justifying its abandonment. It was the Metropolitan branch that first created Washington's Montgomery County suburban "corridor" and, in several places, now forms part of two Metro rapid transit routes. Yet for B&O's first forty years, the Metropolitan branch was the last thing it felt it needed.

And for good reasons. Although Washington became B&O's first major terminal in 1835, the railroad considered its branch there peripheral to its primary purpose, which was to link Baltimore to the midwest. Indeed, the Baltimore-Washington branch was conceived and built as part of the Atlantic seaboard transportation chain, a traffic flow which ran at right angles to B&O's route west. So although the Washington branch prospered modestly, it was left largely on its own while B&O directed its resources toward pushing its main line to the Ohio River and beyond. Its interest in building a line west from Washington was, at best, zero. For one thing, it would have been commercially unproductive: Pre-Civil War Washington was a small, crude and transient town offering little western passenger traffic and virtually no freight business. More significant, the nearby port cities of Georgetown and Alexandria were commercial competitors of Baltimore. They may have been smaller than Baltimore and already declining, but whatever their status B&O's Baltimore backers obviously had no desire to give them any help.

So until the end of the Civil War, whatever western commerce Washington generated got there the hard way. There was the C&O

Canal, which after several long delays finally reached Cumberland in 1850, or a choice of several turnpikes through Maryland or northern Virginia. By rail, passengers took B&O's Washington branch to Relay or Baltimore and transferred there to main line trains. In 1851, for example, travellers could leave Washington at 6 a.m., arrive at Relay at 7:10, perhaps have breakfast at the hotel and catch the Cumberland train at 9:35. However, many people intimidated by the pre-dawn departure time from Washington preferred to take the afternoon train to Relay the day before and spend the night at Relay House.

Since B&O's mind was elsewhere, others tried to promote a new railroad directly west from Washington. In 1853 an assortment of businessmen from Georgetown and Montgomery County organized a company called the Metropolitan Railroad to build from Georgetown to a spot on B&O's main line west of Frederick Junction. Its planned route then continued west to Hagerstown, tunnelling Catoctin and South Mountain on the way. Location work was completed by mid-1854, but afterwards the project lapsed into a coma induced by the high projected construction costs, lack of capital and Baltimore political opposition. Yet it never completely died. It twitched slightly in the late 1850's and again in 1862 as the Civil War dramatized the strategic shortcomings of Washington's western rail connections. By this time the Metropolitan had begun to metamorphose into a potential competitive threat by talking of extending its original route to form a new line between Washington, Baltimore, and possibly Philadelphia, perhaps under the sponsorship of the increasingly aggressive Pennsylvania Railroad.

By the Civil War's end, like it or not, B&O finally moved to build the line itself. Whatever its real reasons, the railroad could rationalize that a western branch into Washington was now justified. The city itself had matured and expanded during the war and certainly had a healthier passenger potential — particularly in conjunction with Garrett's planned extensions to Pittsburgh and Chicago. The federal government, frightened by the near-misses during the war and the obviously awkward rail route for moving troops and supplies anywhere west of Washington, was pushing for a direct line, too. Finally (and probably most critical to Garrett), it was becoming clear that if B&O didn't build the line, someone else might and make it a means of invading B&O territory elsewhere. And indeed, by 1866 the Pennsylvania was maneuvering to get into Washington, which it soon did with outstanding success. B&O took over the old Metropolitan charter in 1865, quickly ran surveys and started building in 1866.

B&O's version of the Metropolitan route began in Washington and joined the original main line just east of Point of Rocks, 42 miles west. Linked with the Baltimore-Washington branch in Washington, it would form an alternate main line between Baltimore and the west — in fact, by running its through passenger trains around the two sides of the triangle formed by the Metropolitan branch and the Washington branch, it could serve both Baltimore and Washington with the same main line trains.

The new Metropolitan branch crossed the Piedmont—pretty, but rugged for a railroad. Typical of the topography is this view west at Waring, between Gaithersburg and Germantown, in March 1979. Credit: H.H. Harwood, Jr.

The balance of the old Metropolitan Railroad's projected line through the mountains to Hagerstown was forgotten.

Laid out on a map the Metropolitan branch was short and direct, but building it was something else. Theoretically, the easiest route from Washington to Point of Rocks was along the Potomac all the way. But this route was already occupied by the C&O Canal and the river bluffs made a parallel line impossibly expensive. Nor was the canal ready to abandon and give up its right of way — although already obsolete, it was flourishing as much as it ever would with growing tonnages of Cumberland coal. In fact, it would reach a record of 974,000 tons in 1875 before slipping into its long decline. Total abandonment would not come until 1924. This meant an inland route through the choppy Piedmont country, shorter than by way of the river but considerably more rugged. Going east from Point of Rocks, the line would have to climb out of the Potomac valley, hurdle Parr's Ridge (the same nemesis that thwarted B&O's early engineers near Mt. Airy), dodge around a continuous string of hills and valleys, then drop back down to the Potomac flats at Washington. There were no watercourses to follow along the way; in fact, the route ran at

A.

B. The Metropolitan branch has changed much since the 1870's, but its breathtaking western gateway looks much the same. A. point of Rocks station, over 100 years old, witnesses a westbound empty grain hopper train come off the "Met" in September 1977. The Old Main Line to Baltimore is at far left. B. Looking west at the junction in 1947. The section of the station nearest the camera predates the spired section behind it—the near portion dates to about 1870, the rest to 1875. KG tower, built in 1903, is now gone from the scene. Credits: A-H.H. Harwood, Jr. B-L.W. Rice; H.H. Harwood collection.

This spindly three-span Bollman truss carried the Met's single track over the Monocacy River west of Dickerson, Md. The C&O Canal aqueduct can be barely made out at the lower left. Credit: C.S. Roberts collection.

Highest point on the Metropolitan branch and summit of the arduous climb out of the Potomac valley is this cut at Parr's Ridge east of Barnesville station. Then and now, eastbound freights usually need helpers to make it. In this April 1979 scene a pair of them drop back down to Brunswick to wait for the next freight east. Credit: H.H. Harwood, Jr.

269

right angles to the drainage pattern, requiring many cuts, fills, dips and several long, high bridges. Although it crossed generally the same type of country as the original main line, the Metropolitan branch had to be a wholly different kind of railroad. . .not quite as curvy, but much more humpy.

Construction started in 1866 at Barnesville, the point where the line crossed Parr's Ridge. For the next three years construction proceeded erratically in scattered sections, then ceased — supposedly for further surveys and property negotiations plus some political problems in Washington, although some long-frustrated central Marylanders began to suspect that the railroad merely wanted to wall off potential competition without actually building the line. Whatever the reason, the enemy was unquestionably approaching. By 1866 the Pennsylvania had picked up the unbuilt Baltimore & Potomac and begun building it; by 1872 it had entered Washington, had taken over the Long Bridge and was heading on south. Perhaps prodded by these events, Metropolitan branch construction resumed about 1871. After some further delay caused by sickness among the building forces, the last rail was laid at Gaithersburg February 8, 1873. Formal service began May 25, 1873.

The finished railroad reflected the haste and uncertain purposes surrounding its creation. Unlike most other B&O lines in the area it was entirely single track, laid with 60 lb. John Brown rail. Its major bridges were either iron Bollman trusses — a design just then verging on obsolescence — or timber trestles put up as temporary expedients. Two elaborate brick stations were built at way points, but several similar structures planned for other communities on the line never appeared. Considering the terrain and obstacles, the branch was well engineered, yet in its earlier years it must have been a rather frightening railroad to ride.

Washington-bound passengers got an impressive welcome to the Metropolitan branch when their train swung over the switch and braked down to a stop at the junction station half a mile east of the Point of Rocks tunnel. The spectacular spired brick Victorian confection stood (and still stands) in the center of the wye between the original main line and the new branch; it was a stop for all trains on both lines and a terminal for several Frederick local runs. (The station, incidently, went through a full cycle of names. Originally it was called Point of Rocks; in 1876 it was renamed Washington Junction and a local stop called Point of Rocks established a quarter of a mile to the west. In December, 1923 it became Point of Rocks again, and remains so today. To further confuse things, Relay had also carried the name Washington Junction until the Metropolitan branch was built.) The station building itself started off life about 1871 as a relatively simple single-story brick structure; it was not until 1875 that it had been expanded into the breathtakingly eclectic monument which survives today.

Accelerating away from Point of Rocks/Washington Jct., the little 4-4-0 and its wood coaches turned southeast, following the north side of the C&O Canal for the next 3½ miles through a wide flood plain and crossing Tuscarora Creek on a 107-ft. Bollman through truss bridge. From Tuscarora the single track swung gradually away from the river and began climbing out of the valley toward Parr's Ridge — a steady and long 1.04%-1.1% grade that would carry the line up 297 feet in the next six miles. On their way up the riverside bluff, passengers suddenly peered down on the Monocacy River, 80 feet underneath, as they rocked across a spidery 730-ft. long four-span Bollman deck truss bridge. Those with sharp eyes could spot the equally impressive but much lower stone canal aqueduct over the river a short distance to the south.

The Monocacy bridge marked the parting from the Potomac, as the river turns south and the railroad heads inland up the ridge. From here to Washington the scenery was woods, fields, subsistence farms and a few crossroads communities. The first was Dickerson, part way up the ridge from the Monocacy where W.H. Dickerson (also the railroad agent) had built a store and post office when the railroad opened. East of Dickerson the track twisted around hillsides as it worked its way up, crossing the Little Monocacy on a scary 76 ft.-high 500 ft.-long timber trestle. Just east of Barnesville station — ten miles from Point of Rocks — the train topped the ridge in a curved cut. At 527.4 feet, the Barnesville summit was the highest point on the line, although 210 feet lower than the Old Main Line's crossing of the same ridge at Mt. Airy. From Barnesville east the up-and-down began: The train dropped down a curving 1% grade to Buck Lodge Creek, passing Boyd's (named for a railroad contractor who had established his construction camp here and afterward settled down as a farmer), then uphill again to Germantown. Midway between Boyd's and Germantown it negotiated a sharp curve and crossed Little Seneca Creek on an even larger wood trestle — this one 106 ft. high and 600 ft. long. East of Germantown it was downhill again, through more curves and cuts as the train dropped into the Great Seneca Creek valley, crossing the stream on still another high (75 feet) long (400 feet) timber trestle. Then uphill on the last major sustained upgrade (much of it close to 1%) through Clopper's to Gaithersburg.

From Gaithersburg into Washington the trip was easy for our east-bound train, but rugged for anything going west as the branch began its long descent again to the Potomac. For the next 14 miles from Gaithersburg to Silver Spring the track gently curved its way down grades ranging from 0.75% to 1.27%, passing little rural settlements along the way: Washington Grove, Derwood, Rockville — the county seat and largest intermediate town on the line — Windham's (later called Randolph), Knowles (Kensington), Forest Glen and Linden. At Rockville, our mid-1870's train stopped at an imposing two-story brick station — the first permanent station east of Point of Rocks and somewhat similar to it in style although considerably more subdued. And at what is now Garrett Park it rolled over the last large bridge on the route, a long four-span Bollman truss over Rock Creek. This one measured 450 feet long and 70 feet high.

Rockville station was one of the earliest structures on the line and now is one of the few reminders of the Met as it was 100 years ago. Built in 1873, the Gothic brick building then served a quiet rural county seat and faced out on a single track. It looked this way in June 1972 as an eastbound mixed freight rolled past. Credit: H.H. Harwood, Jr.

Silver Spring station was a mirror image of Rockville, built five years later in 1878. It stood until 1945 when it was replaced by the present station built on the same foundation. Credit: B&O Museum Archives.

Silver Spring — a small country crossroads seven miles from the Washington terminal — had the only other permanent station building on the branch. This was another two-story brick structure, a mirror image of the one at Rockville, located at the point where the Brookeville turnpike crossed the track. Eastward from Silver Spring the downgrade steepened, averaging 1% all the way into Washington and reaching 1.42% in spots; the track crossed into the District just east of Silver Spring station and dropped past little flag stops at Brightwood (Takoma Park), Stott's (now Chillum), Terra Cotta and Queenstown (later University), entering Washington proper at the present intersection of New York and Florida Avenues. To reach the New Jersey Avenue terminal the line ran south in the center of First Street, N.E. to G Street, where it joined the branch from Baltimore. A single-track wye connection at First & I Streets N.E. — called Metropolitan Junction — allowed trains to head directly toward Baltimore. Since the Washington terminal was stub-end and the through western trains ran to and from Baltimore, it was a regular procedure to turn inbound trains on the wye and back them into the station.

Aside from Silver Spring and Rockville, the few stations on the branch were small frame structures. Two-story brick stations — probably identical to the two already built — were planned for Dickerson, Germantown and perhaps other way points. Possibly the thinly-populated rural nature of the territory in the mid-1870's caused some practical second thoughts; in any event, they were never built. Passing sidings for the single-track line were located at Tuscarora, Barnesville, Boyd, Germantown, Gaithersburg, Washington Grove, Rockville, Knowles and Silver Spring.

The new Metropolitan branch was sent off to a running start. B&O immediately diverted its through passenger trains from the original Patapsco River route, which lapsed into a freight and secondary passenger line. Henceforth, trains to such points as Wheeling, Cincinnati, Pittsburgh, and (after 1875) Chicago ran from Baltimore to Washington, then west over the Metropolitan. Initial service was quite respectable for a brand-new railroad: Four passenger trains a day ran each way — three western expresses and one local — plus one through Washington freight and one way freight. In 1874 an express was added operating between Washington and Harpers Ferry, then running down the newly-extended Shenandoah Valley branch to Staunton, Va. Thus by mid-1875 five passenger runs each way were scheduled over the "Met", the fastest covering the 42 miles from Washington to Point of Rocks nonstop in one hour and 20 minutes, averaging 31.5 m.p.h. — a fairly respectable speed considering the curves, grades, trestles and Washington street running. The two all-stops trains made it in an hour and 50 minutes.

At the time B&O built the Metropolitan branch it also planned, as mentioned earlier, a direct cross-country connection between the Met and the Baltimore-Washington branch, probably for through freights. This line was to leave the Metropolitan at Gaithersburg and head more-or-less directly east, picking up the Patuxent River and following it to Laurel to join the Washington branch. Undoubtedly B&O was trying to find a better route for its growing eastbound coal traffic; although the Met branch and the Gaithersburg-Laurel cutoff would have been hilly and curvy, the Old Main at that time was worse. But the connection never materialized, and the turn-of-the-century rebuilding of the Old Main eventually solved the problem.

Locally, one of the first visible effects of the Metropolitan branch was the development of commercial farming in the Maryland countryside west of Washington. When the railroad was opened, the land between Gaithersburg and the Monocacy River was decribed as "largely covered with pine forest, with the many cleared fields producing little more than sedge grass." The soil was thin and transportation almost anywhere was difficult. But the railroad could bring lime fertilizer down from Frederick cheaply and in large quantities; at the same time, the now-fast transportation to Washington meant a market for milk, vegetables and other perishables. The trees and sedge grass gradually disappeared into productive farms and communities like Gaithersburg and Germantown eventually developed into milling centers.

But the branch was predominantly a passenger line and remained so for 60 years as most freights fought their way over the Old Main Line. By the mid-1880's it had already begun to bulge with trains: three through passenger trains each way plus a Harpers Ferry local, a Weverton local, a Cumberland limited and a run to Shenandoah Junction connecting with the Shenandoah Valley Railroad's Roanoke train. And dodging these 14 trains were five scheduled freights: one each way between Martinsburg and Washington (probably primarily for milk and perishables), one eastbound-only schedule from Washington Junction (probably originating in Frederick) and a round-trip way freight which carried a passenger coach.

It was in this era, too, that B&O passenger advertisments first used

A through express from the west rolls quickly and quietly downgrade through Kensington in 1901. Credit: Montgomery County Historical Society.

the slogan "All Trains via Washington. . .With Stopover Privilege", woven around the Capitol dome to make the point. B&O's new Philadelphia line and its New York connection was certainly not the most direct route between those cities and the midwest, but the Washington stopover was an attractive and hardy selling point. The slogan lived on through the late 1930's; the Capitol dome survived it by becoming the symbol for the railroad itself.

And by the late 1880's the Metropolitan had also started to stimulate a new kind of commercial development: suburbanization. The wooded hills outside Washington may have been an operating nuisance to B&O, but they were a pleasant refuge from the low, steamy and still-malarial city. Before the electric streetcar and paved roads — and even after them — the Metropolitan route provided the fastest transportation combined with some of the most attractive country. Property along the line from Washington to Rockville became a hot target for developers and real estate speculators. Garrett Park, for example, was laid out in 1887 as a Washington version of New York's exclusive Tuxedo Park and Philadelphia's Bryn Mawr. (It was named for B&O president Robert Garrett.) At about the same time Knowles station was given the more fashionable name of Kensington and large frame houses appeared on the hillsides south of the track. Rockville and Forest Glen were promoted both as suburbs and summer resorts. Washington Grove, between Rockville and Gaithersburg, already had been developed as a summer colony and camp meeting site by Washington Methodists and B&O excursion trains regularly carried out crowds on summer weekends to hear the oratory.

A Met branch local has just turned on the wye at Gaithersburg and its crew relaxes before the next trip into Washington. In this photo dating to about 1889, the high peaked roof of the passenger station may be seen dimly behind the first car; the freight house is behind the engine. Both buildings remain today. Credit: Smithsonian Institution.

Forest Glen was both typical of the new railroad suburbs and positively unique unto itself. Its name was no real estate developer's fiction: Nine and a half miles from the Capitol and about 250 feet higher than downtown Washington, the area was rolling, heavily wooded and cut up by small streams running into Rock Creek. In the mid-'80's a real estate syndicate was formed to develop Forest Glen as a summer resort and year-round residential community. Its first and most memorable accomplishment was a large wood resort hotel named Ye Forest Inne, opened in 1887 on a wooded hill across the glen from the B&O track. Ye Forest Inne looked exactly like its name — a rambling rustic, gabled affair with two turrets and a spacious porch running around all sides.

Unhappily, Ye Forest Inne was an almost immediate commercial disaster, but it led directly to one of the most picturesque institutions along the B&O or anywhere else — the National Park Seminary. The hotel was sold in 1894 and converted to one of the more spectacular examples of that peculiar Edwardian educational/social institution, the young ladies' finishing school. Its new owners were determined to make it the most distinctive and fashionable of its type and over the next twenty years the old Ye Forest Inne was expanded and supplemented by an eclectic assortment of buildings scattered haphazardly among the trees and hillsides and interspersed with Victorian statuary and winding walkways. As a boarding school drawing girls from wealthy families along the east coast, the National Park Seminary provided B&O's turreted Forest Glen station with a lively traffic in students, trunks and chaperones along with the more stolid commuters.

Forest Glen station was built in 1887 as an adjunct to the newly-planned suburb and summer resort. A short landscaped driveway led to Ye Forest Inne, later the National Park Seminary. The photo dates to about 1920. Credit: B&O Archives.

WASHINGTON FINALLY GETS WEST:
THE METROPOLITAN BRANCH

With suburban spots such as Forest Glen, Kensington, Takoma Park and Garrett Park beginning to flower — and through passenger, freight and milk traffic growing — B&O was faced with overhauling the Metropolitan branch less than 15 years after it was built. Between 1886 and 1893 it gradually double-tracked the congested inner 21 miles of the railroad between Washington and Gaithersburg, built a turning wye at Gaithersburg in 1888 and began a frequent local train service for the infant suburban communities. Many new stations were built at the same time, either to replace the temporary buildings of the early '70's or to provide accomodations for some new community that had appeared since then. One of the first and finest was a delightful brick station built at Gaithersburg in 1884, designed by E. Francis Baldwin. Others followed soon afterwards, many of them also done by Baldwin: University, D.C. (1890), Takoma Park (1886), Woodside (1892), Forest Glen (1887), Kensington (1891), Garrett Park (1895), Germantown (1891), Boyd (1887), Dickerson (1891) and Tuscarora (1882). Most were attractive frame buildings of differing designs, although at least three (Kensington, Germantown and Dickerson) were similar in appearance. The Baldwin-designed stations at University and Boyd were distinctive masonry structures—

Looking a bit like a gnome's house, Gaithersburg's 1884 Baldwin-designed station was the most picturesque on the Met and a strong contender for the national title. The station and its adjacent brick freight house survive today—more than can be said for the approaching westbound Amtrak turbotrain in this 1972 photo. Credit: Ara Mesrobian.

A.

B. A variety of rural and suburban stations sprouted up along the Met during the late 1880's and early Nineties. (A) Typical of the latter was Takoma Park, originally Brightwood, which got this handsome building in 1886. Here it is shown as originally built and (B) as it looked in its later years. Credits: A—Mary Spears, Takoma Park Historical Society—B-B&O Museum Archives.

University a pleasant stone suburban design with graceful portecochere, Boyd a more elaborate brick building with a massive conical turret. One casualty of the double-tracking project was the long iron Bollman bridge over Rock Creek at Garrett Park; about 1896 the four spindly spans were replaced by an earth fill and stone arch bridge.

Also in 1891 the single-track section west of Gaithersburg was equipped with an automatic block signal system, which B&O boasted was the only one of its kind installed on a single-track line.

The double-tracking, block signals and stations had come none too soon. By the mid-1890's passenger service had reached what would be close to an all-time high. In 1893 no less than 18 trains were scheduled each way: five main-line trips between Baltimore and midwestern cities: one Roanoke connection to Shenandoah Junction: two Harpers Ferry locals; one Frederick local; one to Boyd — and eight Washington-Gaithersburg locals. (And in between, of course, the freights and milk train.) In the years ahead more main line passenger trains would appear, but the local services would drop off as newly-built trolley lines began reaching into Washington's outskirts — and, of course, as autos appeared. In 1892 street railway lines had reached Silver Spring and Takoma Park (they were electrified in 1893); a trolley line was completed to Woodside and Forest Glen in 1897; the little Kensington Railway connected Kensington with Chevy Chase Lake in 1895; a long semi-interurban route reached Rockville in 1900. As a result of these — and probably some initial overoptimism on B&O's part — the railroad had cut the Gaithersburg local runs from eight to four round trips by 1904.

Boyds station was another Francis Baldwin design, built in 1887. It was removed during the 1927 double tracking project. Credit: B&O Museum Archives.

A.

B.

Kensington, Md. (once called Knowles) and University, D.C. were two variations of Francis Baldwin suburban designs. University's stone construction was appropriate to nearby Catholic University, its principal clientele. Built in 1890, it is shown here in 1970 near the end of its life. Kensington, dating to 1891, was identical to Garrett Park, built somewhat later. This 1901 photo shows it as originally built; later the open portion at the left was closed in as a freight shed to replace the tiny structure at far left. Credits: A-H.H. Harwood, Jr.—B-Montgomery County Historical Society.

A.

B.

Most of the Met branch was rural in the 19th Century and stations such as these at Derwood and Germantown were designed to serve the simple needs of the area. According to company records, Derwood dates to 1893, but its design clearly is a product of the mid-1870's. More likely, it was one of the earlier structures on the line. Germantown was built in 1891, photographed in 1969 and burned down by vandals in January 1977. Credits: A-Montgomery County Historical Society—B-H.H. Harwood, Jr.

A.

B.

C. This trio is reproduced primarily as a jarring example of how the Washington metropolitan landscape has changed over the past 60 years. All three photos were taken from the same location at the Georgia Avenue B&O crossing at Silver Spring about 1920. (A) looks north from the grade crossing toward the town of Silver Spring, then just a small collection of stores on the east side of the Forest Glen trolley line. (B) faces south; the single-track side-of-the-road trolley can be seen on the left heading toward Washington. (C) looks west toward the 1878 B&O station. Today, of course, the greatly widened street passes under the railroad tracks, the Metro line shares the railroad right-of-way, the station is gone, and the general surroundings are a sea of asphalt, steel and concrete. Credits (all three photos): B&O Museum Archives.

Yet the pressure on the Met built up as main line schedules were speeded up and equipment got heavier. Half the line was still single-track, with three large wood trestles and at least two obsolete Bollman bridges. True, the 36 scheduled passenger trains of 1893 had dropped to 30 by 1904. But this was mostly the result of the cutback in Gaithersburg locals; the main line expresses had gone from a total of 10 to 14. And freight to Washington continued to grow as the city grew, since the Met was a main artery for food, fuel and building materials. Freight traffic would expand further after 1906 when Potomac Yard gave B&O a competitive connection with the southern railroads.

A start was made in 1896 when the Little Seneca Creek trestle east of Boyd — the worst of the three — was replaced with a curved iron viaduct. Unfortunately however, the sharp curves of the original alignment around Black Hill remained an operating problem for the next 32 years.

When the Pennsylvania Railroad's Leonor Loree assumed command of B&O in 1901, the Met was a clear candidate for his massive modernization program. It did not require the radical surgery that the Old Main Line did, but it did need some dekinking, double-tracking and extensive bridge replacements. In addition, the slowly-blossoming plans for the new Washington passenger terminal and Potomac Yard made future capacity critical.

First priority was the long, high and now-shaky Monocacy River viaduct west of Dickerson. In 1904 its four original Bollman truss spans (which already had been bolstered by additional stone piers about 1893) were replaced by seven less aesthetic but far sturdier steel girder spans... sturdy enough that they still survive there today. At the same time the single-span Bollman truss over Tuscarora Creek to the west got a girder replacement. Like their predecessors, both bridges remained single track structures although designed for expansion later.

This steel trestle across Little Seneca Creek east of Boyds replaced a timber structure in 1896. It in turn was succeeded by a high fill and concrete arch bridge on a different alignment in 1928. Credit: Carlos P. Avery collection.

Loree promptly pulled out the 1873 Bollman truss bridge over the Monocacy River and replaced it with this utilitarian seven-span girder bridge. The rebuilt structure was originally single-track; a set of spans for the second track was added in 1927. Note the odd configuration of the supporting piers. The high piers are original; the shorter stone piers were added in the mid-1890's to help support the Bollman trusses; when the present girder bridge was built, the concrete extensions were added. Both photos were made in April 1979. Credit (both photos): H.H. Harwood, Jr.

Quickly afterwards the rebuilding of other troublesome sections started. Loree decided to defer double-tracking the entire line, but went to work on the two worst bottlenecks: the stiff eastbound grade up Parr's Ridge from Dickerson to Barnesville, which included the Little Monocacy trestle, and the other major hill between Germantown and Gaithersburg, where the double track from Washington ended. And in between those points was the trestle over Great Seneca Creek. By the time the project was completed in 1906 Loree was gone, but the massive Pennsylvania Railroad-style stone viaducts over these two streams are clear marks of the man.

The Dickerson-Barnesville section involved not only double-tracking, but also straightening a series of sweeping "S" curves on the upper part of the hill between the Little Monocacy and Barnesville station —plus, of course, replacement of the "temporary" 1873 timber trestle over the Little Monocacy. To span the ravine cut by the small stream Loree built an awesome triple-arch stone viaduct 331¼ feet long, 76½ feet over the stream bed, with 90-foot arches. Now mostly surrounded by trees, the bridge is still worth a bumpy drive up Mouth of Monocacy Road to see. The new double track began immediately west of Dickerson station (where a tiny single-story interlocking "tower" was built) and ended at the top of the hill by another little interlocking plant just east of Barnesville station. Barnesville got a new frame combination passenger and freight station at the same time.

Between Germantown and Gaithersburg, the second double-track stretch started on the eastbound downgrade half a mile east of Germantown's 1891 frame station (where another single-story interlocking was located) and ended where it joined the earlier double track just west of Gaithersburg. Another three-arch stone viaduct was built over Great Seneca Creek at Waring, this one identical to the Little Monocacy bridge but slightly smaller.

At the same time, the branch also got a few less spectacular improvements: Besides Barnesville, new standardized frame stations appeared at Washington Grove and Buck Lodge and a pair of passing sidings was laid alongside the double track east of Rockville to hold freights out of the way on this busy section. And out at the west end of the branch Loree used a short section of Met right-of-way for his Adamstown cutoff. The cutoff, a completely new six-mile single-track railroad, was really a part of the Old Main Line as explained earlier.

The 1906 rebuilding project had added about seven miles of double track and some decidedly more permanent bridges. When it was finished, though, about a third of the Met branch was still single track and would remain so for 22 years more. The surviving single iron was split in two sections: seven straight miles from Washington Junction to Dickerson, with a passing siding at Tuscarora, and seven rugged curving miles from Barnesville to Germantown. The latter section had many cuts and fills plus the 1896 Little Seneca Creek trestle, in the center of a sharp "S" curve. Boyd station, the midpoint of the section, had a small interlocking plant in the building controlling a busy passing track.

Leonor Loree's Pennsylvania Railroad background inspired some of the same massive stone viaducts Pennsy had been building through the 1890's and early 1900's. This one, finished in 1906, spanned Great Seneca Creek at Waring. A larger twin was built farther west over the Little Monocacy near Dickerson. In March 1979 a westbound rolls over Waring viaduct at 55 m.p.h. making a run for the 1% hill up to Germantown. Credit: H.H. Harwood, Jr.

This standardized frame station was built for Washington Grove during the 1906 double-tracking program. Credit: William F. Smith.

The west end of double track was at Dickerson station, controlled by the little single-story interlocking plant shown in the distance. The 1920 view looks west. Although the freight house and "tower" are gone, the 1891 station building remains. Credit: B&O Museum Archives.

Views of the Met branch in its single track days are surprisingly rare. This, one of the few, shows the line at Buck Lodge about 1920. Credit: B&O Museum Archives.

Nonetheless trains could move faster and considerably more safely. Nonstop expresses now averaged 39 m.p.h. between Washington and Washington Junction. In 1916, seven through passenger trains ran each way over the Met — most of them advertised as "solid vestibuled electric lighted steel trains", and carrying names such as the "Interstate Special" (to Chicago), "Duquesne Limited" (Pittsburgh, of course), "Chicago Limited", "West Virginian" (to Wheeling), and "St. Louis Limited". More prosaically, three locals ran to Gaithersburg, one to Boyd, two to Frederick and one to Hagerstown.

Daniel Willard finally finished the double-tracking job that Loree had left undone. Beginning in 1926 the two remaining sections were rebuilt. Additional steel girder sections were built on the south side of the Monocacy Viaduct and the north side of the short Tuscarora Creek bridge to carry the second track. Between Germantown and Barnesville the existing cuts and fills were widened and the twisting alignment over Little Seneca Creek straightened with a large earth fill and concrete arch bridge. The old trestle footings are now buried in the underbrush about a quarter of a mile north of the new line. The line between Buck Lodge and Boyd was also straightened. A pair of long passing tracks for freights was built just west of Boyd, controlled by newly-established DS tower. Sadly, the handsome brick Boyd station came down to make room for the second track and a nearby grade crossing elimination. The entire project was completed in the fall of 1928 and for the first time the Metropolitan branch was a fully double track railroad.

And just in time, for passenger traffic had peaked simultaneously. By late 1928, a total of 38 passenger trains a day kept Met branch rails warm — 19 each way. Of these 19, eleven were now through runs, led by all-Pullman "Capitol Limited" and "National Limited"; otherwise, two locals ran each way to Frederick, two to Hagerstown or Brunswick, two to Boyd and two to Gaithersburg. By now most of the mid-day locals had disappeared, but the morning and evening commuter peaks were becoming more pronounced. The line also began to see an increasing number of Presidential and VIP specials, since it was the most direct route to the hinterlands. Most freights continued to use the Old Main Line although two through trains generally ran each way between Brunswick and Potomac Yard. These usually set off or picked up cars at Eckington yard in Washington and ran over the Washington branch as far as Hyattsville and the Alexandria branch/PRR trackage to Potomac Yard.

Realignments and double-tracking certainly raised the Met's capacity and eased its operating problems, but those Piedmont hills were still there and the grades much the same as they always were. In fact, since the early 1900's tonnage ratings for the Met have been lower than the Old Main Line. Eastbound, for example, a Q-4 could take only 2,375 tons up the Barnesville grade versus 2,750 tons through Mt. Airy on the Old Main. Freight helpers were the rule, and still are: Eastbound freights usually would get a pusher at Brunswick or Point of Rocks which would cut off at either Barnesville or, more often, Gaithersburg. Westbound freights had an even more gruelling grade from Eckington (Washington) to Silver Spring, but it was shorter (5.2 miles long) and most freights were lighter in that direction. Those that did need help simply got a yard engine from Eckington.

Washington's suburban growth spread rapidly northwest during the 1920's and '30's, partly following the Metropolitan's path. Traditionally, however, the through western trains had made no stops between Washington Union Station and Point of Rocks and the next scheduled pickup point for the "Capitol" and "National" was Martinsburg. In 1936 B&O took what was then an innovative step in passenger marketing: it established a suburban stop for all main-line trains. The spot picked was the 1878 brick station at Silver Spring, just outside the District Line where the railroad crossed Georgia Ave. Silver Spring itself was a somewhat nondescript fringe of the city, but was a major streetcar and bus terminal and — probably more significant — was within easy driving reach of the more prestigious suburbs such as Chevy Chase, Bethesda and northwest Washington. Unfortunately the historic station was deemed inadequate and unfashionable for its new role; immediately after World War II work began on a modern replacement on the site of the original. The new station — still quite active — was opened December 16, 1945, just in time for the Christmas travel rush. But unknown to almost everyone, the old station lives on in a way. In order to get its building permit at a time when wartime material and manpower shortages were still critical, B&O had to build its new station on the old foundations. Thus the form of new Silver Spring followed the old and although its interior layout was roomier, it was still tight for the large postwar passenger loads.

Ex-Buffalo, Rochester & Pittsburgh No. 5143 heads an afternoon westbound local through Forest Glen. The "Castle", a long-time Forest Glen commercial landmark, is at left. Credit: E.L. Thompson.

Freight traffic on the Met traditionally had been kept as light as possible, mostly confined to local Washington business, Brunswick-Potomac Yard runs and way freights. While the line was always a bypass for blockages on the Old Main Line, its hills, heavy passenger traffic and circuity were such that B&O preferred to keep its Baltimore and Philadelphia freights off the Met. Before the Depression and the appearance of good roads and effective truck competition, freight train speed was usually not critical and the railroad was content to live with the lower speeds and coal drag congestion on the Old Main.

But by the late 1930's pressures were building to increase the number of scheduled manifest trains (or "QD's and "Timesavers" as B&O variously called them), tighten their schedules and keep them on time. At the time, the hottest of these were eastbound New York 94 and its westbound counterpart New York 97, usually hauled by doubleheaded Q-4's carrying auxiliary water tenders to minimize stops. Gradually local operating managers began running them around the Met to keep them out of the way of the drags — sometimes surreptiously, since the railroad's top management was concerned about affecting passenger train performance. The routing became more or less permanent and led to more. And in 1938 B&O inaugurated freights 117-118, a high speed overnight New York-Pittsburgh l.c.l. service which was also routed over the Met, running at passenger train speeds.

Indeed, there was getting to be more room on the Met for freight. By the mid 1930's daytime local passenger service had vanished and the branch was carrying primarily the western through trains. These in turn had fallen into a scheduling pattern which bunched them at certain times of the day: outbound from Washington in late afternoon and evening, and inbound in early mid-morning. Except for a few secondary work-

An eastbound freight raises dust at Forest Glen station about 1928.
Credit: E.L. Thompson.

horse trains, the line was pretty much bare of passenger runs the rest of the time. In 1936, thirteen passenger trains ran each way (remember it was 19 in 1928): 11 main line runs, one commuter local to Frederick and one commuter to Brunswick. Soon afterward the terminal of the Frederick run was also switched to Brunswick, leaving a basic two-train Brunswick-Washington commuter service schedule which survived for more than 25 years afterwards. The number of main line trains would drop to a post-depression low of nine each way by 1940 before bulging again during the war years.

But visually at least, the late '30's were not all grim: In 1937 B&O's first (and the country's first) streamlined road passenger diesels arrived on the Met — six two-unit sets of regal Electro-Motive EA/EB's, which were immediately assigned to the "Capitol" and "National" out of Washington. The sight may generate yawns today, but in 1937 (and for years after) passengers waiting in the late afternoon at Silver Spring station were invariably awed as the shining blue, gold, grey and black diesels throbbed up the hill from Washington trailing their heavyweight Pullmans. The "Capitol" was re-equipped in 1938 with blue/grey/gold streamlined (but still heavyweight) cars; the "National" got similar treatment in 1940. And in 1941-42, seven more two-unit passenger diesel

In this atmospheric scene a heavy eastbound freight fights its way to the top of the grade at Gaithersburg in the late 1940's. From here it will drift easily downhill to Washington. Credit: Ara Mesrobian.

sets appeared on other mainliners such as the new "Columbian", "Diplomat" and "Ambassador".Older Pacifics still barked out with the others, including the Brunswick locals. The installation of an automatic train stop system in 1943 allowed higher speeds, too; afterwards passenger trains were allowed 75 m.p.h.

In fact, generally the Met tended to have a slightly more varied motive power diet than the relentless succession of P's and Q's on B&O's other lines in the area. During the 1930's, thanks to wide clearances and Washington Terminal's 100-ft. turntables, the heavy and impressive experimental 4-8-2's 5510 and 5550 regularly handled the "Capitol" west of Washington. And in the early 1950's B&O's home-built T-3 Mountains were assigned to two pairs of mail trains over the Met. In between, odd castoffs occasionally would appear on locals — notably the ex-"Royal Blue" 4-6-4 "Lord Baltimore", by then merely numbered 5340.

Following the frenzy of the war years, when passenger business swelled and freights were routed any way that kept them moving, the Met found itself slowly changing its nature from a high-speed passenger railroad to a fast freight line. It came out of World War II running 14 passenger trains each way, certainly a happier state than the nine of 1940. And by 1947 the number had climbed to 16, which included the fast, luxurious but doomed daytime "Cincinnatian", hauled by its specially streamlined P-7 Pacifics. And in 1949 the completely re-equipped "Colum-

A Q-4-powered eastbound wayfreight eases into Kensington on a summer midday in 1946. Credit: H.H. Harwood, Jr.

bian" appeared with its domes — the first, and for 10 years, the only domes on any eastern railroad. But soon afterwards the decay started: in late 1950 the Met was carrying only 13 passenger trains each way; by 1955 it was 11 as several main liners were consolidated; by 1970 it was only 7, with the "Capitol" (now carrying coaches) the only true name train left. The St. Louis cars of the "National" had been routed over C&O, by now B&O's owner; a semi-local to Cincinnati had taken the "National's" place on B&O, but this was taken off in 1967. Throughout the carnage the two Brunswick commuter locals plugged on, their status unchanged by anything. However, their Pacifics and aging heavyweight coaches were replaced by Budd RDC cars — one run in 1951 and the other in 1953.

The advent of Amtrak May 1, 1971 killed the "Capitol" and all other through services on B&O. Afterwards, the Met's passenger traffic went through an erratic series of gyrations as Amtrak attempted to respond to various political pressures for service between Washington and points in West Virginia and Ohio. Trains appeared, disappeared and changed form and terminals. The most memorable, if short-lived, was a three-car United Aircraft turbotrain set which operated from Washington to Parkersburg in 1972. Present (1979) Amtrak service consists of one through Washington-Cincinnati run — currently in jeopardy — and a commuter round trip to Martinsburg.

At the same time, however, the Brunswick commuter business began its surprising renaissance. Interstate 270 stimulated the suburban development along the northwest corridor started long before by the railroad. Towns like Rockville, Gaithersburg and Germantown turned into an

A stunning exception to the generally bland medium-sized motive power of the 1930's was T-2 No. 5550, here coupling onto the "Capitol" at Washington about 1934. The hefty Baldwin-built Mountain was regular power for this train west of Washington during the mid-Thirties. Credit: H.W. Pontin: H.H. Harwood collection.

In 1951 Budd RDC cars displaced steam on the Washington-Brunswick commuter schedules. During the 1970's commuter traffic expanded dramatically on the Met and at present six RDC and locomotive-hauled trains operate each way on weekdays. Typical is this four-car RDC train braking into Kensington for Washington-bound commuters in June 1972. Credit: H.H. Harwood, Jr.

A brief and forgettable visitor to the Metropolitan branch was a United Aircraft-built turbo-train operated by Amtrak on a Washington-Parkersburg (W. Va.) schedule. Here it heads west through Capitol View in mid-1972. Credit: Ara Mesrobian.

unbroken string of split levels, shopping centers and office parks. Even off-the-beaten-path rural communities such as Boyd, Barnesville and Dickerson have blossomed as "exurbs". An increasing number of Washington commuters from these areas discovered that the railroad was the most practical way of reaching work, particularly in conjunction with Washington's newly opened (in 1976) Metro system. Thanks primarily to a subsidy agreement with the State of Maryland, B&O commuter service on the Met has expanded to a current (mid-1979) total of five trains each way (four to Brunswick, one to Martinsburg), plus the additional Amtrak-operated Martinsburg commuter run. The expanding traffic outgrew B&O's RDC fleet and at least one trip now consists of a mishmash of conventional passenger coaches — some B&O, some C&O, some leased and including one B&O heavyweight — hauled by a diesel.

While the Met's passenger trains went from riches to rags, freight filled the gap, to some extent, at least. Following World War II more scheduled merchandise trains were established, and many were routed around the Met to keep clear of slow freights on the Old Main. (Several parts of the Old Main Line are still limited to 25-35 m.p.h.) In addition, inbound traffic to Washington (primarily perishables, piggyback and building materials) was increasing and more main line freights set off and picked up cars at Eckington. And finally, the development of the Jessup-Fort Meade Junction area as an auto terminal in 1967 required any trains handling Jessup business to use the Met. By 1969, 22 scheduled freights passed over the Met plus such movements as grain extras and even occasional coal trains. The gradual appearance of longer and higher freight cars also worked in the Met's favor — its comparatively gradual curvature allowed normal running speeds, particularly important for piggyback and the large covered hoppers now used to carry grain.

In fact, the Met had become such a preferred freight route that when Agnes devastated the Old Main Line in June, 1972, Chessie's top management came within a hair of abandoning most of it as redundant. While the company debated the economics of abandonment versus the advantages of a bypass and tonnage route, all B&O freight circled through Washington and over the Met, which was now virtually bare of passenger traffic. B&O's operating managers finally prevailed and the Old Main Line was restored in 1974, but its reduced capacity dictated that the Met would remain the major freight route.

Out on the railroad, local freight customers on the Met fell into two clear groups: those in and around Washington and those everywhere else. Washington, of course, was never much more than a consuming city — although as years went on, it consumed heavily. The Met was a major channel for inbound food, building materials, fuel, paper and various manufactured goods. The section from Silver Spring to Washington became a center for cement, brick and coal distribution; coal also was brought into the large terminal north of Union Station and western perishables went to the Eckington team tracks. As Washington expand-

WASHINGTON FINALLY GETS WEST:
THE METROPOLITAN BRANCH

A.

B.

Freights are still frequent on the Met. (A) An eastbound led by SD-35 No. 7409 grinds up the west slope of Parr's Ridge just west of Dickerson in March 1979. In the distance is Catoctin Mountain and Point of Rocks. (B) Shoving on its rear are three GP-9 units. These will go to Gaithersburg, then return light to Brunswick. Credit (both): H.H. Harwood, Jr.

ed outward, the companies handling building materials spread out the line to Kensington and Rockville. Beyond, freight traffic consisted mostly of feed, fertilizer, livestock and other mainstays of agriculture. Feed mills were located at Derwood, Gaithersburg and Germantown —most of which have now disappeared.

The Derwood mill gives an almost industrial background to a passenger local pausing at the 1870-vintage rural station in 1948. Later the mill building burned, taking the station with it. Credit: Lee B. Smith collection.

As the nature of Montgomery County changed so, to some extent, did the complexion of the Met's freight customers. In 1959 Potomac Electric Power Company completed a large coal-fired generating plant southwest of Dickerson, reached by a long spur from the east end of the Monocacy Viaduct. And, typical of the urbanization at the eastern end of the Met, is a large Sears warehouse built at Washington Grove in 1967.

The Met's open right of way through northwest Washington made it a natural and relatively cheap corridor for the city's Metro rapid transit system and in the early 1970's B&O sold a portion of its right-of-way from Rhode Island Avenue to Silver Spring to Metro for $8.5 million. Construction started in 1973 for what was eventually intended to be the Glenmont extension of the Red Line. In order to allow B&O to reach its freight customers on either side of the line to Silver Spring, engineers decided to spread B&O's double track line apart and locate the two Metro tracks between them. The Metro line came down to the surface north of Rhode Island Avenue, burrowed under the westbound Met track, and came back to the surface between the railroad tracks just south of its Brookland station. Metro built its Silver Spring terminal north of the B&O station at Colesville Road; in the process, B&O's eastbound station was removed, but the large westbound station was left untouched. The only other surviving B&O suburban station on the line — the once pretty and now burned-out Baldwin-designed University station — was demolished during the construction.

Metro's Silver Spring line opened in February 1978. West of Silver Spring the rapid transit will eventually tunnel back under the B&O and follow the railroad as far as 16th Street before swinging north to Glenmont. The other end of the Red Line will some day terminate at Shady Grove (Md.), just beyond Rockville and will use the Met's right-of-way through Rockville, displacing the historic brick railroad station in the process. (The station will be saved, but moved.)

So in 1979 the Metropolitan branch is literally a trip through time: It begins in 1875 at the Bavarian spire of Point of Rocks station, adjacent to what's left of the C&O Canal. . .progresses past the Pennsylvania Railroad-era stone viaducts. . .through Silver Spring station, symbol of the unfulfilled postwar passenger hopes. . .and ends racing a Rohr rapid transit train past the shades of little suburban stations.

Between Rhode Island Avenue and Silver Spring, Metro's rapid transit line now occupies the center of the old Met right-of-way, with B&O's main line tracks on either side. An eastbound B&O freight has just beaten a Metro train (in the distance) into Brookland station. Just beyond the overpass in the rear was B&O's pretty stone University station, demolished to make room for the additional tracks. Credit: H.H. Harwood, Jr.

Westbound No. 9 crosses the East-West Highway leaving Silver Spring in May 1950. This site is now the location of Metro's Silver Spring rapid transit and bus station. Credit: E.L. Thompson.

The Detroit-bound "Ambassador" east of Rockville in 1947. Credit: E.L. Thompson.

A trio of F-3's with the westbound "Capitol Limited" accelerate through Georgetown Junction shortly after the passenger stop at Silver Spring. When this photo was made in May 1951, late afternoon train watchers could see a succession of four westbound name trains and a commuter local within two hours. Credit: E.L. Thompson.

A pair of E-7's roar through Kensington station with an eastbound about 1950. Credit: Ara Mesrobian.

IMPOSSIBLE CHALLENGE

CHAPTER 13

GETTING SOUTH THE HARD WAY: THE ALEXANDRIA BRANCH

The Pennsylvania's lightning invasion of Washington between 1870 and 1872 had thrown the B&O into complete disarray. As related in the chapters on the Washington branch and the Washington stations, the PRR not only established a strong passenger route into the city, but managed to elbow the B&O off the Long Bridge — the only direct rail access to Virginia and thus to the south. By mid-1872 — even before the Pennsy had fully finished its Washington-Baltimore line — it had assumed operation of the Long Bridge, rebuilt it and taken over the Alexandria & Washington. In addition, it had extended the A&W south to Quantico, Va., to meet the Richmond, Fredericksburg & Potomac, the northernmost link in the developing chain of railroads through the south. And embarrassingly, the same coup had separated B&O from its own southern satellite, the Orange, Alexandria & Manassas, which terminated at Alexandria, eight miles across the river from B&O's Washington station. The OA&M, which then ran from Alexandria to Lynchburg, was the key to John W. Garrett's ambitions for a route to New Orleans. True, B&O had its Shenandoah Valley route south from Harpers Ferry, but that was uncompleted and ultimately doomed.

Stranded on the north side of the Potomac — in fact, not even at the shore of the river — B&O looked frantically for an alternative route. The river's width coupled with the Pennsylvania line's location and Pennsy's political strength in Washington made a direct assault expensive and success questionable.

Instead the railroad settled on a half-measure: a branch along the east side of the Potomac to a point opposite Alexandria, coupled with a carfloat across the river to reach the OA&M terminal on the Alexandria waterfront. The 12.3-mile branch was built under the name of the Washington City & Point Lookout Railroad. It left the Washington branch at Hyattsville, Md., 5½ miles northeast of Washington and swung south, following the east bank of the Eastern Branch (Anacostia River) and Potomac to a remote and barren point of land protruding into the Potomac opposite the north side of Alexandria's business district. Along the way, it passed through Bladensburg, entered the District near present-day Kenilworth and continued through Benning, Twining City and Anacostia (then called Uniontown). The terminal point was variously called Shepherd's Landing, Marbury Point and (after the railroad arrived) East Alexandria. The Alexandria landing point was slightly less than a mile downriver at Wilkes Street.

The junction at Hyattsville (or Alexandria Junction, as it was listed in B&O operating timetables) was laid out in a wye to allow direct access both north and west. Freights from the west would follow the newly-opened Metropolitan branch into Washington, switch onto the Washington branch a mile north of the Washington station, then follow the Washington branch to Hyattsville — a routing still followed today. Just north of the District line, the branch bridged the Pennsy's Baltimore-Washington main line, then paralleled the Pennsy for three miles through Kenilworth, Benning and Anacostia.

The Alexandria branch joined the Baltimore-Washington line just north of Hyattsville station at an operating point called Alexandria Junction. The scene here shows a freight from Baltimore crossing over on its way onto the branch, which diverges just beyond the camera. An eastbound freight from the branch has just cleared. The date: November 1947. Credit: E.L. Thompson.

The "Alexandria" branch was easy to build, if nothing else. Since it followed the river flatlands with no significant streams to cross and minimal population, construction consisted of not much more than putting track on the ground. Not surprisingly, the job went quickly: Work started at Hyattsville August 1, 1873 and track had been put down to Shepherd's Landing by January 24, 1874. By early March two tugs had arrived at Alexandria and trial trips were run March 10. After fixing some minor problems with the ferry slips, revenue freight service started March 16. Having accomplished its purpose, the Washington City & Point Lookout sold its properties to B&O in November, 1874 and presumably passed out of existence.

For the next 32 years, two tugs normally handled the cross-river service. Oldest was the "Major Henry Bewerton", an iron-hulled tug built by Murray & Hazlehurst in Baltimore in 1857 and lengthened in 1862. ("Bewerton" was a typographical corruption of Brewerton, an Army engineer who worked on the development of Baltimore's harbor and ship channels.) Originally owned by the City of Baltimore, the "Bewerton" was bought by B&O secondhand in October 1872 for its Baltimore harbor operations out of Locust Point. It arrived at Alexandria for the new service in January 1874. Besides the "Bewerton" B&O ordered a new tug, the "Convoy", from Neafie & Levy in Philadelphia; completed in 1873, she was also on the scene at Alexandria when operations began. The carfloats were flat barges fitted with two tracks, each carrying five cars per track. In all probability the floating equipment was traded off with the Baltimore and later Philadelphia marine fleets over the years.

Aside from the marine operations the Alexandria branch was physically and operationally uninspiring. It was flat, mostly straight and single-tracked with minimum facilities. Low wood trestles spanned the small streams along the way. There was a wye and wood pier at Shepherd's Landing and an interchange with the Pennsylvania south of Benning. Although most of the line lay within the District, the area was sparsely populated in the 1870's and aside from the settlement of Uniontown (Anacostia) offered little on-line freight or passenger business.

On the Alexandria side B&O's carfloat terminal was located close to the spot where the Orange, Alexandria & Manassas Railroad's waterfront branch emerged from its Wilkes Street tunnel. (The tunnel is still there, although the rails are now gone.) The OA&M was a post Civil War reorganization of the Orange & Alexandria; B&O's president John Garrett had begun buying its stock in 1866 and by 1872 had picked enough to control the railroad. Two years later — about the time the B&O carfloat operation began — he reorganized it under the unwieldy and pretentious name of the Washington City, Virginia Midland & Great Southern, which everyone promptly shortened as the "Virginia Midland". By this time it had worked its way as far south as Danville, Va. and formed a through connecting route to Atlanta, Chattanooga, Memphis and New Orleans. Unfortunately, the Pennsy's Tom Scott was moving fast ahead of Garrett and by 1874 many of the railroads south of Danville were under Pennsylvania control, so the Virginia Midland had already lost much of its potential.

These two tugs shuttled the carfloats across the Potomac between 1874 and 1906 (A) The *Major Bewerton* steams off Alexandria in 1894. Originally built in 1857, it survived intact, albeit with a large loss of dignity, until 1978. (B) *Convoy*, built in 1873, worked the Alexandria route as well as Baltimore and Philadelphia harbors. She is shown here in Philadelphia in 1950 during her last years. Credits: A—Mariners Museum—B-Steamship Historical Society.

Passenger service on the Alexandria branch led a briefly exciting, confused and dead-end life. For a year after its 1874 opening the line was strictly a freight operation as B&O and its Virginia subsidiary adjusted to the new operational connection and traffic relationship. But John Garrett was not yet ready to give up on the idea of a B&O-operated through passenger service to the south. Early in April 1875 he began running two trains a day between Baltimore and the OA&M/Virginia Midland, using the branch and the tug-powered carfloats. Let the Baltimore *News* of May 16, 1875 describe it:

"The East Alexandria ferry is now in full tide of successful operation, and two trains leave Camden station daily — one at 6:15 a.m. and the other at 10:15 — for Alexandria, Lynchburg, Danville and the South via Shepherd's, the Alexandria terminus of the Baltimore & Ohio Railroad.

The 6:15 a.m. train also takes passengers for Richmond, the steamers of the Richmond, Fredericksburg & Potomac Railroad stopping at Shepherd's and making close connections with the trains. By this route passengers reach Richmond in a fraction over six hours (from Baltimore), and can partake of breakfast on the steamer, besides having a full view of Mt. Vernon and enjoying a delightful trip of about 25 miles on the majestic Potomac.

Upon arriving at Shepherd's, the train for Alexandria, Lynchburg and the south is quickly placed on the steamboat (actually a carfloat) which is provided with double tracks, and started for Alexandria which is directly opposite, the time consumed in the transfer being only about 15 minutes. Everything goes like clockwork, and passengers may feel as secure as though they were on terra firma. The distance from Baltimore to Alexandria is about 49 miles and is run in about an hour and 30 minutes, saving nearly an hour over the route via Washington with its tiresome omnibus transfers...

Travel, since the opening of the route, has increased materially, and Sunday night four well-filled cars composed the train which arrived in this city at 9:50 p.m.

A large amount of freight is conveyed by this route, several trips of the steamer being required daily to make the transfer, ten cars being taken across the river at one time. At Shepherd's everything wears a businesslike aspect, several locomotives and a large number of employees being constantly engaged in shifting cars...

At Alexandria great interest is manifested in the passage of the cars, and large numbers congregate on the wharves every day to witness the operations. A great many ladies cross and recross the river every day on the ferry steamer, 'just for the novelty of the thing'."

The novelty wore off quickly, at least as far as the railroad was concerned. Although present evidence is incomplete, the ferry connection apparently was not as glowingly perfect as the *News* reported it, and the two railroads attempted to work out an all-rail connection. Probably some time in early 1876, they succeeded in setting up an operation whereby Virginia Midland engines and crews ran over the Pennsylvania tracks from Alexandria through Washington to the PRR-B&O interchange near Benning. This was short-lived too; by the evidence of operating timetables, it was gone by late 1876 and B&O never again attempted any north-south passenger services through Washington or Alexandria. During the 1880's it advertised through cars between Washington and the south over the Shenandoah Valley Railroad — now a part of Norfolk & Western — which B&O crossed east of Martinsburg, W. Va. Alexandria branch passenger service withered into a once-daily mixed train — actually simply a way freight operating on a pre-dawn schedule. In 1884 it left Alexandria Junction at 4:20 a.m. and returned from Shepherd's at 5:00 a.m. This finally ceased in the mid or late 1890's.

However, in the early 1880's B&O did run excursion trains from Baltimore to Shepherd's to meet various Potomac passenger steamers. And in addition to the railroad carfloat, it handled a healthy traffic in package freight which was transferred to downriver steamers at the Shepherd dock.

By 1881 Garrett was discouraged with his southern expansion ambitions and sold B&O's Virginia Midland control to an outside financial group which was associated with neither B&O nor Pennsylvania. Pennsy did the same thing, and — except for B&O's abortive Valley branch to Lexington, Va. and Pennsy's very effective line to Quantico — both railroads stayed out of the south forever after. The Virginia Midland was folded into the growing Richmond & Danville system which in 1894 — under the hand of J.P. Morgan — became part of the Southern Railway.

But through all the financial and corporate tradeoffs, the Alexandria carfloat continued on, an important link for both B&O and the Virginia Midland. In 1882 the Virginia Midland bought a one-half financial interest in the tugs and carfloats from B&O, probably a result of the broken corporate tie between the two railroads. And B&O maintained at least a nominal physical presence in Alexandria; in 1890 it built its own freight station at the foot of Wolfe Street.

B&O's other hope — reaching the Richmond, Fredericksburg & Potomac — was not so successful. In 1874 the RF&P's northern terminal was Quantico, Va., 26½ miles south of Alexandria on the Potomac. Here it joined the Pennsylvania's line from Washington and operated through passenger and freight trains between Richmond and Washington via the two railroads. But the RF&P also operated a steamboat pier at Quantico, used by subsidiary Potomac Steamboat Company. Despite its strong Pennsy connection, the RF&P kept the water route as a secondary outlet to Washington and also as a hedge against the Pennsylvania. Using its steamboats, the RF&P managed to maintain the semblance of a passenger connection with the B&O until 1877, when Pennsy pressure stopped it.

But in 1880 B&O and RF&P again tried working together, this time by setting up a carferry route between Shepherd's and Quantico. The Potomac Steamboat Company ordered a full-sized wood hull carferry from Harlan & Hollingsworth that year for the service and rebuilt a Quantico pier to accommodate it. The 239-foot boat was designed for one track on its main deck with cabins above and twin beam engines driving paddle-wheels. But as soon as the Pennsy discovered what was happening it bluntly blackmailed the RF&P by diverting some traffic to the Virginia Midland at Alexandria. The RF&P promptly caved in and the carferry — named the "Excelsior" — was completed as a passenger steamer. It carried passengers for a short while between Washington and Quantico with its open bow and stern, looking every bit like a railroad carferry; in 1881, however, its ends were closed in and it was put on the Washington-Norfolk run. The incongruous-looking "Excelsior" finally burned in 1892, never having fulfilled its original mission.

B&O did eventually establish another railroad connection on its Alexandria branch, although it hardly qualified as a gateway to anywhere. In the railroad construction euphoria of early 1880's a company was formed to build from Washington southeast through rural eastern Maryland to Point Lookout. Its projected route began at a connection with the Alexandria branch in far northeast Washington near Benning and headed east through what is now Seat Pleasant. Under the name of the Southern Maryland, the railroad started some grading east from the B&O about 1883 but eventually expired with no more than about two miles built.

But in 1897 Colorado railroad and mining entrepreneur Otto Mears appeared with a new and grandiose scheme to create an American Monte

The abortive railroad carferry *Excelsior* was meant to form a water bridge between B&O and the RF&P at Quantico, Va. PRR opposition shortstopped the idea and *Excelsior* was completed as a passenger excursion steamer. Credit: Mariners Museum.

Carlo on Chesapeake Bay east of Washington. Essential to his project was a 32-mile railroad to connect the capital with his resort — to be named Chesapeake Beach. For the Washington end of his railroad Mears used the partly-completed right-of-way of the old Southern Maryland, exercising a sort of squatter's rights on the property. Construction of the Chesapeake Beach Railway began in October 1897, starting at a spot on B&O's Alexandria branch north of present Deane Avenue between Benning and Kenilworth. It was able to start service as far as Upper Marlboro late in 1898 and finally opened to Chesapeake Beach in early June, 1900.

Chesapeake Junction, where the CB joined B&O, was about as remote a terminal as the railroad could get and still be within Washington; indeed, in 1898 there was not even a city streetcar line out this far. In April of 1900 the Washington Traction & Electric Company did extend its Columbia (H St.) car line to Seat Pleasant, connecting with the Chesapeake Beach at the extreme western corner of the District Line; afterwards the long trolley line was the major means for Washington passengers to get to the beach trains. But in 1898 the CB also made a trackage rights agreement with B&O to use the Alexandria branch for the four miles between Chesapeake Junction and B&O's Washington branch at Hyattsville. CB's primary object was to tap the Baltimore market by connecting directly with certain Baltimore-Washington trains which stopped at Hyattsville. As part of the contract, B&O built a separate siding in front of its Hyattsville station for CB trains to lay over. Typically, two CB round trips a day were run between Hyattsville and Chesapeake Beach, including an RPO service — the most extensive passenger service the Alexandria branch ever saw.

Bound for the Alexandria branch, a southbound freight eases over the Washington branch crossovers at Alexandria Junction in August 1946. Credit: E.L. Thompson.

Unhappily, neither Chesapeake Beach nor its railroad came close to equaling Mears's dreams. The American Monte Carlo never materialized as such and neither the volume nor the class of clientele at Chesapeake Beach were at the level hoped for. The trackage rights agreement ended July 7, 1913 and afterwards all CB passenger trains ended their runs at the Seat Pleasant trolley terminal. Chesapeake Junction remained the CB's primary freight interchange, although the railroad's totally rural territory produced little freight for CB and B&O to interchange. The junction grew steadily more important after the building of the Benning power plant, but that is a separate story told later in this chapter.

Unhappy with its slow, awkward carfloat and frustrated in its attempts to reach the RF&P, B&O continued to flail about looking for some better way to connect with the Virginia railroads. As early as 1874 the Washington City & Point Lookout (the corporation B&O used to build its Alexandria branch) was attempting to obtain a franchise to extend through Washington and Georgetown to an upriver crossing into Virginia. The most serious try was made in the early 1890's when a new line into Virginia was started, this time leaving the Metropolitan branch and running around the west side of Washington. (The next chapter covers this project.) Naturally this came to nothing also and at the turn of the century B&O was still struggling across the Potomac with its tugs and carfloats. But freight volume improved, if nothing else. In December of 1900, 2,500 cars were floated across the river — an average of over 80 a day.

The Pennsylvania's decision in 1901 to work out a complete realignment and rebuilding of the strategic Washington freight gateway finally extricated B&O from its unhappy situation. That year the machinery was started which shortly would unify both the physical facilities and the commercial relationships of the connecting and competing railroads converging on the Potomac. The aim, in effect, was to establish a freight version of the union passenger station then being planned for Washington. But if anything, the project was more complicated than Union Station, involving some significant corporate changes, revisions of traditional junctions and a radical overhaul of route and yard layout.

At a minimum, physical rebuilding was necessary. North-south freight and passenger traffic was increasing dramatically by the late 19th Century as southern agriculture and industry developed. The perishable business was particularly growing. Yet the Alexandria-Washington layout and facilities had not essentially changed since the Civil War. Passenger and freight trains were transferred over the streets of Alexandria — the Virginia Midland/Richmond & Danville (and its tenant, the C&O) ran north in Henry Street; the Pennsylvania's Washington Southern Railway had a parallel single track a block west in Fayette Street. The Long Bridge was a rebuilt version of the Civil War structure, carrying only a single track. The key Pennsy line to Alexandria was also single track, following the east side of what is now U.S. Route 1. Freight yards were scattered around the area — the Southern's at Alexandria, Pennsy's and B&O's at various spots in Washington.

The essence of the new plan was to establish Alexandria as the common interchange point for all north-south freight traffic. To do this, the RF&P was re-formed as a sort of "union terminal" for the two big southeastern systems terminating in Richmond — the Atlantic Coast Line and Seaboard Air Line. At the same time it was extended north from Quantico to the Alexandria area by taking over the Pennsylvania's Washington Southern Line. The RF&P, in turn, would be jointly and equally controlled by the six railroads directly involved in the Potomac gateway —the Pennsylvania, B&O, Southern, C&O, Atlantic Coast Line and Seaboard. As part of its "union terminal" role, the RF&P would build a new four-track cutoff line through Alexandria, bypassing the congested old street trackage, and an enormous joint freight classification yard north of town in the marshy land near the mouth of Four Mile Run. B&O would be given access to the new yard over the Long Bridge and Pennsy trackage through Washington. And the Long Bridge itself would be replaced by a new steel double-track structure.

Once set, the gateway project rolled rapidly. The Richmond-Washington Co. was created in 1901 as the joint holding company to control the RF&P and the RF&P took over operation of Pennsy's Quantico line the same year. Also in 1901 the new Long Bridge was built — a 13-span truss bridge (including one swing span) which, in altered form, still carries trains today. The new four-track grade-separated alignment carrying RF&P, Southern and C&O through the west side of Alexandria was completed in 1905 including a new union passenger station (which also still stands). And finally the new hump freight classification yard — christened Potomac Yard — was officially opened August 1, 1906.

B&O's entry into Potomac Yard didn't eliminate the need for the Alexandria branch, by any means. To reach the yard, B&O freights followed the branch for 5.7 miles from Hyattsville to a spot south of Benning called Shepherd Junction, where the parallel Pennsy tracks turned west to cross the Anacostia into Washington. At Shepherd Junction a short B&O interchange spur also swung west to tie into the Pennsylvania line at Anacostia Junction at the east end of the Anacostia bridge. Entering the double-track PRR line, B&O's trains passed Anacostia tower, rolled over the low trestle crossing the river and cut across the south side of Washington to the Long Bridge. At the south end of the Long Bridge RF&P property begins; RF&P's RO tower (now demolished; opposite the present Twin Bridges Marriott hotel) switched both B&O and Pennsy Potomac Yard trains onto the yard approach tracks. Typical of most trackage rights arrangements, B&O freights do no local work on the PRR section and are under the direction of PRR (now Conrail) dispatchers.

The Alexandria carfloat was fully shut down October 15, 1906, the slip abandoned, and the two tugs transferred to Philadelphia to work B&O's Delaware River marine services. The tugs, incidentially, proved surprisingly long-lived. The "Convoy" remained in railroad service until it was retired in 1953. The "Bewerton" was sold in 1938 but, believe it or not, survived forty years more as a fishing vessel. When finally scrapped in 1978 at

A.

B.

IN 1906 B&O once again established direct rail connection with the southern railroads—but at the price of trackage rights over the Pennsylvania. (A) Potomac Yard-Philadelphia freight 84 with 110 cars is on Pennsy tracks along Virginia Avenue in southwest Washington in October 1949. (B) On a raw wintry day in 1947 a northbound B&O freight out of Potomac Yard passes RF&P's RO tower at the south end of the Long Bridge in Arlington. This point marks the end of PRR track and the beginning of the RF&P. Pennsy's now-abandoned Rosslyn branch swings off to the right. (Credits: A-E.L. Thompson—B-H.H. Harwood, Jr.

B&O coal destined for the big PEPCo Benning power plant was moved into the plant by an exotic variety of motive power over the years. Originally the plant was switched by electric locomotives operating over the Washington Ry. & Electric Co. and its successor, Capital Transit. Here Capital Transit motor 052 hustles three loads across Kenilworth Avenue about a block east of the B&O-East Washington Ry.-CTCo. interchanges. At this point (called Kenilworth Junction by the streetcar company), car lines to Kenilworth and Seat Pleasant diverged. The photo was taken in March 1949, shortly before the streetcar lines were converted to bus. East Washington diesels took over the power plant transfer work in 1955. EW's 102, a 65-ton World War II-surplus Whitcomb hauls hoppers along the onetime streetcar route at Deane and Minnesota Avenues, N.E. The train is heading for the B&O interchange and is passing under the paralleling B&O and PRR freight Lines. Credits (both): H.H. Harwood, Jr.

the remarkable age of 121 it was the oldest documented self-propelled vessel in the U.S.

With the start of Potomac Yard freight runs in 1906, the Alexandria branch turned into two separate kinds of railroad. The northern half from Hyattsville (Alexandria Junction) to Anacostia Junction carried all of B&O's southern gateway freight traffic, both from the western and northeastern parts of the railroad. It remains today an active, busy line, heavily built and reasonably well maintained. Three miles of this section from Kenilworth to a spot south of Shepherd Junction were double tracked. The lower six miles to Shepherd lapsed into a light secondary branch, living a somewhat checkered life as the nature of the territory along the east shore of the Anacostia and Potomac changed over the years.

The lower half of the Alexandria branch did have one scenic and industrial feature not commonly found on railroad lines. The riverfront flatlands immediately south of Washington developed into an early military aviation center with the establishment of Bolling Field in 1918 and later the adjacent Anacostia Naval Air Station (which took over the original Bolling Field site when Bolling was relocated to the immediate south). The railroad ran alongside both fields and, in fact, later had to be relocated out of the runways as Bolling Field was expanded. During World War II

the installation was obviously sensitive and heavily guarded, causing some mutual problems for B&O and the military. In the words of B&O historian Lawrence Sagle: "The right of way through the field is fenced in and a gate across the track bars entrance. Airplanes had the right of way over trains. Through a telephone tieup between Potomac Yard and the field, the dispatcher had to obtain permission for each train that passed through the field, timed to avoid flights in and out. Armed guards rode the trains to prevent any unauthorized person riding through the grounds."

Otherwise, the area along the Alexandria branch was sort of a back alley for Washington over much of the first half of the 20th Century — and to some extent it still is. B&O freight customer lists of the 1920's and 1930's presented an oddly contrasting combination of necessary but socially disagreeable functions: The stockyards and slaughterhouse at Benning, St. Elizabeth's Insane Asylum (later more euphemistically rechristened St. Elizabeth's Hospital), Washington Steel & Ordinance, Bellevue Magazine (a government arsenal), and the Home for the Aged and Infirm, near Shepherd. Washington Steel & Ordinance was one of the few manufacturing plants of any size ever built in the capital; from 1906 until the Depression it operated a large steel plant on Giesboro Point, now the site of Bolling Field. St. Elizabeth's was reached by a long private spur which wound up the hillside to the hospital on top. This little branch-of-a-branch got national attention from railroad enthusiasts in the late 1950's and early 1960's. The hospital's tiny Porter 0-4-0 saddletank switcher which hauled B&O coal hoppers up to the heating plant was the last active steam locomotive in the area.

But the Alexandria branch's largest single customer was the big electric generating plant on the Anacostia at Benning. Originally built in 1906, it was designed as the central power facility for the onetime Washington Railway & Electric Company, the largest of the city's two street railway companies. Later it was inherited by Potomac Electric Power Company and progressively expanded over the years as the city's major generating plant. The plant actually was reached only by the tracks of WR&E's (later Capital Transit's) Benning trolley line and the streetcar company handled all plant switching and interchange with its own electric locomotives. B&O coal was moved into Benning through an odd series of interchanges which at one time involved three separate carriers to handle the hoppers less than a mile. The problem was that B&O did not connect directly with the streetcar line, which passed underneath the railroad's Deane Avenue bridge. Instead the cars had to be interchanged to the Chesapeake Beach Railway at Chesapeake Junction; the CB track joined WR&E's Benning/Seat Pleasant line about three blocks away at Deane Avenue, where the electric locomotive picked them up and hauled them down alongside Kenilworth Avenue to the power plant.

To avoid the necessity for the CB to switch the cars itself over the three-block stretch between B&O and the trolley interchange, B&O made a contract with the CB in 1919 to allow B&O locomotives to use the track, paying CB a per-car charge for the privilege. Following the abandonment of the hapless CB in 1935, a short segment of its Washington end was reorganized as the East Washington Railroad; the EW existed mostly to serve a few local freight customers near Seat Pleasant and to handle the PEPCo coal interchange. During the late 1930's and early '40's EW's two secondhand 4-4-0's switched the hoppers the three blocks between B&O and Capital Transit. East Washington dieselized in 1946, first with a GE 45-tonner, then an ex-Army 65-ton Whitcomb and finally a former Washington Terminal Alco RS-1. The Seat Pleasant streetcar line was abandoned in 1949; however, Capital Transit continued to switch the Benning plant until January 1955 when it sold the section to the East Washington. The Benning plant continued to be a good B&O coal customer — and virtually the EW's sole support — until 1975 when it switched to oil to meet air pollution requirements. Coal shipments ceased that year although the East Washington wheezed along until early 1978. St. Elizabeth's Hospital had been lost about ten years before — also to oil.

By 1979 there was only one significant customer left on the lower half of the Alexandria branch — the large Blue Plains sewage treatment plant near Shepherd, receiving inbound chlorine. The branch south of Shepherd Junction has been marginal over the past several years, but at the moment is in no immediate danger of abandonment.

The south end of the Alexandria branch may have spent most of the 20th Century as a nondescript industrial spur, but there was a brief and strange moment of glory in the middle of it all. Indeed, the line suddenly sprang to life as the exact fulfillment of John W. Garrett's dream of B&O's own all-rail link across the Potomac. It came 68 years late and lasted only four years when it came, but was an amazing transformation while it lasted.

In the opening days of World War II the government panicked at the obvious vulnerability of the Long Bridge over the Potomac, by far the most important rail link between north and south and the only rail crossing of the river for 55 miles. Furthermore, Potomac Yard was the only facility capable of handling the traffic volume and it was totally tied to the Long Bridge crossing. While enemy air raids were perhaps a remote possibility in 1942, nobody really knew; in addition, sabotage was a very real fear. And in any event, it was dangerous to rely on a single bridge at such a critical spot; even such "normal" events as derailments or traffic congestion could put it out of service or cause serious delays. So almost immediately after Pearl Harbor, military planners started work on an alternate Potomac rail crossing.

B&O's Alexandria branch was the obvious bypass route since, after all, it had originally been built for that purpose. This time, though, a bridge would be built at the point where B&O had been forced to float its cars across years before. The planned bridge would cross the river from a spot slightly north of the old Shepherd's Landing pier, hitting the north side of Alexandria near Third Street. From here a new track was to be built paralleling a Southern Railway branch west into Potomac Yard. There were a few problems: The river was over six-tenths of a mile wide at that point, although mostly shallow; river traffic necessitated a swing bridge; and finally, 36 years of branch-line status for the section between Shepherd Junction and the bridge site had left a light, low-capacity railroad. In fact, the southern tip of the line had been dismantled some years before.

Nonetheless the Army engineers quickly cobbled up a bridge with the same dispatch their Civil War counterparts had done on the Potomac in 1862. Both the speed of the job and material shortages dictated a second-hand structure if possible. Happily, they found a reasonably long steel truss/swing bridge available on the Grand Trunk Western at Saginaw, Mich. and had it dismantled in March, 1942. The Potomac bridge job was a typical spare-no-expense hurryup wartime effort, with a total of about 430 people working two shifts seven days a week. Despite several delays and one severe flood, the bridge was finished by November 1, 1942; the first "train" — a Q-1 and caboose — crossed on December 9. At the same time, the B&O's Alexandria branch was rebuilt with 100-lb. rail, reballasted and signalled.

The completed bridge measured 3,360.5 ft. from abutment to abutment. It consisted of seven through truss spans totalling 1,122 ft. (including a 247-ft. swing span) in the center of the river, flanked by low trestle approaches on each side. The truss portions were supported by bundles of concrete-filled hollow steel pilings; the trestle pilings were mostly timber.

Three F-7's head a long Potomac Yard-bound freight through Chesapeake Junction in January 1955. The high poles at the left mark the parallel Pennsy line; at right is the East Washington interchange. Credit: H.L. Buckley.

Altogether, it was unremarkable from an engineering viewpoint, but impressive nonetheless — and indisputably a Potomac landmark while it lasted.

The emergency bridge, as it was generally known, was government-owned, but operated and maintained by B&O under contract. Technically it was open to all railroads entering Potomac Yard. Normal (non-emergency) traffic over one train a day paid a toll charge.

Use of the bridge tended to be erratic but often exotic. As an "emergency" structure, it was not really meant to carry normal scheduled movements although it was regularly used for overflow traffic — particularly troop trains. Normally only northbound trains were routed over the bridge. Traffic varied from one train a day — the contract minimum, considered necessary to assure the bridge was always in available condition — to anywhere from three to eight trains a day during the traffic peaks of 1943 and 1944. The peak came in October 1943 with 184 trains during the month.

The war's end also meant the end of the bridge. It was closed November 14, 1945 and dismantled about a year later. Afterwards the lower end of the Shepherd branch returned to its normal torpor. Little evidence now shows of the troop trains and heavy freights which once rolled over it.

The war also produced a very special sort of rebirth of passenger service on the Alexandria branch. In Chapter 11 we mentioned President Franklin Roosevelt's penchant for visiting his home at Hyde Park, N.Y. — always by rail and almost always leaving Washington on B&O. The trips were so frequent they almost amounted to regular weekly schedules, causing problems for the Secret Service and White House transportation staff in finding loading points and routings that would keep the Presidential party away from crowded Union Station. After experimenting with several suburban points on B&O and on PRR's Rosslyn (Va.) branch, they settled on a short underground spur into the Bureau of Engraving & Printing off 14th St. in southwest Washington. The spur ran off the Pennsylvania's main line to the Long Bridge, used by B&O's and Pennsy's Potomac Yard freights and southern passenger trains. The Presidential specials were then usually quietly routed over the Alexandria branch to Hyattsville, then sent north over B&O's Washington branch and Philadelphia line.

IMPOSSIBLE CHALLENGE

CHAPTER 14

ANOTHER TRY AT GOING SOUTH: THE GEORGETOWN BRANCH

As a link to the southern railroads, the Alexandria branch and its carfloat across the Potomac was better than nothing, but hardly much more. Compared with the Pennsylvania's direct rail route over the Long Bridge, it was costly, cumbersome, slow and at the mercy of the weather.

Furthermore it gave B&O only partial access to the rail systems that were being pieced together in the South during the 1880's and '90's. The Alexandria carfloat connected only with the Virginia Midland, later a part of the Richmond & Danville and—after 1894—the Southern Railway. This system was oriented primarily to the piedmont region between Alexandria and Atlanta, connecting with lines such as the C&O and Norfolk & Western reaching into the Appalachians. But B&O was effectively sealed off from the direct link to the Atlantic seaboard and Florida, the Richmond, Fredericksburg & Potomac Railroad. At that time the RF&P came only as far north as Quantico, Va., where it joined the Pennsy-built line from Washington. The Pennsy wouldn't interchange with the B&O at Alexandria and had shortstopped the planned B&O-RF&P water link between Shepherd's Landing and Quantico — perhaps just as well, since this would have been even more unwieldy than B&O's short Alexandria carfloat.

B&O's frustrations were only aggravated by the gradual development of agriculture and industry in the south and the formation of large, stable southern railway systems such as the Richmond & Danville /Southern and Atlantic Coast Line. In short, it was becoming an important market and B&O was missing much of it. Yet there wasn't much the railroad could do to improve its position through Alexandria. Bridging the Potomac here was impractical—the river was too wide and too busy and other sites at Washington were no better.

Thus stymied, B&O next decided to try an end run around the other side of Washington. West of Georgetown the river was considerably narrower and carried no commercial traffic, although the topography tended to be hilly. B&O plotted out a route which would leave the Metropolitan branch west of Silver Spring, swing south around the western boundary of the District of Columbia, cross the Potomac west of Chain Bridge, climb out of the Potomac Valley along Pimmit Run, then head more-or-less due south for 40 miles to Quantico, Va. The object, of course, was to connect with the RF&P at its northern terminal; en route, it would cross the Alexandria-Atlanta main line of the Richmond & Danville (later the Southern Railway) at Fairfax Station, Va. The Fairfax Station connection also would interchange with the C&O, which used R&D tracks into Alexandria. At Dunn Loring, Va. the B&O line would also cross the Richmond & Danville's Round Hill branch, a rural secondary line which later became the now-abandoned Washington & Old Dominion.

As a byproduct of the new line, a branch would turn east near the D.C.-Maryland line at Dalecarlia and follow the C&O Canal into Georgetown. Georgetown, of course, predated Washington; as a river port and canal terminal, it was always an important commercial center for this part of the Potomac Valley. By 1890 Georgetown had been politically and economically integrated with Washington and was developing into a small milling, warehousing and distribution center for the evolving metropolitan area. Especially enticing for B&O was its potential as a coal consumption and distribution point, partly an inheritance from its role as a coal terminal on the C&O canal.

Between 1889 and 1891 an odd little group of subsidiaries was created to build various pieces of the project: The Metropolitan Southern (incorporated May 14, 1890), to extend from the Metropolitan branch junction to Dalecarlia; the Metropolitan Western (Feb. 4, 1890), to build the Virginia section of the line from the Potomac bridge to Quantico; and the Washington & Western Maryland (March 2, 1889) to complete the line from Dalecarlia to the Aqueduct Bridge in Georgetown. A fourth company with the mouth-filling name of Georgetown Barge, Dock, Elevator & Railway Co. had already been formed in 1888 to build track along the Georgetown waterfront and in December 1889 had laid its line in Water Street (K St.) from Rock Creek to the Aqueduct Bridge. B&O took over operation of the Georgetown company in December 1891, although it remained isolated from the rest of the system (and from any other railroad) until the Georgetown branch was finally completed in 1910.

(As an aside, this track in Georgetown has always been one of Washington's minor historical mysteries. Since it had no outside track connection for 22 years, and no method of interchanging cars, nobody seems to know what it operated or how. As best can be speculated, it was merely a horse-powered intramural railroad, switching captive cars

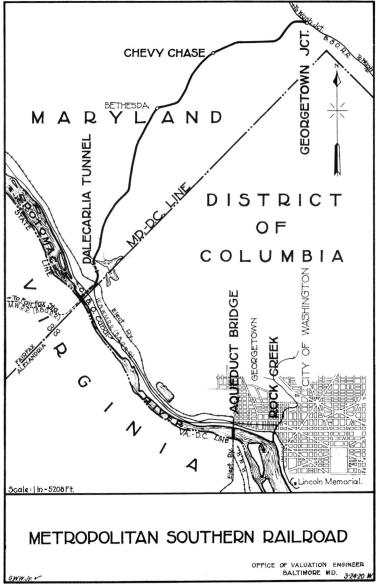

METROPOLITAN SOUTHERN RAILROAD

OFFICE OF VALUATION ENGINEER
BALTIMORE MD. 3-24-20 H.

The Georgetown branch was built under three separate corporate names. The Metropolitan Southern owned the line from Georgetown Junction to the Maryland-D.C. line, including the projected spur to the Potomac River bridge (note the short dashed line following the D.C. boundary near Dalecarlia). Two other companies, shown on this map in lighter lines, completed the branch into Georgetown. Note also the line labelled "Electric Ry.", the scenic Cabin John trolley route. Credit: C.S. Roberts Collection.

between docks and warehouses. When it was originally built, the line apparently intended to continue west along the river and canal to meet the projected B&O line and a trestle was built for it along the river flats just west of Aqueduct Bridge. Rails were never laid on the trestle.)

Construction started on the Quantico and Georgetown project in 1892 and within that year the track had reached Chevy Chase, Md., two miles from the junction with the Metropolitan branch main line. Here it halted—for 17 years, as it turned out. In all probability B&O's increasing financial problems precluded the ambitious route across northern Virginia with its substantial Potomac River bridge, forcing what was assumed to be a temporary delay.

But in the meantime, Chevy Chase was not a total loss as a temporary terminal. Also in 1892 the Rock Creek Railway (later part of the Capital Traction Co.) had completed its long suburban trolley line out Connecticut Avenue to the B&O crossing at Chevy Chase, where it built its carbarn and power house—an excellent inbound coal customer. The spot also developed as an unloading point for building materials for the suburban houses and stores which gradually grew up along the streetcar line. In addition, the trolley company dammed a small stream just south of the carbarn and B&O line, creating an artificial lake and picnic park. The trolley line was abandoned in 1935; Chevy Chase Lake had been long since drained and reverted to a wooded tangle before being overrun by suburbanization in the 1960's. The old wood carbarn, however, managed to survive into the 1950's adapted as a store.

Work on the balance of the branch did not resume until 1909. By this time B&O's situation with its southern connections had substantially changed for the better. As mentioned elsewhere, the Pennsy had turned over its Virginia line to a re-constituted RF&P jointly controlled by the six railroads entering Washington and Richmond...Potomac Yard had been built and B&O given access to the yard over Pennsy trackage. By then the line to Quantico was plainly pointless and was dropped about 1902; however, B&O did keep the planned Virginia route as far as Fairfax Station alive, albeit dormant. The branch was completed from Chevy Chase Lake to Georgetown in 1910 and some slight grading done south of Dalecarlia for the planned route across the river, which was to be the only tangible trace of the Virginia connection.

So in the end the Georgetown branch was yet another symbol of B&O's unfulfilled hopes, materializing as nothing more than a relatively minor local freight spur. But whatever its importance, it certainly was—and is—one of the most picturesque railroad lines anywhere in the area. Within its 11-mile length is a long trestle, a short tunnel, street running, canalside running, an impressive curved truss bridge, the remains of a masonry canal aqueduct, a wooded reservoir, fine views of the Potomac and a general off-the-beaten path atmosphere.

The single-track branch begins at a switch located in the Linden area 1.4 miles west of Silver Spring station originally called Metropolitan

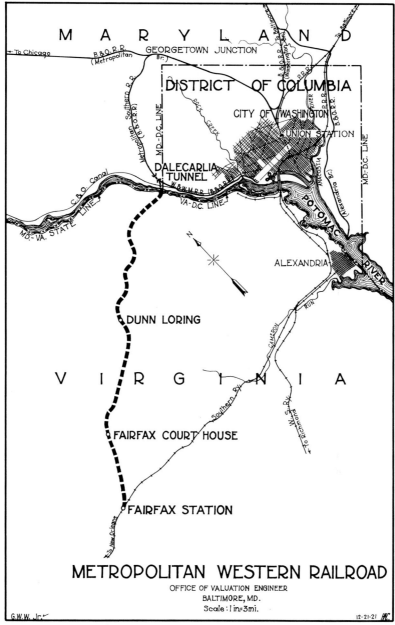

By the time this official company map was made in 1921, the planned extension to Quantico had been given up, but hope still lingered for building the line as far as a Southern Railway connection at Fairfax Station, Va. Credit: C.S. Roberts Collection.

Southern Junction, now Georgetown Junction. About a mile and a half beyond, it crosses Rock Creek Valley on a long (281 feet) high (67 feet) combination wood and steel trestle. The line's largest structure, Rock Creek trestle, was once more so...when first built in 1892 it was a full timber trestle measuring a spectacular 1,400 feet long, advertised as the largest of its type on the B&O system at that time. In 1904 much of it was replaced by fill and a single steel deck plate girder span inserted over the stream portion. It was rebuilt again in 1928 and the steel span replaced; following its dismemberment by Tropical Storm Agnes in 1972 it was further rebuilt and now contains three steel spans.

Next comes Chevy Chase, or Chevy Chase Lake, the original terminal. Until 1935 this was a busy little streetcar-rail junction: Just south of the railroad crossing, Capital Traction's Connecticut Avenue line terminated in a loop; its carbarn and former power house were on the east side of what was then a two-lane country road, abutting the B&O track. The single-track trolley line to Kensington left the loop, crossed B&O, and headed off north along the west side of the road. Now, of course, Connecticut Avenue has been widened, gas stations abound and all traces of the trolley facilities are gone. Only the railroad grade crossing remains, an increasing anachronism in the beltway-spawned sprawl.

Bethesda, the next station, is another onetime country road crossing

Rock Creek trestle as it looked in December 1970, before its partial dismemberment by Tropical Storm Agnes. As originally built, the trestle was 1,400 feet long—reputedly the longest timber trestle on the B&O system. Credit: H.L. Buckley.

now even more overpoweringly suburbanized than Chevy Chase. The branch passed under Wisconsin Avenue (and until 1935, also the single-track trolley line to Rockville) in a cut with a freight station west of the highway. But beyond Bethesda it becomes increasingly wooded as it picks up Little Falls Branch and follows the stream downgrade toward the Potomac, skirting the west side of Dalecarlia Reservoir on the way. A 341-ft. brick-lined tunnel takes the track under a ridge at Dalecarlia; above it, the railroad is completely invisible to auto traffic on MacArthur Boulevard.

At Dalecarlia the line's character changes. South of the tunnel it emerges onto a high bluff overlooking the Potomac, turns east and slowly works its way down the hillside to the river level on grades ranging from 1.3% and 1.5% in some sections. Along the way it crossed over the scenic Cabin John trolley line on a steel girder bridge, swings across Canal Road and the C&O Canal on an intriguing 321'6" three-span curved steel bridge, then parallels the canal into Georgetown. The line reaches the level of the canal towpath at Fletcher's boathouse, opposite the ancient (1801) Abner Cloud house, once part of a small flour milling complex which predated even the canal. Gradually it drops below the canal, reaching the river level near the site of the old Aqueduct Bridge and enters K St. in Georgetown through a massive masonry arch—the last remnant of the bridge. (Aqueduct Bridge was originally built to carry a branch of the C&O Canal across the Potomac on its way to Alexandria.

Q-1 No. 4320 backs into a siding at Chevy Chase Lake to pick up a car. The road crossing is Connecticut Avenue as it looked in 1946. Behind the engine is the onetime Rock Creek Railway/Capital Traction Company carbarn. Credit: H.H. Harwood, Jr.

Bethesda became a major unloading point for inbound building materials and fuel destined for Washington's growing northwest suburbs. An Alco S-2 from B&O subsidiary Staten Island Rapid Transit works south in February 1968. Credit: H.L. Buckley.

A fan excursion for Georgetown poses at the south end of Dalecarlia tunnel in June 1948. MacArthur Boulevard passes directly over the top of the tunnel. Credit: E.L. Thompson.

A.

The truss spans over the C&O Canal and Canal Road were always photogenic, if not greatly unusual. (A) The Georgetown switch run chuffs across in 1948. (B) About five years later, an Alco S-2 switcher rumbles over, also heading for Georgetown. (C) The bridges in 1978, which now look down on a heavy traffic of joggers and bicyclers along the canal. Credits: A-L.W. Rice; H.H. Harwood collection—B-Henry Libby; W.F. Smith collection—C-H.H. Harwood, Jr.

B.

C.

After ten years of difficulties, it was completed in 1843 as a wood truss structure; in 1888 it was rebuilt as an iron highway bridge, and served as a major link between Washington and Virginia until replaced by the present Key Bridge in 1923. Only the hulking twin-arch stone abutment still survives at the Georgetown end, serving as sort of a triumphal arch for the railroad's entry. The arch which the track passes under had to be enlarged when the line was built in 1910 to clear railroad equipment.)

In Georgetown the track runs the length of K Street in the center of the street; at one time, industrial sidings swung off on both sides and a team track yard was located off the street in what is now a parking lot at the southwest corner of Wisconsin Avenue and K. For almost but not all its life, the branch ended on the west side of Rock Creek. In 1914 it was temporarily extended east over the creek and run through the then-undeveloped area of Potomac Park to 23rd Street to carry in materials for the new Lincoln Memorial.

Commercially the branch could best be classed as a coal-and-construction railroad, carrying coal for power plants and retail fuel

Certainly one of the most scenic spots on this highly picturesque branch was the stretch alongside the C&O Canal at Fletchers Boat-house. This northbound enthusiast special has stopped for pictures in October 1954. At the time the branch was completed into George-town, B&O controlled the C&O Canal and thus had little problem locating the line's last three miles on canal property. Credit: Ara Mesrobian.

dealers and building materials destined for the houses and roads growing up around the outskirts of the city. In the earlier days the largest single customer—and, in fact, perhaps the major spur to completing the branch into Georgetown—was a new central power house built on the Georgetown waterfront in 1912 by the Capital Traction Company. CTCo was one of the two large street railway companies serving Washington and the plant—located on the southeast side of Wisconsin Avenue & K Street—generated all electric power for the system. The extensive private sidings and team tracks scattered along K Street served mostly milling, fuel and building supply companies. The only other significant spots on the line were Chevy Chase Lake and Bethesda, also predominantly coal, lumber and cement delivery points.

Unfortunately, B&O lost the Capital Traction generating plant when it was scarcely 21 years old — it was closed in December 1933 when Capital Traction was merged into the Capital Transit Company and the new company switched to commercially-supplied power. Although vacant, the big brick building with its tall twin smokestacks stubbornly

The Georgetown waterfront yards about 1945, before the Whitehurst Freeway and various renewal projects changed the scene. The camera looks east on K Street about a block west of Wisconsin Avenue. In the rear is the former Capital Traction Company streetcar power house; in the foreground are B&O's team tracks and freight office. The area is currently a parking lot. Credit: Columbia Historical Society.

survived as a Georgetown waterfront landmark until it was finally demolished in 1968.

Normally the branch was always a simple one-train-a-day operation, essentially no more than an extended switching run. At present it operates as a local freight based at Eckington yard; in times past a switcher based in Georgetown had merely shuttled cars back and forth to Georgetown Junction, to be handled from there by another local freight. Since there was no wye or turntable at either end of the branch, locomotives were never turned. In steam days the power would be run front-first to Georgetown and backed home to Eckington. The power, incidentally, was almost invariably a switcher of some variety— a D-30 0-6-0 in earlier years, most often an Alco S-1 or S-2 diesel in the late 1940's and 1950's and currently a GP-7 or GP-9. During the late 1940's the branch was worked by a Q-1 2-8-2, but this "big" power was more the exception than rule.

But of course no railroad line in the Washington area has ever been totally routine and the Georgetown branch was no exception. During the Korean war the Army decided to use the branch for moving troops out of nearby Fort Belvoir and Fort Myers, Va. Empty troop trains, complete with passenger diesels, would be hauled backwards down the branch by a switcher and parked in Georgetown, while the troops were bussed over from Virginia. The big E-units would then roar back up the Potomac bluffs with the train, pushed by the switcher. Unhappily for posterity, most of these movements were at night and to the best of anyone's knowledge the sight of a full-scale passenger train over the scenic little spur was never photographed.

The years after World War II brought many changes to the Georgetown waterfront, most of them for the worse insofar as the railroad was concerned. In 1949 the elevated Whitehurst Freeway was built over K Street, leaving the street and tracks below in perpetual gloom. As Georgetown went into the Kennedy era, a movement began to beautify the waterfront, which traditionally had been an industrial backwash out of sight at the bottom of the hill from the heart of the community. By the late 1960's serious work had begun in clearing land, building new office buildings and rebuilding certain historic structures for use as restaurants, offices and trendy shops. The result was the removal of most of the remaining industry in the area, along with much railroad trackage. Eventually the river edge along K Street between 31st and 35th Streets was completely cleared; B&O's team tracks at the southwest corner of Wisconsin and K became a parking lot. At present the K Street area is a transitional mishmash of new buildings, old industry, parking lots and vacant spaces—but the railroad's future is obviously limited. One major coal receiver remains, a federal government-operated steam heating plant near Rock Creek.

Georgetown branch service currently averages only two trains a week, now operating almost entirely for the heating plant. The line has been an off-on abandonment candidate for several years, but for the moment it still hangs on. Presently there is some hope, since the steam plant plans to reconvert entirely to coal again.

A.

B.

Two scenes which typify the atmosphere of the Georgetown branch—a backwoods railroad in the middle of a city. (A) A south-bound switch run at Lyttonsville Road, near Georgetown Junction. February 1968. (B) And alongside the C&O Canal again, opposite the historic Abner Cloud house. Credits: A-H.L. Buckley—B-William F. Smith.

IMPOSSIBLE CHALLENGE

CHAPTER 15

B&O'S THREE AND A HALF TERMINALS IN WASHINGTON

Let's quickly explain that the "half" refers to what is presently (in 1979) called Union Station — the tacked-on undersized appendage behind the original Union Station, which is now in turn the National Visitor Center. It may well turn out that this new terminal is deservedly doomed, to be replaced by none other than the old Union Station. If so, the B&O will have gone through a complete cycle of terminals in the Capital, ending up back where it was in 1907. The sequence could only be called ironic: The railroad spent its first 72 years in Washington struggling through a series of stopgap and outgrown terminal facilities before finally settling into a station which seemingly would serve it for the ages. Now, almost exactly 72 years later, and having abandoned Union Station for yet another inadequate terminal, it may now move back into the same facility.

When the four little Grasshoppers puffed into Washington on August 25, 1835 pulling their procession of inaugural trains, they let off their loads of dignitaries at a temporary platform near First and B Streets, N.W. At the time, B&O had no Washington station and, in fact, no intention of building one. The problem, of course, was money, probably compounded by a bit of pique at the failure of Congress to approve the hoped-for financial aid to the branch. The state of Maryland's involvement in the financing, the necessity to maintain a separate capitalization for the branch and B&O's money needs for its main line construction all discouraged the railroad from spending more than was necessary on the line until business built up. The track and bridges had been well-built, but that was all.

So as a stopgap, B&O bought an existing house at the northwest corner of Pennsylvania Avenue and 2nd Street, N.W. and refitted it as its Washington terminal. It was a narrow three-story brick affair, fronting on

337

Pennsylvania Avenue; originally built as a private home, it had since been turned into a boarding house. Conversion consisted of opening up the rooms on the ground floor into a ticket office and waiting room and adding a small belfry on the roof. Reputedly, the bell was rung ten minutes before train departures. Lest this seem like a superfluous ceremony, remember that "nine o'clock", or whatever, didn't mean the same thing to everyone at that time. In fact, B&O took pains to caution its patrons in a newspaper ad in September, 1835 that: "As there is no standard time in Washington, it is recommended to passengers to be at the depot before the hour named for the departure of trains."

The little house also served as the freight station. Three tracks stub-ended at the station's rear: one passenger loading/unloading track and two shorter tracks inside a wood shed for freight handling.

The railroad's original route into Washington approached the city from the northeast along what is now West Virginia Avenue, turning west on I Street, N.E. and then southwest along Delaware Avenue to about E Street N.E. From here it cut southwest through various blocks, generally following the line of present-day Louisiana Avenue; for its final block it followed the west side of 2nd Street N.W. into the terminal. It should be men-

The original Washington terminal was this converted boarding house at Pennsylvania Avenue and 2nd Street, N.W., shown in this print of unknown origin, indeterminate date and questionable authenticity. It served B&O trains from 1835 to 1851. Credit: B&O Museum Archives.

tioned that in 1835, streets in this area were mostly theoretical. And 2nd Street where it passed the station was more water than street — much of the street bed was occupied by Tiber Creek, a moderate-sized stream which drained the low ground north of the Capitol and flowed on west through a canal to the Potomac.

Altogether, B&O's Washington facilities were minimal and primitive but probably no worse than what it (or any other railroad) had elsewhere at the time. An added irritation, however, was a local restriction against steam locomotives at the Pennsylvania Avenue station. Inbound trains stopped a block north; the locomotive would uncouple, run around its train, recouple on the rear and push it into the station.

On the other hand, service was equally minimal. Initially, two trains a day ran to Baltimore, leaving Washington at 10:15 a.m. and 4:30 p.m. Freight consisted of a nominal two or three inbound cars a day, with virtually nothing outbound — a ratio that has not changed much in 144 years.

But within five years the Pennsylvania Avenue station had become crowded enough so that B&O was forced to move its freight facilities into new quarters somewhere else. It finally picked a plot about a block north-

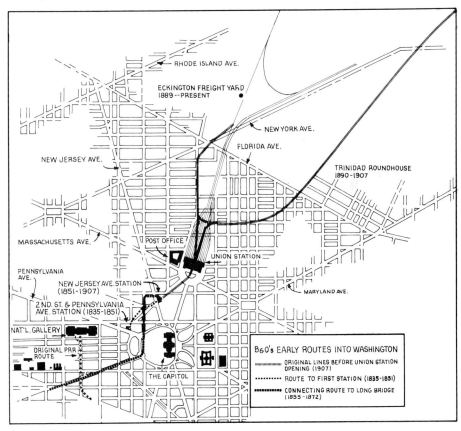

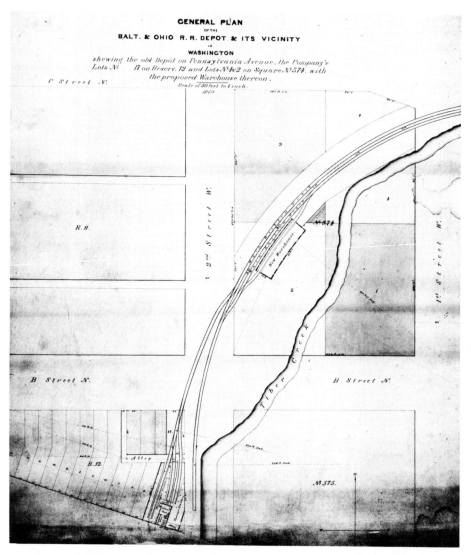

GENERAL PLAN
OF THE
BALT. & OHIO R.R. DEPOT & ITS VICINITY
IN
WASHINGTON
shewing the old Depot on Pennsylvania Avenue, the Company's
Lots N.º 17 on Reserv. 12 and Lots N.º 1 & 2 on Square N.º 574, with
the proposed Warehouse thereon.
Scale of 50 feet to 1 inch.
1840

An extremely rare official drawing of the track layout and placement of facilities at the first Washington station, as they were in 1840. The diagonal line at the bottom is Pennsylvania Avenue. The track at farthest left in the depot was the passenger track; the two short stub tracks behind the building were used for freight. In the center of this map is the new brick freight station, built in 1840 to take the pressure off the obviously cramped facilities at the passenger station. At this time Tiber Creek was an open stream. Credit: B&O Museum Archives.

east of the station on the east side of the square bounded by 1st, 2nd, B and C Streets and built a brand new brick freight house there. The freight station, finished in 1840 or 1841, was typical of B&O's depot layouts at the time with a single track passing completely through the building and all unloading and storage facilities inside. (Ellicott's Mills and Frederick stations had similar interior arrangements.) But it was a landmark structure in one regard: According to at least one architectural historian, its roof — designed by the Austrian-born architect-engineer J.R. Niernsee — was the first iron truss roof in the United States. Also at about this time a small engine house was put up on a vacant plot farther northeast at New Jersey Avenue and C Streets, about three blocks from the end of the track.

By 1848, with traffic slowly building and the Washington branch grinding out steady profits, B&O was ready to face up to building a permanent passenger station which perhaps would be more architecturally appropriate for the capital. It was prodded by plans to raise the street grades immediately north of the Pennsylvania Avenue station, which would require abandonment or substantial rebuilding of the approach tracks anyway. After some bickering with the city over location, it picked the block bounded by New Jersey Avenue, C Street, North Capitol and D Street N.W. — the lot three blocks northwest of the original station which B&O had been partially using for its engine house. The choice wasn't an entirely happy one. Construction started in 1850, but thanks to quicksand and the generally low, boggy land, the job went slower and cost more than was planned.

But ready or not, the railroad decided to shut down its old station— generally described as "filthy" — as quickly as possible. On April 9, 1851 the Pennsylvania Avenue station was closed and trains began using the still-unfinished New Jersey Avenue terminal. The tracks east of New Jersey Avenue were promptly removed and the old station sold. It quickly reverted to type as a tavern, lasting until 1869 when it was finally demolished to make way for new houses. Oddly, the original brick freight house a block away survived at least until the late 1920's, squeezed in between newer buildings halfway up an alley north of B Street between 1st and 2nd Streets.

The New Jersey Avenue station was a distinct and pleasant change from the old boarding house/station/tavern. B&O hired the Baltimore architects Niernsee & Nielsen for the Washington job. Niernsee & Nielsen were just fresh from completing their fine Italianate Calvert Station for the Baltimore & Susquehanna Railroad in Baltimore; for Washington they followed the same architectural style and created another Victorian Italian villa. This one was smaller than Calvert Station but fully as attractive—a single-story brick structure 119 ft. long fronting on New Jersey Avenue with large arched center entrances and set off with a 100-ft. typically Italianate tower. The brick exterior walls were covered with a reddish-brown stucco, with sandstone window sills, doorway arches and coping. The stucco, incidentally, was tinted a shade to match the shade of stone trim.

Inside, said a contemporary reporter, "the saloons for gentlemen and ladies are small but commodious. The walls are panelled with wood, painted to imitate oak; and an agreeable mellow light is distributed through the rooms by the use of yellow curtains. The furniture corresponds in color and character with that of the walls; while arm chairs, benches, etc. are enriched by seats of crimson plush."

The rear of the station opened onto a long two-track trainshed which projected at a northeast angle toward North Capitol Street. The shed was a somewhat odd combination of an iron truss roof supported by square granite columns; it was 340.5 ft. long and 62 ft. wide, with granite walls at each end and two arched doorways at its east (north) end.

As originally built, the new station was intended both as a passenger and freight depot. Expanding business quickly pushed the freight out: In 1856 a frame platform and shed were built on the north side of the station lot along D Street and as the traffic grew more, a larger freight house was later built a block northeast at the southeast corner of North Capitol and E Streets.

Immediately north of the station and shed was a tiny hexagonal brick engine house which, with its single central ventilating cupola, must have

The handsome new station at New Jersey Avenue and C Street as it looked soon after it was opened. The artist perhaps has exaggerated the mucky surroundings—or perhaps not. At this time the street level was low and the ground marshy. At the far left is the little single-stall engine house. The trainshed at the rear actually extended diagonally from the back of the building rather than parallel to it as appears here. Later street grade changes and a large addition to the station substantially changed its appearance. See also the photo in Chapter 10. Credit: B&O Museum Archives.

Two views of the waiting room of the original portion of the New Jersey Avenue station, at it appeared about 1905. Credit (both): Columbia Historical Society.

The rear of the New Jersey Avenue station and trainshed about 1905. A.
As originally built, the shed had two stone arch portals with wood
doors, later removed to provide more clearance and room for an additional track. Note the original granite columns supporting the iron
shed roof. Credit: A-Columbia Historical Society—B-Smithsonian
Institution.
B.

been highly picturesque but was also highly cramped. Measuring only 62 ft. across, it was large enough to squeeze in a single light 4-4-0, but nothing more. But if the size seems surprising for what was supposed to be a major terminal facility, remember that the Washington branch's entire 1850 roster consisted of five engines. It is likely that only one locomotive was normally at the station at any given time, with one laying over at night.

In short, the New Jersey Avenue station and its facilities were handsome and fashionable, albeit modest—but certainly sufficient for the traffic. When it first opened in April 1851 only three regular round trips were being run between Washington and Baltimore; in March 1852 the frequency was increased to four a day, but schedules were such that normally there was only one train in the station at a time.

In 1855 a long spur was run from the new station southwest across the city to the north end of the Long Bridge, the aptly-named mile-long wood highway bridge over the Potomac near the foot of 14th Street. The objective was to connect somehow with the newly-organized Alexandria & Washington Railroad, which was then starting work on its six-mile line to nearby Alexandria. The A&W in turn would connect at Alexandria with the recently-opened Orange & Alexandria, which was heading south via Gordonsville and Charlottesville, Va. The Long Bridge branch started at the New Jersey Avenue station, ran south on First Street as far as Maryland Avenue, then turned southeast following Maryland Avenue on a long diagonal to the bridge. En route the line passed directly in front of the Capitol through the spots now occupied by the Peace Monument and Garfield statue. The A&W finished its line by 1857 but ended it at the south end

This track along Maryland Avenue, S.W. connected B&O's terminal with the Long Bridge. The view is east during the Civil War. Credit: National Archives.

of the Long Bridge; for the next several years, goods and passengers were transferred over the bridge by wagon and carriage (or by a healthy walk). In 1860 B&O's president John W. Garrett appealed to Congress for permission to build a new bridge over the Potomac, but was blocked by Senator Simon Cameron of Pennsylvania — who incidentally was a firm friend of the Pennsylvania Railroad and heavy investor in the Northern Central Railway.

The Civil War abruptly changed the character of both Washington and its branch-town railroad facilities; neither would be the same afterwards. At the time, the compact little New Jersey Avenue complex was the city's only passenger and freight depot. It was suddenly overwhelmed by massive but erratic movements of troops and military supplies. Inbound freight, for example, went from an average of eight cars a day in 1860 to over 400 in late 1861 and early 1862. The hastily-formed military railroad organization quickly put down rails on the Long Bridge, completing the connection between the Maryland Avenue line and the A&W and—for the first time—creating an all-rail route between north and south. The connection over the crowded, limited capacity bridge was a temporary expedient and by 1863 the military had completed a new railroad bridge over the river next to the old. Through movements from the B&O to Alexandria and the south over the First Street-Maryland Avenue route became routine during the war years. Other changes were also made in B&O's Washington facilities: A wye was built in the terminal yard and work was started on double-tracking the entire Washington branch.

The war's end brought back some normality, but "normality" wasn't the same as it was in 1860. Both the city and its railroad traffic had begun to grow rapidly. By 1870, population within the District of Columbia was 131,700—2½ times what it was in 1850; by 1880 it was 3½ times the 1850 figure. In 1868 B&O was scheduling 18 passenger trains in and out of its terminal—nine round trips. And, following the Civil War the federal government had given B&O the right to operate the Long Bridge to Virginia. The railroad thus became a key link in a somewhat loose-jointed all-rail route between New York and New Orleans, handling through cars as far south as Lynchburg, Va., via the Alexandria & Washington and the onetime Orange & Alexandria which had been rechristened in 1866 as the Orange, Alexandria & Manassas.

But the Pennsylvania's unwelcome entry into Washington—plus some physical changes in the city itself — brought B&O additional woe and confusion. By 1870 the Pennsy (through its Baltimore & Potomac subsidiary) had started work on its route into town, approaching from the southeast via Virginia Avenue, swinging north across the Mall at 6th Street, S.W. and ending at a large, ornate terminal at 6th & B Streets N.W. adjacent to Pennsylvania Avenue (B Street is now Constitution Avenue and the terminal site is unrecognizable as such; the west half of the National Gallery of Art now occupies it.) The PRR began partial service as far as Baltimore in 1872 and full through services to New York and various western points in 1873.

In addition, thanks to adroit political maneuvering, the Pennsylvania bought up the Alexandria & Washington in 1870 and at the same time snatched away from B&O the rights to operate over the Long Bridge to connect with the Virginia railroads. The Pennsy's line crossed the A&W/B&O connecting track at Maryland Avenue & 6th Street S.W., giving it an easy end-on connection close to the Penn passenger terminal and, in effect, walling off the B&O.

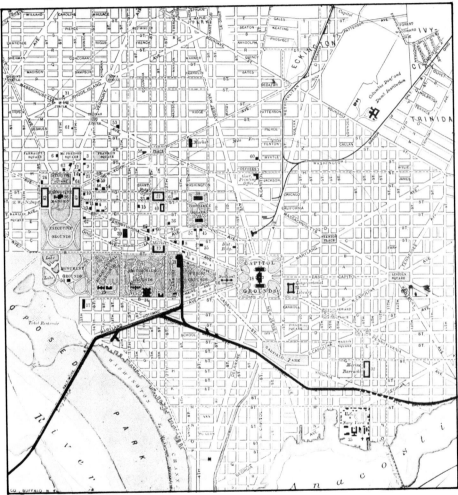

This 1892 map of Washington emphasizes the Pennsy's route through the city with heavy lines—entering from the east on a trestle over the Anacostia (far right), terminating at 6th and B Streets N.W. (center) and crossing the Long Bridge to reach the southern lines (left). B&O's routes and terminal are shown in light lines north of the Capitol. Credit: Enoch Pratt Free Library.

At about the same time, the city decided to raise the grade of several streets in the low, swampy areas drained by Tiber Creek — where, among other things, B&O's New Jersey Avenue station sat. In 1873 both New Jersey Avenue and C Street were raised 15 feet, leaving the station and tracks at their original grade substantially below the new street level. The unfortunate station thus ended up the bottom of a gulch, significantly detracting from both its aesthetics and accessibility. Ramps and stairways had to be built to reach the entrances. At the same time, First Street and the east end of Maryland Avenue — the route of the A&W/B&O connecting track — were also regraded. The A&W (then the owner of the line) was ordered to raise its track to conform to the new grade or lose the line. The PRR-controlled A&W obviously had lost its desire to connect with B&O and chose to lose the line. The track from New Jersey Avenue to 6th & Maryland was dismantled late in 1872, making the B&O terminal a stub-end operation once again. B&O soon ceased being part of any through passenger services between the north and south—forever, as it turned out.

The opening of the Metropolitan branch May 25, 1873 not only added

The wye track connecting the Washington and the Metropolitan branches was located at Delaware Avenue and I Street N.E., about five blocks north of the New Jersey Avenue station. In this photo a Baltimore-Winchester excursion train stops for water on the wye about 1900. The train heads west; the tracks in the foreground are the Washington branch line into the station. This site is now the center of Union Station's terminal throat. Credit: Smithsonian Institution.

more traffic but changed the nature of B&O's Washington facilities and operations. The new line entered the city from the north through Eckington, crossing Boundary Street (now Florida Avenue) just east of 1st Street, N.E. then followed 1st Street south; it joined the Washington branch at the point where 1st Street crossed Delaware Avenue at G Street, N.E. This site is now in the center of the Union Station yard complex. A wye track also connected the two branches about two blocks north at I Street. Since the New Jersey Avenue station was a stub-end terminal located south of the junction of the two branches, through east-west passenger trains had to run around the wye, back down into the station, then head back out to continue their runs. Freights and passenger specials which did not stop at Washington simply bypassed the station around the wye. The wye operation became a permanent and essential fixture of B&O's Washington operations, which was carried through (although at a different location) when Union Station was built.

Unlike its 20th Century successor, however, the first wye was single track and undoubtedly must have given the on-the-ground operating men nightmares in periods of heavy traffic volume. Operating timetables of the 1880's and 1890's were full of this type of straight-faced instruction to train crews: "No. 31 will run around the Y at Metropolitan Junction carefully, looking out for No. 24."

The Metropolitan branch and general traffic growth (even despite increasingly effective Pennsy competition) forced a gradual expansion of B&O's rather constricted facilities and over the next 20 years the pretty little New Jersey Avenue station underwent the same sort of physical stresses as airport terminals did in the 1950's and '60's. Remember that up to 1870, B&O's terminal consisted almost entirely of the single block at the New Jersey Avenue station, reached by running down city streets. Beginning in 1870 and running to 1878 the railroad patched together ownership of the full block immediately northeast of the station property, bounded by North Capitol Street, Delaware Avenue, D and E Streets N.E. B&O's ultimate plan, it was reported, was to build a new passenger terminal here to replace the now-sunken and increasingly overcrowded New Jersey Avenue facility. For the moment, however, storage yards and a freight house were built on the block. The new station, of course, never came and this area remained as the major backup yard for New Jersey Avenue.

Instead of a new station, B&O chose a patchwork rebuilding of the New Jersey Avenue terminal. In 1889 it built a large two-story brick addition on the station's south side, with a second-story entranceway opening directly onto the raised street level at the corner of New Jersey Avenue and C Street. This new section became the station's main entrance, although carriages continued to drive down to the older entrance at the lower level. It also became the most prominent feature of the terminal, adding a bulky, Romanesque look to the once-trim single-story villa design.

At the same time the railroad relocated its completely inadequate yard and service facilities to spots farther out on the two branches, away from the congested and constricted area around the station and junction. In

The rebuilt and expanded New Jersey Avenue station as it looked about 1895. The level of both intersecting streets had been raised 15 feet in 1873, submerging the original section of the station (the left hand portion in this photo). The addition on the right, with street level entrance, was built in 1889. Credit: U.S. Commission of Fine Arts.

The interior of the 1889 addition, looking toward the street entrance. Credit: B&O Museum Archives.

The New Jersey Avenue station in its last hours in 1907, abandoned and in the process of demolition. Union Station can be seen behind it on the right. Credit: E.G. Hooper; H.H. Harwood collection.

1888 it bought land on the Metropolitan branch at Eckington, north of Boundary Street (Florida Avenue) and proceeded to build a new freight yard. Eckington yard became B&O's primary Washington freight terminal, handling local switching for most Washington freight customers. (Before the yard was built, Washington's only freight facilities were the freight station tracks near the New Jersey Avenue station, and whatever storage tracks could be temporarily snatched away from passenger use. Cars which could not be accommodated at Washington immediately usually had to be held at Martinsburg, Baltimore or Point of Rocks.) Today, after much rebuilding and expansion, it still is B&O's key Washington freight yard. Property was also bought in 1890 in the then-undeveloped Trinidad area, on the east side of the Washington branch tracks midway between Boundary Street and Mt. Olivet Road. Here a new roundhouse and machine shop were built, along with coach storage and servicing facilities. Trinidad, it turned out, would not share Eckington's longevity; it was abandoned in 1907 when Union Station was completed and the B&O route through Trinidad dismantled.

And as Washington's population pushed outward in the 1880's and 1890's, a string of attractive little suburban stations was also built along both branches. A frame "suburban" station was built on the Metropolitan branch at Eckington in 1890; called Boundary station, it was located near what is now Florida and New York Avenues approximately where B&O's present Eckington freight office stands. Also in 1890 a handsome stone and wood station — designed by the notable Baltimore architect E. Fran-

The short-lived "suburban" station at Boundary Street (Florida Avenue) and New York Avenue in Washington, built in 1890 and razed about 1906 when the new Eckington freight house was built. The grade crossing in the foreground is now Florida Avenue. Credit: Columbia Historical Society.

cis Baldwin — was built at Catholic University, where Michigan Avenue crossed the Metropolitan branch. Three miles further out, a picturesque 1½-story turreted wood station was put up in 1886 at Takoma Park near Blair Road and 4th Street N.W.—probably another Baldwin design. (It was enlarged in 1890.) On the inner end of the Washington branch, single-story frame stations appeared at Langdon (1891), Branchville (1890), and Riverdale (1890), the last two also done by Baldwin. Riverdale, incidently, was originally paid for by a local developer, the Riverdale Park Co.; B&O agreed to pay back the station's cost after the developer had built 75 homes. The Riverdale Park Company finally got its money back in 1905 and the railroad took ownership of the station. Hyattsville, west of Riverdale, already had a large and ornate brick station designed by Francis Baldwin in 1883-84.

Despite B&O's Washington station and yard improvements, its operating situation was beginning to border on the impossible. By 1893 the New Jersey Avenue station — which, you'll recall, was originally designed for eight trains a day in and out — was handling an astonishing 98. And many of these were bunched at certain times of the day, notably early morning, late afternoon and early evening. For example, in the hour between 8 a.m. and 9 a.m., 11 trains arrived or departed, and at 8:30 a.m. there were three simultaneous scheduled movements in and out. In the space of 13 minutes around 4:30 p.m., six trains arrived or left the station. Keep in mind that the station had, at most, four usable terminal tracks. . .that most movements required turning on the wye and backing in. . .that both main lines into town ran down city streets with numerous grade crossings. . .that light engines, empty equipment and freight trains had to be moved in between the scheduled trains. . .and that switches were manually operated and communications were by Morse code telegraph. All things considered, the job of moving this volume of traffic in and out of the terminal must have been heroic, to put it mildly. And, interestingly, most of the through east-west trains were scheduled in and out of the station in ten minutes — with the brief exception of the new "Capitol Limited" in the mid 1920's, faster than the B&O was ever able to accomplish later in the spacious luxury of Union Station. How smoothly it was all done is not recorded, but somehow it *was* done. And in comparing this performance with that of railroad terminals today — with their larger yards, lighter traffic and radio communication — one can't help thinking that the art of railroading has gone backwards.

If the operating situation was bad for B&O, the grade crossing problem was worse for the city. Both B&O and Pennsylvania entered the city on the surface and, to one degree or another, used city streets to approach their terminals. B&O's two lines occupied three different streets for varying lengths and crossed 24 others at grade. Only North Capitol Street—which crossed the terminal tracks at the entrance to the trainshed—had been carried over the tracks on a narrow iron bridge. One of the worst spots was the H Street crossing, about five blocks north of the station. H Street was the main route to the northeast section of town and carried a busy streetcar line. It also had the misfortune of crossing the railroad right in the center of the wye where the two branches joined so that it got the maximum of trains—many of them backup movements. Not surprisingly, there were several serious accidents at the crossing. The sections of Delaware Avenue and First Street, N.E. occupied by the railroad were virtually unusable by normal vehicular traffic. Less dangerous but perhaps more emotionally and aesthetically bothersome was the Pennsy's approach to its station directly across the Mall.

Beginning about 1885, city officials started pressuring B&O to eliminate its grade crossings and a firm plan was developed in 1897-98. But with B&O then in receivership, things languished until the turn of the century. By then, a new concept was developing for planning the entire city — or rather a return to Washington's original concept. The "city beautiful" movement had begun, and the McMillan Commission was formed to realize it.

Washington's railroad facilities were a screaming priority and development of a new station plan became the McMillan Commission's first project. Not only were the old facilities inadequate and the grade crossing situation intolerable, but the entire railroad layout was an offensive industrial intrusion in the center of what was supposed to be a classic system of vistas, broad avenues, parks and strategically-placed public buildings. As a start, in February 1901 Congress had passed bills specifying separate new stations for both the B&O and Pennsylvania along with a general grade crossing removal program for both railroads. In response B&O created a new subsidiary — the Washington Terminal Company — in December 1901, as the corporate vehicle to build its new station.

The two-station plan was a throwback to the B&O's and Pennsy's brutally competitive relationship of the late 19th Century; common sense and the McMillan Commission planners knew that a single, great gateway to the city was the sensible solution. And, almost coincidentally, the atmosphere to accomplish it was there. By late 1901 B&O was under the Pennsylvania's control, and while the rivalry certainly wasn't gone, it was put within practical bounds. In addition, the Pennsylvania's president at the time was the expansive A.J. Cassatt, a man most sympathetic to monument building. Quickly, all the parties united on a single union station project. In February 1903 Congress passed another bill eliminating the provision for separate stations, and work began immediately. B&O's Washington Terminal Company was picked as the entity to build and operate the new station and was reorganized as a joint company with B&O and PRR each taking 50% of its stock. The southern lines, all of which had been tenants in the old Pennsy station, were to remain merely tenants in the union station, with no ownership interest.

The new union station's site was to be chosen by the McMillan Commission members: architects Daniel H. Burnham and Charles F. McKim, sculptor Augustus St. Gaudens and landscape architect Frederick Law Olmsted, Jr.; the building itself was designed by Burnham, architect of the 1893 Columbian Exposition. In short, Union Station's location and looks were to be determined by the "city beautiful" planners rather than railroad engineers. It is interesting to speculate what the B&O would have done for a new station if left to its own devices.

The station was properly viewed as the city's gateway and given a highly visible and symbolic location. The Commission placed it on Delaware Avenue immediately north of the Capitol. The full park concept wasn't fully realized until 1931. During and after World War I, some of the area was cluttered by temporary buildings. Burnham's design was, at a minimum, monumental — a massive Roman Beaux-Arts temple direct from the Columbian Exposition, 663 ft. long and 211 ft. wide and built (of course) of white marble and granite. Its general waiting room was 220 ft. long and 130 ft. wide, under a barrel-vaulted roof rising 97¼ feet above it.

The station's chosen site was only about three blocks northwest of B&O's New Jersey Avenue station, so the new terminal trackage and support facilities were laid out to follow roughly the route of the Washington branch into the city. The route was completely realigned, however, and ownership was split, with Washington Terminal owning the portion between Union Station and Florida Avenue, and the individual railroads (B&O and PRR) owning the lines north and east of Florida Avenue. This meant considerable rebuilding for both B&O and PRR. B&O's new Washington branch alignment began at what was called Montello station, slightly northwest of what is now New York and Montana Avenues; it swung southwest from the old right-of-way (which later became West Virginia Avenue) in a straight line, following present New York Avenue

Grandiose hardly seems adequate to describe Union Station. Fortunately its facade remains intact today, although its interior is another story. Credit: B&O Museum Archives.

(which at that time did not exist east of Florida Avenue). The Metropolitan branch was straightened out at Eckington and brought into the Washington branch just east of New York and Florida Avenues; the connecting wye was then placed in the area around Mt. Olivet Road and T Street, N.E.

The Terminal Company's coach yards and engine terminal were located adjacent to the B&O trackage in this area; although operated by WT, they were jointly built and owned by B&O and Pennsy and leased to the Terminal.

Since the Penn's original line had come into the city from the southeast, via Benning, it had to build an entirely new six-mile cutoff from Landover east to the B&O at Montello, then paralleling B&O to Florida Avenue where both roads joined the WT property. This 1.2 mile parallel stretch became sort of a mini-racetrack for certain simultaneously-scheduled eastbound B&O and Pennsy trains as they accelerated away from Washington — an exciting little break for both crews and passengers to enliven otherwise dull trips to Philadelphia and New York.

Washington Union station was finally completed in 1907. B&O began using it first — at 2:52 a.m. Sunday October 27, the "Duquesne Limited" for Pittsburgh left New Jersey Avenue and the old station was closed. Union Station's first train, B&O No. 10, arrived from Pittsburgh the same morning at 6:50. The Pennsylvania and southern lines began using the new station three weeks later, on November 17. Afterwards, both B&O's New Jersey Avenue station and Pennsy's 6th and B terminal were demolished and the approach tracks taken up. Now, after the regrading and redevelopment of the Capitol and Mall areas, absolutely no trace of either facility exists. Similarly, B&O's original grade-level route into town has totally disappeared into the city's street system and into Union Station's viaduct, station building and plaza.

Union Station is only four years old as B&O Pacific 2107 takes out a New York express on a cold morning in 1911. Hopper cars for the coal delivery trestles can be seen at the right. Credit: Smithsonian Institution; C.B. Chaney collection.

B&O's Washington branch and Pennsy's passenger line paralleled
one another past Washington Terminal's Ivy City engine terminal
and coach yards. Both lines had been built new as part of the terminal
project. A. This view looks north from the 9th Street bridge in the early
1940's as the Washington-bound "Royal Blue" crosses over onto the
wye. New York Avenue is at far right. B. Train 518 for Baltimore accelerates away from Washington at the same location. The 9th Street
bridge is behind the train and "F" tower partly hidden behind the smo-
kebox of the 5314. April 1947. Credits: A-B&O Museum Archives—B-
E.L. Thompson.

A.

B.

Since Union Station was only partly B&O, the full details of its career are not germaine to this book and certainly they defy a quick summary. In fact, Union Station fully deserves a book of its own, as architectual and engineering history, social history and political history — a book that would do some justice to its role in Washington's unique urban development; its service to presidents, visiting dignitaries and varieties of lesser politicians; its handling of the incredible World War II traffic loads, not to mention the more ordinary transient hordes of tourists; the near-catastrophic "Federal Express" wreck of January 15, 1953; the decline of the 1960's and "Amtrak-ization" of the 1970's; the costly comedy of errors which created the National Visitor Center and "new" Union Station in 1976. And for the strict railroad enthusiast, there was the motive power — steam, electric, diesel, RDC and gas-electric — of five determindly independent railroads, all of whom believed in distinctive locomotives. Plus, of course, the trains — which at one time or another reached points as disparate as Portland, Me., Montreal, Key West, New Orleans, Memphis, St. Louis, Detroit (with brief through cars to Los Angeles and Fort Worth), and, of course, Chicago.

But here let's only briefly touch on B&O's 20th Century operations at Union Station. B&O generally was assigned the western half of the station's 20 upper-level terminal tracks; the Pennsylvania had the others, somewhat more strategically located in the station's center, while the southern lines (and their PRR connections) used the 12 lower-level tracks at the east side. B&O made extensive use of its Ivy City/Eckington wye to ease its station operations: All through trains between western points and Baltimore or New York ran over the wye, backed into Union Station, and were usually switched and reassembled before heading out again. Even many trains terminating in Washington were wyed and backed in to save turning equipment and to allow locomotives to clear immediately. The double-track wye was thus a busy place, with passenger moves, through freights and westbound freights stopping to pick up or set off cars at Eckington yard. Two towers controlled the operation: "F" on the east end at Ivy City (located at the present 9th Street bridge), and "QN" on the west, at Rhode Island Avenue. "F" was removed in 1951, but "QN", in altered condition, is still very active and a key point in B&O's Washington operations. The south leg of the wye was controlled by Washington Terminal's "C" tower between New York and Florida Avenues, which also marked the junction of the PRR line and the beginning of WT property. ("C" became a casualty of Metro construction in 1973.) Along with all other Union Station users, B&O's locomotives were turned and serviced at Washington Terminal's Ivy City engine terminal; normally they were assigned the easternmost ready tracks and were thus usually most visible from passing trains.

Through most of the first half of the century B&O's Washington passenger services fell into four distinct categories: First and most important were the through trains to the west, to such cities as Pittsburgh, Chicago, Detroit, Cleveland, Cincinnati and St. Louis. In these areas B&O had a clear edge over competing PRR services via Baltimore and Harrisburg and

Most inbound B&O passenger trains turned on the wye and backed into Union Station. This Baltimore-Washington run has just come off the west leg of the wye at QN tower (to the rear) at Rhode Island Avenue and is backing down over the Metropolitan branch main tracks. June 1947 was the date. Credit: E.L. Thompson.

Washington Terminal's spacious twin coach yards, as seen from the New York Avenue bridge about 1932. In the foreground is equipment for B&O's "Columbian" and "Capitol Limited". Pennsy and B&O Washington branch approach tracks are at the far right. The left hand portion of this yard is now used as the Metro rapid transit shop and storage yard. Amtrak uses a rebuilt portion of the yard on the right. Credit: E.L. Thompson.

A. The scenes at Union Station's old train gates were always bittersweet—the names of now-gone trains on blue and white boards but also the sweaty summertime crowds trying to get out of town. B&O was allocated the tracks at the west side of the huge station concourse. Credits: A-Ara Mesrobian—B-B&O Museum Archives.

dominated the markets as long as people rode on trains. Its second major
service — Washington-New York — was never as fortunate; despite comparable mileage, B&O never matched the Pennsylvania from the beginning. Pennsy's entry into Manhattan in 1910 and electrification in 1935
merely solidified B&O's secondary status; in addition, the Penn continued
as the sole connecting carrier between New York and the south, as well as
Washington and New England. B&O was always the "courteous, comfortable" way to get to Philadelphia and New York, but the PRR was the
people-hauler — the "great red subway" of World War II days. The abrupt
end of B&O's Washington-New York service on April 26, 1958 was sad but
no great surprise.

But between Washington and Baltimore — B&O's third major service
— B&O was considerably more competitive and, in fact, still operates after
a fashion. Compared to the Pennsy, B&O's intermediate local territory
was better developed and its Baltimore stations better situated; it thus normally handled a major share of city-to-city traffic and a heavy local business. Through the 1930's and 1940's B&O scheduled a relatively consistent
26 trains each way between the two cities, slightly over half of which were
locals or Baltimore-Washington limiteds and the rest through trains to
New York. Sadly, it fell apart in the late 1950's and 1960's. The completion
of the Baltimore-Washington Parkway and later beltways at each city, the

B.

abandonment of the New York trains in 1958 and the short-haul low-revenue nature of the business made it unpatronized and uneconomic. In 1979 only four round trip weekday commuter schedules remained, well filled but state subsidized. Ironically, B&O's 1979 service frequency is now back at what it was in 1852.

B&O's fourth distinct Washington-based service was the local runs on the Metropolitan branch to various short-run terminals such as Gaithersburg, Boyd and Brunswick. Originally begun as a rural accommodation service, it rapidly turned into a commuter operation as the country towns along the line turned into suburbs. Through most of its history it was definitely secondary in traffic volume to the Washington-Baltimore local route and underwent the same decline in the 1950's-60's, particularly after the completion of Interstate 270. But it then went through a reverse twist and by the late 1970's was carrying record loads and far outstripping what was left of the Baltimore-Washington service. The odd upswing was the product of Montgomery County's explosive growth and — expressways to the contrary — the impossibility of rush-hour driving in downtown Washington. Transfer of financial responsibility for the service from the railroad to the state of Maryland has kept it growing.

As a byproduct of the Union Station project in 1905-07, B&O's Washington freight facilities were also rebuilt. The original Metropolitan branch right-of-way north of New York Avenue was redeveloped as the railroad's primary local freight terminal for the metropolitan area. A large brick l.c.l. freight house was built at the corner of New York and Florida Avenues; immediately north of it extensive team tracks and unloading facilities were laid out to handle inbound carload shipments. The 1889 Eckington freight yard was expanded and has undergone several subsequent expansions. It and the Eckington freight station/team track complex remain B&O's primary freight handling facilities for the Washington metropolitan area. LCL and most inbound perishable business has since disappeared, but beginning in 1955 the terminal has handled steadily growing amounts of piggyback traffic. Eckington yard is also the terminal for switching and local freight runs in the area. In the past it was also put to occasional extracurricular use as a "Pullman city." During Presidential inaugurations and other special occasions, chartered sleeping cars would be parked at the freight team tracks and, in effect, used by their occupants as hotels. Particularly memorable were the times when the army brought cadets and parade units into Eckington in special trains, at the same time converting the big brick freight house into a mess hall.

B&O has also retained freight rights on the west side of Washington Terminals's property south of Florida Avenue to Union Station. As part of the terminal project, it built a large coal delivery terminal for retail fuel dealers in the block bounded by N, M and First Streets, N.E.; the six long, wood coal unloading trestles were always a landmark for railroad passengers coming into Union Station until they were gradually dismantled between 1977 and 1979. B&O also served several warehouses along First Street just west of the Terminal tracks.

Eckington freight yard was sometimes pre-empted by special trains for Presidential inaugurations. In one of the last such occasions, West Point cadets have arrived for John F. Kennedy's inauguration in January 1961. Credit: Ara Mesrobian.

The rapid decay of passenger traffic during the 1960's and Union Station's increasingly insupportable taxes and maintenance costs led B&O and Pennsy to look for ways of getting out of the station — or at least getting out of its expenses. Unhappily for the two owners, its heroic architecture and size made it virtually impossible to simply walk away from, much less tear down. But by the mid-sixties the railroads at least had made it clear that something had to be done. Some sympathy and interest finally developed from the federal government, the only institution in Washington which could logically use such a structure or pay for it. By early 1968 a plan was developed to convert the station to a national visitor's center, a sort of grandiose reception room for Washington's Bicentennial tourists and those who would follow afterwards. The initial vision was a complete transportation center, combining rail and intercity bus terminals, tour bus terminals and a massive 4,000-car parking garage for both tourists and passengers. The railroad terminal would be relocated to a new and obviously smaller structure directly behind the existing Union Station, underneath the planned parking garage.

B&O and Pennsy were more than anxious to sell Union Station outright, but unfortunately at that time it was deemed politically unpalatable for the government to lay out a large lump sum for immediate purchase. Instead, a complex plan had to be worked out requiring the two owning railroads to jointly pay for converting the old station to the visitor center as well as building the new station and parking garage. In exchange, the government (via the Department of the Interior) would then lease the facility for at least 25 years at a rental designed to give the railroads a rapid return on their investment and relieve them of most of their costs. The estimated cost, to be provided by the railroads, was $16 million; their annual rental would range from $3.3 to $3.5 million a year.

Congress passed legislation creating the National Visitor Center March 12, 1968 and the lease/financing agreement with the two railroads was signed in December of that year. In the interim, the Pennsylvania had been merged into Penn Central.

But what promised to be a practical and creative re-use of a notable building quickly turned into a nightmare of delays, planning errors, cost overruns, passenger purgatory, and — ultimately — facilities that seemed to dissatisfy everyone. Obviously it is a story of it own, and not yet a finished one.

To summarize it as briefly and—under the circumstances—as objectively as possible: First, Penn Central's bankruptcy in June, 1970 effectively nullified the crucial financing agreement, since PC was in no position to contribute its half of the investment commitments. Chessie, B&O's parent, finally picked up the pieces alone by consenting to furnish the financing and manage the project. A new agreement was signed in September, 1972 and work on the new railroad station and parking garage began in 1973. Ground was formally broken for the Visitor Center rebuilding in March, 1974 under a now-frantic timetable to have the Center completed by the Bicentennial in July 1976. By this time costs had already mounted to the point where the 4,000-car garage was cut back to 1,200 cars and Congress had to provide extra funds to cover the escalating conversion costs. The bus terminal idea had also been discarded.

Next came a lawsuit from Amtrak in 1974. Amtrak's takeover of most rail passenger services May 1, 1971 had added a new party to the project. Although Amtrak owned no part of the facilities, it was plainly the primary user and wanted a say in what was done with them. But apparently nobody seriously consulted with Amtrak, whose traffic was increasing beyond what it felt was the capacity of the planned terminal. As a result it brought suit claiming dissatisfaction with the design of the new station and its ownership structure. This in turn froze Chessie's payments into the project and by September 1974 work had stopped. The problem was finally resolved by a redesign of the new station and more government money to keep the work going in the meantime. The station building went ahead, but all work on the scaled-back parking garage ceased because of further cost overruns.

The ordeal technically ended July 27, 1976 when the Visitor Center was formally dedicated. Not surprisingly, by this time the project had cost over four times the original estimate and had not been completed according to the plan. Along the way, part of the east end of the old Union Station concourse had been demolished and a giant hole opened in the center of the main waiting room floor for a sunken theater — which hardly endeared the project to the preservationists it was supposed to please. And in the intervening three years, railroad passengers had endured gruelling hikes through the old station dodging construction and struggling over temporary walkways and through narrow passages to reach the trains far behind.

The new railroad station — usually described in the press as a "motel lobby" — proved to be cramped and inaccessible. Most passengers still had to troop all the way through the Visitor Center to get there — the equivalent of 1½ blocks. On the other hand, without the parking garage or, indeed, a clear purpose, the plushy redone Visitor Center was vastly underused. Almost universal unhappiness at the outcome dictated yet another study, this one commissioned by the federal Department of Transportation. The report, released in late 1977, recommended that the new station be dismantled and the old Union Station be partially re-reconverted as a railroad terminal again. The cost, to be picked up by the Department of Transportation this time, was estimated at $45 million, which would include finishing the now-useless parking garage. There, at this point, the project lies.

While the Visitor Center project was limping off to its start, B&O and Washington Terminal also sold sections of right-of-way to the Washington Metropolitan Area Transit Authority for part of what would eventually be the Red Line Metro route to Silver Spring. The sale included a right-of-way along the west side of WT's viaduct and approach tracks and a large area north of New York Avenue for Metro's main shop and storage yard.

Work on the Metro line started in 1970, and by late 1971 track was being laid in the new storage yard near Eckington. As part of the same project, B&O relocated its Metropolitan branch passenger main line to the east of the Metro route and built a new spur to the west of Metro to reach its freight sidings north of Union Station. Metro construction work at its subway entrance just north of Union Station got caught in the Visitor Center construction tangle during 1972-73, one of the many delays the subway itself suffered. Operation finally started as far as Rhode Island Avenue on March 27, 1976.

So, by 1979 B&O's passenger presence in Washington had shrunk to a handful of subsidized commuter trains idling in the gloom under an unfinished parking garage, hemmed in by Metroliners on one side and rapid transit trains on the other — and tucked back behind the sumptuous but mostly silent onetime Union Station. It's obviously not much after the days of 98 trains a day, Presidential specials, the all-Pullman "Capitol Limited", the "Royal Blue" and whatever else. But with all other trains in Washington now lettered Amtrak, it's some sort of accomplishment that most of the cars still carry the name "Baltimore & Ohio". The first railroad into town is at least still represented.

An 1893 DAY IN THE LIFE OF B&O'S NEW JERSEY AVE.
STATION, WASHINGTON, D.C.
June, 1893

Movement and Time		Train	Branch To or from
Leave	5:00 AM	No. 140 local to Baltimore	Wash. Br.
Arrive	5:30 "	**No. 4 from Grafton, Cincinnati	Met. Br.
Lv.	5:40 "	No. 4 express to Baltimore	Wash. Br.
Lv.	6:25 "	No. 49 local to Gaithersburg	Met. Br.
Arr.	6:30 "	No. 141 local from Baltimore	Wash. Br.
Lv.	6:35 "	No. 142 local to Baltimore	" "
Lv.	7:15 "	No. 144 limited to Baltimore	" "
Arr.	7:25 "	No. 56 local from Gaithersburg	Met. Br.
Arr.	7:30 "	No. 143 local from Baltimore	Wash. Br.
Arr.	7:40 "	No. 10 from Pittsburgh	Met. Br.
Lv.	8:00 "	No. 510 express for Phila., New York	Wash. Br.
Arr.	8:00 "	No. 145 local from Baltimore	" "
Lv.	8:05 "	No. 10 express to Baltimore	" "
Arr.	8:10 "	No. 515 express from Phila., New York	" "
Arr.	8:20 "	No. 60 local from Boyd	Met. Br.
Lv.	8:30 "	No. 146 local to Baltimore	Wash. Br.
Arr.	8:30 "	No. 147 limited from Baltimore	Wash. Br.
Arr.	8:30 "	No. 52 from Washington Jct.	Met. Br.
Arr.	8:55 "	No. 149 express from Baltimore	Wash. Br.
Lv.	9:00 "	No. 57 local to Gaithersburg	Met. Br.
Arr.	9:00 "	No. 62 local from Gaithersburg	" "
Lv.	9:15 "	No. 200 express for Annapolis Jct.	Wash. Br.
Arr.	9:20 "	No. 42 from Martinsburg	Met. Br.
Lv.	9:30 "	No. 42 limited to Baltimore	Wash. Br.
Arr.	9:30 "	No. 44 from Shenandoah Jct.	Met. Br.
Lv.	10:00 "	No. 512 express to Phila., N.Y.	Wash. Br.
Arr.	10:05 "	No. 151 local from Baltimore	" "
Arr.	10:30 "	No. 17 limited from Baltimore	" "
Lv.	10:40 "	No. 17 local to Harpers Ferry	Met. Br.
Arr.	11:10 "	No. 5 express from Baltimore	Wash. Br.
Arr.	11:20 "	No. 505 from Philadelphia	" "
Lv.	11:30 "	No. 5 to Pittsburgh & Chicago	Met. Br.
Arr.	11:30 "	No. 64 local from Gaithersburg	" "
Lv.	12:00 N	No. 508 express to Phila. & N. Y.	Wash. Br.
Lv.	12:15 PM	No. 150 local to Baltimore	" "
Lv.	12:45 "	No. 61 local to Gaithersburg	Met. Br.
Arr.	12:45 "	No. 153 express from Baltimore	Wash. Br.
Lv.	1:30 "	No. 204 express to Annapolis Jct.	" "
Arr.	1:55 "	No. 155 local from Baltimore	" "

**Sleepers on No. 4 are parked for occupancy until 7:00 a.m.

B&O'S THREE AND A HALF TERMINALS IN WASHINGTON

Movement and Time		Train	Branch To or from
Arr.	2:10 "	No. 2 from Grafton & Cincinnati	Met. Br.
Lv.	2:20 "	No. 2 express to Baltimore	Wash. Br.
Arr.	2:35 "	No. 18 from Martinsburg	Met. Br.
Lv.	2:40 "	No. 502 express to Phila. & N.Y.	Wash. Br.
Arr.	3:00 "	No. 501 express from Phila. & N.Y.	" "
Lv.	3:00 "	No. 61 local to Gaithersburg	Met. Br.
Lv.	3:15 "	No. 18 limited to Baltimore	Wash. Br.
Arr.	3:20 "	No. 1 express from Baltimore	" "
Lv.	3:25 "	No. 156 local to Baltimore	" "
Lv.	3:30 "	No. 1 to Cincinnati & St. Louis	Met. Br.
Arr.	3:30 "	No. 66 local from Gaithersburg	" "
Arr.	4:05 PM	No. 8 from Grafton, Wheeling & Chicago	Met. Br.
Lv.	4:15 "	No. 8 express to Baltimore	Wash. Br.
Arr.	4:20 "	No. 159 local from Baltimore	" "
Lv.	4:28 "	No. 158 limited to Baltimore	" "
Lv.	4:30 "	No. 51 local to Washington Jct.	Met. Br.
Arr.	4:30 "	No. 511 express from Phila. & N.Y.	Wash. Br.
Lv.	4:31 "	No. 160 local to Baltimore	" "
Lv.	4:33 "	No. 65 local to Gaithersburg	Met. Br.
Lv.	5:00 "	No. 506 express to Phila. & N.Y.	Wash. Br.
Arr.	5:20 "	No. 41 limited from Baltimore	" "
Lv.	5:30 "	No. 41 to Harpers Ferry	Met. Br.
Lv.	5:30 "	No. 162 limited to Baltimore	Wash. Br.
Lv.	5:35 "	No. 67 local to Gaithersburg	Met. Br.
Lv.	5:35 "	No. 164 local to Baltimore	Wash. Br.
Arr.	6:00 "	No. 54 local from Gaithersburg	Met. Br.
Arr.	6:00 "	No. 7 from Baltimore	Wash. Br.
Lv.	6:15 "	No. 7 to Grafton, Wheeling & Chicago	Met. Br.
Lv.	6:20 "	No. 166 limited to Baltimore	Wash. Br.
Lv.	6:30 "	No. 168 local to Baltimore	" "
Arr.	6:40 "	No. 163 local from Baltimore	" "
Lv.	7:05 "	No. 69 local to Gaithersburg	Met. Br.
Arr.	7:05 "	No. 165 limited from Baltimore	Wash. Br.
Arr.	7:20 "	No. 6 from Pittsburgh & Chicago	Met. Br.
Lv.	7:30 "	No. 6 express to Baltimore	Wash. Br.
Arr.	7:40 "	No. 509 express from Phila. & N.Y.	" "
Arr.	7:40 "	No. 74 local from Gaithersburg	Met. Br.
Arr.	7:53 "	No. 167 local from Baltimore	Wash. Br.
Lv.	8:00 "	No. 516 express to Phila. & N.Y.	" "
Lv.	8:05 "	No. 170 local to Baltimore	" "
Arr.	8:20 "	No. 201 express from Annapolis Jct.	" "
Arr.	8:30 "	No. 76 local from Gaithersburg	Met. Br.
Arr.	8:30 "	No. 9 limited from Baltimore	Wash. Br.
Lv.	8:40 "	No. 9 to Pittsburgh	Met. Br.
Arr.	8:40 "	No. 116 from Grafton	" "

Movement and Time		Train	Branch To or from
Lv.	9:00 "	No. 16 limited to Baltimore	Wash. Br.
Arr.	9:15 "	No. 507 express from Phila. & N.Y.	" "
Lv.	9:40 "	No. 75 local to Boyd	Met. Br.
Arr.	10:05 "	No. 205 express from Annapolis Jct.	Wash. Br.
Arr.	10:40 "	No. 169 local to Baltimore	" "
Arr.	10:52 "	No. 503 express from Phila. & N.Y.	" "
Arr.	10:55 "	No. 78 local from Gaithersburg	Met. Br.
Lv.	11:10 "	No. 43 to Shenandoah Jct.	" "
Lv.	11:30 "	No. 77 local to Gaithersburg	" "
Lv.	11:30 "	**No. 514 express to Phila. & N.Y.	Wash. Br.
Lv.	11:35 "	No. 174 local to Baltimore	" "
Arr.	12:20 AM	No. 3 express from Baltimore	" "
Lv.	12:35 "	No. 3 to Cincinnati & St. Louis	Met. Br.
Arr.	12:45 "	No. 171 local from Baltimore	Wash. Br

**Sleepers for No. 514 parked for occupancy at 10:00 p.m.

Same train in and out   Through car(s) between trains

Most B&O passenger trains have disappeared from the Washington scene, but the scene itself is still exciting. In January 1973 three trains pass one another alongside New York Avenue at Ivy City. At the left, an Amtrak GG-1 picks up speed northbound on the onetime Pennsylvania line. Next to it, a B&O freight has just come around the wye on its way toward Baltimore. At the right, a westbound B&O freight is slowing for a stop to pick up cars at Eckington yard. Credit: H.H. Harwood, Jr.

IMPOSSIBLE CHALLENGE

CHAPTER 16

INTO HAGERSTOWN'S BACK DOOR:
THE WASHINGTON COUNTY BRANCH

At the time B&O began building out of Baltimore, Hagerstown was a small crossroads village. But the roads that crossed in the town were important and the general area had potential. The little town sat in the center of the Great Valley—the fertile, thousand-mile-long trough running roughly southwest between the easternmost ridges of the Appalachians. Immediately north of Hagerstown it went by the name of the Cumberland Valley; a short distance south in Virginia, it was the Shenandoah Valley. Hagerstown was located where the turnpike running through this valley crossed the road from Baltimore to Cumberland, connecting with the National Road west. Baltimore was about 75 miles to the east, overland. The Potomac River was only six miles southwest of Hagerstown at Williamsport, a sister town which eventually would become the busiest port on the C&O Canal between Georgetown and Cumberland. When B&O surveyors first came through the area in 1827, Hagerstown's industrial potential was far in the future; then, it was mostly a rural trading center and collection of inns and taverns serving the turnpike trade.

The railroad surveyors were exploring all possible routes B&O could follow to Cumberland, generally following the north side of the Potomac. One such route they found swung away from the Potomac Valley at what is now Weverton, followed a narrow defile north to Hartman's Gap, crossed northwest into the Antietam valley as far as a spot of Funkstown, then returned to the river at Williamsport. Although inland from the Potomac and hilly, this line would have been considerably straighter than the twisty river between Weverton and Williamsport. But it was only one of several alternatives for the railroad and eventually was rejected in favor of following the Potomac all the way.

However, by the early 1830's the route briefly came to life again. The legal scuffle with the C&O Canal over rights to the north bank of the Potomac to Cumberland put B&O's planned route in serious doubt and again an inland line near or through Hagerstown was considered. Spurred by this hope, Washington County legislators managed to incorporate a proviso in an 1836 state transportation aid bill which specified that B&O must locate its route through Boonsboro and Hagerstown or lose $1 million of the aid. But by then B&O engineers had reached the obvious conclusion that it was suicidal to fight through the continuous string of ridges north of the Potomac; if they couldn't use the immediate north side of the river, the only reasonable alternative was along the south side—state politics notwithstanding. Accordingly, they crossed the river at Harpers Ferry and began building west from there. The railroad collected its state aid anyway, but Hagerstown got no B&O.

The little town didn't stay frustrated long. When the Cumberland Valley Railroad built southwest from Harrisburg to Chambersburg, Pa. in 1837, the communities in the valley south of Chambersburg determined to connect with it. They finished their Franklin Railroad from Hagerstown to Chambersburg in February 1841. The Franklin's immediate success was not overwhelming, seeming to justify B&O's decision to go the other way; within two years the lightly-built road had deteriorated to the point where locomotives could not use it. After passing through a series of foreclosures and repossessions—interspersed with erratic operations—it was finally taken over by the Cumberland Valley in 1859, rebuilt and reopened a year later. Afterwards Hagerstown had a strong rail link to the east—but the Cumberland Valley fed railroads leading to Philadelphia, not Baltimore. Baltimore and Washington could only be reached by a roundabout routing from Hagerstown to Harrisburg, then south from Harrisburg over the Northern Central—157 miles versus the direct turnpike distance of about 75 miles.

The lack of a railroad to Baltimore still irritated the farmers and politicians of Washington County. After all, Baltimore was considerably closer than Philadelphia, was in Maryland and was really Hagerstown's "natural" outlet. The problem was that the topography east of Hagerstown was anything but easy. Although the town itself was in the center of the broad, level valley, the valley ran the wrong way to get to Baltimore. To get east, any railroad had to cross the Blue Ridge, which as it extended south split into two spurs—South Mountain and Catoctin. Nonetheless, Hagerstown constantly hatched railroad projects eastward. One of the more serious of these was the Metropolitan Railroad, organized in 1853 to run from Hagerstown to Washington, tunneling both ridges on the way. Money for such an ambitious project was not forthcoming from the rural countryside and despite some lingering efforts the Metropolitan never got started. It did reappear in partial form after the Civil War as B&O's Metropolitan branch, but the portion to Hagerstown was forever dead.

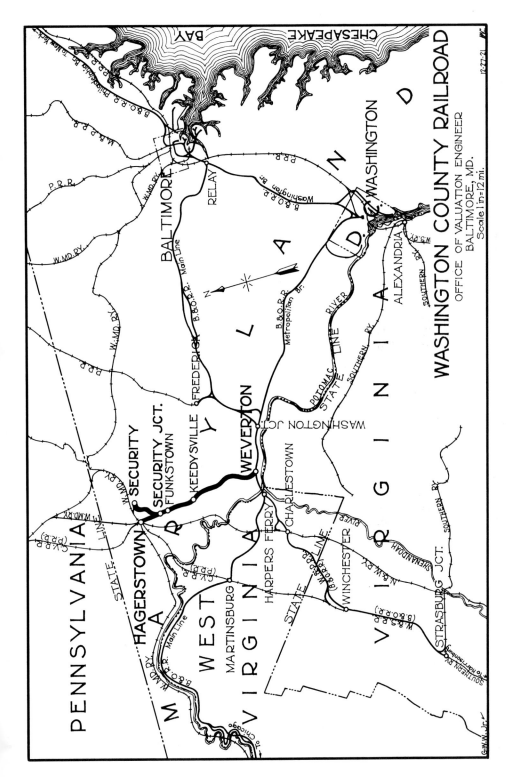

WASHINGTON COUNTY RAILROAD

OFFICE OF VALUATION ENGINEER
BALTIMORE, MD.
Scale 1 in.=12 mi.

Sporadically through the 1840's and '50's efforts were also made to promote a branch into Hagerstown from the B&O main line using the old survey route from Weverton. But B&O would not finance the line itself and—again—local money was insufficient. One product of these local efforts was the incorporation of the Washington County Railroad in March 1864 to build such a branch. Following the end of the Civil War, Washington County politicians and businessmen called on John W. Garrett and managed to persuade him to help build the line. B&O put up three-quarters of the Washington County Railroad's capital; the county government and various private sources contributed the rest. B&O was to lease and operate the branch, although the Washington County Railroad remained a separate company because of the outside financing and separate mortgage.

The branch began at Weverton and ran roughly due north to Hagerstown, 23.7 miles, following Israel Creek and Antietam Creek most of the way. Construction began in 1866 and the last rail was laid November 21, 1867. Commercial operation began December 1, 1867 and—symbolic of the line—the first revenue consignment was a load of wheat.

Hagerstown may have accomplished its dream by getting the B&O, but to B&O Hagerstown was no bonanza. The town was still small— about 5,500 people when B&O arrived—and was still essentially a rural trading center, crossroads and county seat. Furthermore, the now well-established Cumberland Valley Railroad continued to haul most of the area's commerce, channeling it through Philadelphia and New York. The Washington County Railroad showed a deficit in its early years and John W. Garrett grumbled in 1869 that B&O "could conveniently transport in one week all the business that it has been in its power to obtain in the sixteen months elapsed since the opening of the road."

To aggravate B&O's problem, the Western Maryland Railway completed its direct line over the mountain from Baltimore to Hagerstown in June 1872. To be sure, the WM of 1872 was no particular pillar of strength either—it was a rural railroad too, and at that time its Baltimore terminal was remote and makeshift. In 1872 Western Maryland ended at Fulton, on the west side of Baltimore; by 1876 it managed to reach downtown at Hillen Street via trackage rights through the Pennsylvania tunnels. But it was not until 1904 that the railroad had truly competitive port facilities in Baltimore. WM's Hagerstown-Baltimore route was somewhat more direct than B&O's through Weverton (87 miles vs. B&O's 99) and, if nothing else, Western Maryland helped to divide an already thin traffic even thinner.

But whatever its commercial and financial status, the Washington County branch was picturesque and pretty—and even now mostly detached from the Twentieth Century. Turning north from the main line at Weverton, the branch followed Israel Creek up a narrow valley walled in by South Mountain on the east and Elk Ridge to the west. The single track crisscrossed the creek no less than 17 times on wood trestles as it climbed out of the Potomac Valley and over the ridge on a steady upgrade ranging from 1.07% to 1.68%.

The Hagerstown branch joined B&O's main line at Weverton, Md., west of present-day Brunswick. This view, taken in the early 1920's, looks east on the main line; the branch is to the rear of the station. This station dates to 1888, a replacement of the original 1868 structure. Credit: B&O Museum Archives.

At Beeler's Summit, 6.8 miles north of Weverton, it topped the ridge and dropped down a somewhat steeper grade (1.41% to 1.88%) for about four miles to Eakle's Mill, the bottom of the hill, where a passing siding and water tank were located. Between Eakle's Mill and Keedysville the branch emerged from the hills into the Great Valley, picking up Antietam Creek leading to Hagerstown. From here on north it followed a straight but up-and-down path through low hills and open farming country. The branch entered Hagerstown from the south, ending a block from the center of town at a compact terminal inside the block bounded by Antietam Street, South Potomac, West Baltimore and South Jonathan (Summit Avenue).

Structures on the line—with a few notable exceptions—tended to be minimal. For the branch's opening in 1867 B&O built a frame station at the Weverton junction for passengers transferring to main line trains. It was fairly large (120 feet long) and included a separate ladies' waiting room and a restaurant. In 1888 it was replaced by a smaller but quite fashionable frame station equipped with a squat circular tower and scalloped shingle siding. Also at Weverton was a water station and a

The branch's rural atmosphere is beautifully caught in this 1952 view in the open Antietam Creek valley of a "southbound" way freight south of Hagerstown. Credit: Philip R. Hastings.

turntable for engines ending their runs there—originally wood, replaced in 1874 with an iron Sellers-patent turntable.

At the Hagerstown end the original facilities consisted of a 101 foot-long two-story brick freight house, a 50 foot turntable and a small frame engine house. There is no record of the original passenger station, if indeed there was one. However, in 1891 B&O rebuilt its Hagerstown terminal, replacing the freight house and building an attractive new passenger station. The two-story stone and wood structure was another product of Baltimore architect E. Francis Baldwin and was a larger version of his University suburban station in Washington; it had a rounded agent's bay, graceful curved stone *porte-cochere* and wood gables. Baldwin also designed the nearby frame freight station—not nearly so distinguished, but with small gables that gave it more style than the usual freight house.

In between the two terminals was a scattering of tiny farming and mill communities whose names conveyed their atmosphere—Garrett's Mill, Clagett's, Rohrersville, Eakle's Mill, Keedysville, Breathed's. The largest of these—Keedysville—scarcely exceeded 400 people even in the 1970's. So, not surprisingly, their stations amounted to little or nothing. In fact at three locations—at Rohrersville, Breathed's and Roxbury—the railroad simply used space in a country store or combination store-mill alongside the track. In these cases the space was apparently free, in exchange for use of right-of-way property. Other stations on the line in the early 1900's included small open shelters at Stonebraker, Garrett's Mill and Augusta, all built in 1903; a tiny closed frame station at Brownville, also built in 1903; a frame passenger station and separate freight house at Gapland, (originally called Clagett's) both dating to 1891, and both designed by Francis Baldwin. Keedysville got a standardized frame combination freight and passenger station in 1913. Ball's Road and Fiery Siding also were equipped with 1903 wood shelters.

Bridges were similarly unspectacular—with one exception. By and large the Washington County branch was originally mostly a timber trestle railroad, particularly along Israel Creek; to some extent it remained so over its life. Several short Bollman trusses spanned the Little Antietam at Keedysville and some road crossings. Many of the timber trestles and trusses were replaced between 1889 and 1898 with steel I-beams and girders except the three Little Antietam spans, which got new girders in 1900 and 1913. The most impressive structure on the line of any type—and it was impressive by any standards—was the 746 foot long, 75 foot high bridge over the Antietam north of Keedysville. Originally this was a combination truss and trestle affair, with at least two Bollman deck trusses—one about 167 feet, the other about 106 feet— and a trestle approach on the south side. By about 1900 the Bollman trusses were unable to cope with the loads and the bridge was rebuilt as a full timber trestle; in 1909 an 84 foot girder span was installed over the creek portion. With some patching, it survived in this form until dismantled in 1979.

A.

In 1891 this pretty little passenger terminal was built at the corner of Summit Avenue and Antietam Street. It was torn down shortly after World War II, replaced by a gas station and replaced again by the Hagerstown *Herald-Mail* building. Credits: A-Gary Schlerf collection—B-C.T. Mahan collection.

B.

In short, the Washington County line was a prototypical pastoral branch. In fact, even as late as 1920 three quarters of its length was laid with 67-lb. relay rail dating to the 1880's. And the line had one typical hazard of back-country branches: its track—especially along Israel Creek—was a favorite sunning spot for copperheads in the summer.

Commercially it followed that the branch had a beginning and end, but very little middle. Between Weverton and Hagerstown the freight was thin and almost entirely agricultural, plus such agriculture-related activities as tanning. But whatever strength the line would ever have lay at Hagerstown and its immediate surroundings.

Hagerstown finally began to blossom by the 1880's. In 1880 the Shenandoah Valley Railroad (now part of Norfolk & Western) arrived in town from the south, and soon had completed a line to Roanoke. Working closely with the Cumberland Valley/PRR, the Shenandoah Valley/ N&W formed a major through rail route between the south and the Atlantic seaboard. The ability to reach north, east and south easily by rail spurred the establishment of Hagerstown as a manufacturing center and its industry and population grew quickly. By 1900, its population was almost exactly double what it was in 1880.

Through the 1890's and early 1900's the city continued to develop as a railroad junction point, which in turn further stimulated industrial development. In 1892 the Western Maryland had extended west to join B&O's main line at Cherry Run, W.Va., giving the city a strong western link. In 1886 WM also established a connection with the Reading at Shippensburg, Pa. and eventually developed a second through route to the Philadelphia, New York and New England markets which more or less paralleled the Cumberland Valley/PRR routes. The route from Cherry Run to the northeast via Hagerstown soon became an important secondary means for B&O to reach the seaboard cities; under the name of the Central States Dispatch Route, B&O, WM and various connecting railroads operated tightly-coordinated through freight services. And finally, Western Maryland completed its own main line to Connellsville, Pa. in 1912, giving it direct access to lines to Pittsburgh and the midwest.

B&O's Washington County line thus ended up as the only branch in a city now served by multiple main lines leading everywhere. Incongruously, heavy B&O coal drags and CSD manifest freights regularly roared into the city on WM's main line over the Cherry Run interline route—but B&O's own line remained tucked away in its own detached backwash. A variety of freight customers did develop in Hagerstown's south side along the branch—lumber dealers, furniture manufacturers, sheet metal fabricators, a paper products manufacturer and a taxicab builder. The railroad's team tracks, located in the center of the retail district, also did a good business.

But the branch's biggest freight stimulus—indeed, its savior—came with the construction of the Security (Antietam) branch in 1916. This 3.7-mile spur left the branch just south of Hagerstown and followed the Antietam in an arc around the east side of town to Security. At Security it

A.

Rohrersville in action and at rest. The "station", typical of several along the branch, was a private store with desk space for the railroad agent. In the late 1930's view an E-27 Consolidation heads south toward Weverton; in 1979 the scene was much the same, except that the railroad was now abandoned and awaiting the wrecking crew. Credits: A-Charles Summer—B-H.H. Harwood, Jr.

B.

joined the Western Maryland's main line to Baltimore but, more important, reached the plant of Security Cement & Lime (later North American Cement and presently Marquette). The cement plant developed into Hagerstown's largest single industry and, of course, B&O's largest customer. Several smaller shippers and receivers also later located on the Security branch—primarily lumber and furniture companies, fuel dealers and later a large scrap dealer.

In addition to whatever traffic it could generate itself, the Washington County branch was occasionally useful to both B&O and Western Maryland as an emergency detour route. Since it connected B&O's big Brunswick yard with the key junctions at Hagerstown, it could be used as an alternative routing around tieups at many spots on both railroads. It usually would get such a workout at least once or twice a year. In a typical case, in late 1947 the "Capitol Limited" and several other main-line passenger trains were detoured over the branch to get around a derailment at Martinsburg, W.Va. But by the early 1960's its track had deteriorated to the point where it was permanently barred as a passenger detour. The generally open line was also a good bypass route for certain high or wide shipments.

B&O's Hagerstown passenger schedules never outgrew the classic branch line mold. For the entire time passenger trains operated over the line all of them made all local stops, handling people, mail and express at the little towns and road crossings. When the line was opened, service

Keedysville looked like this about 1907. The train is "southbound". Credit: Gary Schlerf collection.

consisted of three round trips a day between Hagerstown and the main line junction at Weverton—a pattern which remained basically the same for the next 60-odd years. From the 1880's through the late 1920's the regular passenger runs were supplemented by a southbound-only mixed train, leaving Hagerstown in late afternoon. By the late 1920's the basic three-train service had built up to four (plus the one-way mixed); briefly in the 1929-30 period it hit a peak of five trips each way, although by then the mixed had been taken out of the schedule.

Passenger running times reflected the nature of the business—that is, casual. In the early days of the branch trains took one hour and ten minutes to cover the 23.7 miles. By the 1890's this had been cut to an hour, which became an unvarying standard until the late '20s when a few runs were able to make it in 55 minutes.

Through the late 19th Century the Hagerstown trains tied up at Weverton and all passengers transferred there for Baltimore, Washington or wherever. Beginning in the early 1900's several of the branch trains were scheduled as through runs directly to Baltimore and Washington, in effect by merging them with Metropolitan branch and Old Main Line local schedules. As a result these were mostly all-stops locals and tended to be excruciatingly slow, but at least they got there without a change. Washington was reached from Hagerstown in three hours flat; the fastest through schedule to Baltimore took three hours and 35 minutes, although at times the schedules were over four hours. (Western Maryland's fastest Hagerstown-Baltimore service trips varied in frequency over the years, but generally there was one Baltimore schedule each way and one or two Washington trips.)

By 1929 gas-electric cars based at Brunswick had been substituted for two of the steam trips on the branch and the mixed ceased carrying passengers. The through steam-powered Baltimore and Washington runs were continued at least through 1930, but as the Depression deepened passenger service on the branch was brutally (but probably belatedly) slashed. By 1936 only one train was left—a gas-electric operating out of Brunswick which also covered the Brunswick-Frederick local services during the same day. This run came up to Hagerstown in late morning and left after 1 p.m. This basic service hung on virtually unchanged through World War II and after; it finally died November 1, 1949. The pretty stone station in Hagerstown had already come down by the time service ended and a gas station built on the site.

A five-day-a-week local freight continued to roll over the line hauled by a 2-8-2 and, later GP-9's. Cement and scrap from Security, plus paper, lumber and furniture to and from Hagerstown kept the branch alive. What little business was on the line south of Hagerstown gradually evaporated, finally leaving a feed mill at Breathed's as the only customer by 1975.

When the ICC permitted B&O and C&O to exercise direct management control over the Western Maryland in 1968, the handwriting for the

A.

The mighty Antietam trestle in two of its three incarnations. Originally a combination of trestle and iron Bollman deck trusses, it was rebuilt as a full wood trestle about 1900 and given a steel span in 1909. Credits: A-Frank A. Wrabel collection—B-B&O Museum Archives— C-H.H. Harwood, Jr.

B.

C.

A cement car for Security gets switched in Hagerstown in 1952. Credit: Philip R. Hastings.

Trains like this operated through local schedules between Hagerstown and Washington or Baltimore in the 1920's. The photo shows B-18 No. 2024 at the Summit Avenue station in the late '20's. Credit: C.S. Roberts collection.

Washington County branch appeared on the wall. Since virtually all of the branch's business was concentrated at the Hagerstown-Security end—where there were already two direct WM connections—it became less necessary to support the entire branch merely to maintain a competitive B&O line at Hagerstown. With WM now an integral part of the Chessie family, it was less important which pocket the revenue went into. As a result it made economic sense to turn over the Hagerstown section to WM and dismantle the pretty but unproductive 20-odd miles to Weverton.

The abandonment application was submitted to the ICC March 17, 1975. In it B&O asked to abandon the entire branch except for about a mile at Hagerstown and 1.2 miles at Security, with these two tips to be leased to Western Maryland. Later this was amended to include the line south of Hagerstown as far as Roxbury, 5½ miles, where a large scrap auto shredding operation had been established in early 1975. The case took over three years to plod through the ICC, but in the meantime the branch required some urgent track renewal work to keep it operating. Rather than spend money which would be largely wasted, B&O decided to shut it down ahead of time and reroute the Hagerstown traffic over WM from Cherry Run. On February 13, 1976 it took 18 miles of the branch out of service between Weverton and Roxbury. Three days a week a B&O crew was taxied from Brunswick to Hagerstown where it picked up a Western Maryland diesel and caboose and switched the cars between the WM interchanges and B&O sidings.

ICC approval finally came through June 19, 1978, although labor negotiations delayed the formal Western Maryland takeover until November 15. The balance of the Washington County branch, now overgrown after three years of inactivity, remained in place until 1979 when it was finally taken up. The compact little Hagerstown terminal yard, including the site of the passenger station, is now occupied by the new Hagerstown *Herald Mail* building. But oddly, the Washington County Railroad—the original company formed to build the line—still exists, long since a B&O subsidiary but still with some outside stockholders.

Not long afterwards, gas-electric trains looking like this took over the Hagerstown runs. This particular scene dates to Nov. 1, 1949, the last day of service. Credit: Russell Wilcox.

The daily Hagerstown local freight fights its way through Pleasant Valley foliage at Gapland, six miles north of Weverton, in September 1949. Credit: Charles T. Mahan, Jr.

In the last days of Hagerstown passenger service, the gas-electric train loaded in a paved-over open lot off Antietam Street. The gas station at the left occupies the site of the onetime passenger station. This view dates to Nov. 1, 1949 and the train is about to make its last run to Brunswick. Credit: Russell Wilcox.

The station is gone, passenger service is gone, but steam still rules what is left on the Washington County branch in this 1952 scene at the Antietam Street terminal. The passenger station stood at the far left; a hand-operated turntable is out of the picture at the lower left. The Hagerstown *Herald-Mail* building now occupies most of this site. Credit: Philip R. Hastings.

The 4145, handling the Brunswick-Hagerstown local freight, gets turned by its crew at the Hagerstown yard before heading home. The photo dates to October 1952. Credit: Philip R. Hastings.

The Hagerstown-Brunswick local freight, headed by 2-8-2 4145, leaving Hagerstown for Weverton in 1952. Credit: Philip R. Hastings.

The wayfreight treads cautiously over the Antietam Creek trestle on its way "south" in September 1969. Credit: Lee B. Smith.

36   TIME TABLE. | 4

BALTIMORE & OHIO RAILROAD.

Washington County Branch.   1876

To take effect at 5.50 A. M., Monday, June 5th, 1876.

EASTWARD.

STATIONS.	Dist. Bet.	Wh. Dist.	No. 915 (Pas'ng'r)	No. 911 (Pas'ng'r)	No. 919 (Pas'ng'r)	No. 931 (Freight.)	No. 905 (Pas'ng'r)
			A. M.	A. M.	P. M.	P. M.	P. M.
Hagerstown............ ....leave			6 15	9 00	12 15	4 10	5 35
Breathed's....................	6¾	6¾	6 31	9 17	12 32	4 40	5 52
Keedysville........	4½	11¼	6 42	9 29	12 44	5 01	6 04
Eakles' Mill................ ..	2	13¼	6 47	9 34	12 50	5 12	6 09
Rhorersville............... ...	2¾	16	6 54	9 42	12 58	5 25	6 17
Beeler's Summit................	1¼	17¼	6 57	9 45	1 02	5 31	6 20
Claggett's....................	1	18¼	7 00	9 48	1 05	5 37	6 23
Brownsville............	1¼	19½	7 03	9 52	1 09	5 43	6 27
Bartholow's...............	1¼	20¾	7 06	9 56	1 14	5 49	6 31
Weverton.............arrive	3½	24¼	7 15	10 05	1 25	6 05	6 40
			A. M.	A. M.	P. M.	P. M.	P. M

NOTES.

ALL TRAINS DAILY, EXCEPT SUNDAY.

No. 915 meets 940 at Rhorersville at 6.54 A. M.   900 will wait indefinitely at Weverton for 915.

No. 919 meets 914 at Breathed's at 12.32 P. M.   914 will take the siding and wait until 12.45, P. M., if necessary, for 919.   919 will not wait after 12.35 P. M. for 914.   912 will wait indefinitely at Weverton for 919.

All trains will leave Hagerstown and Weverton on prompt time whether overdue trains of the same class have arrived or not, except as provided for in notes.   Freight trains will avoid passenger trains indefinitely.

S. SPENCER,   F. MANTZ,
  Supervisor of Trains.   General Supervisor of Trains.

C. E. WAYS,   THOS. R. SHARP,
  Agent at Hagerstown.   Master of Transportation.

36 TIME TABLE. | 4

BALTIMORE & OHIO RAILROAD.
Washington County Branch. | 1876

To take effect at 5.50 A. M., Monday, June 5th, 1876.

WESTWARD.

STATIONS.	Dist. Bet. Wh. Dist.		No. 940 (Freight.)	No. 900 (Pas'ng'r.)	No. 914 (Pas'ng'r.)	No. 912 (Pas'ng'r.)	No. 902 (Pas'ng'r.)
			A. M.	A. M.	A. M.	P. M.	P. M.
Weverton...............leave			5 50	7 25	11 35	1 40	6 55
Bartholow's.....................	3½	3½	6 05	7 35	11 45	1 50	7 05
Brownsville.....................	1¼	4¾	6 11	7 38	11 48	1 53	7 08
Claggett's.....................	1¼	6	6 18	7 42	11 51	1 56	7 11
Beeler's Summit..............	1	7	6 24	7 45	11 54	1 59	7 14
Rhorersville.....................	1¼	8½	6 30 A / 6 54 L	7 49	11 58	2 02	7 17
Eakles' Mill................	2¾	11	7 08	7 57	12 06	2 09	7 24
Keedysville.....................	2	13	7 19	8 03	12 12	2 15	7 30
Breatheds'.....................	4½	17½	7 43	8 15	12 24 A / 12 32 L	2 27	7 42
Hagerstown............arrive	6¾	24¼	8 15	8 35	12 45	2 45	8 00
			A. M.	A. M.	P. M.	P. M.	P. M.

NOTES.

ALL TRAINS DAILY, EXCEPT SUNDAY.

No. 940 meets 915 at Rhorersville at 6.54 A. M.

No. 900 will wait indefinitely at Weverton for 915.

No. 914 meets 919 at Breathed's at 12.32 P. M. 914 will take the siding and wait until 12.45 P. M., if necessary, for 919. 919 will not wait after 12.35 P. M. for 914.

No. 912 will wait indefinitely at Weverton for 919.

All trains will leave Weverton and Hagerstown on prompt time, whether overdue trains of the same class have arrived or not, except as provided for in notes. Freight trains will avoid Passenger trains indefinitely.

Main Stem Rules and Regulations apply to the Washington County Branch.

Read Carefully the new Rules on page 43, Time Book 18.

IMPOSSIBLE CHALLENGE

CHAPTER 17

EPILOGUE: RAISING THE GHOSTS OF THE PAST

As the humdrum diesels drone past hauling their hi-cube boxcars and trilevel auto carriers, some trainwatchers wistfully shut their eyes and play Miniver Cheevy: "Ah, if only I had been around here to watch the 'Royal Blue'. . .or a pair of Consolidations wheeling wood gondolas back to the mines. . .a Winans Camel, maybe. . ." It's a futile exercise, of course, unless you're willing to settle for looking at the cold metal in the B&O Museum (which is not too bad an alternative). But don't completely despair of witnessing the past now. The little Grasshopper locomotives may be gone, but many of the bridges they rolled over are still there. In fact, so is some of the track structure if you know where to look. Stations stand which once served William Mason woodburners; so do shop buildings which repaired the ornate Royal Blue Line coaches and parlor cars. There are cuts, embankments and a culvert which never even saw steam power. And the ghosts of Jonathan Knight, Caspar Wever and Benjamin Latrobe still lurk underneath footpaths and behind thickets along the Patapsco Valley.

So, if you're willing to study the stationary part of the railroad, you'll find a lot of living history out there. In fact, the archeological aspect of railroading can be fully as fascinating as the locomotives and cars — if for no other reason than it is far less explored and known. This chapter therefore will introduce you to the survivors of B&O's pioneering days which still exist in one form or another in the area west and south of Baltimore — and give you plenty of fresh air and exercise at the same time.

Let's begin with a group of the earliest railroad bridges anywhere in the country. You probably know of two of them, but there are many others you may not:

Like it or not, we have to start with the obvious: the Carrollton Viaduct (oldest surviving railroad bridge in the U.S., completed 1829) and the Thomas Viaduct (oldest multiple-arch railroad bridge — 1835 — and an awesome structure in its own right).

Many people know the Carrollton from pictures; few have seen it on the spot and for good reason. Although located near the center of Baltimore and almost underneath Interstate 95, it isn't easy to get to. The best and safest access is through the Carroll Park Golf Course — enter from Washington Boulevard and follow Gwynns Falls upstream for the equivalent of about five blocks. This route will put you close enough to take in its 297-foot length and 80-foot single stone arch, but not so close as to become intimate with the junkyard immediately behind it. On the west side of the bridge, a now-buried small arch once spanned a dirt country road. Although the Carrollton viaduct ceased carrying the main line over 126 years ago, it is still well-trodden. Now at the east throat of an active freight yard (Yard "A" in B&O's Baltimore Terminal), it is used by switchers, yard transfer runs and a few road freights making pickups and setoffs.

The Thomas Viaduct (1833-35) is considerably more accessible. The

Carrollton Viaduct is well worth the struggle to see, even if some of its surroundings have lost their 19th Century country estate atmosphere. At the time this April 1975 photo was taken, the small arch at the far left (which once crossed a wagon road) was still visible. It has since been buried. Credit: H.H. Harwood, Jr.

"traditional" photo location for the bridge (made famous and a bit tired by several generations of B&O publicity pictures) is at the Relay end and requires a short hike down the track from Railroad Avenue. (Note the stone mileposts on both sides of the track, about midway there.) But a better spot to appreciate the viaduct's size and aesthetics is from the river level at the Elkridge end. Simply take Washington Boulevard (U.S. Route 1) to Levering Road in Elkridge, then turn north. Shortly you'll pass directly under the bridge and can choose several good spots to contemplate its length (612 feet) and eight 58-foot arches sweeping gracefully away from you. Wait around for a while and you're likely to see action of some sort — the bridge carries virtually all of B&O's merchandise freight traffic, plus four weekday morning and evening Washington commuter runs.

The Thomas Viaduct is normally thought of as something eternal, and indeed it probably will be. But few people know that B&O came perilously close to abandoning the structure several times in its history. The details of the abortive Relay cutoff are related in Chapter 11. In essence, property was acquired for a direct bypass route between Halethorpe and Elkridge, passing behind the present Seagram (Calvert) distillery. The cutoff was partly graded but never completed — although thought was given to building it as late as 1969. Part of the property was subsequently sold to Seagram, ending all further consideration. Trains still grind around the curves and over the viaduct, and likely will as long as trains run here, while only a railroad-owned pole line marks the would-be replacement route.

After these two stunning structures anything else is apt to be an anticlimax. But don't stop there. Scattered along the Old Main Line and the Washington branch are many fine smaller masonry relics of the "stone railroad" of the 1830's. To be sure, almost every one of these would fit easily inside one of the Thomas viaduct's arches. Yet they can offer something the Thomas and Carrollton viaducts cannot — the thrill of discovering some 150-year-old bridge deep in the woods or under some fill, unseen and unappreciated for three-quarters of a century or more.

One of these, in fact, is almost next to the Carrollton viaduct. If not quite as spectacular, it is equally as old — or at least part of it is. This 20-foot arch and high stone embankment crosses a little ravine formed by Gwynns Run, a lateral tributary to Gwynns Falls. As it stands now, Gwynns Run bridge is a composite of two important phases of the B&O's development in Baltimore: Its older section (the north side of the bridge) dates to the original main line construction from Mount Clare in 1828-29. In 1848, when the branch to Locust Point was built (and which in 1853 also became the main line into Camden station), the junction was established at the east end of the bridge and the bridge extended on its south side to carry the new track. Unfortunately, Gwynns Run is even harder to get to than the Carrollton viaduct. Aside from hiking west down the track from Monroe Street (not recommended), the best route into it is over the service road which follows the north perimeter of Carroll Park Golf Course.

A.

The Thomas Viaduct between Relay and Elkridge offers history, engineering aesthetics and action. (A) In this view from the south-west side, southbound freight NE-87 is heading toward Potomac Yard from Philadelphia about 1974. (B) During the "Chessie Steam Special's" memorable two-year tour of B&O, C&O and Western Maryland lines, the ex-Reading 4-8-4 has its yellow and red train rolling toward Washington on a Baltimore-Harpers Ferry Excursion. This trip was May 8, 1977. Credits: A-Bill Rettberg—B-H.H. Harwood, Jr.

B.

Beyond the Carrollton Viaduct, the railroad's severe struggles to conquer the rough terrain west of Baltimore can still be sensed at two points: At the spot where Patapsco Avenue crosses over the railroad at the present southwestern city boundary, one may look directly down into the infamous "Deep Cut". Long ago widened for four tracks, it no longer looks very deep; the hill itself, now engulfed in urbanization, hardly seems formidable. The sight is perhaps a lesson in how our sense of scale — and with it our sense of awe — has been cut down by our own creations. Just west of Halethorpe is the high fill and stone bridge over Gadsby's Run, now called Herbert Run — another symbol of the company's early obsession with enduring engineering works. When viewed from stream level, the 57-foot fill is still impressive, particularly when a passing train provides proportion. The little 25-foot stone arch underneath was extended in 1875 when the embankment was widened to carry four tracks. Oddly, however, it appears that both sides of the bridge are the original masonry and that the newer brick arch was inserted in the center. To reach Gadsby's/Herbert Run, drive west on Hollins Ferry Road to it's dead-end and walk down to the stream immediately beyond.

Elsewhere out on the Old Main Line, the hard-core railroad archeologist can find enough other bridge relics to justify a healthy two days of exploring. A few are only partial remnants, but most are still in reasonably pristine shape. But one caution to the overenthusiastic searcher: Many of the stone bridges on the present Old Main Line are not original — they date to the 1901-06 rebuilding program. (Leonor Loree liked masonry fully as much as the B&O's early directors.) These "new" stone arches include some of the more prominent ones, such as several visible from Interstate 70 east and west of Mt. Airy and the interesting twin-arch bridge east of Mt. Airy.

Let's go up the Patapsco a bit and see the remains of the two other large bridges (Carrollton was the first) dating to the railroad's original construction — the Patterson and Oliver Viaducts. The Patterson carried the old line over the river at Ilchester, about two miles east of Ellicott City. As completed in 1830, it was a stolid but attractive four-arch structure — two 55' foot arches over the river and a smaller 20-foot arch at each end over country roads. Unhappily it lasted in this form only 38 years; the 1868 flood swept away three of the arches, leaving only the roadway arch at the west end. The east end abutment was completely rebuilt and a long single-span iron Bollman truss erected across the river. During 1902-03 a completely new line was blasted through Ilchester, tunnelling the high granite hillside which the original line had respectfully circled around, and crossing the river upstream. The old line was abandoned, the Bollman span dismantled and the remains left to nature. The single surviving arch of the Patterson viaduct stands amid the trees next to River Road and the rebuilt east abutment and masonry retaining wall of the old line can be clearly seen directly across the river.

The Oliver viaduct, also built in 1829-30, sat in the center of Ellicott City and, in fact, was virtually integral with the station. Two of its three 20-

The 57-foot fill over Gadsby's Run west of Halethorpe helped soak up some of B&O's original capital, as did the stone arch over the stream. The fill and bridge originally carried a double track line. When this section was widened for four tracks in 1875, B&O's engineers—who apparently had a sense of history even then—preserved the original facade of the bridge by separating it and inserting a new section in the center rather than simply extending it on either side. Credit: H.H. Harwood, Jr.

foot wide arches spanned Ellicott City's main street (which also formed the route of the Frederick turnpike — the main route to the west from Baltimore — and the Columbia Pike to Washington) while the arch closest to the station crossed Tiber Creek, a small stream. The Oliver was dismembered at roughly the same time as the Patterson, but in this case its undoing was traffic, not water. The two roadway arches proved too constricted even for mid-19th Century wagons; they were removed in 1868, but the stone center pier was left in place. By the mid-1920's the pier also became too tight and dangerous for the masses of autos, trucks, buses and streetcars now crowding through the town. Between 1928 and 1931 the street was widened, the center pier removed, and the railroad bridge was rebuilt with a pair of prosaic girder spans. But one-third of the original Oliver Viaduct — the single span over Tiber Creek — still survives, tucked inconspicuously in between Main Street and the station.

Beyond these two easily-seen survivors, the going gets a bit tougher but the specimens are mostly healthier. Backtracking eastward from Ellicott City, take River Road toward Ilchester. About a mile from Ellicott

This is what remains of the Oliver Viaduct in Ellicott City. As originally built in 1829-30, two arches of identical size spanned the Frederick turnpike (now Main Street) immediately to the right. They were removed in 1868. In this 1975 photo, Ellicott City station was in the process of renovation. Credit: H.H. Harwood, Jr.

City, you'll see a small stone bridge on the railroad line directly across the river. This point on the railroad — and a point is all it is — is called Lees, the site of the now-demolished emergency World War II coaling station. The stone bridge you see is "new", built in 1903 when a small curve was straightened out here during the relocation project. What you don't see is the original 1830 bridge, almost identical, hiding behind the later one. Should you want a closer look, you'll have to hike in, either west from Ilchester (.8 mile) or east from Ellicott City (1.3 miles).

Also in the Ellicott City vicinity is a nice stone bridge over Sucker Run, opposite Oella. This single 20-foot arch is another 1831 original, rebuilt

Typical of several long-abandoned and seldom seen original stone arches is this one over Line Run, on a bypassed section of the 1831 alignment just northeast of Davis tunnel. Several others still stand, some in service, on the section west of Daniels. Credit: H.H. Harwood, Jr.

after the 1868 flood. It is still in active use, and requires more right-of-way walking to reach.

Considerably safer and more productive is the area west of Daniels. In the 2½ miles along the south bank of the Patapsco between Daniels and Davis are the remains of the two famous Elysville bridges (successively wood truss and two generations of Bollman iron trusses), three abandoned stone arch bridges (two of them probably original and one dating to about 1870), one fine 1831 bridge still in service, and, at one point, three successive railroad alignments. This stretch also dramatically illustrates the turn-of-the-century rebuilding of the Old Main Line — the present railroad line, completed in 1907, is on a completely new location on the north side of the river, and with the help of two tunnels and two long steel girder bridges, cuts a relatively straight line through the winding river valley.

This is entirely a hiking or bicycling jaunt; there's no way to cover it by car, although a State Park service road (no motor vehicles!) now runs over most of the old right-of-way, making the going quite easy. To get there, take Old Frederick Road to Daniels Road, then follow Daniels Road down into the valley. The road will dead-end at what was once the thriving mill town of Elysville/Alberton/Daniels, now a desolate ruin. The brick and frame workers' houses were levelled in 1968 and the mill buildings were ravaged by Agnes in 1972. A 1977 fire finished off the little that was left. A short distance upstream from the present railroad bridge are the abutments and piers of the original "lower" Elysville bridge, first built in 1838 as part of a pioneering relocation project. The original (1831-38) line followed the south bank of the river west from here. The Park road now occupies this roadbed — park where it begins and start hiking. The long-abandoned railroad line follows the bend of the river, hemmed in by rocky ledges on the left. Around this bend are the remains of the "upper" Elysville bridge — a pair of abutments and a cut-down pier — where the 1838 cutoff rejoined the original line. The old line can now be followed easily for almost two miles along the south side of the river, with the present line mostly in sight along the north side. Along the way you'll note Dorsey's Run tunnel on the new line, built in 1906 and 1,022 feet long. In this same area is the first substantial relic on the old line — a large early 1830's stone culvert crossing a stream. A short distance farther is another large stone culvert, this one with a brick arch signifying that it was probably built or rebuilt after the Civil War. Immediately west is a wide, curved cut where the line sliced a slight bit off a river bend. Beyond, the new line crosses the river to our side, slices across the path of the old line, and dives into Davis tunnel. The Park road ends here, but the old roadbed picks up again as a path on the north side of the new line and winds around the river bend which Davis tunnel shortcuts. A short way north on this path the old road crosses another stream on a well-preserved stone bridge — probably another 1831 survivor. The old line then rounds the bend and meets the present line as it emerges from Davis tunnel. From here west to Sykesville the present line follows essentially the original alignment, although many minor twists and kinks have been eased. But don't stop quite yet. Follow the present line a little bit farther west from Davis Tunnel to the spot where it crosses Davis

Creek (perhaps a third of a mile) and climb down (carefully!) to take a look at the fine stone bridge. Yet another early-1830's product, this 13-foot single arch is one of the few left on the Old Main Line which still carries trains.

Aside from this Daniels-Davis section, finding early structural relics is pretty much a scattered here-and-there proposition. Four small stone bridges of varying dates from 1831 to 1903 can be found on the present line between Woodstock and Marriottsville. East of Henryton, another early (1831-1850) alignment can be traced a short distance to the south of the present Henryton tunnel. Until it was replaced in 1850 by what was then called the Marriottsville tunnel (rebuilt as Henryton tunnel in 1903), the original line swung abruptly south, crossed the river on a single 40-foot stone arch bridge and cut through a hillside. The double-track rock cut is still there and fairly impressive, but aside from some random granite blocks, all traces of the bridge have been wiped out.

Otherwise, two early 1830's stone bridges are still in service at Doub, southwest of Frederick — one 20-foot span over Tuscarora Creek and a smaller one about two-thirds of a mile south of the crossing. Another stands at Monrovia, slightly to the south of the present line on a fragment of the original alignment, later used as a spur. A few similar small bridges exist elsewhere, but have been extended, reinforced and resurfaced to the point where they have lost their original form.

Farther west and much more impressive is the main line bridge over Catoctin Creek, between Point of Rocks and Brunswick — a large granite and limestone structure of two 50-foot arches. This one is only half historic. Like little Gwynns Run, it is now a composite bridge — the north side is original (about 1834); the south side is a 1902 extension. To reach it, hike west down the C&O Canal towpath from Lander about 0.6 mile. (On the way there, you may spot another small 11-foot arch, partly original and partly built in the late 1860's.) The railroad is busy through here and, like the Thomas Viaduct, a modest amount of patience will usually produce a train.

Finally, the single-span bridge over Israel Creek at Weverton is, as best can be determined, original. With a 25-foot span, it is one of the bigger "small" early bridges. Incidentally, within a few hundred feet of one another at this location are three early stone bridges over the creek — one for the C&O Canal, one for the railroad and one for the old road to Harpers Ferry.

The Washington branch no longer offers much for the old stone bridge fanatic. Although never substantially rebuilt as the Old Main Line was, a combination of floods, suburbanization and new track construction has largely wiped out the traces of this "stone railroad." The larger bridges all died young — an 1847 freshet removed the Little Patuxent bridge near Savage and the Northwest Branch bridge at Bladensburg; in 1863 another flood took out the Big Patuxent span at Laurel. All that's left of even moderate interest is an original 1835 15-foot arch over Bascom Creek at Harwood and a brick-lined 1870 arch of about the same size over Deep Run at Dorsey. There's also a little one almost hidden immediately north of U.S. Route 1

Hardly fearsome any more, this is the path of the 5% grade of inclined Plane no. 3 down the west slope of Parr's Ridge. The photo was taken from the top of the ridge looking west. Credit: H.H. Harwood, Jr.

where it passes under the railroad at Elkridge. Try to spot it as you whiz by — if you're quick you'll notice that the east side is all-stone and original; the west is a brick-lined 1863 product dating to the double-tracking.

Tracing the Parr's Ridge planes presents the greatest challenge. After over 140 years, nature has done a fairly effective job of blanketing the route. But it's the man-made changes which make the job impossible in many spots. One of the worst offenders was the B&O itself: the 1901 Mt. Airy cutoff obliterated the bases of Planes 2 and 3 and most of the route of Plane 4. The U.S. Route 40 bypass — now Interstate 70 — also helped complete the wipeout of the west end of the line. Yet there are still some traces of this ill-begotten system, including one masonry bridge. This book won't attempt a foot-by-foot guide to the route. Much of it is now private property, in woods, fields, underbrush, driveways and back yards. However, there are a few reasonably accessible points to observe both the general route and some of the better specific remnants. You can begin with the base of Plane 1, which was immediately west of Twin Arch Road (southeast of Mt. Airy) about 300 feet north of B&O's present (1901) twin arch bridge on the Mt. Airy cutoff. The spot is marked by a private lane leading west up the hill. Plane 1 paralleled this lane slightly to the north in a shallow cut, still mostly visible.

The best evidences of the planes — such as they are — can be found on what was the "level" section connecting Planes 1 and 2 on the east side of the ridge. To reach it, go north on Maryland Rt. 27 from the I-70 interchange and turn right (east) at Rt. 144 (Old National Pike). Follow this road down the hill into the little settlement of Parrsville, turning half-right on the rutted dead-end road leading to the railroad track. You're now on the original alignment of the National Pike; until 1931 it crossed the railroad at grade at the bottom of the hill on its way east. Just before reaching the track, look hard on the north side of the road. Hidden in a tangle of brush is a 10-foot stone arch over a small stream. This is the sadly decomposed remnant of what was once the twin-arch bridge which crossed both the stream and the National Pike. All that remains now is the single stone arch itself, devoid of any other masonry. The 20-foot road arch undoubtedly was knocked down shortly after the planes were abandoned; some time later the grade over the stream arch was cut down so that vehicles could be driven over it from the road. Immediately north of here the level portion of the planes route can be clearly followed. Most of it is now a private driveway leading into a small quarry, which includes a small cut and a fairly impressive fill over a gully.

The summit of the planes on top of Parr's Ridge is south of Ridgeville on Ridge Road (old Rt. 27) close to the spot where it dead-ends at I-70. The point where the planes passed under the road is now marked by B&O's pole line following over the top of Mt. Airy tunnel. Considerable imagination must be used to find traces of the old cut here, but the line of Plane 3 can be seen as a path dropping down through the woods to the west. Midway down this hill is a fill and a rock cut, the last tangible traces anyone has found. From here on west, things become speculative. The base of Plane 3

409

was about where B&O's Mt. Airy Junction is now and the heavily graded Mt. Airy cutoff has pretty well scrambled the topography once occupied by the western level section and Plane 4. The base of Plane 4 and the original railroad grade west along Bush Creek have been smothered by the six lanes of Interstate 70, which partly occupies their bed.

A brief, surprising and somewhat spooky glimpse into another unhappy phase of B&O's infancy appeared suddenly when Tropical Storm Agnes ravaged the Patapsco valley in June 1972. The flood which came close to killing the Old Main Line also uncovered several sections of the original stone roadbed—still in place. Back in 1838 when the railroad finally faced up to its engineering error and replaced the unyielding stone with wood ties and iron T rails, it had simply covered over the stone and started over again on top. The surging waters which swept under the tracks washed away ballast and earth built up over the intervening 134 years and revealed the buried mistakes—somewhat directly under the present track, sometimes marching away from the track on some ancient alignment.

Three separate sites were discovered where clear lines of stone roadbed could be traced, plus some random blocks elsewhere which had been used in later fills. The first, slightly west of the bridge at Ilchester, was the most fascinating. Here a double set of stone blocks had appeared, each one different. One—the old westbound track—was made up of rectangular blocks which had carried wood stringers topped with iron strap rails. (The iron fittings were still attached to some.) The eastbound track consisted of continuous stone stringers aligned to carry an iron strap rail along their inner edges.

Another section was found just off the south portal of Union Dam tunnel, close to where U.S. Route 40 crosses the river. At Union Dam, three straight rows of the stone stringers (a track and a half) reached almost 200 feet in almost perfect alignment (that is, as perfect as is possible with a track system like this). They lay on a part of the original line abandoned since 1902 when the tunnel cut across a sharp river bend. Finally, a 150-foot double line of similar stringers showed up west of the Old Frederick Road crossing at Hollofield, probably representing the one-time westbound track.

Sadly, most of these phantoms have since quietly disappeared. The Ilchester and Hollofield sites sat spang on the present right-of-way and were soon reburied as the line was repaired. Although a few stones were pulled out for preservation beforehand, most are still there underneath the new fill and ballast. Since they were safely away from the operating line, the Union Dam stringers were left alone by railroad workers; their awkward location and weight (up to a ton apiece) pretty well protected them from souvenir collectors. But neglect, natural erosion, and general tramping has covered them over again. At least they are there, ready for anyone who may want to establish a small shrine to a famous false start.

*　　*　　*　　*

A.   Jonathan Knight's granite roadbed appeared all too briefly after Tropical Storm Agnes in June 1972. (A) At Ilchester, both the rectangular block system and slightly later stone stringers were revealed side by side. In this view, looking east, the line of blocks up the center marks the south rail of the original westbound track; the adjacent line of stone stringers to the right carried the north rail of the eastbound track. Note the difference in elevation between the original line and

the present grade. (B) West of Ellicott City, both tracks had been laid   B.
with stone stringers. Here at Union Dam, south of Hollofield, the
camera looks west along the well-preserved westbound track. Only a
single line remains from the eastbound track at the left; the other was
removed some years ago to accommodate a sewer line. Credit
(both): H.H. Harwood, Jr.

To most people—even railroad archeologists—stations are a considerably more fascinating subject than small stone bridges or fragments of roadbed. And at the least, most of them can be approached without fighting through brambles, poison ivy or loose ballast. The west end of the Baltimore division can still offer a first class collection of stations. Like railroad lines everywhere, there have been numerous casualties— particularly during the past 20 years—as passenger services were cut back and local freight agencies eliminated. And, for better or worse, B&O has consistently believed in clean housekeeping (and the resultant tax savings); when it closed a station, it usually tore it down. Hence the survivors are few and scattered, but what remains is exceptionally high in both architectural and antiquarian interest. In fact, out of the 14 older stations still standing in this area in early 1979, nine are either now on the National Register or have been nominated; a tenth is part of a National Register Historic District. And at least three of these could easily be classed as nationally notable. (These numbers, incidentally, do not include Washington Union Station—half-owned by B&O—which is in a class by itself.)

Like the bridges, we have to begin with the best-known. It's hardly a secret that the country's oldest station (and probably the world's oldest) stands on the B&O in this area—although there's been some argument over which station it is. Bravely but positively, we nominate Ellicott City. This two-story stone structure dates to 1831 and served briefly as the railroad's first terminal as B&O built its way west up the Patapsco valley. Actually it was not originally designed as a passenger station and apparently not formally used as one until about 1856. It was built as a "depot" in the original sense of the word—an early form of multi-purpose building housing an operating/construction office, freight unloading facilties and inside locomotive storage. As best can be deduced, early passengers used the Patapsco Hotel on the north side of Main Street, which adjoined the track and had its own platform access. (It still stands, too.) The station is somewhat oddly laid out—since the track is elevated here, the entrance is at ground level, with waiting room and office space above. Originally, a track entered at the south (east) end. Ellicott City station is now safe in the hands of Historic Ellicott City, Inc. and currently undergoing restoration as a museum along with the attractive little 1885 brick freight house nearby. Between the station and freight house is a partially-excavated turntable pit originally built in 1863 to turn engines from the Ellicott's Mills local trains.

The other contender for "oldest station" prize is, of course, Mt. Clare in Baltimore—reputedly built in 1830. But strong evidence says it isn't and wasn't. It was built in 1851 as an adjunct to the Mt. Clare shop expansion and growth of the West Baltimore neighborhood at that time. This little two-story polygonal brick building served only about two years as a passenger station; afterwards it was supplanted by Camden and became strictly a shop office building and freight agency until its rehabilitation as the entranceway to the B&O Museum complex. But whatever its true

Ellicott City's 1831 station—the country's oldest—in its latest incarnation as a museum. Between the stone station and the 1885 freight house (at far left) is the partly-excavated 1868 turntable built to turn the power for the Ellicott City passenger local. An eastbound freight eases past on the now-single track Old Main Line in May 1979. Credit:

Although long advertised as the "oldest station", Mt. Clare most probably really dates to 1851. For at least 80 years, the building itself has been confused with its site—which was indeed the spot (or very close to it) where the country's first passenger service began. This vintage photo, taken about 1890, shows Mt. Clare looking dishevelled but still with its original roof. The roof was later slightly altered and covered with slate. Credit: Smithsonian Institution.

age, it marks one of the most historic sites in railroading—the point where passenger operations on the B&O first started in 1830.

Second in significance to Ellicott City is Camden station, B&O's primary Baltimore terminal since the mid-1850's. (This book's scope does not extend to Mt. Royal station, built in 1896 for the Philadelphia-New York service, but don't overlook it in your itinerary.) Camden presently has the distinction of being the oldest American metropolitan passenger terminal still in active service. Elsewhere in Baltimore, the onetime Philadelphia, Wilmington & Baltimore Railroad's 1850 President Street station is the oldest such terminal, but passenger trains have not used it since 1911.

Camden has been a remarkably fluid building over its lifetime and its appearance has never stayed put for too long. A makeshift terminal was first established at the Camden site in 1853; the "permanent" station (the central part of the present building) was opened in 1857, topped by a tall central tower and backed by a long wood trainshed. Two wings were added in 1863-65 each with a small tower at its end. The central tower soon turned out to be structurally unstable and was cut down to a sort of large cupola. The wood trainshed was replaced by a shorter iron one in 1886. Then in 1892 an additional trainshed was built on the east side of the original one as facilities were rearranged to accommodate the planned Howard Street tunnel. With the opening of the Howard Street tunnel in 1896, a lower-level platform was added at the tunnel entrance at the east end of the station. At about the same time, a brick baggage room was also built onto the east end. In 1904 the end of the west wing was chopped off to make room for the Camden warehouse office building. The waiting room and concourse were remodeled, front entrances changed, some windows bricked up and a street-side canopy added—all during the early 1900's. A 1951 renovation removed the trainsheds, the third floor of the east wing and single central cupola, but cleaned, painted and otherwise refurbished the somewhat motheaten building inside and out. In 1977 the street-side canopy came off and in 1978 the brick baggage room and onetime passageway to the low-level platform were removed—putting Camden several steps back toward its original appearance. It still serves eight weekday Washington commuter schedules and, for the moment, some company offices. As of early 1979 the railroad was working with a developer and restoration architects to find a new commercial use for the old terminal.

While at Camden, be sure to take in the adjacent Camden warehouse, best viewed from its Eutaw Street side. Normally people don't get too excited over warehouses but Camden is spectacular by anyone's standards. This awesome structure is a truly classic turn-of-the-century railroad warehouse, a design long since made obsolete by single-floor industrial-park warehouses but still defiantly standing there. Consider its dimensions: three blocks long, eight stories high, containing 430,000 sq. ft. of storage space. It was built in sections between 1899 and 1904; the office building in front came in 1905. Originally, Barre Street passed

A.

Camden station as it is today, after a long and hard life. (A)In 1975, the ugly street side canopy still obstructed the station's lower portions; (B) By 1977 it was gone, leaving a scar and altered ground-floor windows. Carefully compare this view with those in Chapters 4 and 8. Particularly note how the third floor of the wing nearest the camera has been deftly removed, replacing the original cornice so that the surgery is hardly noticeable. Credit (both): H.H. Harwood, Jr.

B.

under the building and crossed Camden station yard at grade. Camden warehouse is currently vacant (except for storage of company records on its top floor), but is to be included in the redevelopment plans along with the station.

Stations elsewhere in the area are widely scattered, but almost all are worth a visit. Coincidentally, most of these survivors were probably designed by one man—E. Francis Baldwin (1837-1916), a notable late Victorian Baltimore architect. Baldwin's name nowadays rings few bells in Baltimore, but he created several of the city's more notable landmarks of his period—the Maryland Club, Fidelity Building, Old City College, Mt. Royal Station (all still standing), the fondly-remembered Rennert Hotel and many Catholic churches around the city. Two widely-known local industrial structures were also Baldwin designs—the 1884 Mt. Clare passenger car shop roundhouse and adjoining print shop (now the central attraction of the B&O Museum) and the onetime United Railway & Electric Co.'s Carroll Park shops, today the main shop and office of Baltimore's bus system.

Massive Camden warehouse, seen here from South Eutaw Street, is certainly one of the more challenging problems in adaptive re-use of a building. It is to be preserved and somehow integrated into the railroad-sponsored Camden redevelopment project. Credit: H.H. Harwood, Jr.

The B&O Museum and the remains of the Mt. Clare shop complex still contain a fine array of late 19th Century industrial buildings. (A) This air view looking east was taken in 1975; since then the shop structures nearest the camera have been demolished, but three others survive. (B) Best is the 1884 Museum "roundhouse" actually built as a passenger car shop and designed to provide maximum working space and lighting. When visiting it, be sure to look up into the cupola—it's the closest you'll come to an industrial cathedral. (C) This is probably the oldest building on the property now; it's exact construction date is unknown, but most evidence points to the late 1860's. Its most recent active use was a passenger car shop and it now houses some Museum equipment. (D) The final notable survivor is the 1882 bridge shop near the center of the shop grounds. Credits: B-B&O Museum Archives; all others: H.H. Harwood, Jr.

B.

C.

D.

But to this author, Baldwin's best creations were the smaller stations put up at many locations in the B&O system during the architect's full-time stint with the railroad in the late 1870's and early '80's. He designed at least 30 of these, each of them distinctive, picturesque and appealing. In fact—although not quite as inventive (or eccentric)—Baldwin came close to being a Baltimore version of Frank Furness, his famous Philadelphia contemporary who created such a memorable assortment of stations for the Reading, the Pennsylvania and the B&O's Philadelphia extension. Sadly, Baldwin has never received serious study and his prodigious output is still largely undocumented, but an effort is now under way which may finally give this interesting architect his due.

Moving west up the Old Main Line from Ellicott City, the first survivor is at Sykesville. Probably a Baldwin design, it is typical of the brick beauties he turned out on the B&O in the early 1880's. Sykesville station is a 2½-story asymmetrical brick Queen Anne-style structure built in 1883-84. It's a combination passenger and freight station replete with Victorian touches: multiple gables, arched windows and doorways, elaborate brickwork and decorative woodwork on the gables. The building is still essentially original except for the loss of its small *porte-cochere* on the street side and a few boarded windows. Incidentally, while you're at Sykesville, look at the nondescript two-story wood building immediately north of the station on the same side of the street—now a small restaurant. This stands alongside the original railroad alignment through town, now still used as a dead-end siding. Maybe—just maybe—this was an earlier station.

Next west is Mt. Airy, a long single-story brick combination station dating to 1875-82. (The central portion was built in 1875; it was later extended on each end.) The original main line through Mt. Airy (which in turn succeeded the inclined planes) is now partially abandoned, but the station has survived successively as a feed store and now an antique shop with almost no outward change from its railroad days.

At Frederick the "new" 1854 passenger terminal stands at the corner of Market and All Saints Streets, now under the care of the city and restored to its original appearance after years of degradation as a food market and furniture store. This building succeeded the original 1832 stone station, a block to the east; it dates to B&O's brief fling with Italianate architecture in the early 1850's and is a little sister of the Washington and Wheeling terminals built in the same period, with a squat three-story tower. In 1892 it was expanded with a single-story addition on its east end and a platform canopy. The station was reached by a single track running down All Saints Street dead-ending at the station; trains loaded and unloaded at curbside. The 1832 station remained as a freight house until 1911, when it was demolished and replaced by a wood frame freight station on the same site. In a typical B&O touch to maintain a link with its past, the small cupola of the original was transferred to its successor and remained there until a few years ago when the building was altered.

Point of Rocks station, at the junction of the Old Main Line and the

This fine 1884 Francis Baldwin-designed station stands in Sykesville in good condition but essentially unused. Credit: H.H. Harwood, Jr.

After several ups and downs, Frederick's 1854 Italianate station is slowly on its way to restoration. Since this 1975 photo was taken, the large plate glass ground floor windows have been removed and the windows rebuilt as they were originally. The single railroad track once dead-ended at the rear of the parked car on the left. Credit: H.H. Harwood, Jr.

Mt. Airy station, which currently looks a bit better than this 1971 view, was built in three sections, starting in the middle in 1875. It is now on a dead-end spur, once the 1838 main line over the top of Parr's Ridge. Credit: H.H. Harwood, Jr.

Metropolitan Branch is neither the oldest nor most historically significant in the area, but it's probably the best known. Point of Rocks has been pictured in many publications and seems to be a favorite subject for amateur photographers and painters on any decent day in the year. And rightfully so. An exhilarating conglomeration of shapes and polychrome masonry culminating in a high cupola and spire topped with an iron finial, it is the prototype High Victorian Gothic railroad station. Detailed architectural analysis is almost beside the point; almost the whole Victorian bag is there: gabled and hipped roof sections; gabled, hipped and jerkinhead dormers; carved bargeboards; gothic arched windows; ornate finials; scalloped shingles; polychrome bands of granite and sandstone. The architect: Francis Baldwin, of course. The station sits inside the Y formed by the two lines with symmetrical exterior. Its construction date is commonly given as 1875; however, it was actually built in two sections at different times, the rearmost (east) end being the oldest and probably dating to about 1871. For its first 40 years or so, the station was called Washington Junction and was originally meant to be a major transfer point between Washington trains on the newly-built Metropolitan branch and Old Main Line local services. With the decline of Old Main Line passenger service and the development of nearby Brunswick as the railroad's primary operating terminal, Point of Rocks gradually became little more than a way station; its pretentious architecture now seems strangely misplaced in the tiny town. But it still serves as a railroad maintenance office as well as a stop for Washington-Brunswick commuter trains.

Also at Point of Rocks are some other relics of interest to the railroad archeologist: an odd two-story brick building behind the station whose original purpose is now a mystery; a tool house, probably dating to 1874; and the foundations of the onetime KG tower, on the south side of the Met branch track alongside the station. This two-story wood tower was built about 1905 and closed in 1959.

West of Point of Rocks are two more stations: Brunswick and Harpers Ferry. Both are wood frame buildings of essentially ordinary design; both are contemporaries (Brunswick was built in 1891, Harpers Ferry in 1894); both are currently in good health as Amtrak and commuter stations. And, oddly, both have been relocated from their original sites.

Point of Rocks station must be viewed rather than described. The rear portion (to the right) is the original building, probably built in 1870 or '71; the front dates to 1875. Credit: H.H. Harwood, Jr.

Brunswick is the more distinctive of the two, with Palladian windows set in twin gables and some scalloped shingles to give some flair to its otherwise conventional layout. Baldwin is (again) responsible for it. Built at the time that the new railroad town of Brunswick was just beginning to evolve out of the old canal/river village of Berlin, the station was first located about nine blocks east at what was supposed to become a residential development. At a date unknown—but undoubtedly soon afterward—it was moved to its present site near the center of town. In the early 1900's the yard was expanded and the track layout changed, separating the east and westbound main lines by about a block. A smaller and plainer standardized wood station was built in 1908 to serve eastbound trains and the older station limited primarily to westbound traffic. The eastbound station was damaged by fire in 1978; however, it still stood in mid-1979 and may be incorporated in the developing Brunswick Museum complex.

Harpers Ferry station was built as part of the 1894 relocation project which included the tunnel (on the Maryland side) and new steel truss bridge over the Potomac which eliminated the right-angle curves at each end of the old alignment. Originally it stood at the south end of the bridge, where the present Shenandoah Valley branch turns off, and incorporated an interlocking tower at its east end. When the present main line bridge was built on still another new alignment in 1931, the old station was frugally moved over, interlocking tower and all. The tower has since been removed, but otherwise the station is mostly original.

The Metropolitan branch has four late 19th Century stations—two wood and two brick—all of them attributed to Francis Baldwin. Going east from Point of Rocks, they are:

(1) *Dickerson* (1891): A small single-story frame structure, one of the last survivors of a standardized B&O/Baldwin design repeated at several locations in Maryland. (The recently-deceased stations at Germantown and St. Denis were similar.) Dickerson's primary architectural distinctions are its elaborately ornate construction date ("B&O 1891") on its small track-side gable and an unusual "V"-shaped agent's bay.

(2) *Gaithersburg* (1884): This little brick gem is probably the most purely delightful design in the area and one of the most charming "country" stations anywhere. Unquestionably a Baldwin building, its wood trim, brickwork and general feeling are very similar to Sykesville. But the combination of its smaller size, high steeply-pitched gable roof and round spindle brackets give it the look of some elf's house. The station was rebuilt somewhat when the railroad was double-tracked through here in 1905 and at some point it appears that part of the roof overhang was trimmed back. Nonetheless, Gaithersburg remains in near-pristine shape, still a well-used commuter station.

(3) *Rockville* (1873): Built for the opening of the Metropolitan branch, Rockville is now the oldest survivor on the line. It is a two-story brick building very similar in style to Point of Rocks, although a bit more

Gaithersburg was a rural crossroads when B&O built this station in 1884. Now an active commuter stop, its station is one of the most distinctive Victorian confections anywhere. Credit: H.H. Harwood, Jr.

Rockville's 1873 Gothic station still displays its polychrome banding, trim and roof slates. Designed by the same architect as Gaithersburg, it is considerably more conventional but still creative and colorful. Soon to be evicted by Metro construction, it will be moved and preserved. Credit: H.H. Harwood, Jr.

subdued and conventional in layout. In all probability it was done by the same architect (meaning Francis Baldwin) and, among other things, has the same polychrome masonry treatment, gothic arched windows, polychrome slates and wood trim style. If Point of Rocks is the zenith of "Railroad Gothic," Rockville is at least a first-class specimen of the breed. Incidentally, an identical twin once stood at Silver Spring and, apparently, similar stations were originally planned for Dickerson and Germantown but never built. Rockville station is slated for preservation by the city, but impending construction of the Metro rapid transit line will force its relocation.

(4) *Kensington* (1891): A larger variation of the B&O/Baldwin standard single-story frame design found at Dickerson, this one with a freight house at the east end. (The freight addition was made some time in the early 1900's). Kensington has the same little gable as Dickerson with the same elaborately intertwined "B&O 1891" lettering inside. It's still a commuter stop in a rapidly suburbanizing area, with high-rises closing in. Yet it's still not the least difficult to look at the station and imagine that the milk train is almost due, while the little single-truck Kensington Railway trolleys wait in front to take passengers down to Chevy Chase Lake.

Indeed, all four of these Metropolitan branch survivors are graphic symbols of the time when the region was rural and the stations marked farm trading centers, milling villages and summer resorts for upper-class Washingtonians. The final station on this line—Silver Spring—is the herald of what came after. A large but bland brick box, it was built in 1945 to serve the growing residential sections in northwest Washington—replacing the "obsolete" Rockville twin which had stood on the spot since 1878, when Silver Spring was a small country town.

There's one other station on the Metropolitan branch, which is picturesque and historic—but not a station. The little brick structure now at Barnesville—complete with B&O station sign—actually was a Washington Gas Light Company metering station at Rockville, built in 1933. When its owner threatened demolition in 1976, some imaginative souls saved it, had it trucked 23 miles to Barnesville and set it up to serve railroad commuters. The "station" was opened in early 1977, replacing the long-gone original Barnesville station.

And finally, the Washington branch. Only one station still stands on this line, but it is an excellent one. Laurel, built in 1884, is another Baldwin brick beauty—a 1½-story Queen Anne style structure with typically Baldwin arched windows, brickwork, brackets and decorative wood trim. Its asymmetrical roof is an oddity—partly gabled, partly hipped and mostly humpbacked, it helps give the station a different appearance from every viewing angle. So far, Laurel has been well preserved, is listed on the National Register and is a commuter stop. Another survivor until recently was Beltsville, demolished in 1978. The loss is not devastating. Built in 1905 to succeed a more picturesque little 1871 station, Beltsville was an austere standardized single-story frame design put up at count-

Looking like it always belonged there, Barnesville "station" is actually a 1933 gas metering station from Rockville, saved and moved here by preservationists in 1977. The view looks west down the 1% Parr's Ridge grade. Credit: H.H. Harwood, Jr.

Laurel station, another 1884 Francis Baldwin charmer, is showing slight signs of neglect but is essentially in sound shape. It is still used by both commuters and railroad maintenance crews. Credit: H.H. Harwood, Jr.

less points on the B&O during the early 1900's—a classic country station design not basically different from Dickerson and Kensington, but devoid of their decorative touches. Coming only 14 years after those two stations, it graphically marked the B&O's transition from the erratic but aesthetic 19th Century to Leonor Loree's no-nonsense efficiency.

Before ending this chapter and returning to the present, let's briefly look at a few more bridges. There are several others at least worth a side trip, one of which has extremely high historic significance—almost the equal of the Carrollton or Thomas Viaducts, although far less known.

By all means head for Savage, Md., about a mile to the west of U.S. Route 1 north of Laurel. Here a now-abandoned B&O branch crossed the Little Patuxent River to reach the old Savage Mill. The bridge is no less than a genuine iron Bollman truss, the last of its kind and an amazing survivor. The design dates to the early days of iron railroad bridges, when engine weights, train speeds and fire hazard began to catch up with the capabilities of wood trusses and trestles. This particular iron truss was first patented by Wendel Bollman, B&O's Master of Road (i.e., Chief Engineer) in 1852; about one hundred Bollman bridges big and small were built everywhere on the B&O over the next 20 years. Yet this unique spidery design was never widely popular and was confined mostly to the B&O and its subsidiaries as well as to some highway bridges in the Baltimore area. The two-span Savage bridge was originally built in 1869 for mainline use at some unknown location; it was moved to Savage in 1887 and single-tracked. Although the spur into Savage was abandoned in 1947 when the mill closed, both bridge and track remained in place. The rails were finally removed several years ago and a pedestrian walkway substituted. Howard County currently owns the priceless structure (which is listed on the National Register and also declared a Historic American Civil Engineering Landmark by the ASCE), but thus far little has been done to restore it.

As we mentioned earlier in this book, B&O's early fixation with stone bridges ended by the mid-1830's; afterwards, most new construction was wood, then iron. But Leonor Loree's reconstruction of the railroad in the early 1900's briefly brought back masonry, with some memorable results. Much of this work was done elsewhere on the railroad—notably the Brandywine bridge at Wilmington and the relocation near Lodi, Ohio, but the Maryland area got a few substantial samples. Most were built on the Metropolitan branch, where wood trestles and Bollman bridges had spanned the many ravines on the hilly line. These couldn't be called historic, but they're aesthetic and impressive. Two are decidedly above average: the Little Monocacy bridge, half a mile east of Dickerson (follow Mouth of Monocacy Road out of town), and the Waring Viaduct over Big Seneca Creek about 1½ miles east of Germantown. Both are massive three-arch stone viaducts built in 1905-06 to replace single-track wood trestles. Little Monocacy has the edge in statistics: 331.25 feet long, 76.5 feet above the stream bed, with 90-foot arches. Waring comes close: 274 feet long, 74 feet high, with three 65-foot arches.

The rare—indeed unique—Bollman truss spans at Savage. The bridge is owned by Howard County, which plans to restore it including its original colorful livery. The track has been removed since this 1969 photo and replaced by a walkway. Credit: H.H. Harwood, Jr.

"New" but nonetheless notable—and definitely off the beaten path—is this 1906 triple-arch viaduct over the Little Monocacy east of Dickerson. Each of its arches measures 90 feet across. Credit: H.H. Harwood, Jr.

And if you're not completely satiated with stone arches by now, you might take in the much smaller—but still interesting—1901 twin-arch on the Old Main Line Mt. Airy cutoff between Watersville and Mt. Airy. Its two 16-foot arches span a branch of the Patapsco (just a small creek at this point) and Twin Arch Road. Should you go hunting for the traces of Plane 1, you'll use this bridge as your landmark.

Harpers Ferry was once a bridge fan's paradise. In fact, for about five years in the early 1930's three generations of B&O bridges (and three separate main-line alignments) existed side by side—beginning on the east with an 1870 Bollman truss and girder combination and ending with the 1931 girder bridge. The old Bollman bridge (which in turn sat on the site of the original wood bridge) was wiped out by the 1936 flood, leaving only its piers; the other two, of course, remain in railroad service. The one-time main line bridge of 1894 is at least mildly interesting; it consists of $3\frac{1}{2}$ through truss and four deck girder spans, and is 896.5 feet long. When in main line service it carried two tracks, with the Shenandoah Valley branch junction located at its west (south) end. As part of the 1930-31 realignment the bridge was single-tracked for use by Valley branch trains only, with the junction relocated inside the tunnel on the Maryland side.

And we'll end with a little bridge that has only marginal historic or engineering interest. It's simply an oddity. On the south side of Maryland

A true ghost bridge, this ordinary little Pratt truss span off Maryland Route 32 at Guilford has not seen a track, much less a train, in over 50 years. It once carried a spur over the Little Patuxent to the granite quarries. Credit: H.H. Harwood, Jr.

Route 32 at Guilford (about two miles west of U.S. Route 1 near Savage) you'll spot a light steel truss forlornly lost in the woods, crossing the Little Patuxent. This short, skewed pin-connected Pratt truss is typical of many turn-of-the-century light duty bridges; it was built in 1901 when B&O extended its Savage branch up to the granite quarry at Guilford. The line was abandoned in 1928, but the bridge was retained as part of a private driveway. Eventually the driveway too was abandoned and the bridge stripped of its decking. Yet it still sits there intact, having now lived almost twice as long out of railroad service as in—but until about four years ago, was carried as an "active" bridge on B&O's books.

If you've staggered through this archeological tour—or even just a part of it—you have seen the richest and most concentrated collection of historic railroad structures anywhere. In fact, it's a bit like a giant family attic full of mementoes from all stages of growth from infancy to adolescence to maturity. And the accomplishments, stresses and mistakes of each age speak through the stone, brick and iron no less than those personal keepsakes up in the attic do to you. Don't ask what stage of growth—or decline—the railroad is at now—it's too conjectural and irrelevant here anyway. The point is that perhaps you've learned to be more sensitive to the clues which tell the story of a life.

IMPOSSIBLE CHALLENGE

THE PARR'S RIDGE PLANES

As B&O's engineers worked their way west toward the Potomac, they hit their first genuine obstacle—a low ridge running roughly north-south across central Maryland slightly more than halfway between Baltimore and Point of Rocks. Locally called Parr's Spring Ridge, it forms the divide between the Patapsco/Patuxent watersheds to the east and the Monocacy on the west. At this point the Patapsco petered out, ending the easy grade the railroad had been following out of Baltimore. The next available watercourse was Bush Creek, a small stream leading down to the Monocacy and eventually to the Potomac. But Bush Creek was on the west side of the ridge; to get to it, the rails had to get over the hill first—somehow.

Averaging something less than 800 feet above sea level (and 884 feet at its highest), Parr's Spring Ridge is hardly much of a mountain. Nonetheless, it rises abruptly on either side—particularly on the west side, where most of B&O's anticipated traffic would be coming from. For example, on the most direct line between the Patapsco and Bush Creek, the ridge climbs about 200 feet in 1.73 miles on the east side, then drops 250 feet in slightly less distance on the west. Lower summits and easier grades were available by twisting the line a bit and adding some extra mileage, but the best route the surveyors could find still produced a continuous grade of almost 1.6% for about two miles on either side of the ridge.

Unhappily, too, there was no practical alternate route—in one form or another, and under one name or another, Parr's Spring Ridge runs through most of this section of the state. In fact, the ridge later created

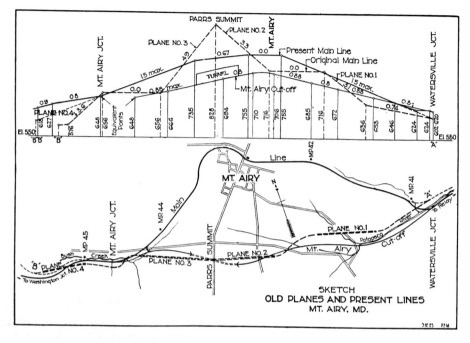

SKETCH
OLD PLANES AND PRESENT LINES
MT. AIRY, MD.

B&O's three routes over Parr's Ridge. At the bottom of the map is the original line of the inclined planes (in dashed lines) and the 1902 Mt. Airy cutoff, the present main line through the ridge. The original route of the Frederick Turnpike (now Md. Rt. 144) follows these two lines just to the north. The 1838 line over the summit (labelled "Main Line" on this map) shows swinging to the north through Mt. Airy. It is now a stub-end branch; the section between Mt. Airy and Watersville Junction has been abandoned. Note the substantial difference in elevation between the present Mt. Airy cutoff and the base of Plane no. 4—a dramatic example of how the entire grade was re-engineered in 1901-02.

Since this map was made in 1923, several changes have been made in the road system shown. Interstate 70 now runs along the south border of the map, crossing to the north of the railroad in the vicinity of Plane no. 4. Maryland Rt. 27 now runs northeast across the midpoint of Plane no. 2. The old Frederick Turnpike no longer crosses the railroad between Planes 1 and 2, although the road may still be followed as far as the crossing on the west side of the track. Credit: Baltimore & Ohio R.R.

operating problems of various degrees for every other railroad built west or north from Baltimore: the Western Maryland Railway west of Westminster, another Western Maryland line near Lineboro, the Northern Central (Baltimore & Susquehanna) at New Freedom, Pa., and B&O's own Metropolitan branch at Barnesville, Md.

Surveyors first climbed around the ridge in 1828, but were apparently intimidated by the topography and passed on without staking out a definite route. Even as the B&O began laying rails west of Ellicott City in early 1831 nobody had yet firmly figured out how to get over Parr's Spring Ridge. By this time the problem had a new dimension added: B&O was just on the threshold of steam power—it knew steam would work and probably ultimately would be its sole motive power, but that was about all. In mid-1831 its only working experience was with the pea-sized "Tom Thumb"—strictly a slapped-together demonstrator—plus the motley collection of rejects submitted for the locomotive competition and the semi-successful little "York", itself little more than a demonstrator. Jonathan Knight thus had no real idea of the ultimate capabilities of steam power and was conservative in locating the line; already he had set a 0.7% maximum grade for any steam-operated portions of the railroad. Clearly there was no way to hold to 0.7% across Parr's Spring Ridge without enormously expensive (and, in 1831, perhaps impossible) grading and tunnelling. Knight saw only one solution: inclined planes, the method already successfully used by the Quincy Granite railroad and the Delaware & Hudson Canal Company, and then being planned for the Allegheny Portage Railroad. He worked out a sequence of four inclined planes— two on each side of the ridge—interspersed with a long level section between each of the two pairs of planes. The planes closely followed the route of the Frederick turnpike over the ridge in a fairly direct line between the projected railheads at the Patapsco and Bush Creek. Moving from east to west, they looked like this:

Plane 1 began in an open field about 1.8 miles west of Watersville, Md., at what is now Twin Arch Road, where stables and a shelter station were built. The plane was 2,150 feet long and rose 80.4 feet, mostly through a shallow cut, giving it a grade of 3.7%.

At the top of this plane a long (3,774 feet) level section carried the line in a gradual "S" curve over a gully and across a small stream and the Frederick turnpike. Because of a difference in elevation between the railroad and turnpike and the presumed need to keep the rail line level, a bridge had to be built over the road. This was originally intended to be a simple wood structure, but in keeping with B&O's fixation with stone the end product was a twin-arch rough masonry bridge crossing the turnpike and adjacent stream side by side. (The roadway arch was 20 feet wide; the stream arch 10 feet.)

Plane 2, 3,000 feet long, then rose 99.6 feet to the top of the ridge, following a hillside south of the Frederick turnpike and reaching a summit of 828 feet above sea level. Its average grade was 3.3%;

actually the first 2,800 feet rose at 3.2%, the next hundred feet at 4.2% and the final hundred feet at 5%. At the summit the line ran level for 600 feet in a 20-foot-deep cut, passing under a state road (now Ridge Road, old Maryland Rt. 27) which crossed the line on a wood bridge.

Plane 3, the steepest and longest, dropped down the west side of the ridge following another hillside, still just a short distance south of the turnpike. This plane was 3,200 feet long through several cuts and fills; it fell 159.6 feet for a steady and somewhat harrowing grade of 5%.

There followed another long level section, this one 3,687 feet, which included another "S" curve, a 12-foot masonry culvert and an 80-foot temporary wood trestle.

Plane 4 then brought the line down to Bush Creek at a 576-foot elevation; it was 1,900 feet long and dropped 81.4 feet for a slightly milder 4.3% average grade.

As inclined planes go, the Parr's Ridge line was not particularly steep—5% was the worst and the average was closer to 4%. The Allegheny Portage Railroad—also considered a fairly easy line—averaged 8% and bordered on 10% in some spots; the Belmont plane at the Philadelphia end of the State-built Philadelphia & Columbia Railroad was 6.7%. The original Quincy (Mass.) Granite railroad had a 26.7% incline, and one of the later Mauch Chunk (Pa.) planes was a bloodcurdling 28.6%.

One of the more visible remnants of the planes, this is a portion of the "level" section between Planes 1 and 2. The view looks west toward the hamlet of Parrsville, where the line crossed the Frederick Turnpike. Note the fill in the distance over a small ravine. Credit: H.H. Harwood, Jr.

Although most of the railroad had already been located as far as Point of Rocks before 1831, Knight delayed determining the final alignment of the planes until early June, 1831—possibly hoping for some kind of miracle. Construction work started quickly after and probably was completed in November.

Thanks to the relatively mild grades on the planes and the light traffic of the early 1830's, Knight was able to postpone installing stationary steam engines to work the inclines—prudently, as it turned out. Locations for engines and hoisting machinery were staked out at the summit and at the heads of Planes 1 and 4, a foundation started at the summit and some wheels and sheaves bought. But "temporarily," horses and mules hauled the cars up the inclines while a special brakeman rode them down the other side.

But as the straining animals pulled the trains over the ridge, the railroad sweated heavily over the obvious expense and delays of the operation—particularly as the speed and economy of steam locomotives became apparent. By mid-1834 the first of the heavier "grasshoppers"— the 7½-ton "Arabian"—had been delivered and went into regular service hauling the Baltimore-Frederick train as far as the foot of Plane 1. On December 2, the "Arabian", coming back from the Harpers Ferry line opening, ran up Planes 4 and 3 with two carloads of dignitaries, stopping and starting on the grade as it went. The demonstration was apparently more for show than for scientific testing, but at the least it proved that the old 0.7% grade limit was plainly invalid. It also gave the railroad an excellent excuse for further postponing the installation of stationary steam engines on its unloved planes or, for that matter, spending any money whatever to improve them.

As additional Grasshoppers went into service in 1835 and early 1836, B&O decided it was time to test their capabilities more formally. During late March of 1836 several speed/tonnage trials were made on the Washington branch. And, on March 22, 1836, the newly-delivered "Andrew Jackson" was run out to Parr's Ridge with a trainload of city officials for another assault on the hill. The 8½-ton Grasshopper charged up Plane 1 hauling its tender, three four-wheeled cars and one double truck car—a total trailing weight of 17¼ tons—and managed to surmount the 3.7% grade at 5 m.p.h. Plane 2 with its final 4.2% and 5% was tougher. Near the summit the train was stopped and the three four-wheelers uncoupled. Left with its tender and a loaded eight-wheel car— 12¼ trailing tons—the little "Jackson" started up again and chugged to the top with its safety valve popping.

From these experiments the railroad concluded that steam could haul what it considered reasonable loads at reasonable speeds up grades of over 2%. The implications for B&O's future route through the Alleghenies were enormous, but for the moment Parr's Ridge was the primary problem. Surveyors were immediately sent out again to find a route across the ridge which would eliminate the misbegotten planes. Working through 1836 and into 1837, they eventually settled on a lower summit

(755 feet) at the site of future Mt. Airy, about a mile north of the point the planes topped the ridge. Their new 5½-mile line left the original route about a mile east of the foot of Plane 1, climbed over the hill in a wide arc and rejoined the old line just west of the base of Plane 4.

The new Mt. Airy line quickly became the most important improvement project of the early McLane regime. By late 1838 it had been finished and for the first time locomotives could travel the entire length of the railroad.

The Mt. Airy route added only a nominal nine-tenths of a mile to the B&O's total mileage, but it was no particular bargain to build or operate. Construction was far from easy: A long, deep rock cut was required at the summit just east of Mt. Airy station, followed by a heavy fill on the west and lesser cuts and fills down the west slope. Worse, the new line had sustained grades of 1.58% on either side. Of course, anything was better than the inclined planes, but Parr's Ridge remained an operating headache for almost 65 years afterwards. It was, in fact, the worst grade on the B&O main line between Baltimore and Cumberland.

Needless to say, the planes were abandoned and quickly forgotten. In fact, so little remembered were they afterwards that no accurate graphic representation of them has yet been uncovered. But in a way, they came back from the dead. As B&O began the job of rebuilding its railroad in 1900, Parr's Ridge again became a priority problem. Still another new alignment was laid out through the hill, following almost exactly the direct line of the old planes—but this time doing what the engineers of 1831 could not. The railroad was relocated a total of ten miles through the area. A 2,758-foot tunnel was drilled through the ridge, passing under the summit at the precise point the planes went over the top; a long fill on the west side of the ridge brought the line down to the level of Bush Creek on a far more gradual grade than the old route. (In fact, it did not reach the grade of the old line until Monrovia, seven miles west of Mt. Airy.) The result was a grade across Parr's Ridge of 0.83% westbound and 0.88% eastbound—close to the ideal sought by Jonathan Knight 70 years before. The cutoff was completed in August 1902 at a cost of $1.3 million; it had cut the grade almost in half and eliminated close to a mile of roundabout routing through Mt. Airy as well as several curves in the process. The 1838 Mt. Airy line remained in place for passenger service and local freight customers at Mt. Airy, but was downgraded to branch line status and single-tracked. Its east leg was finally retired in 1957, but the west half still survives.

A few physical traces of the planes also remain, although they are widely scattered and well-hidden. Chapter 17 tells you where to look for them. And oddly enough, the railroad continues to commemorate them, probably without remembering why. Present B&O operating timetables carry the cryptic designations "East Plane" and "West Plane" to identify the two ends of a key passing siding on the west slope of the Mt. Airy cutoff. These refer to Plane 4 station, a onetime flagstop on the line in this area—which in turn marked the approximate location of the base of inclined Plane no. 4, considerably below the present track level. In the days of the planes, a small "locomotive" terminal existed here—a stable for the horses and probably a shed for one of the Grasshoppers. When the Mt. Airy line was built in 1838, the terminal remained as a helper engine station for trains climbing the steep grade over the ridge. By the 1860's it was a key operating location, usually assigned two helper engines, with an engine shed, water and coaling facilities, and telegraph office. The Mt. Airy cutoff ended the days of Plane No. 4 as an operating station—in fact it literally buried it—but the name hung on for the little hamlet which had grown up there.

The inclined planes may have left a more meaningful mark, although hard-core railroad historians might debate the point. According to the testimony of John E. Spurrier, a B&O operating official who began his railroad career at Plane No. 4 telegraph station in 1862, an incident on the inclines inspired the first use of sand for railroad locomotives. Said Mr. Spurrier:

" Christian Smith was engineman of the Grasshopper engine which hauled a train from Baltimore to Plane No. 1, and Thomas Spurrier (operated another Grasshopper) from Plane No. 4 to Frederick. Mr. Smith told of a wet, slippery and foggy morning when his engine lost time account of slipping and arrived at Plane No. 1 late. Spurrier was at No. 4 with his engine to take the train to Frederick. The train did not show up at the time expected, and Spurrier walked to No. 3 to look for or meet it, leaving his engine at the bottom of the planes (at No. 4). In making the stop to cut off the team (at the summit) and run the cars down the grade by gravity, the brake failed. C. Smith said that Tom Spurrier was standing there and had the presence of mind to kick a little dirt or gravel onto the rail which caused the brake to hold and stop the car.

" Mr. Smith said that it came to him then and there that if a little dirt would cause the brakes to hold, it would likely prevent his engine from slipping, and he at once rigged a box for gravel, dry dirt and sand, and contrived a method of getting the sand to the rail by boring a hole in the bottom of the box and fastening a piece of tank hose from the box to the rail. The sand valve was a piece of square wood to fit over the auger hole. The block was fastened to a lever or wire so as to be moved from over the hole so the sand could drop. He discovered he could make time over wet rail and told his plan to the Master Mechanic, who rigged up a better sand box and had one put on each engine as fast as they could be made.

" Mr. Smith died a poor man. He gave up railroading during the Civil War and bought a little farm on the top of Maryland Heights at Harpers Ferry where he ended his days, many times wishing he had patented the use of sand on locomotives. If he had, no doubt both Smith and Spurrier would have been wealthy instead of poor."

The west slope of Parr's Ridge as it is today. The westbound freight is emerging from Mt. Airy tunnel near Mt. Airy Junction. The approximate route of Plane no. 3 can be seen on the hillside to the upper right of the train. Credit: H.H. Harwood, Jr.

A B&O ARCHEOLOGIST'S ITINERARY
OLD MAIN LINE — MAIN LINE

Miles from Camden Sta.	Location	Structure	Constr. Date	Comments
0.0	Baltimore	Camden station	1857-63	
		Camden warehouse	1899-1904	
0.8 (MC)		Mt. Clare station	1851	Now B&O Museum; Nat. Reg., NHL
		Pass. car roundhouse	1884	Now B&O Museum; Nat. Reg., NHL
		2 shop buildings	c.1870, 1883	Last of older Mt. Clare shop buildings
1.9 (MC)		Gwynns Run bridge	1829, 1848	
2.1 (MC)		Carrollton viaduct	1829	Most serious original construction obstacle; now widened for 4 tracks
3.5	W. Baltimore	"Deep Cut"	1828	
5.9	Halethorpe	Herbert/Hubbard (ex-Gadsby's) Run fill & bridge	1830, 1875	Largest original fill; stone bridge extended 1875 but original
10.7	Ilchester	Patterson viaduct	1830	Remains; one arch survives
11.5	Lees	Small stone bridge	1830	Adjacent to 1903 bridge
12.8	Ellicott City	Station	1831	Now museum; Nat. Reg., NHL
		Oliver viaduct	1830	Remains; one arch survives
		Freight station	1884	Part of museum
		Truss Bridge over Patapsco	1905	Siding to DCA Plant
13.4	Oella	Sucker Run Bridge	1831	Now reburied
14.9	Union Dam	Stone roadbed	1831	Only piers remain
17.9	Daniels	Elysville bridge	1838+	On orig. line, abandoned
19.2 to 19.8	W. of Daniels	3 stone bridges	1831, 1870	On present line
20.3	Davis	Davis Creek bridge	1831	On present line
21.8 to 24.6	Woodstock to Marriotsville	3 stone bridges	1831, c.1848	
28.8	Sykesville	station	1883	Nat. Register
37.8	SE of Mt. Airy	twin arch stone bridge	1901	On Mt. Airy cutoff
		base of Plane 1	1831	North of bridge

38.5	Ridgeville, Parrsville	Planes grading & stone bridge	1831	
39.6	Mt. Airy	Station	1875-82	
46.7	Monrovia	Stone bridge	1831	On old alignment adjacent to present line
58.2	Frederick	Station	1854	In Nat. Reg. Hist. Dist.
61.8	Doub	Tuscarora Creek bridge	1832	On present line
65.2	Point of Rocks	Station	c.1871, 1875	Nat. Register
68.9	Catoctin	Catoctin Creek bridge	1833, 1902	
72.1	Brunswick	Station (WB)	1891	In Nat. Reg. Hist. Dist.
75.8	Weverton	Israel Creek bridge	1833	
78.2	Harpers Ferry	Valley branch bridge	1894	Originally main line bridge
		Station	1894-5	Relocated 1931 to new line

(MC) = Located on Mt. Clare branch

WASHINGTON BRANCH

7.2	Relay	Thomas viaduct	1833-35	
10.4	Harwood	Bascom Creek bridge	c.1835	
11.5	Dorsey	Deep Run bridge	1870	Little Patuxent R. at Savage Mill
—	Guilford	Little Patuxent bridge	1901	Line abandoned
19.4	Laurel	Station	1884	Nat. Register
31.3	Hyattsville	Alexandria Jct. tower	c.1900	Wood interlocking tower

METROPOLITAN BRANCH

Miles from Washington Union Sta.	Location	Structure	Constr. Date	Comments
6.9	Silver Spring	Station	1945	
10.4	Kensington	Station	1891	Nat. Register; to be moved
16.0	Rockville	Station	1873	Nat. Register
21.1	Gaithersburg	Station	1884	
24.4	Waring	Stone viaduct	1906	Big Seneca Creek
34.3	E. of Dickerson	Stone viaduct	1906	Little Monocacy River
34.8	Dickerson	Station	1891	
36.3	Dickerson (West)	Monocacy bridge	1872, 1904, 1928	Piers of orig. Bollman deck truss survive; north side girder spans blt. 1904; south 1928

GEORGETOWN BRANCH

	Location	Structure	Constr. Date	Comments
2.9*	Washington, D.C.	C&O Canal bridge	1909	Canal Rd. & Arizona Ave.

*—Miles from Georgetown

Nat. Register—Listed on National Register or nominated for National Register.

NHL—National Historic Landmark

447

IMPOSSIBLE CHALLENGE

BIBLIOGRAPHY/REFERENCES

Much of the specific data on facilities and operations in this study comes from a wide variety of unpublished internal company records and reference publications. This included, among other things, Engineering Department track charts and bridge diagrams, Accounting Department property inventory records, operating timetables dating from 1843 onwards, station and siding lists from 1896 on, and the like. It should be mentioned that the construction dates of stations and bridges found in company records must be used with extreme caution; apparently the loss of many property records in the 1904 Baltimore fire and the somewhat casual record keeping of the 19th Century have resulted in many present-day inaccuracies.

Similarly, there have been preserved in the B&O Museum Archives and other company offices much historic correspondence, descriptive data and written reminiscences. One of the most amazing of these is a collection of handwritten reminiscences of John E. Spurrier, a B&O Baltimore division operating official who began his career in 1862 and retired about 1919. Apparently under the prodding of Daniel Willard, Mr. Spurrier set down an awesome amount of his memories of 19th Century operations and people and also transcribed many telegrams and other documents from the Civil War. His papers have been preserved largely intact in at least two separate collections.

Generally available published material used in this study included the following:

BOOKS, MONOGRAPHS, REPORTS, ETC.

Richard Sanders Allen, *Covered Bridges of the Mid-Atlantic States;* Bonanza Books, New York, N.Y., 1959

American Railway Guide, 1851; Curran Dinsmore & Co., New York, N.Y. 1851

Baltimore & Ohio Railroad, *Address of John W. Garrett, President, Made on April 14, 1869 at the Monthly Meeting of the Board of Directors of the Baltimore & Ohio Railroad;* B&O Railroad, Baltimore, Md. 1869

Baltimore & Ohio Railroad, *Address of John W. Garrett, President, Made on May 8, 1870 at the Monthly Meeting of the Board of Directors of the Baltimore & Ohio Railroad;* B&O Railroad, Baltimore, Md., 1870

Baltimore & Ohio Railroad, *Annual Reports,* 1828-1960

Baltimore & Ohio Railroad, *Corporate History of the Baltimore & Ohio Railroad Co., as of June 30, 1918;* Office of Valuation Engineer, Baltimore & Ohio Railroad, Baltimore, Md., October 24, 1922

Baltimore & Ohio Railroad, *Correspondence Between the Secretary of War and the President of the Baltimore & Ohio Railroad in Relation to Additional Routes between Washington and New York;* Baltimore & Ohio Railroad, Baltimore, Md., 1862

Baltimore & Ohio Railroad (ed.), *Laws and Ordinances Relating to the Baltimore & Ohio Rail Road Co.;* collected and published by the Baltimore & Ohio Railroad, Baltimore, Md., 1850

Carroll Bateman, *The Baltimore & Ohio: The Story of the Railroad that Grew Up with the United States;* Baltimore & Ohio Railroad, Baltimore, Md., 1951

T.H.S. Boyd, *History of Montgomery County, Maryland, 1650-1879;* orig. published 1879; reprinted 1968 by Regional Publishing Co., Baltimore, Md.

J. Snowden Bell, *The Early Motive Power of the Baltimore & Ohio Railroad;* orig. published by Angus Sinclair Co., New York, 1912; reprinted 1975 by Glenwood Publishers, Felton, Cal.

Alex. Brown & Sons, *The Early Correspondence of Alex Brown & Sons with Regard to the Building of the Baltimore & Ohio Railroad;* Alex Brown & Sons, Baltimore, Md., 1927

G.H. Burgess and Miles C. Kennedy, *Centennial History of the Pennsylvania Railroad Co.;* Pennsylvania Railroad Co., Philadelphia, Pa. 1949

Chessie System, The Story So Far: *The Birth and Growth of America's Railroads;* Chessie System, Cleveland, Ohio, 1977.

Michel Chevalier, *History and Description of the Channels of Communication in the United States, Vol. II;* Paris, 1841

Ray Eldon Hiebert and Richard K. MacMaster, *A Grateful Remembrance: The Story of Montgomery County, Maryland;* jointly pub. by the Montgomery County Government and the Montgomery County Historical Society, Rockville, Md., 1976

Cecelia M. Holland, *Ellicott City, Mill town U.S.A.;* privately published, 1970

Edward Hungerford, *The Story of the Baltimore & Ohio Railroad* (2 volumes); G.P. Putnam's Sons, New York, N.Y., 1928

E.M. Killough, *A History of the Western Maryland Railway;* Western Maryland Railway, Baltimore, Md., 1938

B.H. Latrobe, *Report of the Chief Engineer upon the Expediency of Resuming the Reconstruction of the Baltimore & Ohio Rail Road Between Baltimore and Harper's Ferry;* Baltimore & Ohio Railroad, Baltimore, Md., Nov. 12, 1845

S.H. Long and W.G. McNeill, *Narrative of the Proceedings of the Board of Engineers of the Baltimore & Ohio Railroad Co. . . . .;* privately published, Baltimore, Md. 1830

Louis N. Markwood, *The Forest Glen Trolley and the Early Development of Silver Spring;* jointly pub. by the National Capital Historical Museum of Transportation and the Montgomery County Historical Society, Arlington, Va., 1975

John H. Merriken, *Annapolis Short Line — The First Cars;* Capital Traction Quarterly, Vol. 1, No. 6, Springfield, Va., 1966

Donald B. Myer, *Bridges and the City of Washington;* U.S. Commission of Fine Arts, Washington, D.C., 1974

National Register of Historic Places, Nomination Forms for the following structures or locations:
> Brunswick, Md. historic district
> Harpers Ferry, W.Va. bridge sites
> Rockville, Md. station
> Sykesville, Md. station

All unpublished reports in files of National Register of Historic Places, U.S. Dept. of the Interior, Washington, D.C.

Official Guide of the Railways (under various names), various years, 1868-1971

Richard E. Prince, *Southern Railway System — Steam Locomotives and Boats;* Richard E. Prince, Green River, Wyo., 1965

Richard E. Prince, *The Richmond-Washington Line and Related Railroads;* Richard E. Prince, Millard, Nebr., 1973

Milton K. Reizenstein, *The Economic History of the Baltimore & Ohio Railroad, 1827-1853;* Johns Hopkins Press, Baltimore, Md., 1897

L.W. Sagle and A.F. Staufer, *B&O Power;* Alvin F. Staufer, Medina, Ohio, 1964

Walter S. Sanderlin, *The Great National Project: A History of the Chesapeake & Ohio Canal;* orig. pub. by Johns Hopkins Press, Baltimore, Md., 1946; reprinted 1976 by Arno Press, New York, N.Y.

J. Thomas Scharf, *History of Baltimore City and County;* Louis H. Evarts, Philadelphia, Pa., 1881

Wm. P. Smith, *History and Description of the Baltimore & Ohio Railroad,* by 'A Citizen of Baltimore'; John Murphy & Co., Baltimore, Md., 1853

John F. Stover, *Iron Road to the West: American Railroads in the 1850s;* Columbia University Press, New York, N.Y., 1978

John F. Stover, *Railroads of the South, 1865-1900: A Study in Finance and Control;* Univ. of North Carolina Press, Chapel Hill, N.C., 1955

Henry S. Tanner, *A Description of Canals and Railroads in the United States,* orig. pub. by T.R. Tanner and J. Disturnell, New York, N.Y., 1840; reprinted 1970 by Augustus M. Kelley, New York, N.Y.

Charles A. Varle, *A Complete View of Baltimore. . . .To Which is Added a Detailed Statement of an Excursion on the Baltimore & Ohio Railroad to the Point of Rocks;* S. Young, Baltimore, Md., 1833

R.M. Vogel (ed.), *Some Industrial Archeology of the Monumental City and Environs, A Guide for S.I.A. Tourists;* Society for Industrial Archeology,. Washington, D.C., April, 1975

Constance W. Werner, et al., *Georgetown Historic Waterfront, Washington, D.C. A Review of Canal and Riverside Architecture;* jointly pub. by U.S. Commission of Fine Arts and Office of Archeology and Historic Preservation, National Parks Service, Washington, D.C., 1968

Ames W. Williams, *Otto Mears Goes East: The Chesapeake Beach Railway,* Meridian Sun Press, Alexandria, Va., 1975

T.J.C. Williams, *History of Frederick County, Maryland;* L.R. Titsworth Co., Hagerstown, Md., 1910

T.J.C. Williams, *A History of Washington County, Maryland;* J. M. Runk and L.R. Titsworth, Hagerstown, Md., 1906

_____, *Legislative Investigation of the Washington Branch of the Baltimore & Ohio Railroad: Joint Proceeding of the Maryland Legislative Session of 1906, In the Matter of the State's Interest in the Washington Branch of the Baltimore & Ohio Railroad,* April 2, 1906

ARTICLES IN MAGAZINES, BULLETINS, NEWSPAPERS, INCLUDING SHORT UNPUBLISHED MANUSCRIPTS

Carlos P. Avery, "The Trestles Over Little Seneca Creek, B&O Metropolitan Branch, at Boyds, Md.", unpublished manuscript, April, 1979

Robert Braunberg, "B&O's Mt. Airy Inclines, Parrs Ridge", unpublished manuscript, 1973

Michel S. Franch, "Camden Station: Vivid Past, Cloudy Future", Baltimore *Sunday Sun Magazine,* March 16, 1975

John P. Hankey, "Rains, Raging Rivers and the B&O, or the Flood of 1972", *B&O Railroader,* Vol. 1, No. 6 (November-December, 1972)

Herbert H. Harwood, Jr., "Horse Era Railroading by the Harborside", *Railfan,* February, 1978

Herbert H. Harwood, Jr., "Mt. Clare, America's Oldest Station — Or is It?" *Railroad History 139,* 1978

John E. Merriken, "Annapolis & Elk Ridge", National Railway Historical Society Bulletin, vol. 38, no. 6, 1973

Dianne Newell, "The Short-Lived Phenomenon of Railroad Station Hotels", *Historic Preservation,* July-Sept., 1974

Lawrence W. Sagle, "America's Oldest Railroad Shops—Mt. Clare", Railway & Locomotive Historical Society Bulletin 127, 1972.

Lawrence W. Sagle, "Baltimore & Ohio Stations in Baltimore", Railway & Locomotive Historical Society Bulletin 106, 1962

Lawrence W. Sagle, "The Baltimore & Ohio in Carroll County, Maryland", unpublished manuscript in B&O Museum archives

Lawrence W. Sagle, "Emergency Potomac Crossing", *Railroad Magazine,* December, 1946

Charles B. Thomas, "The Development of Railroads in Washington", Railway & Locomotive Historical Society Bulletin 105, 1961

A.W. Thompson, "The Magnolia Cut-Off Improvement on the Baltimore & Ohio Railroad", Proceedings of the Engineers' Society of Western Pennsylvania, vol. 30, Nov. 24, 1914

E.L. Thompson, "Beyond Ellicott's Mills", *Trains,* September, 1944

E.L. Thompson, "Definition of a Redball", *Trains,* June, 1966

Washington Topham, "First Railroad into Washington and its Three Depots", Columbia Historical Society, Vol. 27, 1923

Robert M. Vogel, "The Engineering Contributions of Wendel Bollman", Paper 36, U.S. National Museum Bulletin 240, Smithsonian Institution, 1964

J.H. White, Jr. and R.M. Vogel, "Stone Rails Along the Patapsco", *IA,* The Journal of the Society for Industrial Archeology, vol. 4, no. 1, 1978

_____ , "American Railroads: The Baltimore & Ohio", *The Family Magazine,* circa 1831

_____ , "Depot of the Baltimore and Washington Railroad at Washington, U.S.", *Illustrated London News,* April 23, 1853, p. 309

_____ , "Reconstruction Work on the Baltimore & Ohio", *Railway Age,* June 28, 1907, p. 1221

TUNNELS BETWEEN BALTIMORE AND HARPERS FERRY
OLD MAIN LINE/MAIN LINE

Miles from
Camden Sta.*

10.4 ILCHESTER

1,404.2 ft. long, all on tangent; 30 ft. wide.
Built 1902-03. Drift tunnel through medium granite and mica schist ledge. A portion of the roof was heavy and required timber support, which was left in place when permanent lining was built. Lining and portals are brick; coping and keystone are granite. Most brick came from Zanesville, Ohio; some from Thornton, W.Va.

14.9 UNION DAM

810 ft. long, all on 7° curve; 30 ft. wide.
Built 1902. 80 ft. of east end is cut and cover; balance drift through medium granite and mica schist ledge. Lining brick; portals sandstone from Grafton, W.Va. and Somerset, Pa.

19.0 DORSEY'S RUN

1,022.1 ft. long; (782.5 ft. on curve); 30 ft. wide.
Built 1906. Drift tunnel through medium granite and mica schist ledge. A portion of the roof required timber support which was left in place when permanent lining was built. Lining brick; portals sandstone.

19.8 DAVIS

496.6 ft. long, all on 4° curve; 30 ft. wide.
Built 1906. Drift tunnel through medium granite and soft mica schist ledge. There was a cave-in at the east portal during construction, and a portion of the original timbering was left in place when the permanent lining was built. Lining brick, with concrete haunches where fall occurred; portals sandstone.

25.1 HENRYTON

430.4 ft. long (30.7 ft. at east end on 4°45′ curve) 30 ft. wide.
Originally built 1849-50 as single-track tunnel; rebuilt for double track 1865. Rebuilt to present configuration 1903. Drift tunnel through medium granite and mica schist ledge. Brick lining and portals, with concrete coping and footings.

29.6 SYKESVILLE

239.7 ft. long, all tangent; 30 ft. wide.
Built 1903. Drift tunnel through medium granite ledge, seamed and unstable. Lining and portals brick; copings concrete.

33.6 **WOODBINE**

385.3 ft. long, all tangent; 30 ft. wide.

Built 1902. Drift tunnel through medium to somewhat soft gneiss ledge. Lining and portals brick; copings limestone from Marriottsville; footings concrete.

39.9 **MT. AIRY**

2,757.6 ft. long (981.7 ft. at east end on 1°15' curve; balance tangent); 30 ft. wide.

Built 1902. Drift tunnel through medium talcose slate ledge. A portion of the roof caved in near the west end during construction. The tunnel was first timbered, then lined with brick, the timbering being left in place. Portals sandstone; concrete footings.

51.3 **HARTMAN**

215 ft. long, all on 6° curve; 30 ft. wide.

Built 1901-02. Drift tunnel through hard to medium trap, serpentine and sandstone ledge, seamed with medium to soft shale. Brick lining; portals limestone; concrete footings.

65.7 **POINT OF ROCKS**

798.8 ft. long (704.5 ft. at east end on curve and spiral; balance tangent); 30 ft. wide.

Originally built 1867-68. Rebuilt to present configuration 1902. Drift tunnel through hard gneiss, granite and serpentine ledge. Lining and portals brick; coping concrete. Traffic detoured around tunnel during 1902 enlargement.

67.3 **CATOCTIN**

494.1 ft. long (331.6 ft. at east end on 5° curve; balance tangent); 30 ft. wide.

Originally built 1867-68. Rebuilt to present configuration 1902-03. Originally self-supporting. Drift tunnel through hard gneiss, seamed with hard to soft serpentine ledge. Lining and portals brick; concrete copings.

77.8 **HARPERS FERRY**

924.7 ft. long, all tangent; 28 ft. wide at east portal, 54'11" wide at west portal.

Originally built 1893. Enlarged and masonry lined 1895-96. West end belled out with new portal 1930. Combination cut and cover and drift tunnel, through hard granite and quartz ledge, and medium gneiss and serpentine ledge. Originally the tunnel was about 36 ft. shorter on each end, with limestone portals. Extended on each end with backfill on extensions to protect them from rock falls. Present east portal brick; arch portion of lining and most of bench walls brick; remainder of bench walls limestone. Spandrel filling in cut and cover portion is of limestone. West portal and lining concrete.

The original alignment (now Shenandoah Valley branch) of tunnel was on a curve at the west end; present main line alignment is tangent.

GEORGETOWN BRANCH

4.7** DALECARLIA

340.9 ft. long, all tangent; 18 ft. wide.
Built in 1910. Drift tunnel, through decayed sandy mica schists, and soft to medium hard mica schist and gneiss ledge. Lining and portals brick; granite copings; some concrete under steps of the portals.

**Distance from end of the track at Georgetown

454

Photo Album

Heading for Brunswick, a short local freight bangs through Harpers Ferry on a murky January day in 1948. Power is E-24 2237, a Pennsylvania Railroad design bought during the Loree era. Credit: C. T. Mahan, Jr.

The eastbound "Ambassador" for Baltimore passes JD tower at Alexandria Junction, north of Hyattsville station on the Washington branch, in August 1946. Credit: E. L. Thompson

The Viaduct Hotel-Station in its last days, about 1947. By then the building was vacant and boarded. It came down in 1950. Credit: E. M. Cummings

Train 6, the eastbound "Capitol Limited" with three F-3's, nears Washington on a May 1949 morning. The location is Georgetown Junction, west of Silver Spring. Credit: E. L. Thompson

Where Annapolis steam trains and interurban cars once rolled, GP-30 6914 takes a single car along the Fort Meade branch in 1972. The line was built by the Annapolis & Elk Ridge, later operated by the Washington, Baltimore & Annapolis, and finally sold to B&O in 1935 when the WB&A died. Credit: John P. Hankey

A westbound RDC train pops out of Point of Rocks tunnel on its way to Brunswick in the early 1970's. Compare this photo with the 1870 scene in Chapter 7 taken at the same location. The eastbound track on the right was built around the tunnel in the 1960's to provide better clearances. Credit: John P. Hankey

Parr's Ridge is conquered again as three F-7's struggle toward the summit with a coal train in 1975. Three more units were wide open at the rear. Credit: John P. Hankey

The entire Brunswick-Washington RDC fleet rolls through Jessup on its way to a date with a fan excursion the following day. Credit: Bill Rettberg

A

B

C

The last days of the Pratt Street switch run in 1972.

A-A pause at Pratt and Fremont Avenue. This area now has been completely cleared for the boulevard connecting with Interstate 95.

B-Several blocks farther east, at Pratt and Hanover Streets. The "Leep Inn" and all its neighbors are also now gone and Pratt Street widened and repaved.

C-The end of the run at President and Aliceanna Streets, near the old City Dock. The onetime PW&B President Street passenger terminal is at the far right, behind the tractor. Credit: John P. Hankey

One of the last full-scale through passenger trains to operate out of Baltimore, the "National Limited", accelerates past Ostend Street in 1965. Credit: H. H. Harwood, Jr.

On its way from Ellicott City to Baltimore, the "Baltimore Birthday Express" emerges from Ilchester tunnel. The run, hauled by two Western Maryland F-7's, celebrated the city's 250th anniversary August 11, 1979.
Credit: H. H. Harwood, Jr.

TIMETABLE

The timetables reproduced
on the following pages
were taken from
the B&O's Employee Timetable 31A
effective 12:01 AM EST June 24, 1935.

WESTWARD.

FIRST CLASS.

Washington Sub-Division. TIME-TABLE No. 31A. June 24, 1935.

Dist. from Balt. (Camden Sta.)	Train Order Sta.	Station	Siding Cap.	13 DAILY Ex. Monday	141 DAILY Ex. Sun. and Holid's	511 DAILY	143 DAILY Ex. Sunday	111 DAILY	◆145 DAILY Ex. Sun. and Holid's	147 DAILY Ex. Sunday	35 DAILY	149 DAILY	15 DAILY	27 DAILY	645 Sat'day ONLY
				A.M.	A.M.	A.M.	A.M.	A.M.	A.M.	A.M.	A.M.	A.M.	P.M.	P.M.	P.M.
	DN	MT. ROYAL STATION.		3.21		S 6.14		S 7.15	S 7.45	S 9.00	S 9.57	11.00	S 12.12	S 1.14	
	DN	CAMDEN STATION.		S 3.26 / 3.41	5.45	S 6.19 / 6.30	6.42	S 7.20	S 7.50	S 9.05	S 10.02 / 10.04	S 11.05	S 12.17 / 12.19	1.18 / 1.19	1.30
0.7	DN	BAILEY.													
1.5	DN	CARROLL.													
2.1		MOUNT WINANS.			F 5.50										F 1.35
3.0		WEST BALTIMORE.			F 5.53										F 1.38
4.1		LANSDOWNE.			F 5.56		F 6.49								F 1.41
5.4	DN	HALETHORPE.		3.51	F 5.58	6.45	F 6.52	7.28	7.58	9.13	10.12	11.13	12.28	1.27	F 1.44
6.7		ST. DENIS.			F 6.00										F 1.47
7.2		RELAY.			S 6.03		S 6.55	S 7.30	S 8.01						S 1.50
7.8		ELK RIDGE.			F 6.05		F 6.57								
9.7		HANOVER.			F 6.09		F 7.00								
10.4		HARWOOD.			F 6.10		F 7.01								
11.5		DORSEY.	32	3.59	F 6.12	6.53	F 7.03	7.34	8.05	9.19	10.18	11.18	12.34		
13.0		MONTEVIDEO.			F 6.14										
13.9		JESSUP.			F 6.16		F 7.07								
14.5		BRIDEWELL.			F 6.18		F 7.08								
16.0		FT. GEO. G. MEADE JCT.	56	4.05	S 6.21	6.58	S 7.11	7.39	F 8.10	9.23	10.22	11.22	12.38	1.36	
17.6		SAVAGE.			F 6.23		F 7.14								
19.4		LAUREL.	38		S 6.27	7.02	S 7.18	S 7.43	S 8.13			S 11.26			
21.2		OAK CREST.			F 6.30		F 7.21								
21.7		CONTEE.			F 6.31										
23.1		MUIRKIRK.		4.13	F 6.34	7.06	F 7.24		F 8.18						
24.3		AMMENDALE.			F 6.36		F 7.26								
25.8		BELTSVILLE.	66		F 6.39		F 7.28								
26.8		SUNNYSIDE.			F 6.40		F 7.30								
28.0		BRANCHVILLE.			F 6.44		F 7.33								
28.4		BERWYN.		4.18	F 6.47	7.12	F 7.34								
29.6		COLLEGE PARK.			F 6.50		F 7.37								
30.6		RIVERDALE.			F 6.52		S 7.41								
31.3	DN	ALEXANDRIA JCT.	63	4.21	6.54	7.15	7.42	7.56	8.27	9.36	10.35	11.39	12.52	1.48	
31.6		HYATTSVILLE.			S 6.57		S 7.44								
32.5		BRENTWOOD.			F 7.00		S 7.46								
34.1		LANGDON.			F 7.03		F 7.49								
35.1		IVY CITY ROUNDHOUSE.													
35.5	DN	F TOWER.		Y 4.26	7.09	7.20	7.51	8.00	8.34	9.40	10.39	11.43	Y 12.56	1.52	
36.1	DN	NEW YORK AVE.			7.12	7.22	7.53	8.02	8.37	9.42	10.41	11.45	1.02	1.54	
36.8	DN	WASHINGTON.			A 7.15	A 7.25	A 7.57	A 8.05	A 8.40	A 9.45	A 10.44	A 11.48	A 1.05	A 1.57	
				A.M.	A.M.	A.M.	A.M.	A.M.	A.M.	A.M.	A.M.	A.M.	P.M.	P.M.	P.M.
		Time over Sub-Division		.45	1.30	.55	1.15	.45	.50	.40	.40	.43	.46	.38	.20
		Average speed per hour		46.8	24.5	40.3	29.2	49.0	44.3	55.2	55.2	51.3	48.0	58.1	21.6

Passenger trains will not exceed a speed of 75 miles per hour.

Speed as shown in Special Instruction 5, and such other restrictions as may be in effect, will not be exceeded.

◆ Indicates Gas or Diesel-Electric Train.

WESTWARD.

FIRST CLASS.

Washington Sub-Division.
TIME-TABLE No. 31A.
June 24, 1935.

Distance from Baltimore (Camden Station.)	Train Order Stations	Station	Passing Sidings Capacity in Cars	♦151 DAILY Ex. Sunday	5 DAILY	153 DAILY	1 DAILY	47 DAILY Ex. Sunday	♦159 DAILY Ex. Sunday	165 DAILY Ex. Sunday	523 DAILY	167 DAILY	3 DAILY	117 DAILY Ex. Sat. & Sunday	125 DAILY Ex. Sunday	7 DAILY
				P.M.	P.M.	P.M.	P.M.	P.M.	P.M.	P.M.	P.M.	P.M.	P.M.	P.M	P.M.	P.M.
	DN	MT. ROYAL STATION.		2.00	S 3.32		S 5.26				S 7.03		S 9.54	10.03		S10.47
	DN	CAMDEN STATION.		S 2.05	S 3.37 3.39	4.00	S 5.31 5.34	5.35	5.40	6.20	S 7.08 7.09	8.35	S 9.59 10.03	S10.08 10.15	10.25	S10.52 10.56
0.7	DN	BAILEY. 0.7														
1.5	DN	CARROLL. 0.8														
2.1		MOUNT WINANS. 0.6							F 5.46	F 6.25						
3.0		WEST BALTIMORE. 0.9							F 5.49	F 6.27						
4.1		LANSDOWNE. 1.1						5.43	F 5.52	S 6.30		S 8.42				
5.4	DN	HALETHORPE. 1.3		2.13	3.48	4.09	5.43	5.46	F 5.56	F 6.33	7.17	8.44	10.12	10.24	10.34	11.05
6.7		ST. DENIS. 1.3							F 5.59	S 6.35						
7.2		RELAY. 0.5		S 2.15		S 4.12		S 5.50	S 6.01	S 6.37		S 8.46				
7.8		ELK RIDGE. 0.6							F 6.04	F 6.39		F 8.48				
9.7		HANOVER. 1.9							F 6.08	F 6.42		F 8.51				
10.4		HARWOOD. 0.7							F 6.10	F 6.44						
11.5		DORSEY. 1.1	32	2.19	3.54	F 4.18	5.49		F 6.13	S 6.46		F 8.54	10.19	10.32	10.42	11.12
13.0		MONTEVIDEO. 1.5							F 6.16	F 6.48						
13.9		JESSUP 0.9		F 2.23		F 4.22			S 6.18	S 6.50		F 8.57				
14.5		BRIDEWELL. 0.6							F 6.20	F 6.52						
16.0		FT. GEO. G. MEADE JCT. 1.6	56	2.26	3.58	4.25	5.53		S 6.24	S 6.55	7.26	9.00	10.23	10.37	10.47	11.16
17.6		SAVAGE. 1.6							F 6.26	F 6.58						
19.4		LAUREL. 1.8	38	S 2.30		S 4.30			S 6.30	S 7.02		S 9.05	U10.26		F10.50	
21.2		OAK CREST. 1.8								F 7.05						
21.7		CONTEE. 0.5								F 7.06						
23.1		MUIRKIRK. 1.4				4.36				F 7.09						
24.3		AMMENDALE. 1.2							F 6.36	F 7.11		W 9.11				
25.3		BELTSVILLE. 1.0	66						F 6.39	F 7.12						
26.1		SUNNYSIDE. 0.6								F 7.13						
28.0		BRANCHVILLE. 1.3								F 7.16						
28.4		BERWYN. 0.4				F 4.41				F 7.17						
29.6		COLLEGE PARK. 1.2							F 6.45	F 7.19		R 9.17				
30.6		RIVERDALE. 1.0							F 6.46	F 7.21						
31.8	DN	ALEXANDRIA JOT. 0.3	63	2.43	4.11	4.45	6.06		6.48	7.22	7.38	9.20	10.38	10.51	11.01	11.30
31.6		HYATTSVILLE. 0.9							S 6.49	S 7.23						
33.8		BRENTWOOD. 1.6							F 6.51	F 7.25						
34.1		LANGDON. 1.0								F 7.27						
35.1	DN	IVY CITY ROUNDHOUSE. 0.8														
35.3	DN	F TOWER.		2.47	4.15	4.50	6.10		6.55	7.30	7.42	9.25	Y10.43	Y10.55	Y11.06	Y11.35
36.1	DN	NEW YORK AVE. 0.7		2.49	4.17	4.52	6.12		6.57	7.32	7.44	9.27	10.49		11.12	11.40
36.8		WASHINGTON.		A 2.52	A 4.20	A 4.55	A 6.15		A 7.00	A 7.35	A 7.47	A 9.30	A10.52		A11.15	A11.43
				P.M.	P.M.	P.M.	P.M.	P.M.	P.M.	P.M.	P.M.	P.M.	P.M.	P.M.	P.M.	P.M.
		Time over Sub-Division		.47	.41	.55	.41	.15	1.20	1.15	.38	.55	.49	.40	.50	.47
		Average speed per hour		47.0	53.8	40.3	53.8	28.5	27.6	29.2	58.1	40.3	44.8	52.9	44.3	47.0

Passenger trains will not exceed a speed of 75 miles per hour.
Speed as shown in Special Instruction 5, and such other restrictions as may be in effect, will not be exceeded.
♦ Indicates Gas or Diesel Electric Train.

EASTWARD.

FIRST CLASS.

Distance from Washington	Train Order Stations.	Washington Sub-Division. TIME-TABLE No. 31A. June 24, 1935.	Passing Sidings Capacity in Cars.	528 DAILY	118 DAILY Ex. Sunday and Monday	140 DAILY Ex. Sun. and Holid's	10 DAILY	46 DAILY	142 DAILY Ex. Sunday	144 DAILY Ex. Sunday	18 DAILY	48 DAILY Ex. Sunday	2 DAILY	6 DAILY	◆146 DAILY Ex. Sunday	4 DAILY	32 DAILY Ex. Sat. and Sunday
				A. M.	A. M.	A. M.	A. M	A. M.	A. M.	A. M.	A. M.	A. M.	A. M	A. M	A. M.	A. M.	P. M.
	DN	WASHINGTON.		1.00			6.20		6.22	7.15	7.30		8.00	9.00	10.00	11.30	12.10
		0.7															
0.7	DN	NEW YORK AVE.		1.03			6.23		6.25	7.18	7.33		8.03	9.03	10.03	11.33	12.13
		0.8															
1.8	DN	F TOWER.		1.05	5.05		6.25		6.27	7.20	7.35		8.05	9.05	10.05	11.35	
		0.9															
1.7		IVY CITY ROUNDHOUSE.															F12.15
		1.0															
8.7		LANGDON.							F 6.29								F12.17
		1.6															
4.5		BRENTWOOD.							F 6.31	F 7.23							F12.19
		0.9															
4.8		HYATTSVILLE.							S 6.34	F 7.25							S12.22
		0.3															
5.5	DN	ALEXANDRIA JCT.	34	1.10	5.10		6.29		6.35	7.26	7.39		8.09	9.09	10.09	11.39	12.23
		0.7															
6.8		RIVERDALE.							F 6.36	F 7.27							F12.25
		1.0															
7.8		COLLEGE PARK.							F 6.38	F 7.29							F12.28
		1.3															
8.4		BERWYN.	60	1.13					F 6.41	F 7.31	7.43						F12.30
		0.4															
8.8		BRANCHVILLE.							F 6.42	F 7.33							
		1.8															
10.6		SUNNYSIDE.							F 6.44								F12.34
		0.9															
11.5		BELTSVILLE.	19						F 6.45	F 7.37							F12.36
		1.0															
12.5		AMMENDALE.							F 6.47	F 7.39							F12.38
		1.2															
13.7		MUIRKIRK.	95	1.19	5.17		6.36		F 6.49	F 7.41	7.47		8.16	9.16	10.17	11.46	F12.41
		1.4															
15.1		CONTEE.							F 6.52								
		9.5															
16.6		OAK CREST.								F 7.44							
		1.8															
17.4		LAUREL.		1.23		5.25			S 6.56	S 7.48 / 7.54 18	S 7.51 144				S10.21		S12.48
		1.8															
19.2		SAVAGE.				F 5.27			F 7.00	F 7.57							F12.52
		1.6															
20.8		FT. GEO. G. MEADE JCT.	94	1.27	5.24	F 5.29	6.43		S 7.03	F 8.00	7.54		8.23	9.23	10.24	11.53	S12.55
		1.5															
22.3		BRIDEWELL.				F 5.32			F 7.06	F 8.03							
		0.6															
22.9		JESSUP.				F 5.34			S 7.08	F 8.04							F12.59
		0.9															
23.8		MONTEVIDEO.				F 5.36			F 7.11	F 8.06							F 1.01
		1.5															
25.5		DORSEY.		1.32		F 5.39			F 7.14	F 8.09	7.58						F 1.04
		1.1															
26.4		HARWOOD.				F 5.41			F 7.17	F 8.12							F 1.06
		0.7															
27.1		HANOVER.				F 5.43			F 7.19	F 8.14							F 1.08
		1.9															
29.0		ELK RIDGE.				S 5.47			S 7.23	F 8.18							S 1.12
		0.6															
29.6		RELAY.				S 5.50		S 7.02	S 7.26	F 8.20		S 8.00			S10.33		S 1.15
		0.8															
30.4		ST. DENIS.				F 5.52		S 7.04	S 7.29			F 8.04					S 1.17
		1.3															
31.4	DN	HALETHORPE.		1.40	5.35	F 5.54	6.53	F 7.07	F 7.32	8.23	8.06	F 8.08	8.33	9.33	10.35	12.03	F 1.20
		1.3															
32.7		LANSDOWNE.				F 5.57		S 7.12	F 7.36			S 8.11					S 1.23
		1.1															
33.8		WEST BALTIMORE				F 6.00		F 7.14				8.13					
		0.7															
34.7		MOUNT WINANS.				F 6.02		F 7.17	F 7.40			F 8.16					
		0.6															
35.3	DN	CARROLL.															
		0.8															
36.1	DN	BAILEY.				F 6.06		F 7.20									
		0.7															
36.8	DN	CAMDEN STATION.		S 1.50 / 1.55	S 5.45 / 5.55	A 6.10	S 7.02 / 7.05	A 7.25	A 7.47	A 8.33	A 8.15	A 8.22	S 8.41 / 8.43	S 9.42 / 9.44	A10.45	S12.11 / 12.13	A 1.32
	DN	⅜ MT. ROYAL STATION.		S 2.05	6.01		S 7.11						S 8.49	S 9.50		S12.19	
				A. M.	A. M.	A. M.	A. M.	A. M.	A. M.	A. M.	A. M.	A. M.	A. M.	A. M.	A. M.	P. M.	P. M.
		Time over Sub-Division...		.50	.40	.45	.42	.23	1.25	1.18	.45	.22	.41	.41	.45	.41	1.22
		Average speed per hour....		44.3	52.9	25.8	52.5	18.7	25.9	28.2	49.0	19.1	53.8	52.5	49.0	53.8	26.9

Passenger trains will not exceed a speed of 75 miles per hour.

Speed as shown in Special Instruction 5, and such other restrictions as may be in effect, will not be exceeded.

◆ Indicates Gas or Diesel Electric Train.

EASTWARD.

FIRST CLASS.

Distance from Washington	Train Order Stations	Washington Sub-Div. TIME-TABLE No. 31A. June 24, 1935.	Passing Sidings. Capacity in Cars.	504 DAILY	656 Sat. ONLY	650 Sat. ONLY	150 DAILY	♦152 DAILY Ex. Sunday	28 DAILY	156 DAILY Ex. Sat. & Sunday	8 DAILY	158 DAILY Ex. Sunday	160 DAILY Ex. Sun. and Holid's	164 DAILY Ex. Sunday	16 DAILY	♦166 DAILY	14 DAILY
				P. M.	P. M.	P. M.	P. M.	P. M.	P. M.	P. M.	P. M.	P. M.	P. M.	P. M.	P. M.	P. M.	P. M.
	DN	WASHINGTON. 0.7		1.00	1.25	1.45	3.00	4.00	4.15	4.50	5.00	5.08	5.30	6.20	7.15	10.30	11.50
0.7	DN	NEW YORK AVE. 0.8		1.03	1.28	1.48	3.03	4.03	4.18	4.53	5.03	5.11	5.33	6.23	7.18	10.33	11.53
1.5	DN	F TOWER. 0.2		1.05	1.30	1.50	3.05	4.05	4.20	4.55	5.05	5.13	5.35	6.25	7.20	10.35	11.55
1.7		IVY CITY ROUNDHOUSE. 1.0															
3.7		LANGDON. 1.6				F 1.52						F 5.14		F 6.26			
4.3		BRENTWOOD. 0.9				F 1.54						S 5.16		F 6.28			
5.2		HYATTSVILLE. 0.3				F 1.57						S 5.18		S 6.30			
5.5	DN	ALEXANDRIA JCT. 0.7	34	1.09	1.34	1.58	3.09	4.09	4.24	4.59	5.09	5.19	5.39	6.31	7.24	10.39	12.00
6.2		RIVERDALE. 1.0				S 2.00						F 5.21		F 6.32			
7.2		COLLEGE PARK. 1.2				F 2.03						F 5.24		F 6.34			
8.4		BERWYN. 0.4	60		1.38	F 2.05		4.13			5.03	F 5.27	5.43	F 6.36		10.43	
8.8		BRANCHVILLE. 1.8				F 2.07						F 5.29		F 6.37			
10.6		SUNNYSIDE. 0.9				F 2.10						F 5.32		F 6.40			
11.5		BELTSVILLE. 1.0	19			F 2.12						F 5.34					
12.5		AMMENDALE. 1.2				F 2.14											
13.7		MUIRKIRK. 1.4	95	1.16	1.42	F 2.17	M 3.17	4.17		5.07	5.16	F 5.38	5.48	F 6.44	7.32	10.48	12.07
15.1		CONTEE. 0.5				F 2.20						F 5.40					
16.6		OAK CREST. 1.8				F 2.22						F 5.41					
17.4		LAUREL. 1.8			S 1.46	S 2.26	S 3.21	S 4.21		S 5.11		S 5.45 / 5.55 (160/158)	5.52 (158)	S 6.49	7.36	S 10.52	S 12.11
19.8		SAVAGE. 1.6				F 2.30						F 5.57					
20.8		FT. GEO. G. MEADE JCT. 1.5	94	1.23	1.49	F 2.34	3.24	4.24	4.36	5.14	5.23	S 6.01	5.55	S 6.54	7.40	10.55	12.15
22.8		BRIDEWELL. 0.6				F 2.37	F 3.26										
22.9		JESSUP. 0.9				F 2.39	S 3.27					S 6.04		F 6.58		S 10.57	
23.8		MONTEVIDEO. 1.6				F 2.41											
24.8		DORSEY. 1.1				F 2.45	R 3.29					F 6.08		F 7.02			
26.4		HARWOOD. 0.7				F 2.47						F 6.10		F 7.04			
27.1		HANOVER. 1.9				F 2.49						F 6.12					
29.0		ELK RIDGE. 0.6				S 2.53						S 6.16	F 6.05	S 7.08			
29.6		RELAY. 0.5			G 1.58	S 2.56	S 3.37				G 5.23	S 6.18	F 6.07	S 7.10		S 11.07	
30.1		ST. DENIS. 1.3				S 2.58						F 6.20	F 6.08	F 7.12			
31.4	DN	HALETHORPE. 1.3		1.33	2.00	F 3.01	3.40	4.35	4.45	5.25	5.33	6.22	6.10	F 7.14	7.52	11.10	12.28
32.7		LANSDOWNE. 1.1				F 3.04						F 6.24		F 7.17			
33.6		WEST BALTIMORE. 0.9															
34.7		MOUNT WINANS. 0.6															
35.5	DN	CARROLL. 0.8															
36.1	DN	BAILEY. 0.7															
36.8	DN	CAMDEN STATION.		S 1.41 / 1.43	S 2.08 / 2.10	A 3.15	A 3.48	A 4.43	4.52	S 5.33 / 5.35	S 5.42 / 5.44	A 6.31	6.18 / 6.20	A 7.25	S 8.00 / 8.03	A 11.18	S 12.38 / 12.50
	DN	MT. ROYAL STATION		S 1.49		A 2.15		S 4.58		A 5.40	S 5.50	A 6.25			S 8.09		S 12.56
				P. M.	P. M.	P. M.	P. M.	P. M.	P. M.	P. M.	P. M.	P. M.	P. M.	P. M.	P. M.	P. M.	A. M.
		Time over Sub-Division		.41	.43	1.30	.48	.43	.37	.43	.42	1.23	.48	1.05	.45	.48	.48
		Average speed per hour		53.8	51.3	24.5	46.0	51.3	59.6	51.3	52.5	26.6	46.0	33.9	49.0	46.0	46.0

Passenger trains will not exceed a speed of 75 miles per hour.

Speed as shown in Special Instruction 5, and such other restrictions as may be in effect, will not be exceeded.

♦ Indicates Gas or Diesel Electric Train.

WESTWARD.

FIRST CLASS.

Distance from Washington	Train Order Stations	Metropolitan Sub-Division. TIME-TABLE No. 31A. June 24, 1935.	Posting Sidings Capacity in Cars.	25 DAILY	29 DAILY Ex. Monday	11 DAILY	55 DAILY Ex. Sunday	♦73 DAILY Ex. Sunday	15 DAILY	31 DAILY Ex. Sunday	5 DAILY
				A. M.	A. M.	A. M.	A. M.	A. M.	P. M.	P. M.	P. M.
	DN	WASHINGTON. 0.9		12.04	......	8.35	......	......	1.20	2.00	4.35
0.9	DN	NEW YORK AVENUE. 0.8		12.07	......	8.38	......	......	1.23	2.03	4.38
1.7	DN	QN TOWER. 0.9		12.09	4.36	8.40	......	......	1.25	2.05	4.40
2.6		UNIVERSITY. 1.2								F 2.07	
3.8		TERRA COTTA. 0.4								F 2.09	
4.4		CHILLUM. 1.0								F 2.11	
5.3		LAMOND. 0.5								F 2.13	
5.7		TAKOMA PARK. 0.5								S 2.15	
5.9		NORTH TAKOMA. 0.7								F 2.16	
6.9		SILVER SPRING. 0.9	76	12.19	4.46	8.50	......	......	1.35	F 2.19	4.49
7.8		WOODSIDE. 0.5								F 2.20	
8.5		GEORGETOWN JUNCT. 0.4		12.21	4.48	8.52	......	......	1.37	2.21	4.51
8.7		LINDEN. 0.5								F 2.23	
9.3		FOREST GLEN. 0.7								F 2.26	
9.9		CAPITOL VIEW. 0.5								F 2.28	
10.4		KENSINGTON. 1.5		12.24	4.51	8.55	......	......	1.40	S 2.30	4.53
11.9		GARRETT PARK. 1.3								F 2.33	
13.8		RANDOLPH. 1.6								F 2.35	
15.0		AUTREY PARK. 1.0								F 2.40	
16.0		ROCKVILLE. 1.2	48	12.30	4.57	9.01	......	......	1.46	S 2.42	4.59
17.3		WESTMORE. 1.3								F 2.45	
18.5		DERWOOD. 1.6								F 2.48	
20.1		WASHINGTON GROVE. 1.0								S 2.51	
21.1		GAITHERSBURG. 0.5		12.36	5.03	9.06	......	......	1.52	S 2.54	5.04
21.6		WARD 0.9									
22.5		BROWN. 1.2								F 2.57	
23.7		CLOPPER. 0.7								F 2.59	
24.4		WARING. 1.5								F 3.00	
25.9		GERMANTOWN. 2.2		12.42	5.09	......	......	......	1.58	F 3.04	
28.4		BOYD. 0.7								F 3.09	
29.1		DS TOWER. 0.7	93	12.46	5.13	9.15	......	......	2.02	3.10	5.12
29.8		BUCK LODGE. 2.8								F 3.11	
32.6		BARNESVILLE. 2.2		12.50	5.17	9.19	......	......	2.06	F 3.17	5.16
34.8		DICKERSON. 3.7		12.53	......					F 3.21	
38.5		TUSCARORA. 3.7								F 3.25	
42.2	DN	POINT OF ROCKS. 3.1		1.01	5.27	S 9.32	......	......	2.19	S 3.33	5.26
45.3		CATOCTIN. 3.8									
49.1	DN	BRUNSWICK. 2.4		1.10	5.36	S 9.50	10.10	10.15	S 2.27	S 3.42	5.35
51.5		KNOXVILLE. 0.8					F10.15	F10.19			
52.3	DN	WEVERTON.		1.14	5.40	9.55	S10.20	F10.21	2.32	S 3.53	5.39
				A. M.	A. M.	A. M.	A. M.	A. M.	P. M.	P. M.	P. M.
		Time over Sub-Division............		1.10	1.04	1.20	.10	.06	1.12	1.53	1.04
		Average speed per hour............		44.8	47.4	39.2	19.2	32.0	43.5	27.7	49.0

Passenger trains will not exceed a speed of 70 miles per hour between Washington and Point of Rocks, and 50 miles per hour between Point of Rocks and Weverton.

Speed as shown in Special Instruction 5, and such other restrictions as may be in effect, will not be exceeded.

♦ Indicates Gas-Electric Train.

474

WESTWARD.

Distance from Washington	Train Order Stations	Metropolitan Sub-Division. TIME-TABLE No. 31A. June 24, 1935.	Passing Sidings Capacity in Cars.	FIRST CLASS.								
				♦75	19	77	37	1	9	117	3	7
				DAILY Ex. Sunday	DAILY	DAILY Ex. Sunday	DAILY Ex. Sunday	DAILY	DAILY	DAILY Ex. Sat. & Sunday	DAILY	DAILY
				P. M.	P. M.	P. M.	P. M.	P. M.	P. M.	P. M.	P. M.	P. M.
	DN	WASHINGTON. 0.9		......	5.00	5.10	5.45	6.30	8.15	......	11.06	11.59
0.9	DN	NEW YORK AVENUE. 0.8		......	5.03	5.13	5.48	6.33	8.18	......	11.09	12.02
1.7	DN	QN TOWER. 0.9		......	5.05	5.15	5.50	6.35	8.20	11.03	11.11	12.04
2.6		UNIVERSITY. 1.2		......	......	......	F 5.51	......				
3.8		TERRA COTTA. 0.4		......	......	......	F 5.53	......				
4.2		CHILLUM. 1.0		......	......	......	F 5.54	......				
5.2		LAMOND. 0.5		......	......	......	F 5.56	......				
5.7		TAKOMA PARK. 0.5		......	......	F 5.22	S 5.59	......				
6.2		NORTH TAKOMA. 0.7		......	......	F 5.24	......					
6.9		SILVER SPRING. 0.9	76	......	5.15	S 5.26	F 6.02	6.45	8.30	11.13	11.21	12.14
7.8		WOODSIDE. 0.5		......	......	F 5.27	F 6.04	......				
8.3		GEORGETOWN JUNCT. 0.4		......	5.17	5.28	6.05	6.47	8.32	11.15	11.23	12.16
8.7		LINDEN. 0.5		......	......	F 5.30	......					
9.2		FOREST GLEN. 0.7		......	......	S 5.32	S 6.07	......				
9.9		CAPITOL VIEW. 0.5		......	......	F 5.34	F 6.08	......				
10.4		KENSINGTON. 1.5		......	5.20	S 5.36	S 6.10	6.50	8.35	11.18	11.26	12.19
11.9		GARRETT PARK. 1.3		......	......	F 5.40	S 6.13	......				
13.2		RANDOLPH. 1.8		......	......	F 5.43	......					
15.0		AUTREY PARK. 1.9		......	......	......	.	......				
16.9		ROCKVILLE. 1.2	48	......	5.26	S 5.49	S 6.21	6.56	8.41	11.24	11.32	12.25
17.9		WESTMORE. 1.3		......	......	F 5.52	F 6.24	......				
18.5		DERWOOD. 1.6		......	......	......	F 6.26	......				
20.1		WASHINGTON GROVE. 1.0		......	......	S 5.57	S 6.29	......				
21.1		GAITHERSBURG. 0.5		......	5.32	S 6.01	S 6.32	7.02	8.47	11.30	11.38	12.31
21.6		WARD. 0.9		......	......	......	F 6.33	......				
22.5		BROWN. 1.2		......	......	......	F 6.34	......				
23.7		CLOPPER. 0.7		......	......	F 6.07	F 6.36	......				
24.4		WARING. 1.5		......	......	......	F 6.37	......				
25.9		GERMANTOWN. 2.5		......	5.38	S 6.12	S 6.40	7.08	8.53	11.35	11.44	12.37
28.4		BOYD. 0.7		......	......	S 6.17	S 6.43	......				
29.1		D8 TOWER. 0.7	93	......	5.42	6.18	6.44	7.12	8.57	11.38	11.47	12.40
29.8		BUCK LODGE. 3.8		......	......	F 6.20	F 6.46	......				
33.6		BARNESVILLE. 2.2		......	5.46	S 6.26	S 6.50	7.16	9.01	11.42	11.51	12.44
34.8		DICKERSON. 3.7		......	5.49	S 6.31	F 6.54	7.19	9.04	11.45	11.54	12.47
38.5		TUSCARORA. 3.7		......	......	F 6.37	F 6.59	......				
42.2	DN	POINT OF ROCKS 3.1		5.30	C 5.57	S 6.47	A 7.05	7.27	9.12	11.52	12.02	12.55
45.3		CATOCTIN 3.8		F 5.35	......	F 6.52	......					
49.1	DN	BRUNSWICK 2.4		A 5.42	6.06	A 6.58	......	7.36	S 9.24	12.01	S12.16	1.04
51.5	DN	KNOXVILLE 0.8		......	......	......	......					
52.3	DN	WEVERTON.		......	6.10	......	......	7.40	9.29	12.05	12.21	1.08
				P. M.	P. M.	P. M.	P. M.	P. M.	P. M.	A. M.	A. M.	A. M.
		Time over Sub-Division..........		.12	1.10	1.48	1.20	1.10	1.14	1.02	1.15	1.09
		Average speed per hour		34.5	44.8	27.2	30.4	44.8	42.4	49.2	41.8	45.4

Passenger trains will not exceed a speed of 70 miles per hour between Washington and Point of Rocks, and 50 miles per hour between Point of Rocks and Weverton.

Speed as shown in Special Instruction 5, and such other restrictions as may be in effect, will not be exceeded.

♦ Indicates Gas-Electric Train.

EASTWARD.

Distance from Weverton.	Train Order Stations.	Metropolitan Sub-Division. TIME-TABLE No. 31A. June 24, 1935.	Passing Sidings. Capacity in Cars.	FIRST CLASS.							
				118	**10**	**38**	**18**	**2**	**78**	**20**	**6**
				DAILY Ex. Sunday and Monday	DAILY	DAILY Ex. Sunday	DAILY	DAILY	DAILY Ex. Sunday	DAILY	DAILY
				A. M.	A. M.	A. M.	A. M.	A. M.	A. M.	A. M.	A. M.
	DN	**WEVERTON.** 0.8		3.55	4.53	....	6.02	6.27	......	7.23	7.32
0.8		KNOXVILLE 2.4		......	......	......	......	......	......	......	......
3.2	DN	BRUNSWICK 3.8		3.59	4.57	...... S 6.08	6.31	6.40	7.27	7.36	
7.0		CATOCTIN 3.1							F 6.44		
10.1	DN	POINT OF ROCKS 3.7		4.08	5.06	S 5.34	6.18	6.40 S 6.53	7.36	7.45	
13.8		TUSCARORA. 3.7				F 5.38			F 6.59		
17.5		DICKERSON. 2.2		4.16	5.14	F 5.43	6.27	6.50 S 7.05	7.44	7.53	
19.7		BARNESVILLE. 2.8		4.20	5.18	F 5.48	6.32	6.55 S 7.10	7.48	7.57	
22.5		BUCK LODGE. 0.7				F 5.52			F 7.14		
23.2		DS TOWER. 0.7	99	4.24	5.22	5.53	6.36	6.59	7.15	7.52	8.01
23.9		BOYD. 2.5				S 5.54			S 7.16		
26.4		GERMANTOWN. 1.5		4.28	5.27 S 5.58		6.41	7.04 S 7.19	7.56	8.05	
27.9		WARING. 0.7				F 6.00					
28.6		CLOPPER. 1.2				F 6.02			F 7.23		
29.8		BROWN. 0.9				F 6.05					
30.7		WARD. 0.5				F 6.07					
31.2		GAITHERSBURG. 1.0		4.34	5.33 S 6.09		6.48	7.10 S 7.28	8.02	8.11	
32.2		WASHINGTON GROVE. 1.6				F 6.12			S 7.30		
33.8		DERWOOD. 1.3				F 6.15			F 7.33		
35.1		WESTMORE. 1.2				F 6.18			F 7.35		
36.3		ROCKVILLE. 1.0	42	4.39	5.39 S 6.21		6.54	7.16 S 7.37	8.08	8.16	
37.3		AUTREY PARK. 1.8				F 6.23					
39.1		RANDOLPH. 1.3				F 6.26			F 7.41		
40.4		GARRETT PARK. 1.5				S 6.29			S 7.43		
41.9		KENSINGTON. 0.5		4.44	5.45 S 6.32		7.00	7.22 S 7.46	8.14	8.22	
42.4		CAPITOL VIEW. 0.7				F 6.33			F 7.48		
43.1		FOREST GLEN. 0.5				S 6.35			F 7.50		
43.6		LINDEN. 0.4				F 6.36			F 7.52		
44.0		GEORGETOWN JCT. 0.5		4.47	5.48	6.37	7.03	7.25	7.53	8.17	8.25
44.5		WOODSIDE. 0.9				F 6.38					
45.4		SILVER SPRING. 0.7		4.48	5.50 F 6.40		7.05	7.27 S 7.56	8.19	8.27	
46.1		NORTH TAKOMA. 0.5				F 6.41			F 7.57		
46.6		TAKOMA PARK. 0.5				S 6.42			F 7.59		
47.1		LAMOND. 1.0				F 6.43					
48.1		CHILLUM. 0.4				F 6.45			F 8.02		
48.5		TERRA COTTA. 1.2				F 6.46			F 8.03		
49.7		UNIVERSITY. 0.9				F 6.48			F 8.07		
50.6	DN	QN TOWER. 0.8		Y 4.55 Y 5.57		6.50	7.12	7.35	8.10	8.25 Y 8.33	
51.4	DN	NEW YORK AVE. 0.9			6.02	6.52	7.14	7.37	8.12	8.27	8.38
52.3	DN	WASHINGTON.			A 6.05 A 6.55 A 7.17 A 7.40 A 8.15 A 8.30 A 8.42						

			A. M.	A. M.	A. M.	A. M.	A. M.	A. M.	A. M.	A. M.
	Time over Sub-Division.. Average speed per hour...		1.00 50.6	1.12 43.5	1.21 31.2	1.15 41.8	1.13 42.9	1.35 31.0	1.07 46.8	1.10 44.8

Passenger trains will not exceed a speed of 50 miles per hour between Weverton and Point of Rocks, and 70 miles per hour between Point of Rocks and Washington.

Speed as shown in Special Instruction 5, and such other restrictions as may be in effect, will not be exceeded.

EASTWARD.

				FIRST CLASS.							
Distance from Weverton.	Train Order Stations.	**Metropolitan Sub-Division.** TIME-TABLE No. 31A. June 24, 1935.	Passing Sidings. Capacity in Cars.	**32** DAILY Ex. Sunday	**4** DAILY	**♦74** DAILY Ex. Sunday	**8** DAILY	**16** DAILY	**54** DAILY Ex. Sunday	**26** DAILY	**12** DAILY
				A. M.	A. M.	P. M.	P. M.	P. M.	P. M.	P. M.	P. M.
	DN	**WEVERTON.** 0.8		S 9.42	10.07	F 2.14	3.15	5.57	F 7.32	9.04	10.23
0.8		KNOXVILLE. 2.4		F 9.44	......	F 2.16	......	......	F 7.33	......	......
3.4	DN	BRUNSWICK. 3.8		S 9.49	10.11	S 2.20 3.10	3.19	6.01	A 7.37	S 9.14	10.27
7.0		CATOCTIN. 3.1		......	......	F 3.15	......	......	......	......	......
10.1	DN	POINT OF ROCKS. 3.7		S10.03	10.20	A 3.21	S 3.29	6.10	......	9.23	10.36
13.8		TUSCARORA. 3.7		F10.08	......	......	......	......	......	......	......
17.6		DICKERSON. 2.2		F10.13	10.29	......	3.37	6.19	......	9.32	10.44
19.7		BARNESVILLE. 2.8		F10.18	10.33	......	3.42	6.23	......	9.36	10.48
22.5		BUCK LODGE. 0.7		F10.22	......	......	......	......	......	......	......
23.2		DS TOWER. 0.7	99	10.24	10.37	......	3.46	6.27	......	9.40	10.52
23.9		BOYD. 2.5		S10.25	......	......	......	......	......	......	......
26.4		GERMANTOWN. 1.5		S10.30	10.41	......	3.51	6.31	......	9.44	10.57
27.9		WARING. 0.7		......	......	......	......	......	......	......	......
28.6		CLOPPER. 1.2		F10.34	......	......	......	......	......	......	......
29.1		BROWN. 0.9		......	......	......	......	......	......	......	......
30.7		WARD. 0.5		......	......	......	......	......	......	......	......
31.8		GAITHERSBURG. 1.0		S10.50 4	10.47 32	......	3.58	6.37	......	9.50	11.03
32.8		WASHINGTON GROVE. 1.6		F10.52	......	......	......	......	......	......	......
33.8		DERWOOD. 1.3		......	......	......	......	......	......	......	......
35.1		WESTMORE. 1.2		......	......	......	......	......	......	......	......
36.3		ROCKVILLE. 1.0	42	S10.57	10.53	......	4.04	6.43	......	9.56	11.09
37.3		AUTREY PARK. 1.8		......	......	......	......	......	......	......	......
39.1		RANDOLPH. 1.3		......	......	......	......	......	......	......	......
40.4		GARRETT PARK. 1.5		F11.03	......	......	......	......	......	......	......
41.9		KENSINGTON. 0.5		F11.07	10.59	......	4.10	6.49	......	10.02	11.15
42.4		CAPITOL VIEW. 0.7		......	......	......	......	......	......	......	......
43.1		FOREST GLEN. 0.5		F11.11	......	......	......	......	......	......	......
43.6		LINDEN. 0.4		......	......	......	......	......	......	......	......
44.0		GEORGETOWN JUNCT. 0.5		11.14	11.01	......	4.13	6.51	......	10.05	11.17
44.5		WOODSIDE. 0.9		......	......	......	......	......	......	......	......
45.4		SILVER SPRING. 0.7		F11.17	11.03	......	4.15	6.53	......	10.07	11.19
46.1		NORTH TAKOMA. 0.5		......	......	......	......	......	......	......	......
46.6		TAKOMA PARK. 0.5		F11.22	......	......	......	......	......	......	......
47.1		LAMOND. 1.0		......	......	......	......	......	......	......	......
48.1		CHILLUM. 0.4		......	......	......	......	......	......	......	......
48.5		TERRA COTTA. 1.2		......	......	......	......	......	......	......	......
49.7		UNIVERSITY. 0.9		F11.34	......	......	......	......	......	......	......
50.6	DN	QN TOWER. 0.8		Y11.36	Y11.08	......	Y 4.22	Y 6.58	......	10.15	11.25
51.4	DN	NEW YORK AVENUE. 0.9		11.41	11.12	......	4.27	7.02	......	10.17	11.27
52.3	DN	WASHINGTON.		A11.45	A11.15	......	A 4.30	A 7.05	......	A10.20	A11.30
				A. M.	A. M.	P. M.	P. M.	P. M.	P. M.	P. M.	P. M.
		Time over Sub-Division.......... Average speed per hour............		2.03 25.5	1.08 46.1	1.07 9.0	1.15 41.8	1.08 46.1	.05 38.4	1.16 41.2	1.07 46.8

Passenger trains will not exceed a speed of 50 miles per hour between Weverton and Point of Rocks, and 70 miles per hour between Point of Rocks and Washington.

Speed as shown in Special Instruction 5, and such other restrictions as may be in effect, will not be exceeded.

♦ Indicates Gas-Electric Train.

WESTWARD.

Baltimore Division. West End. TIME-TABLE No. 31A. June 21, 1935.

FIRST CLASS.

Distance from Relay	Train Order Stations	Station	Passing Sidings Capacity in Cars	381 DAILY Ex. Sunday A.M.	645 Sat'day ONLY P.M.	♦75 DAILY Ex. Sunday P.M.	47 DAILY Sunday P.M.
		RELAY. 0.6		...... S 1.50	......	S 5.50	
0.6		AVALON. 0.4		...... F 1.52	......	F 5.52	
1.0		GLENARTNEY. 0.4		...... F 1.53	......	F 5.53	
1.4		VINEYARD. 1.0		...... F 1.54	......	F 5.54	
2.4		ORANGE GROVE. 1.1		...... F 1.56	......	F 5.56	
3.5		ILCHESTER. 1.1		...... F 1.58	......	S 5.58	
4.6		GRAY. 1.0		...... F 2.00	......	F 6.00	
5.6		ELLICOTT CITY. 0.6		...... S 2.03	......	S 6.04	
6.2		OELLA. 2.9		...... F 2.05	......	F 6.06	
9.1		H S CABIN 0.8	112	...... 2.10	......	6.11	
9.4		HOLLOFIELD. 1.3		...... F 2.12	......	F 6.13	
10.7		ALBERTON. 2.6		...... S 2.15	......	S 6.16	
13.3		DAVIS. 1.3		...... F 2.20	......	F 6.21	
14.6		WOODSTOCK. 2.6		...... S 2.23	......	S 6.25	
17.2		MARRIOTTSVILLE. 0.8		...... F 2.29	......	F 6.31	
18.0		HENRYTON. 1.7		...... F 2.31	......	F 6.33	
19.7		GORSUCH. 1.9		...... F 2.34	......	F 6.37	
21.6		SYKESVILLE. 1.3		...... S 2.39	......	S 6.44	
22.9	N	GAITHER. 1.2	91	...... F 2.43	......	F 6.49	
24.1		HOODS MILL. 2.0		...... S 2.46	......	S 6.53	
26.1		MORGAN. 0.9		...... F 2.50	......	F 6.58	
27.0	D	WOODBINE. 2.4		...... A 2.54	......	S 7.01	
29.4		WATERSVILLE. 0.9		......	......	F 7.07	
30.3		WATERSVILLE JCT. 2.1		......	......	7.10	
32.4		MOUNT AIRY. 1.8		......	......	S 7.18	
34.2	DN	MT. AIRY JCT. 1.7	50	......	......	F 7.22	
35.9		PLANE 4. 1.3		......	......	F 7.25	
37.2		BARTHOLOW. 2.3		......	......	F 7.27	
39.5		MONROVIA. 3.5		......	......	F 7.33	
43.0		IJAMSVILLE. 3.1		......	......	F 7.40	
46.1		REEL'S MILL. 1.3	119	......	......	F 7.46	
47.4	DN	FREDERICK JCT. 2.6	26	S 5.06	......	5.02	A 7.48
50.0		LIME KILN. 1.7		F 5.10	......	F 5.06	
51.7		BUCKEYSTOWN. 2.0		F 5.13	......	F 5.10	
53.7		ADAMSTOWN. 0.2		S 5.17	......	F 5.15	
53.9		ADAMSTOWN JCT. 0.7		......	......		
54.6		DOUB. 3.4		F 5.19	......	F 5.18	
58.0	DN	POINT OF ROCKS.	100	A 5.26	......	S 5.26	

				A.M.	P.M.	P.M.	P.M.
Time over District				.20	1.04	.24	1.58
Average speed per hour				31.8	25.3	26.5	24.1

EASTWARD.

Baltimore Division. West End. TIME-TABLE No. 31A. June 21, 1935.

FIRST CLASS.

Distance from Point of Rocks	Train Order Stations	Station	Passing Sidings Capacity in Cars	46 DAILY Ex. Sunday A.M.	48 DAILY Sunday A.M.	♦74 DAILY Ex. Sunday P.M.	370 DAILY Sunday P.M.
	DN	POINT OF ROCKS. 3.4		......	S 3.35	7.10	
3.4		DOUB. 0.7		......	F 3.40	F 7.15	
4.1		ADAMSTOWN JCT. 0.2		......			
4.3		ADAMSTOWN. 2.0		......	F 3.43	F 7.18	
6.3		BUCKEYSTOWN. 1.7		......	F 3.47	F 7.22	
8.0		LIME KILN. 2.6		......	F 3.51	F 7.25	
10.6	DN	FREDERICK JCT. 1.3	25	...... S 5.57	A 3.55	A 7.33	
11.9		REEL'S MILL. 3.1	125	...... F 6.01			
15.0		IJAMSVILLE. 3.5		...... S 6.07			
18.5		MONROVIA. 2.3		...... S 6.15			
20.8		BARTHOLOW. 1.3		...... F 6.20			
22.1		PLANE 4. 1.7		...... F 6.25			
23.8	DN	MT. AIRY JCT. 1.8		...... F 6.30			
25.6		MOUNT AIRY. 2.1		...... S 6.41			
27.7		WATERSVILLE JCT. 0.9		......	6.50		
28.6		WATERSVILLE. 2.4		...... F 6.53			
31.0	D	WOODBINE. 0.9		...... S 6.58			
31.9		MORGAN. 2.0		...... F 7.01			
33.9		HOODS MILL. 1.2		...... S 7.05			
35.1	N	GAITHER. 1.3	112	...... F 7.08			
36.4		SYKESVILLE. 1.9		...... S 7.11			
38.3		GORSUCH. 1.7		...... F 7.15			
40.0		HENRYTON. 0.8		...... F 7.19			
40.8		MARRIOTTSVILLE. 2.6		...... F 7.21			
43.4		WOODSTOCK. 1.3		...... S 7.27			
44.7		DAVIS. 2.6		......			
47.3		ALBERTON. 1.3		...... S 7.34			
48.6		HOLLOFIELD. 0.3		...... F 7.37			
48.9		H S CABIN 2.9	117	...... 7.38			
51.8		OELLA. 0.6		...... F 7.43			
52.4		ELLICOTT CITY. 1.0		6.48 S 7.45			
53.4		GRAY. 1.1		F 6.50 F 7.47			
54.5		ILCHESTER. 1.1		S 6.53 S 7.50			
55.6		ORANGE GROVE. 1.0		F 6.55 F 7.52			
56.6		VINEYARD. 0.4		F 6.57 F 7.54			
57.0		GLENARTNEY. 0.4		F 6.58 F 7.55			
57.4		AVALON. 0.6		F 7.00 F 7.56			
58.0		RELAY.		S 7.02 S 8.00			

				A.M.	A.M.	P.M.	P.M.
Time over District				.14	2.03	.20	.23
Average speed per hour				25.0	23.1	31.8	27.1

Passenger trains will not exceed a speed of 40 miles per hour.

Speed as shown in Special Instruction 5, and such other restrictions as may be in effect, will not be exceeded.

♦ Indicates Gas or Diesel Electric Train.

WESTWARD.

Distance from Weverton.	Train Order Stations.	Washington County Sub-Division. TIME-TABLE No. 31A. June 24, 1935.	Passing Sidings. Capacity in Cars.	FIRST CLASS. *♦73 DAILY Ex. Sunday A. M.
	DN	WEVERTON. 1.2		F10.21 .....
1.8		STONEBRAKER. 0.8	2	F10.23 .....
3.0		GARRETT'S MILL. 1.3		F10.26 .....
3.5		AUGUSTA. 1.1		F10.29 .....
4.4		BROWNSVILLE. 1.4	2	F10.32 .....
6.8	D	GAPLAND. 1.0	11	S10.35 .....
6.8		BEELER'S SUMMIT. 1.4	9	F10.37 .....
8.8		ROHRERSVILLE. 2.9	15	F10.40 .....
11.1		EAKLE'S MILL. 1.5	48	F10.46 .....
18.6	D	KEEDYSVILLE. 1.9	14	S10.51 .... .
14.8		SHOWMAN. 1.0		F10.55 .....
16.8		BURTNER. 1.5		F10.57 .....
17.0		BREATHEDS. 1.2	12	F11.00 .....
18.8		ROXBURY. 1.8	5	F11.03 .....
80.0		BALLS ROAD. 0.4		F11.07 .....
80.4		FIERY SIDING. 1.7	7	F11.08 .....
81.7		FUNKSTOWN. 0.8	6	F11.11 .....
88.8		CORBETT. 1.2		F11.13 .....
88.7		HAGERSTOWN.	134	A11.16 .....
				A. M.
		Time over Sub-Division........ Average speed per hour........		.55 25.8

EASTWARD.

Distance from Hagerstown.	Train Order Stations.	Washington County Sub-Division. TIME-TABLE No. 31A. June 24, 1935.	Passing Sidings. Capacity in Cars.	FIRST CLASS. *♦74 DAILY Ex. Sunday P. M.
		HAGERSTOWN. 1.2	124	1.15 .....
1.8		CORBETT. 0.8		F 1.18 .....
1.0		FUNKSTOWN. 1.3	6	F 1.20 .....
3.8		FIERY SIDING. 0.4	7	F 1.22 .....
3.7		BALLS ROAD. 1.8		F 1.23 .....
5.5		ROXBURY. 1.2	5	F 1.26 .....
6.7		BREATHEDS. 1.5	12	F 1.28 .....
8.1		BURTNER. 1.0		F 1.31 .....
9.1		SHOWMAN. 1.5		F 1.33 .....
11.1	D	KEEDYSVILLE. 1.9	14	S 1.38 .....
18.6		EAKLE'S MILLS. 2.9	48	F 1.41 .....
16.8		ROHRERSVILLE. 1.4	15	F 1.47 .....
16.9		BEELER'S SUMMIT. 1.0	9	F 1.50 .....
17.6	D	GAPLAND. 1.4	12	S 1.55 .....
19.8		BROWNSVILLE. 1.1	2	F 2.00 .....
80.4		AUGUSTA. 1.3		F 2.04 .....
81.7		GARRETT'S MILL. 0.8		F 2.07 .....
88.6		STONEBRAKER. 1.8	2	F 2.10 .....
88.7	DN	WEVERTON.		F 2.14 .....
				P. M.
		Time over Sub-Division........ Average speed per hour........		.59 24.1

Passenger trains will not exceed a speed of 30 miles per hour between Weverton and Beeler's Summit and 35 miles per hour between Beeler's Summit and Hagerstown.

Speed as shown in Special Instruction 5, and such other restrictions as may be in effect, will not be exceeded.

* Train 73 is superior to Train 74, Weverton to Hagerstown.

WESTWARD.

Distance from Frederick Junction.	Train Order Stations.	Frederick Sub-Division. TIME-TABLE No. 31A. June 24, 1935.	FIRST CLASS.		
			★♦487 DAILY Ex. Sunday P. M.	37 DAILY Ex. Sunday P. M.	47 DAILY Ex. Sunday P. M.
	DN	FREDERICK JCT. 2.4	4.00	7.35	7.50 ....
8.4		GROVE. 2.6	F 4.06	F 7.41	F 7.56 ....
8.6		FREDERICK.	A 4.10	A 7.45	A 8.01 .•.......
			P. M.	P. M.	P. M.
		Time over Sub-Division...... Average speed per hour......	.10 21.6	.10 21.6	.11 19.6

EASTWARD.

Frederick Sub-Division. TIME-TABLE No. 31A. June 24, 1935.	FIRST CLASS.		
	38 DAILY Ex. Sunday A. M.	48 DAILY Ex. Sunday A. M.	★♦488 DAILY Ex. Sunday P. M.
FREDERICK. 1.2	4.55	5.45	4.50 ....
GROVE. 2.4	F 4.59	F 5.49	F 4.54 ....
FREDERICK JCT.	A 5.05	A 5.55	A 5.00 ....
	A. M.	A. M.	P. M.
Time over Sub-Division...... Average speed per hour......	.10 21.6	.10 21.6	.10 21.6

Passenger trains will not exceed a speed of 30 miles per hour.

Speed as shown in Special Instruction 5, and such other restrictions as may be in effect, will not be exceeded.

★ Train 487 is superior to Train 488, Frederick Junction to Frederick.

♦ Indicates Gas-Electric Train.

STATION LIST

The Station List shown on the following pages was reproduced from B&O Official List (Form 6) No. 18 effective February 1, 1917.

LEGEND

C—Coupon Ticket Office   L—Livestock Facilities
D—Derricks or Cranes   S—Track Scales
G—Frog and Switch Removed   V—Third Track
W—Water Tank

Passing	Company	Joint	Private	Telegraph Call	Station Number	STATIONS AND SIDINGS with character references, population (census of 1910), and additional index references	County	Miles from	Bay View
						Baltimore Belt Railroad			
142	235			BA	181	**Bay View—S W** (614,700)..........Md.		90.6	0.0
	37				183	Gay Street......................	"	92.8	2.2
	10				183B	Clifton Park....................	"	93.3	2.7
			5		183 D	McShane Bell Foundry Co........	"	93.3	2.7
			4		183C	Clough & Malloy................	"	93.3	2.7
						Harford Road Tunnel............	"	93.5	2.9
	15				183A	Harford Road...................	"	93.5	2.9
			4		183E	P. Flanigan & Sons	"	93.5	2.9
	8				184A	Jenkins Lane...................	"	93.9	3.3
			7		184G	American Paving & Contracting Co.	"	93.9	3.3
				SF	184F	Waverly Tower.................	"	94.0	3.4
	4				184C	Waverly Motor Siding...........	"	94.0	3.4
			11		184E	The Linde Air Products Co.......	"	94.1	3.5
			7		184B	James J. O'Meara...............	"	94.2	3.6
	22				184 H	Dietrich Brothers..............	"	94.2	3 6
	6				184 D	York Road (Waverly)............	"	94.2	3.6
						York Road Tunnel..............	"	94.3	3.7
						Guilford Ave. Tunnel...........	"	94.5	3.9
						St. Paul Street Tunnel..........	"	94.6	4.0
						Oak Street Tunnel.............	"	94.7	4.1
				HU	185J	Huntingdon Ave. Tunnel.........	"	94.9	4.3
					185	Huntingdon Ave. Tower.........	"	95.0	4.4
	38		3		185K	Huntingdon Ave. Yard—**V W**......	"	95.0	4.4
	6				185L	Indian Refining Co.............	"	95.0	4.4
	8				185M	Baltimore Electrical Commission..	"	95.0	4.4
	4				185N	H. G. Von Heine...............	"	95.0	4.4
			7		185 D	Orenda Coal Co.................	"	95.0	4.4
	18				185E	D. M. Andrew Co.—**V**...........	"	95.0	4.4
	13	8			185C	Maryland Lime & Cement Co.....	"	95.0	4.4
		3			185A	American Ice Co................	"	95.0	4.4
	10				185F	Sisson Siding (W. Sisson & Sons)—**V**	"	95.2	4.6
						Oak Street Junction (M. & P. Transfer)—**V**............	"	95.3	4.7
	75				185B	Oak St. (North Ave. Yard)—**D V**...	"	95.3	4.7
	20				185P	Enterprise Fuel Co.............	"	95.3	4.7
			3		185H	W. J. Chapman Coal Co..........	"	95.3	4.7
	4				185G	National Building Supply Co......	"	95.4	4.8
						North Avenue Tunnel—**V**......	"	95.5	4.9
				NA	186C	North Avenue Tower............	"	95.6	5.0
	5				186 D	International Harvester Co........	"	95.6	5.0
	10				186	Rullman & Wilson—**D**.........	"	95.6	5.0
		10			186A	**City Pumping Station**...........	"	95.6	5.0
						Mt. Royal Tunnel—**V**..........	"	95.8	5.2
					186B	Mt. Royal Passenger Station—**C V**..	"	95.9	5.3
	10			RM		Mt. Royal Tower—**V**...........	"	95.9	5.3
						Howard Street Tunnel..........	"	96.7	6.1
					188	Camden Station—**C W** (860)........	"	97.5	6.9
				CA		Camden Cut Tower.............	"	97.5	6.9
34	16			DX		Lee Street Tower—**W** (865)..........	"	97.6	7.0
	16				188A	Hamburg Street (867).............	"	97.8	7.2

Siding Capacity Cars 42 feet long				Telegraph Call	Station Number	STATIONS AND SIDINGS with character references, population (census of 1910), and additional index references	County	Miles from	
Passing	Company	Joint	Private						

Passing	Company	Joint	Private	Telegraph Call	Station Number	STATIONS AND SIDINGS	County	Miles from	
						Baltimore City District—Con.		Park Junct.	Bay View.
						Baltimore Belt Railroad—Con.			
						Baltimore, P. 558,485...............Md.			
				{GO} {J M}		General Offices—**C**..................	"		
						127 E. Baltimore St................ ● "		Alice-anna St.	West Balto.
						Mt. Clare Branch			
	8				B100	Baltimore, Aliceanna St.............Md.	"	0.0	4.8
	6				B100C	Fleet Street.....................	"	0.1	4.7
	6				B100B	Baltimore Sewerage Commission...	"	0.1	4.7
	38				B100A	President St..................	"	0.1	4.7
			3		B100F	W. G. Scarlett & Co.............	"	0.1	4.7
	4				B100G	Coca Cola Co...................	"	0.3	4.5
		2			B100E	Frey & Son Siding.............	"	0.5	4.3
	6				B100 D	C. A. Gambrill Mfg. Co........	"	0.5	4.3
	10				B101C	Company Siding (Cheapside)......	"	0.6	4.2
		2			B101A	A. Reiter.....................	"	0.7	4.1
		3			B101B	Egerton Bros..................	"	0.7	4.1
			2		B101D	John Deere Plow Co............	"	0.9	3.9
	7				B101E	Howard St., Morris & Co.........	"	1.0	3.8
		1			B101 N	Swift & Co....................	"	1.0	3.8
		3			B101 M	Pittsburgh Plate Glass Co.......	"	1.0	3.8
	4				B101F	Eutaw St., Armour & Co........	"	1.1	3.7
		2			B101 I	Sulsberger & Sons Co............	"	1.1	3.7
		2			B101P	A. Schauman..................	"	1.3	3.5
		4			B101 K	Henry Sonneborn & Co.........	"	1.3	3.5
		3			B101G	Pratt St., Quemahoning Coal Co...	"	1.4	3.4
		3			B101 H	Simmons Mfg. Co..............	"	1.4	3.4
		3			B101J	Crane & Co. (2 Sidings—3 cars each)	"	1.4	3.4
		2			B101R	Southern Bedding Co............	"	1.4	3.4
	4				B102 D	Penn St., Anheuser Busch Brewing Co......	"	1.5	3.3
	4				B102A	Consolidated Gas Electric Light & Power Co......	"	1.5	3.3
		4			B102J	The Gandy Belting Co...........	"	1.5	3.3
			3		B102H	Boston Iron & Metal Co.........	"	1.6	3.2
	33				B102C	McHenry St., Bartlett, Hayward & Co......	"	1.7	3.1
	109				B102E	Poppleton Street Yard—**D L**......	"	1.8	3.0
	10				B102B	Oats Elevator—**S**.............	"	1.8	3.0
	434				B102	Mt. Clare—**C S W**...............	"	2.0	2.8
	5				B102F	H. G. Von Heine...............	"	2.0	2.8
	9				B102G	Consolidation Coal Co..........	"	2.0	2.8
		4			B103J	Frank F. Graham..............	"	2.1	2.7
	10				B103	Cumberland Coal Co............	"	2.2	2.6
		7			B103 M	Magee Bros...................	"	2.3	2.5
		8			B103 K	Alma Manufacturing Co........	"	2.3	2.5
	975				B103A	Mt. Clare Junction—**S** (840)....	"	2.9	1.9
		40			B103B	Wilkins (Wilkins Hair Co.)......	"	2.9	1.9
					B103 N	Carroll Viaduct...............	"	3.2	1.6
	9				B103P	Greenwald Packing Co..........	"	3.4	1.4
	523			SX	B103C	**Claremont—L**..................	"	3.4	1.4
	10				B103U	D. B. Martin Co...............	"	3.4	1.4
	29				B103 D	Calvin T. Davidson...........	"	3.4	1.4
	14				B104A	Curtis Bay Junction (965).......	"	4.2	0.6
	114				192	West Baltimore (891)..........	"	4.8	0.0
								Carroll	Mt. Clare Junct.
					B103A	Baltimore, Mt. Clare Junct.—**S** (827).	"	1.0	0.0
		9			B103L	Balto. High Grade Brick Co......	"	0.6	0.4
		53			B103E	United R'y & Electric Co.......	"	0.5	0.5
	122				B103 H	Industrial Track, Wicomico St.....	"	0.3	0.7
	69				B103F	Lumber and Scrap Yard Tracks....	"	0.3	0.7
	5				B103X	Dump Track..................	"	0.3	0.7
	15				B103Q	Kosse Shoe & Scheyler..........	"	0.4	0.8
		10			B103V	Levering Bros.................	"	0.5	0.9
		7			B103R	Chesapeake Terra Cotta Co.......	"	0.5	0.9
		12			B103S	Ellicott Machine Co...........	"	0.9	1.3
	8				B103Y	Baltimore Gas Appliance Co......	"	0.9	1.3
	4				B103G	American Radiator Co.........	"	1.0	1.4
	4				B103 W	{R. Goldstein & Son............ {American Wool Stock Co.......	"	1.1	1.5
	11				B103T	Baltimore Bargain House Siding...	"	1.1	1.5
	8				B103AA	Team Track..................	"	1.1	1.5
	32				B103Z	Agri Manufacturing Co........	"	0.3	0.7
	60				B103AB	Carnegie Steel Co. Switch Lead....	"	0.1	0.9
				CX	189G	Carroll (886, 995)............	"	0.0	1.0
						Relay Branch		Park Junct.	Camden Station.
	262				188	Camden Station—**C W** (780)........Md.		97.5	0.0
						Camden Warehouses..............	"		
				DO		Dispatchers Office................	"		
						Main Office....................	"		
						Pullman Office.................	"		
				DX		Lee Street Tower (782)..........	"	97.7	0.2
	69				188E	Blue Line Yard................	"	97.8	0.3

Passing	Company	Joint	Private	Telegraph Call	Station Number	STATIONS AND SIDINGS with character references, population (census of 1910), and additional index references	County	Park Junct.	Camden Station
						Baltimore City District—Con.			
						Relay Branch—Con.			
						Baltimore (Concluded)............Md.			
	85				188A	Hamburg St. (785)................ "		97.9	0.4
					188F	Produce Yard.................... "		97.9	0.4
			1		188H	C. D. Kenny Co.................. "		98.0	0.5
	80				188 D	Eutaw Street Track.............. "		98.0	0.5
•			6		188G	Terminal Heating & Freezing Co.. "		98.0	0.5
	12			BY	188B	Bailey—D S W (910)............. "		98.3	0.8
	1				188C	Schlitz Brewing Co.............. "		98.4	0.9
	6				189P	Baltimore Distilling Co......... "		98.4	0.9
	8				189B	Hannis Distilling Co............ "		98.4	0.9
				RN	189P	Russell Street Tower............ "		98.5	1.0
	58				189	Warner St....................... "	Baltimore City	98.6	1.1
	4				189C	Kidd & Buckingham Lumber Co.. "		98.6	1.1
			38		189 K	Maryland Electric Ry's Yard..... "		98.6	1.1
						Jos. McCarthy.................. "			
	18				189R	Union Carbide Co............... "		98.7	1.2
						Mutual Manifold Co............. "			
		15			189 D	Wooster St., New Gas House...... "		98.7	1.2
			5		189E	H. B. Davis & Co. Siding........ "		98.8	1.3
76					189 H	South Passing Track............. "		98.9	1.4
71					189J	North Passing Track............. "		99.0	1.5
				CX	189G	Carroll (855, 995).............. "		99.2	1.7
86					190B	North Passing Track............. "		99.4	1.9
86					190C	South Passing Track............. "		99.4	1.9
			4		190A	Maryland Glass Corporation...... "		99.8	2.3
					190	Mt. Winans...................... "		100.0	2.5
					192	West Baltimore—V (835)......... "		102.0	4.5
						*Yard Limit Board.............. "		102.4	4.9
					193	Lansdowne, P. 750—V............ "		103.0	5.5
		6			193B	Brandau Coal Yard—V........... "		103.0	5.5
					194	Monumental—V.................. "	Baltimore	103.8	6.3
		11			194B	Standard Compressed Yeast Co.... "		103.8	6.3
					195	Halethorpe. P. 110—V.......... "		104.5	7.0
		10			196	St. Denis—V................... "		106.0	8.5
					196B	Hellman Siding—V.............. "		106.2	8.7
				RX	197A	Relay Tower—W V.............. "		106.4	8.9
					197	Relay P. 1200—V (1035, 1810)..... "		106.5	9.0
						Locust Point Branch			Bailey
				BY	B200	Baltimore, Bailey D S W (872).......Md.		98.3	0.0
		17			B200G	U. S. Asphalt & Refining Co...... "		98.3	0.0
			9		B200A	Diggs No. 1..................... "		98.5	0.2
		33			B200E	Baltimore Pearl Hominy Co....... "		98.5	0.2
			6		B200F	Hilgartner Marble Co............ "		98.5	0.2
		9			B200B	Hilgartner...................... "		98.6	0.3
		5			B200C	Hilgartner...................... "		98.6	0.3
12	27				B200 D	Leadenhall Street............... "		98.7	0.4
		13			B201	Keen & Hagerty................. "		98.8	0.5
		11			B201A	Chapman Siding................. "		98.9	0.6
	5				B201B	Old Gas House.................. "		98.9	0.6
	4				B201C	J. M. Raffel Co................ "		99.0	0.7
		35			B201 X	Thomsen Chemical Co........... "		99.0	0.7
		1			B201E	Standard Oil Co................ "		99.0	0.7
					B201 D	American Oil Co................ "		99.0	0.7
			2		B201G	Jos. H. Mewshaw............... "		99.1	0.8
			2		B201F	Pabst Brewing Co............... "		99.2	0.9
	2				B201 H	P. Kennedy..................... "		99.3	1.0
		9			B201L	Matthai, Ingram & Co.......... "		99.3	1.0
					B201V	W. J. Hooper M'f'g Co......... "		99.5	1.2
	353			RV	B201	Riverside—W.................. "		99.5	1.2
		16			B201J	Maryland Tel. & Tel. Co........ "		99.5	1.2
		2			B201 W	A. D. Meushaw................. "	Baltimore City	99.8	1.5
			24		B201 R	Columbia Paper Bag Co......... "		99.8	1.5
		13			B201S	W. C. Kaiss.................... "		99.8	1.5
	21				B201 U	H. P. Nivison.................. "		99.8	1.5
	20				B201T	Fort Avenue Switch............. "		99.8	1.5
			2		B201P	Chesapeake Paper Board Co..... "		99.9	1.6
		6			B202	Torsch Packing Co.............. "		100.2	1.6
	13				B202B	Piedmont—Mt. Airy Guano Co.... "		100.2	1.9
	14		32		B202C	Armour & Co................... "		100.3	2.0
		21			B202J	McLean Warehouse.............. "		100.4	2.1
		30			B202E	Detrick Fertilizing Co.......... "		100.4	2.1
		4			B202F	Baltimore Retort & Fire Brick Co. "		100.4	2.1
	21				B202G	G. Ober & Sons Co............. "		100.5	2.2
	2				B202 H	D. F. Haynes & Son............ "		100.5	2.2
			8		B202 D	Price & Heald.................. "		100.5	2.2
		6			B202A	Hughes Furniture Co........... "		100.5	2.2
		17			B202 K	McLean Contracting Co......... "		100.6	2.3
	10				B202M	Baltimore Dry Docks & Shipbuilding Co........ "		100.7	2.4
	30				B202 N	Immigration Pier............... "		100.7	2.4
	3963				B203	Locust Pt. {Agents Office / Y. M. Office. D S W / Elevators....} "		100.9	2.6
			10		B203A	Coastwise Shipbuilding Co....... "		101.0	2.7

Passing	Company	Joint	Private	Telegraph Call	Station Number	STATIONS AND SIDINGS with character references, population (census of 1910), and additional index references.	County	Miles from	

Baltimore City District—Con.

Locust Point Branch—Con.

								Locust Point	Locust Point
......	20	......	......	......	B216	Wolf Street...................Md.		By Water	By Water
......	22	......	......	......	B217	Hendersons Wharf................. "			
					B218	Fell St. Tobacco Warehouse....... "			
					B218D	Fell Street Station................ "			
					B218E	Southern Packing Co............. "			
......	7	......	......	......	B218A	Booth Packing Co............... "			
......	9	......	......	......	B218B	Southern Can Co.............. "			
......	......	......	2	......	B218C	}	Baltimore City		
......	......	......	......	......	B219	Chase's Wharf Station.............. "			
......	......	......	18	......	B222	American Agricultural Chemical Co. (Canton)................. }			
......	4	....	35	......	B223	Baugh Chemical Co. (Canton)..... " }			

Curtis Bay Branch

								Park Junct.	Curtis Bay Junct.
......	14	......	......	......	B104A	Curtis Bay Junction (834)...........Md.		100.5	0.0
......	1	......	......	......	B300A	Iron Hill Sand Co................. "	Balto.	100.7	0.2
153	......	......	......	......	B300	Hull Passing Siding................ "		101.0	0.5
......	25	......	......	......	B302	**Clifford** (1005).................... "		102.2	1.7
......	......	......	......	......	B302B	Patapsco......................... "		102.7	2.2
......	10	......	......	......	B303	Brooklyn.......................... "		103.5	3.0
......	......	......	......	......	B304	Crisp (1010)...................... "		104.3	3.8
......	1205	......	......	......	B304A	Crisp Yard........................ "		104.5	4.0
......	......	......	......	......	B304B	Stone House Cove—**W**........... "		104.9	4.4
......	......	12	......	......	B304C	Team Track...................... "		101.9	4.4
......	......	14	......	......	B304D	Curtis Bay Chemical Co........... "		104.9	4.4
......	......	10	21	......	B305 D	Maryland Car Wheel Works....... "		105.3	4.8
......	......	12	......	......	B305F	Maryland Car Wheel Works....... "		105.4	4.9
......	......	......	2	......	B305B	Monarch Engineering & Mfg. Co.... "		105.4	4.9
......	12	......	......	......	B305G	Locust Street Track.............. "	Anne Arundel	105.5	5.0
......	......	20	365	......	B305C	Baltimore Car & Foundry Co...... "		105.5	5.0
......	3300	......	......	......	B305E	Curtis Bay Yard.................. "		105.5	5.0
......	49	......	10	......	B305 K	Standard Wholesale Phosphate Co.. "		105.6	5.1
......	49	......	......	......	B305	Curtis Bay....................... "		105.8	5.3
......	......	......	16	......	B305H	Curtis Bay Distilling Co.......... "		105.9	5.4
......	......	......	......	......	B305M	Standard Guano Co............... "		105.9	5.4
......	9	......	......	......	B307	Curtis Bay Coal Pier—**S**........... "		105.9	5.4

South Baltimore Branch

							Balto. City		Carroll
......	......	......	......	CX	189G	Carroll (855, 886)...................Md.		99.3	0.0
......	......	......	......	WP	B351E	Westport Tower.................... "		99.9	0.6
......	34	......	......	......	B351	**Westport**........................ "		100.0	0.7
......	......	......	14	......	B351G	Consolidated Gas Electric Light & Power Co................. "		100.0	0.7
......	......	10	......	......	B351A	Carr-Lowery Glass Works.......... "		100.0	0.7
......	......	......	2	......		Maryland Veneer & Basket Co..... "	Baltimore	100.0	0.7
......	......	12	......	......	B351B	Chesapeake Iron Works........... "		100.0	0.7
......	3	......	......	......	B351 D	Fish House Road Tower............ "		100.3	1.0
......	......	65	......	......	B351C	Baltimore Vitrified Clay Co........ "		100.3	1.0
......	......	......	......	......	B351F	Westport Paving Brick Co. No. 2... "		100.5	1.2
......	25	......	......	......	B302	Clifford (968)...................... "		101.3	2.0

Sea Wall Branch

									Crisp
......	47	......	......	......	B304	Crisp (971).....................Md.		104.3	0.0
......	500	......	......	......	B380	Storage Yard..................... "		104.8	0.5
......	45	......	......	......	B381	Factory Site Commission.......... "		105.3	1.0
......	......	33	......	......	B381A	Ellicott Machine Co.............. "		105.4	1.1
......	......	......	30	......	B381B	Furst Concrete Scow Const. Co ... "		105.5	1.2
......	......	......	7	......	B381C	Montgomery Chemical Works...... "		105.7	1.4
......	......	38	......	......	B382	Rasin—(Rasin Fertilizer Co.)..... "	Anne Arundel	105.8	1.5
......	......	22	......	......	B382A	Rasin Monumental Co............. "		105.8	1.5
......	61	......	......	......	B382C	F. S. Royster Guano Co.......... "		105.8	1.5
......	......	......	85	......	B382D	Prudential Oil Corporation........ "		105.9	1.6
......	114	......	......	......	B382E	Storage Tracks·.................. "		105.9	1.6
......	......	......	72	......	B383B	U. S. Asphalt & Refining Co...... "		106.6	2.3
......	68	......	......	......	B383	Wagners Point (Martin Wagner Co.).. "		106.6	2.3
......	461	......	......	......	B383A	Sea Wall Branch Extension........ "		106.7	2.4
......	......	......	5	......	B383C	The Texas Co..................... "		106.7	2.4

MAIN LINE

								Camden Station	
......	8	......	......	......	197	Relay—**W**—(901,1210)...............Md.		106.5	9.0
......	......	......	......	......	197A	Avalon........................... "		107.2	9.7
......	......	......	......	......	198	Glenartney........................ "		107.6	10.1
......	......	......	......	......	198A	Vineyard.......................... "	Baltimore	108.0	10.5
......	......	......	......	......	199	Orange Grove..................... "		109.0	11.5
......	......	......	......	......		Ilchester Tunnel................. "		109.9	12.4
......	12	......	......	......	200	Ilchester, P. 650.................. "	Howard	110.1	12.6
......	......	......	......	......	201	Lees—**W**........................ "		110.9	13.4
38	......	......	......	......	202	Gray—**W**........................ "		111.2	13.7
......	......	......	19	......	202B	Fisher & Carozzi................. "		111.2	13.7

484

Siding Capacity Cars 42 feet long

Passing	Company	Joint	Private	Telegraph Call	Station Number	STATIONS AND SIDINGS with character references, population (census of 1910), and additional index references	County	Miles from Park Junct.	Miles from Camden Station
						MAIN LINE—Con.			
		22			202A	Crusher Siding—(Albert Webber)..Md.		111.6	14.1
	30				202C	Patapsco Mills (Gambrill M'l'gCo.) "		111.9	14.4
	26			MS	203	Ellicott City, P. 1,800—L. "	Howard	112.2	14.7
		6			203A	Radcliffe Siding—(J. F. Radcliffe). "		112.3	14.8
	5		9		203B	W. J. Dickey.		112.8	15.3
	5				203C	Oella, P. 516.		112.8	15.3
	18		2		205	J. W. Dickey & Sons.		114.3	16.8
						Union Dam Tunnel.		114.4	16.9
255				HS	206A	HS Tower.		115.7	18.2
	8				207	Hollofield.		116.0	18.5
	12				208	Alberton, P. 862.		117.4	19.9
			8		208A	James A. Gary.		117.4	19.9
						Dorsey's Run Tunnel.	Balto.	118.6	21.1
	2				209	Eureka Mining and Operating Co...		118.9	21.4
						Davis Tunnel.		119.4	21.9
	5				211A	Fannie R. Frost Siding.	Howard	119.5	22.0
					211	Davis.		119.8	22.3
	10		762		212A	Putneys Bridge—(Guilford & Watersville Granite Co.).		120.3	22.8
	9			WS	212	Woodstock, P. 208—D.		121.1	23.6
	3				312A	Maryland Spar & Flint Co.		121.6	24.1
	13				215	Marriottsville, P. 60—W.		123.6	26.1
						Henryton Tunnel.		124.4	26.9
	11				216	Henryton, P. 30.		124.5	27.0
	4				217	Gorsuch.		126.2	28.7
					219A	Warfield.		127.4	29.9
			9		219B	Copper Mining Co.		128.1	30.6
	24			U	219	Sykesville, P. 900—L.		128.1	30.6
	8		150		220	Springfield State Hospital.		128.5	31.0
						Sykesville Tunnel.		128.9	31.4
262	30			G	221	Gaither, P. 110—W.	Carroll	129.4	31.9
	14				222	Hood's Mill. P. 35—L.		130.7	33.2
		4			222A	Hammond Bros.		130.7	33.2
	6				224	Morgan, P. 128.		132.6	35.1
						Woodbine Tunnel.		133.0	35.5
	3				225B	A. H. Gosnell.		133.3	35.8
	26				225	Woodbine P. 200.		133.3	35.8
	2		6		225C	J.M.Delashmutt & Sons Coal-Trestle and Elevator.		133.3	35.8
	9				225A	Newport.	Howard	133.8	36.3
	8				227	Watersville, P. 150.		136.0	38.5
	6			WX	228	Watersville Junction (1160).	Carroll	137.1	39.6
	56				230	Mount Airy, P. 850—L.		138.9	41.4
	17				232A	Mount Airy Junction "Y".		140.4	42.9
56	7			MA	232	Mount Airy Junction—W (1163).		140.9	43.4
					234	Plane No. 4, P. 63.		142.4	44.9
	9				235	Bartholow, P. 80.		143.7	46.2
	82				237	Monrovia, P. 75—L.		146.0	48.5
				RO	238	Monrovia Tower.		146.5	49.0
	8				241B	Westport Paving Brick Co.		149.3	51.8
	8				241	Ijamsville, P. 90.		149.4	51.9
					241A	Dennis.		150.1	52.6
						Hartman Tunnel.		150.6	53.1
243	35			RS	244	Reel's Mill—W.		152.6	55.1
					245A	Araby, P. 25.		153.7	56.2
64	28			FE	245	Frederick Junction—W (1140).		154.0	56.5
					248	Lime Kiln, P. 200.		156.5	59.0
		19			248B	M. J. Grove Lime Co.—Lime Kiln.		156.5	59.0
			9		248A	Baker & Son.		156.9	59.4
	9				248B	{ Excelsior Creamery Co. / Chapin Sachs Mfg. Co.		156.9	59.4
	11				248C	Buckeystown Packing Co.		156.9	59.4
			14		249	Keller (O. J. Keller Lime Co.).	Frederick	157.6	60.1
			30		249A	C. F. Thomas & Son.		157.7	60.2
	14				250	Buckeystown, P. 450.		158.2	60.7
			8		252C	G. L. Thomas.		160.0	62.5
		8			252A	Adamstown Packing Co.		160.0	62.5
	8				252	Adamstown, P. 208—L.		160.2	62.7
					252B	Adamstown Junction (1164).		160.4	62.9
	7				253	Doub, P. 218.		161.1	63.6
115	17			KG	256	Washington Junct.—C W (1165, 1364).		164.5	67.0
	27				256A	Point of Rocks, P. 375—L.		164.8	67.3
						Point of Rocks Tunnel.		165.1	67.6
						Catoctin Tunnel.		166.7	69.2
	13				259	Catoctin P. 75.		167.6	70.1
					261	East Brunswick Tower.		169.4	71.9
						Yard Limit Board.		170.4	72.9
	2533				262	East Yard—V.		170.5	73.0
		19			263B	B. F. Crampton Siding—V.		171.3	73.8
						Brunswick (Transfer), P. 4,500—V.		171.4	73.9
				WB	263A	West End Yard—S V W.		171.4	73.9
	6			UN	263	Brunswick Station—C V.		171.5	74.0
		3			263C	Gross (W. L. Gross)—V.		171.5	74.0
	20				263D	Stock Pen Siding—L V.		171.6	74.1
	16				263E	Wenners—V.		172.0	74.5
	3573				264	West Yard—V.		173.5	76.0
	13				265	Knoxville, P. 363—V.		173.8	76.3
				VO	266A	Weverton Tower—V W.		174.5	77.0
	12				266B	Potomac Refining Co.	Wash-ington	174.6	77.1
	23			WE	266	Weverton—W (1170, 1600).		174.6	77.1
						Yard Limit Board (1601).		174.7	77.2

Siding Capacity Cars 42 feet long

STATIONS AND SIDINGS
with character references, population (census of 1910), and additional index references

Passing	Company	Joint	Private	Telegraph Call	Station Number	Stations and Sidings	County	Miles from (Park Junct.)	Miles from (branch junct.)
						Frederick Branch		Park Junct.	Frederick Junct.
				FE	245	Frederick Junction—W (1097)........Md.	Frederick	154.0	0 0
	44				B423F	M. J. Grove Lime Co.	"	156.5	2.5
					B423	Grove	"	156.5	2.5
		7			B423 D	M. J. Grove Lime Co. Siding—G..	"	156.5	2.5
			24		B423E	Tabler Lime & Stone Co	"	156.6	2.6
14					B423C	The Frederick City Abattoir Co...	"	156.6	2.6
	10				B423A	Ramsburg Siding	"	156.7	2.7
27		36			B423B	Passing Siding	"	156.9	2.9
	10				B424B	Frederick Brick Works	"	157.0	3.0
	10				B424 D	Baltimore & Washington White-Cross Milk Co	"	157.1	3.1
6					B424A	Colt-Dixon Packing Co	"	157.2	3.2
		7			B424 H	S. A. Brown	"	157.2	3.2
		7	1		B424E	J. M. Newman	"	157.3	3.3
134					B424C	Frederick Yard—L S W	"	157.3	3.3
23					B424 H	Canning Hill Siding	"	157.3	3.3
	6				B424F	Detrick Milling Co	"	157.3	3.3
	10				B424G	Markel & Ford	"	157.4	3.4
	2				B424J	Ramsburg Fertilizer Co	"	157.4	3.4
				FD	B424	**Frederick, P. 10,411—C**	"	157.5	3.5
						Mount Airy Cut-Off			Watersville Junct.
				WX	228	Watersville Junction (1085)..........Md.	Howard	137.1	0.0
						Mount Airy Tunnel	Carroll	139.7	2.6
	8				231	Shippers' Siding	Frederick	140.3	3.2
				MA	232	Mount Airy Junction—W (1086)	"	140.6	3.5
						Adamstown Cut-Off			Adamstown Junct.
				AX	252B	Adamstown Junction (1109)....Md.	Frederick	160.4	0.0
7				KG	256	Washington Junct.—C W (1111, 1364)	"	166.2	5.8
						Washington County Branch			Weverton
33				WE	266	Weverton P. 75—W (1150, 1600)......Md.	Washington	174.6	0.0
	3				D 0	Savage Distilling Co	"	174.7	0.1
	5				D 1	Stonebraker	"	175.8	1.2
13					D 2	Garrett's Mill	"	176.6	2.0
	3				D 3	Augusta	"	177.9	3.3
13				JA	D 6	Brownsville, P. 75	"	179.0	4.4
					D 6	Gapland, P. 65	"	180.4	5.8
11					D 7	Beeler's Summit	"	181.4	6.8
18					D 8	Rohrersville, P. 200	"	182.8	8.2
12					D 11	Eakle's Mill, P. 120	"	185.7	11.1
					D 12	Keedysville Water Station—W	"	186.4	11.8
15				KD	D 13	Keedysville, P. 426—C L	"	187.2	12.6
					D 15	Showman	"	189.1	14.5
					D 16	Burtner	"	190.2	15.6
15					D 18	Breatheds, P. 130—L	"	191.6	17.0
6					D 18A	Roxbury, P. 23	"	192.8	18.2
					D 20	Balls Road	"	194.6	20.0
7					D 21	Fiery Siding	"	195.0	20.4
	3				D 22A	W. H. Bixler	"	196.3	21.7
7					D 22	Funkstown, P. 600	"	196.3	21.7
					D 22B	Security Junction (1205)	"	196.9	22.3
					D 23	Corbett	"	197.1	22.5
	22				D 23B	Pope Manufacturing Co	"	197.4	22.8
	16				D 23A	Danzer Lumber Co	"	197.5	22.9
	11				D 23C	Hagerstown Electric Light Co	"	197.6	23.0
	5				D 23E	Hollinsworth Wheel Co	"	197.6	23.0
	3				D 23 D	Barnes & Son	"	198.0	23.4
		5			D 24A	Hollinsworth Wheel Co	"	198.4	23.8
		32			D 24B	Western Md. Interchange	"	198.4	23.8
144				HA	D 24	**Hagerstown, P. 16,507—C D L S W.-**	"	198.4	23.8
						Antietam Branch			Security Junct.
					D 22B	Security Junction (1191)..............Md.	Washington	196.9	0.0
					DA 4	**Security**	"	200.5	3.6
9		26			DA 4A	Security Cement & Lime Co	"	200.5	3.6
						Washington Branch			Relay
					197	**Relay—W (901, 1055)**..............Md.	Balto.	106.5	0.0
	6				C .0	Viaduct (Viaduct Printing Co.)....	"	106.7	0.2
	14				C 1	Elk Ridge, P. 1,000	"	107.1	0.6
		8			C 1A	J. H. Toomey & Son	"	107.1	0.6
24					C 1B	Murray Siding	"	107.9	1.4
17					C 3	Hanover, P. 200	"	109.1	2.6
					C 3A	Har-Wood	Howard	109.9	3.4
	10				C 4	Smith Siding (Josevius Smith)	"	110.3	3.8
37					C 4A	Dorsey Passing Siding	"	110.6	4.1
8					C 5	Dorsey (Wesley Grove) P. 85	"	110.9	4.4
					C 6	Montevideo, P. 25	"	112.4	5.9
21					C 7	Jessup, P. 315	"	113.3	6.8
		72			C 7A	Bridewell (Maryland House of Correction)	"	113.8	7.3

Passing	Company	Joint	Private	Telegraph Call	Station Number	STATIONS AND SIDINGS with character references, population (census of 1910), and additional index references	County	Miles from Park Junct.	Relay
						Washington Branch—Con.			
88	68			PA	C 9	**Annapolis Junction,** P. 125 ....Md.		115.4	8.9
	15				C 10	Savage, P. 900 (*1260*) .... "	Howard	116.9	10.4
	76				C 12C	Md. State Fair Grounds .... "		118.4	11.9
48	20				C 12	Laurel, P. 2600—**W** .... "		118.8	12.3
	1				C 12A	Standard Oil Co. .... "		118.9	12.4
		11			C 12B	Wm. Numsen & Son .... "		118.9	12.4
					C 13	Mistletoe Springs .... "		120.0	13.5
					C 14	Oak Crest .... "		120.5	14.0
	13				C 15	Contee, P. 75 .... "		121.1	14.6
	18				C 16	Muirkirk, P. 200 .... "		122.4	15.9
			10		C 16A	C. E. Coffin .... "		122.4	15.9
34					C 17	Ammendale, P. 150 .... "		123.6	17.1
19	32				C 18	Beltsville, P. 300 .... "	Prince George	124.7	18.2
					C 19	Sunnyside .... "		125.6	19.1
67	16				C 21	Branchville, P. 380 .... "		127.4	20.9
					C 21A	Berwyn, P. 1,200 .... "		127.8	21.3
					C 21B	Lakeland, P. 400 .... "		128.3	21.8
					C 22	Paint Branch—**W** .... "		128.5	22.0
	7				C 23	College, P. 150 .... "		128.9	22.4
	7				C 24	Riverdale, P. 1300—**L** .... "		130.0	23.5
85	26			JU	C 24A	Alexandria Junction (*1270*) .... "		130.5	24.0
	28				C 24B	Hyattsville, P. 2,500 .... "		130.9	24.4
	11				C 25	Brentwood, P. 3,800 .... "		131.9	25.4
	6				C 26A	J. C. Lang ....⎫		132.4	25.9
	1					Aman Bros ....⎭	"		
					C 26	Rives .... D. C.		132.5	26.0
	6				C 27	Langdon, P. 419 .... "		133.4	26.9
					C 27C	Pathfinder Publishing Co. ...... "		133.4	26.9
					C 27D	District Tile & Brick Co. .... "		133.4	26.9
		27			C 27A	Corby Co. .... "		133.4	26.9
19				F	C 27B	F. Tower—**W** .... "		134.6	28.1
					C 30	New York Ave. (*1295*) .... "	District of Columbia	136.5	30.0
				DC H	C 31	{**Union Station—C** .... "⎫ {**Washington,** P. 331,069 .... "⎭		137.5	31.0
				WC		New York Ave. and 15th St., N. W. Washington—**C** .... "			
						619 Penna. Ave., **Pass—C** ...... "			
						619 Pennsylvania Ave., **Frt** ...... "			
						Patuxent Branch		Savage	
					C 10	Savage (*1824*) .... Md.	Howard	116.9	0.0
	26				C101	Savage Factory .... "		118.0	1.1
	17				C101A	Gabbro .... "		118.8	1.9
	14				C103A	B. F. Pope Siding .... "		119.8	2.9
	28				C104C	Maryland Granite Co .... "		121.2	4.3
	30				C104	Guilford—**W** .... "		121.2	4.3
					C104E	Howard Granite Co .... "		121.2	4.3
						Alexandria Branch	Prince George	Alexandria Junct.	
28		12		JU	C 24A	Alexandria Junction (*1843*) .... Md.		130.5	0.0
					C151	Washington, Baltimore & Annapolis Electric Railway Siding ...... "		131.1	0.6
	27				C151A	Bladensburg, P. 463 .... "		131.2	0.7
					C153	Beaver Dam .... "		133.5	3.0
					C154	Kenilworth .... D. C.		134.1	3.6
		30			C154A	**Chesapeake Junction** (Chesapeake Beach R'y) .... "	District of Columbia	134.6	4.1
			10		C154B	*Washington R'y & Electric Co. (Chesapeake Beach R'y)* .... "		134.6	4.1
	11				C155	Deanwood, P. 500 .... "		135.1	4.6
		10			C155 D	Jos. Swift Sand & Gravel Co .... "		135.4	4.9
	23				C155A	Washington Union Stock Yards—**L** "		135.6	5.1
		6			C155C	Washington Cold Storage and Slaughtering Co. .... "		135.6	5.1
	16			BN	C155B	**Benning** .... "		135.8	5.3
	246				C156	**Anacostia Junction** .... "		136.4	5.9
					C160	*Long Bridge (Penna. R. R.)* .... "		140.8	10.3
					C164	*Potomac Yard—**L S W** (Wash. So. R'y)* .... Va.	Alexandria	144.7	14.2
	5				C157	Twining City, P. 716 .... D. C.		137.4	6.9
	39				C158	Uniontown, P. 9,491 .... "		138.5	8.0
	5				C158A	S. M. Frasier .... "		138.5	8.0
		36			C159	St. Elisabeth Insane Asylum ..... "	District of Columbia	139.3	8.8
	80				C162A	Chemical Products Co .... "		142.2	11.7
		21	200		C162B	Washington Steel & Ordnance Co. "		142.3	11.8
	53				C163	Shepherd—**W** .... "		143.0	12.5
						Metropolitan Branch		Relay	
					C 30	New York Ave. (*1254*) .... D. C.		136.5	30.0
		14			C 30C	Union Trust & Storage Co .... "		136.9	30.4
	15				C 30 D	Swift & Co. .... "		136.9	30.4
		20			C 31E	National Mortar Co .... "		137.0	30.5
	121				C 31Y	M Street Yard .... "		137.0	30.5
	602				C 31 D	New York Avenue Freight Station, Washington—**D** .... "⎫		137.1	30.6
		2			C 31K	District Commissioners .,....... "⎭		137.1	30.6

487

Passing	Company	Joint	Private	Telegraph Call	Station Number	STATIONS AND SIDINGS with character references, population (census of 1910), and additional index references	County	Miles from Park Junct.	Relay

Metropolitan Branch—Con.

Passing	Company	Joint	Private	Telegraph Call	Station Number	Station	County	Park Junct.	Relay
			10		C 31M	Col. Geo. A. Truesdale...........D. C.		137.1	30.6
	7				C 31F	National Biscuit Co..............	"	137.6	31.1
	6		6		C 31 H {	Schlitz Brewing Co........	" }	137.6	31.1
						Great Bear Spring-Water Co......	"		
	360				C 31C	T Street Yard—S W............	"	137.7	31.2
			25		C 31A	Barber & Ross................	"	137.8	31.3
		19			C 31J	Monumental Brewing Co. (543)...	"	137.9	31.4
						Marvin S. Young Printing Co. }			
	13				C 31N {	Daniels Realty Co...........	"	137.9	31.4
						Loose Wiles Biscuit Co........ }			
		6			C 31B	A. Malnati..................	"	137.9	31.4
	526			QN	C 31G	Q. N. Tower.................	"	138.1	31.6
	6				C 32B	Pintsch Gas Co..............	"	138.3	31.8
	38				C 32	University..................	"	139.0	32.5
		6			C 32C	A. D. V. Burr..............	"	139.1	32.6
						Yard Limit Board...........	"	139.2	32.7
	33				C 33	Terra Cotta. P. 600...	"	140.1	33.6
	11				C 33A	National Terra CottaWorks(Thos. Somerville Co.)...	"	140.1	33.6
	24				C 33B	Washington Silicate Brick Co....	"	140.1	33.6
					C 34	Chillum	"	140.6	34.1
		4			C 35A	Lamond (J. Lamond).............	"	141.6	35.1
		3			C 35B {	Angus Lamond Siding..........	" }	142.1	35.6
						Wm. Watkins, Coal............	"		
	11				C 35	Takoma Park, P. 5,000........	"	142.1	35.6
		6			C 35C	Columbia Brick & Coal Co	"	142.2	35.7
	5				C 36A	North Takoma................Md.		142.7	36.2
50	15			SG	C 36	Silver Spring, P. 4,500........	"	143.3	36.8
		13			C 36B	Wilkins & Jordan.............	"	143.3	36.8
					C 37A	Fenwick.....................	"	143.9	37.4
					C 37	Woodside, P. 300.............	"	144.2	37.7
	32				C 38A	Georgetown Junct. (1370).......	"	144.5	38.0
	3				C 38	Linden, P. 150...............	"	145.1	38.6
	10			FN	C 39	Forest Glen, P. 225..........	"	145.6	39.1
					C 39B	Capitol View	"	146.3	39.8
	16				C 40	Kensington, P. 800...........	"	146.9	40.4
					C 41	Rock Creek—W...............	"	147.7	41.2
	8				C 42	Garrett Park, P. 175.........	"	148.3	41.8
					C 42A	Windham....................	"	149.2	42.7
					C 43	Randolph, P. 30.............	"	149.4	42.9
	20				C 44	Halpine....................	"	150.6	44.1
					C 45	Autrey Park	"	151.4	44.9
97	12				C 46	Rockville, P. 1,500........	"	152.4	45.9
	7				C 46A	Hickerson Bros.and Holland&Clark	"	152.4	45.9
					C 47	Westmore...................	"	153.6	47.1
	17				C 48	Derwood, P. 170.............	"	154.9	48.4
	32				C 50	Washington Grove, P. 300.....	"	156.5	50.0
		5			C 50A	J. L. Burns and Herbert Bryant & Son......................	"	157.1	50.6
64	38				C 51	Gaithersburg, P. 900—L......	"	157.5	51.0
					C 51A	Ward......................	"	158.0	51.5
		14			C 52	Brown (G. W. Brown).........	"	158.9	52.4
	2				C 53	Clopper, P. 25.............	"	160.1	53.6
					C 55	Waring—W..................	"	160.8	54.3
69				GM	C 55A	Germantown Tower...........	"	162.0	55.5
	5				C 56	Germantown, P. 250—L.......	"	162.3	55.8
59	16			DS	C 58	Boyds, P. 200—L............	"	165.0	58.5
	17				C 60	Buck Lodge, P. 83...........	"	166.3	59.8
34	13			BA	C 62A	Barnesville Tower...........	"	169.2	62.7
	18				C 62	Barnesville, P. 125—L.......	"	169.3	62.8
	26				C 65	Dickerson, P 150—L.........	"	171.5	65.0
52				DN	C 65A	Dickerson Tower............	"	171.6	65.1
	95				C 68A	Government Stone Siding......	"	172.5	66.0
51	7				C 68	Tuscarora, P. 26—L.........	"	175.1	68.6
					C 71	Sugar Loaf.................	Frederick	177.6	71.1
54	27			KG	256	Washington Junct.—C W—(1111, 1165)		178.6	72.1

Georgetown Branch

Passing	Company	Joint	Private	Telegraph Call	Station Number	Station	County	George town Junct.	
					C 38A	Georgetown Jct (1331)..............Md.		144.5	0.0
	2				C201	M. J. Grove Lime Co.............	"	145.8	1.3
	12				C202	Chevy Chase, P. 5,000..........	"	146.5	2.0
	2				C202B	T. W. Perry.................	"	146.5	2.0
	15				C202A	Team Track.................	"	146.6	2.1
		4			C203A	Chevy Chase Fuel & Supply Co....	"	147.9	3.4
			12		C203B	J. H. Miller & Son Coal Trestle....	"	147.9	3.4
	7				C203D	Real Estate Trust Co.........	"	147.9	3.4
	19				C203	Bethesda, P. 1,000............	"	147.9	3.4
	2					C. D. Rigsbee.............	"	147.9	3.4
	4				C206	Dalecarlia Reservoir........	"	150.6	6.1
						Dalecarlia Tunnel...........	"	150.7	6.2
	5				C209	C. & O. Canal Co...........D. C.		154.0	9.5
		1			C210	Southern Building Supply Co....	"	155.3	10.8
		8			C211A	Capitol Traction Co.........	"	155.3	10.8
	17				C211C	Rosslyn Supply Co..........	"	155.4	10.9
		22			C211B	Consolidation Coal Co	"	155.5	11.0
	29				C211	Georgetown(West Washington)—D S	"	155.5	11.0
				10	C212	Lincoln Memorial Track........	"	157.7	12 2

488

ERRATA

Page 35, first paragraph—McLane was elected President in December 1836 but was not on the job full time until July 1837.

Page 53, first paragraph—The PW&B and its predecessor, the Baltimore and Port Deposit, used B&O's Pratt Street station after late 1836. The joint arrangement quickly overloaded the terminal and caused some joint unhappiness. By about 1839 the PW&B had built its own freight station at President Street and in 1850 opened its own passenger terminal there.

Page 104, Relay Station plans—It is believed that the "storage room" shown on the first floor plan was originally the main dining room.

Page 206, fifth paragraph—The single exception to the "stone standard" was a five-span 125 foot long bridge over Paint Branch near Berwyn. On this bridge, the piers were stone but the superstructure was wood.

Page 232, third paragraph—Several of these trains were meant to form a connection for Washington passengers going south over the Virginia Midland. . .obviously an unwieldy, doomed route.

Page 239, top—Also built in this decade were stations at Scagg's (now Branchville) in 1873 and Brentwood—the latter identical to Hanover.

Page 239, bottom—Although the Bay Ridge line was built strictly as a route to the resort, it briefly found itself part of a through route for freight to the Eastern Shore. For less than a year, between 1890 and 1891, a carferry shuttled cars across the bay to Claiborne where they were delivered to the Baltimore and Eastern Shore Railroad. The B&ES at that time was a newly-built independent railroad running across the Delmarva Peninsula to Salisbury and Ocean City. The Bay Ridge connection apparently was unsatisfactory, and soon afterwards the B&ES gave it up and operated its carferry directly to Baltimore.

Page 365, second paragraph—The Metro shop and yard was built on the site of one of WT's two former coach yards; the second coach yard was rebuilt as Amtrak's passenger car storage and service facility.

Page 425, bottom—People looking at Point of Rocks station are almost always amazed that such a fine Victorian building has survived in such pure form, not realizing that much isn't original but rather the result of careful restoration. In July 1931 the station was struck by lightning and badly gutted. Considering the Depression and the railroad's desperate financial situation at the time, a "prudent" management probably would have demolished it or rebuilt it in austere, truncated form. But apparently Daniel Willard's sense of history overrode his prudence. . .B&O completely rebuilt Point of Rocks in its original form, replacing roof sections, windows, 19th Century brickwork and ornate wood trim.

For those readers deeply interested in B&O history, we highly recommend membership in the non-profit BALTIMORE AND OHIO RAILROAD HISTORICAL SOCIETY. . . write for details to the Society at P.O. Box 13578, Baltimore, MD 21203.

INDEX

490

Brown, Alexander-18
Brown, George-5
Brown, John-74, 270
Brownville-375
Brunswick (Berlin) town, yard, station, etc.-71, 78, 84, 105, 119, 122-124, 127, 135, 137, 144, 147, 150, 158, 160, 162, 169, 175, 177, 178, 269, 289, 291-297, 362, 373, 380, 381, 386, 389, 391, 392, 407, 425-427
Buckeystown-89, 147, 164, 180
Buck Lodge-286, 288, 289
Buck Lodge Creek-271
Budd RDC cars-187, 258, 260, 294, 295, 296, 358
Buffalo, Rochester & Pittsburgh Railroad-290
Bush Creek-11, 25, 36, 46, 49, 82, 94, 121, 137, 143, 144, 147, 160, 163, 410, 437, 439, 440, 442
Buzzard's Rock-24

Cabin John-323, 327
Calvert Street Station-55, 58, 59, 341
Camden & Amboy Railroad-201
Camden Street Station-56, 58, 60, 68, 70, 74, 75, 94, 102, 107, 110-113, 129-133, 151, 152, 170-172, 176, 177, 182, 195, 210, 213, 217, 234, 257, 260, 307, 399, 413, 416, 417, 419
Camden Warehouse-150, 151, 196, 416, 419
Camden Yard-121, 151
"Camel" locomotives-32, 43, 63, 64, 68, 70, 96, 97, 115, 397
Camp Meade Junction-247
Canton-11, 107, 129, 231
"Canton" ferry-107
Canton Viaduct-15
"Capitol Limited" train-168, 254, 259, 260, 289, 290, 292-294, 301, 353, 359, 365, 380
Capitol Transit-314, 316, 317, 333
Carroll, Charles-2, 3, 12, 15, 146
Carroll's-113, 171
Carroll Tower-113, 151, 171
Carrollton Manor-11, 146
Carrollton Viaduct-15, 16, 18, 56, 94, 398, 399, 402, 431
Cassatt, A.J.-133, 134, 135, 228, 234, 250, 354
"Castle", Forest Glen-290
Catoctin-89, 90, 94, 297, 370
Catoctin Creek-31, 71, 407
Catoctin Mountain-26, 29, 30
Catoctin Station-92, 185
Catoctin Tunnel-137, 148, 150, 185, 266
Catonsville-153
Central States Dispatch Route-377
Chambersburg-370
Charles Town-42, 74
Charlottesville-345
Chase's Wharf-107
Chattanooga-227
Cherry Run-377, 386
Chesapeake Bay-202, 239, 310
Chesapeake Beach-310, 311

Chesapeake Beach Railway-240, 310, 311, 316, 317
Chesapeake Junction-310, 311, 316, 318
Chesapeake & Ohio Canal-4, 9, 29, 30, 31, 32, 71, 74, 79, 84, 92, 93, 105, 123, 148, 202, 205, 265, 267, 269, 270, 294, 299, 322, 327, 330, 332, 335, 369, 370, 407
Chesapeake & Ohio Railroad (Chessie)-135, 180, 184, 296, 311, 312, 321, 322, 364, 381, 386, 401
Chevy Chase-290, 324, 326, 327
Chevy Chase Lake-279, 326, 327, 333, 429
Chicago-91, 97, 227, 232, 259, 260, 266, 273, 289, 358
Chicago Junction (Willard)-98, 173
"Chicago Limited" train-289
Cincinnati-55, 91, 97, 232, 273, 294, 358
Civil War-3, 42, 43, 46, 47, 49, 58, 64, 68, 72, 75, 83, 95, 100, 102, 107, 116, 122, 125, 127, 150, 168, 205, 219, 220, 223, 228, 232-234, 265, 266, 305, 311, 318, 345, 346, 370, 372, 406, 443
Clagett's (Gapland)-375
Cleveland-358
Clifford's-113, 151, 170, 171
Cloud, Abner House-335
Cole, Major Henry A.-84
College Station (College Park)-234, 235, 239, 262
Columbia-4
"Columbian" train-178, 250, 293, 359
Connellsville-377
Conrail-182, 194, 232, 312
"Consolidation" locomotives-137, 151, 160, 249, 251, 378, 397
Contee-204
"Convoy" tug-108, 305, 306, 312
Cooper, Peter-26
Cornerstone (First Stone)-2, 3, 133, 134
Cowen, John-136
"Crab" locomotives-32, 39, 41, 63
Cumberland-4, 8, 9, 30-32, 39, 42, 43, 46, 74, 79, 82, 88, 98, 121, 160, 162, 164, 177, 178, 180, 257, 266, 274, 369, 370, 442
Cumberland Valley-369
Cumberland Valley Railroad-370, 372, 377
Curtis Bay-11, 54, 110, 113, 121, 157, 168, 178, 180
Curtis Bay Pier-157

Dalecarlia-322, 324
Daniels-see Elysville
Danville-305, 307
Davis-138-140, 176, 183, 406, 407
Davis Creek-406
Davis, Phineas-27, 29, 32, 41, 42, 207, 210
Davis Tunnel-140, 405, 406
Deep Cut (Great Cut)-16, 17, 107, 110, 402
Deep Run-204, 407
Deer Park-98
Delaware & Hudson Canal Company-439
Delaware River-202, 312
Derwood-277, 281, 298

492

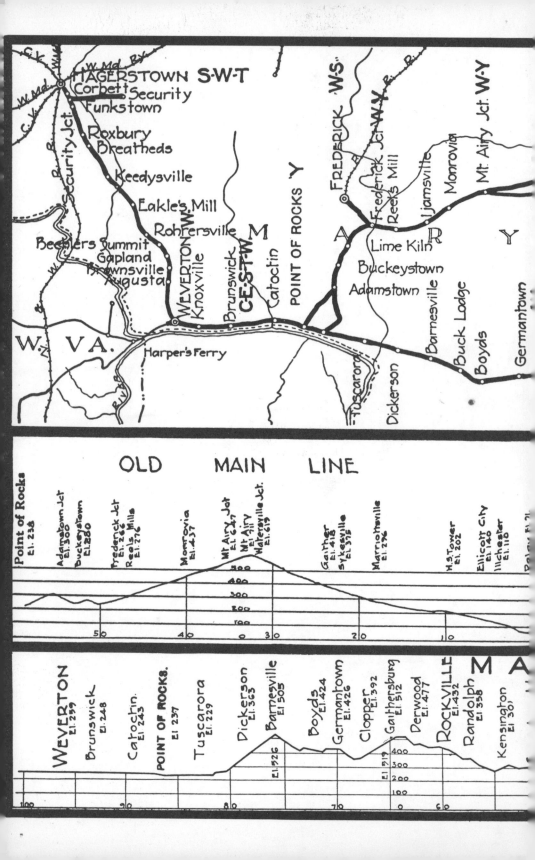

OLD   MAIN   LINE